KIM WILDE
Pop Don't Stop: A Biography

By Marcel Rijs

All rights reserved. No part of this publication may be reproduced, stored in a retrieval system, or transmitted in any form or by any means, electronic, electrostatic, recording, magnetic tape, mechanical, photocopying or otherwise, without prior permission in writing from the publisher.

The publisher makes no representation, express or implied, with regard to the accuracy of the information contained in this publication and cannot accept any responsibility in law for any errors or omissions.

The right of Marcel Rijs to be identified as the author of this work has been asserted by them in accordance with sections 77 and 78 of the Copyright, Designs and Patents Act 1988. No part of this book may be reproduced in any form without permission from the publisher except for the quotation of brief passages in reviews.

A catalogue record for this book is available from the British Library.

This edition © This Day In Music Books 2021. Text ©This Day In Music Books 2021

ISBN: 978-1-8383798-6-5

Cover photograph by Anton Corbijn. Front and back cover concept by Liz Sánchez.
Interior page layout and design by Gary Bishop. Additional interior page photography and design by Ian T Cossar.

This Day In Music Books, Bishopswood Road, Prestatyn, LL19 9PL

THIS DAY IN MUSIC BOOKS

www.thisdayinmusicbooks.com

Email: editor@thisdayinmusic.com

Exclusive Distributors: Music Sales Limited 14/15 Berners St London W1T 3JL

© Sheila Rock

KIM WILDE

CONTENTS

FOREWORD BY KIM WILDE	6
INTRODUCTION	7
CHAPTER 1: BEGINNINGS	8
CHAPTER 2: CHILDHOOD	18
CHAPTER 3: KIDS IN AMERICA	32
CHAPTER 4: DEBUT ALBUM	40
CHAPTER 5: SELECT	49
INTERVIEW: ANTON CORBIJN	65
CHAPTER 6: CATCH AS CATCH CAN	67
CHAPTER 7: TEASES & DARES	79
CHAPTER 8: ANOTHER STEP	93
INTERVIEW: RICHARD BLANSHARD	110
CHAPTER 9: CLOSE	112
CHAPTER 10: LOVE MOVES	128
CHAPTER 11: LOVE IS	143
INTERVIEW: GREGG MASUAK	154
CHAPTER 12: THE SINGLES COLLECTION 1981-1993	157
CHAPTER 13: NOW & FOREVER	168
INTERVIEW: MARTIN ZANDSTRA	178
CHAPTER 14: TOMMY	179
CHAPTER 15: BETTER GARDENS	189
CHAPTER 16: CUMBRIAN FELLSIDE GARDEN	208
CHAPTER 17: NEVER SAY NEVER	221

INTERVIEW: SABRINA WINTER	239
CHAPTER 18: COME OUT AND PLAY	246
INTERVIEW: NICK BEGGS	261
CHAPTER 19: SNAPSHOTS	263
CHAPTER 20: WILDE WINTER SONGBOOK	283
INTERVIEW: CASE EAMES	308
CHAPTER 21: HERE COME THE ALIENS	311
INTERVIEW: STEVE NORMAN	327
CHAPTER 22: SHINE ON	329
END NOTES	338
ACKNOWLEDGEMENTS	367

FOREWORD BY KIM WILDE

In 2020 Marcel told me that he was keen to write the story of my professional career and he wanted to seek my approval. I was naturally happy to agree as it was clear to me that my blessing was the best birthday gift I could give to Marcel in his 50th year. As it turned out, this book was the best gift he could have given me for my 60th.

I first met Marcel in early 2001 at a fundraising gig for our Village Day in Codicote, Hertfordshire at the Campus West Theatre in Welwyn Garden City. Fabba, the Abba tribute band, approached me through local musician Andy Skelton to accompany them on some classic Abba tunes, and also persuaded me to perform 'Kids in America' – something I hadn't done since retiring in 1996, when my husband and I were married and we started our family.

In retrospect this performance became my unlikely 'comeback' gig - soon after I joined an 80's tour and, before I knew it, I was back on the rollercoaster... music had returned to claim me once more and I fell in love with 'Kids in America' all over again.

Since that day in 2001, Marcel has provided continuous support to my career and become a good friend. With his thorough and organised mind, he has now produced a document which accurately charts the definitive path of my career but which never allows the facts and figures to obscure his true passion... the music.

Starting at the very beginning, from the early days of what would become known generally as *pop music*, Marcel maps the incredible birth of rock'n'roll in the late 1950s with the career of my Dad, Marty Wilde, before diving headlong into his comprehensive account of my own from the early 1980s.

Together with my Dad and brother, Ricky Wilde, our lives have, to this day, been shaped and inspired by *pop music*. During 2020 – and at the age of 81 – my father released an album of vibrant new songs and this year, 2021, my definitive Greatest Hits album will be released, celebrating the 40th anniversary of the release of 'Kids in America' and including a new single called 'Shine On', a duet with pop's ultimate icon, Boy George.

In these uncertain times there is, at least, one thing of which I'm absolutely sure, and I know that Marcel would agree: Pop Don't Stop!

INTRODUCTION

I was just nine years old when Kim Wilde's debut single 'Kids in America' was released. I was already listening to the Top 40 charts at that time, thanks to my older brother and sister who watched *Toppop* (the Dutch version of *Top of the Pops*) every week. Like many young people I was a fan of pop groups like Abba and Boney M, but Kim was something else: it seemed like she could take on the world all on her own.

She kept releasing singles that grabbed my attention, and soon enough I was buying her records. I fell in love with each and every song. It didn't take long before I started buying her singles and albums. I loved the stories that those songs told, and as the years progressed I noticed that the lyrics of Kim's songs were becoming ever more personal. But what struck me most was the melodies. Somehow those melodies resonated with me more than those of any other musician out there.

When I created a website about Kim Wilde back in 1998, it was my response to the fact that there was almost no information about her on the internet. This surprised me: this was one of Britain's most successful female singers and it seemed like the world had forgotten about her! All the information I'd amassed during the past two decades was thrown on that website, and this snowballed into many good things: getting to know fellow fans all over the world, amassing even more information about Kim Wilde and her father Marty Wilde, and best of all: friendships that last until the present day. I also got to know Kim herself, something I never imagined when I watched her on TV as a young lad. She contributed messages, diaries and photographs to the website and I got to know a genuinely lovely lady.

Writing this book was inspired by the same surprise I felt when I made the website. It is, of course, a story 'from the outside in', using magazine articles, TV and radio broadcasts and the occasional interviews with people who have worked with her through the years. The astonishing tale of a woman who excelled not only in music but also in gardening, writing and presenting had to be told. You will find it in this book. And like the song says, 'there's no end to this story'.

Marcel Rijs
February 2021

CHAPTER 1:
BEGINNINGS

Reginald Leonard Smith was born in a nursing home in Blackheath, South London on 15 April, 1939, the only son of Reginald and Jessica Smith. Reginald Sr. was a Sandhurst-trained Sergeant. During World War II, he was moved to the Royal Hotel in Capel Curig, North Wales, which was requisitioned in 1942 by the Royal Military College and used as a training camp, where officer cadets from Sandhurst took part in live firing military exercises in Snowdonia's mountainous areas. Reginald Sr. helped train new Army recruits for the War effort. His wife and son followed him.

Marty: **"After the war my Dad was a tram driver, then a bus driver, but my Mum had a heart defect so she couldn't work."**[1]

Reg's father was a big influence on him. When the radio was on, he would sing along to the songs being played, and would start to harmonise. From the age of two or three, his father got him to sing a song called 'The Son Of Sargent Smiffy' to his Army pals. The seeds of the love for music were sown.

Marty: **"My grandma was a fortune teller and devastatingly accurate. She'd read tea leaves and tell people their fate. I was a baby when she said I'd be a singer and travel the world – which, in her lifetime, was unheard of. She told my parents to make sure I got whatever I needed musically. And they did. They didn't tell me until much later that she predicted the whole thing."**[2]

After the war, they moved back to Greenwich, on 92 Woolwich Road, and Reginald Jr. began school at Halstow Road Primary School. He was there for several years before he went on to Charlton Central Secondary Modern School. One of the boys in that school brought in a ukelele one day. Reg thought it was a very interesting instrument and asked his parents to buy him one. He learned to play the instrument quite quickly and would go on bus rides, playing George Formby songs on his ukelele on the upper deck to amuse people.

Marty: **"Because I was so lousy at school, I wasn't doing very well, and I didn't have great self-esteem as a youngster. Playing my ukelele and singing suddenly got me noticed, I felt respected at last and my self-esteem grew."**[3]

Popular singers like Frankie Laine, Johnny Ray and Guy Mitchell were his favourites, but Reg's interest in music didn't stop at the popular genre. One teacher in school started bringing in classical music. Reg latched on to it almost immediately. He heard the beauty of the melodies while the other boys started looking out the window and got a bit fidgety.

CHAPTER 1: BEGINNINGS

He attended a youth club at the local Sunday school in the Charlton and Blackheath Baptist Church and sang in the choir. After leaving school at the age of 15, he considered himself 'totally unqualified for the real world', but became a messenger boy in the City of London for a firm of brokers in Rood Lane, Eastcheap.

During these years he dreamed of a career in music and of becoming a singing star. Having played the ukelele for some years, he bought a guitar during his teens – the instrument of choice for teenagers at during the 1950s. With a group of friends he formed a group called Reg Smith and the Hound Dogs, mainly playing popular skiffle songs.

Marty: "We used to do Lonnie Donegan-type material, skiffle, and then I went to see *Blackboard Jungle*, which was a great film, and that was the first time I heard rock'n'roll properly, with Bill Haley at the opening credits of the film starting off with 'Rock Around The Clock'. [It was] an incredible vibe for a young person who'd never heard that kind of sound before. I watched the film and I knew immediately, four bells coming down on the jackpot. And I met the band and said, 'Skiffle is out, from now on it's rock'n'roll!'"[4]

Another artist who influenced Marty greatly was a certain American singer by the name of Elvis Presley, with his self-titled album from 1956 a revelation.

Marty: "Something about Elvis´ voice touched me deeply, as no other singer had ever done before in my young life, in just the same way it had inspired millions of other young people around the world. The passion Presley evoked in those early Sun songs is quite stunning, and when you listen to his ability to paint rhythmic pictures with his voice and induce a sexiness to the lyrics of the songs, the effect was mind-blowing, and I tell you it hit me like a ton of bricks."

Renaming themselves Reg Patterson and the Hound Dogs (the new surname a tribute to American heavyweight boxer Floyd Patterson), they switched to an Elvis and Jerry Lee Lewis repertoire, playing some gigs in the South of England, until Reg was approached by Joe Brunnely, a music publisher with contacts in London.

Joe offered him two weeks' work as a solo artist in the West End of London. One week would be at the Blue Angel nightclub, and the second at the Condor Club in Soho, which attracted lots of the personalities and stars of the day, such as Sterling Moss, and – according to rumours – Princess Margaret.

Whilst earning £1 a night plus a bowl of spaghetti, Reg was noticed by Larry Parnes, who, as Tommy Steele's manager, was the most powerful manager in the UK. But when Larry went backstage to speak to him, he was told Reg had gone home rather swiftly, as he had to take the last bus home to Greenwich from Wardour Street. Larry managed to obtain Reg's address from the owners of the club though, and the following day he headed down to Greenwich with a contract in his pocket, approaching Reg's parents to sign him up as he was underage.

Marty: "My tribute to Larry is this: he arrived at my house with my name on a contract, and he'd not even seen me. That, for me, was the real talented, hungry manager. Larry came down to Greenwich on a Sunday.'" [5]

Marty: "I used to go to church [on Sunday] and I came home in the afternoon and my mother said there's been a knock on the door. And I said yeah, so what does he want? She said, 'Well, he wants to manage you.' So I asked 'Who is it?'. She said: 'Larry Parnes'. Immediately my ears pricked up, and my father said, 'Who's Larry Parnes?'. I said: 'He manages Tommy Steele'. Tommy was the biggest thing around at that time. And Larry had a contract. I don't know how he did it, but he had a contract with my name on it and my address, and he brought that contract down, and we'd never even met."[6]

Larry: "He didn't want to sign up with me. Marty was a very independent fellow, even at 18, 19 years old, and he felt that because Tommy and I were having such success together, it wouldn't be a good thing if he signed with me. I assured him that it wouldn't make any difference. Eventually he went into another room and had a confab with his mother and father, and they persuaded him, I think, to sign the contract with me."[7]

It was Larry Parnes who thought up Reg's stage name. Parnes explained in an interview: "His real name was Reg Smith. He was a big tall lad of six foot four, who had to be kept friendly yet had to be kept wild. Hence Marty Wilde: Marty's very friendly and Wilde shows that little wild trait in him."[8] Reg himself wasn't sure, but when he saw it in print he was convinced of its billing strength. And the name stuck.

Marty: "I always loved fighting... heavyweight fighting has always been one of my great passions, so I called myself Reg Patterson, my real name being Reg. I lopped off the Smith and put in the Patterson, because Floyd Patterson was the then world champion, and I thought he was marvellous! Larry thought the name was awful, and said, 'I think your first name should be Marty', and I said 'Come off it, that sounds like some crew-cutted American nerd!' But he insisted... he'd seen this film with Ernest Borgnine in, and said I had a lot of the qualities of 'Marty'... I said 'I've not even seen the film!' He said, 'Well, the name would really suit you.' We were always gamblers – he taught me that. I was a shocking gambler, I'd gamble on two flies crawling up a wall! And he said, 'All right, I'll flip a coin and heads I win, tails you lose!' And he won. And then it came to the surname. I wanted Patterson, again, but he's said, 'I think it should be Wilde', and I've gone, 'Oh no! No, no, no... I can't be 'Wilde'... that's terrible!' And he won again, so there I was, saddled with this Marty Wilde name... but after about a week, it really dawned on me what a great name it was!"[9]

His first live appearance as Marty Wilde took place in 1957 at the Trocadero Theatre in London's Elephant and Castle, as part of a 'package' show.

CHAPTER 1: BEGINNINGS

Marty: "The Elephant and Castle boys were and still are tough boys. How I got out of there alive I'll never know. I'm staggered they didn't storm the theatre and rip me to shreds." [10]

Together with Colin Hicks (Tommy Steele's brother) and The Most Brothers, he went on a countrywide tour in October that year. The first Marty Wilde single was 'Honeycomb', a version of Jimmie Rodgers' US No.1 hit. It was released on 78rpm shellac discs on the Philips label, but failed to chart. Nevertheless, Wilde was promoted vigorously and appeared frequently on BBC Television's pop music programme *6.5 Special*.

Marty: "The *6.5 Special* was the first real pop programme that I was lucky enough to appear on. It was a friendly sort of a show, with lots of teenagers and musicians enjoying music of all styles. My favourite memory was when a certain lady lost her temper with the orchestral conductor – took her wig off and threw it at him. But I can't say who it was." [11]

Two more single releases, 'Love Bug Crawl' and 'Oh Oh, I'm Falling in Love Again' didn't chart, but then in the summer of 1958, Marty had a hit. 'Endless Sleep' was originally written and recorded by American rockabilly singer Jody Reynolds (1932/2008). The song tells the story of a young man desperately searching for his girlfriend, who, after an argument, has flung herself into the ocean. The label persuaded a reluctant Reynolds to change the lyrics to give the song a happy ending. Marty's version peaked at No.4 in the UK singles chart.

Meanwhile, Marty's agent Larry Parnes persuaded influential producer Jack Good to make Wilde the resident star of his new television programme, *Oh Boy!*. A pilot episode was broadcast on 15 June 1958, featuring Marty as one of the stars in the programme, alongside The Dallas Boys, The John Barry Seven, Lord Rockingham's XI, Ronnie Carroll, Bertice Reading, Cherry Wainer, Red Price, Neville Taylor and the Cutters, Dudley Heslop, Kerry Martin, and 16-piece vocal group the Vernons Girls.

The show returned on screen in September 1958, with Marty and a very young Cliff Richard among the performers. A week later, Marty was scheduled to appear but didn't because of problems with his voice. This was unfortunate, as he'd just released 'Misery's Child' as his new single. Being unable to promote the song on the show meant that it didn't chart. Together with Vince Eager, Marty instead sang the Everly Brothers' 'Bird Dog' on the show broadcast on 4 October 1958.

Larry Parnes complained to Jack Good that Cliff Richard was getting the best songs to sing and received more publicity than Marty Wilde. He threatened to withdraw Marty – who was signed for the first six shows of *Oh Boy!* - from the series after the 18 October show. Jack Good suspected Parnes of being greedy, his stable of stars already dominating the series. So Jack released Marty, who had wanted to remain, leaving Cliff solely as the main star attraction. On October 18, 1958, Marty appeared on the show for the last time that year.

Marty's debut single 'Honeycomb' 78rpm label

Bad Boy Danish 7" single

Kim as a baby © Wilde Productions

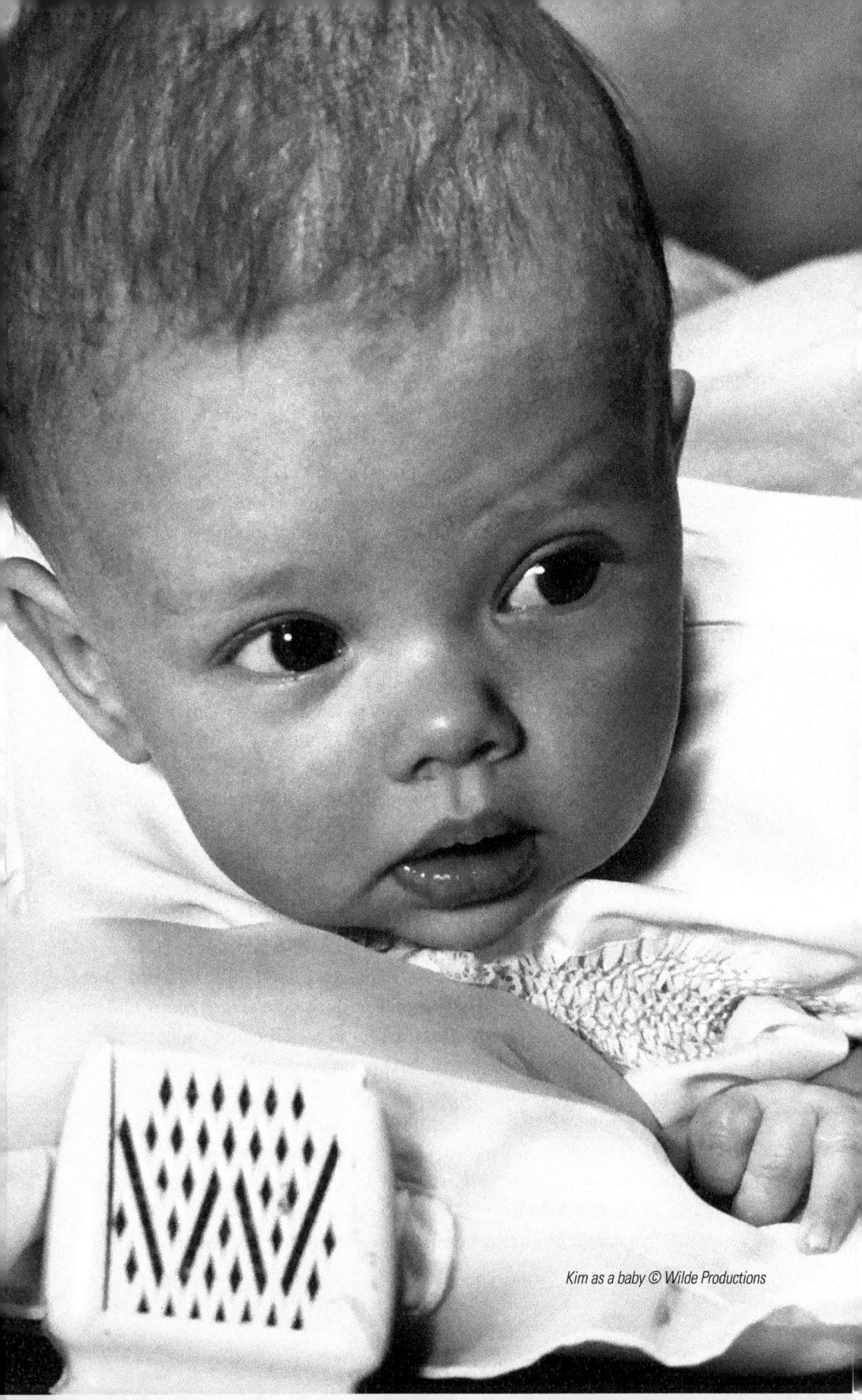

Marty was not happy about his agent's move, wanting to terminate his contract with Parnes, but by December, the *NME* reported that the two had patched up their quarrel.

Marty: "Everything is straightened out now. I was really upset about leaving the *Oh Boy!* show, but Larry and I have had a discussion, and have agreed to co-operate fully."[12]

Marty's next single, 'Donna' was a cover of a song by Richie Valens, who died on 3 February 1959 in the infamous plane crash that also killed Buddy Holly and J.P. Richardson, a.k.a. The Big Bopper. Entering the UK single charts on 12 March 1959, the single spent 16 weeks in the hit parade, peaking at No.3.

When Marty Wilde returned to *Oh Boy!* on February 7, he joined Cliff Richard on three numbers. A week later, Marty did a comedy duet with Shirley Bassey, appearing on every show until the final edition on 30 May 1959.

Looking at the few recordings of the show that still exist today, you notice that the girls are screaming loud during Marty's performances, much like the girls did during the 1960s when The Beatles broke through.

Marty: "It was just part of the job, really. I never took that side seriously. I looked in the mirror and I wasn't what I wanted to be. I'd like to have been five times more handsome. (...) I didn't like my voice, I didn't like my face."[13]

During the show's run, Marty released his first album, *Wilde About Marty*. It didn't include any of his chart hits, but rather versions of 'Blue Moon Of Kentucky', 'High School Confidential', 'All American Boy' and other rock'n'roll songs. He also had another hit single, 'A Teenager In love', written by Doc Pomus and Mort Shuman, and that became his signature song and biggest hit, reaching No.2 in the UK singles chart in the summer of 1959.

After leaving *Oh Boy!*, Marty Wilde and Cliff Richard were booked to appear in their first Royal Variety Show, held at Manchester on 23 June 1959. Unfortunately, the event was not recorded for television (as opposed to the 1960 show, recorded by ATV and surviving to this day in the archives of Carlton International).

Oh Boy! did not return, but in September 1959 Jack Good produced a new show, *Boy Meets Girls*. Featured as the host, compere and resident singer, Marty had one of the busiest times in his career. Besides the premiere of the new show, he also released a new single – 'Sea of Love', which he performed on the first show – and his first feature movie premiered, *Jet Storm*.

In the script, his role was described as 'a successful, super popular teenage star taking a plane trip to New York'. Fact and fiction blended together as some fans made their way to London Airport where the filming took place. Director Cy Endfield was satisfied that Marty would fit the role perfectly.

Cy Endfield: "No doubt about his talent. I knew that after I'd tested him with

CHAPTER 1: BEGINNINGS

various girls before we finally chose Jackie Lane to co-star with him. His name will look good on the billing. But that's strictly by the way."[14]

Jet Storm was also co-written by Cy Endfield. In the film, Ernest Tilley (Richard Attenborough), a former scientist who'd lost his daughter two years earlier in a hit-and-run accident, tracks down James Brock (George Rose), whom he believes responsible for the accident, boarding the same plane on a flight from London to New York. Tilley threatens to blow himself up and everyone on board as an act of vengeance. The film also starred Stanley Baker as Captain Bardow, David Kossoff as Doctor Bergstein, and Patrick Allen as terrified passenger Mulliner.

Part of the deal was that Marty recorded the title song, which he co-wrote with Endfield. *Jet Stream* was the intended name of the movie, the song title remaining unchanged when the movie was renamed.

Meanwhile, Marty had met Joyce Baker, one of the Vernons Girls, while they were both starring in *Oh Boy!* After a relatively brief courtship – seven or eight months – Marty married Joyce, aged 18 and originally from Huyton, then part of Lancashire, on 2 December 1959 at Christ Church, Greenwich. Parnes arranged for Marty to spend the night before the wedding under his roof, while Joyce stayed with Marty's parents.[15] Crowds gathered two hours before the ceremony.[16] Police eventually had to hold back the crowds whilst press photographers and film media covered the event. The ceremony was in part stage-managed by Parnes, with Cherry Wainer playing the organ, four of the Vernons Girls as bridesmaids and all 16 in the choir. One of the girls, Jean Ryder, sang 'Ave Maria' during the service. After the wedding, they went to a Chinese restaurant for their reception.

Honeymooning in the United States, Joyce bought Marty a £60 monogrammed ring, but he lost it while swimming in the sea at Bournemouth, where they had a bungalow for the summer season in 1960.

Marty: "It must have become loose on my finger in the water and slipped off without my noticing. I missed it when I reached the beach".[17]

Meanwhile, the Rev. Gerald Hawker got into trouble with his congregation after putting up a sign in early 1960 with the words, 'Getting married? This church was good enough for Marty Wilde.'[18]

Joyce later admitted that the switch to becoming a housewife wasn't easy on her.

Joyce: "When I retired from dancing and got married, I couldn't even boil an egg, let alone do anything else. I wasn't really up on anything, so it was mostly boil-in-the-bag stuff in those days."[19]

The marriage was considered to be a bad career move at the time.

Marty: "Pop stars were discouraged from openly having girlfriends back then, let alone wives. But I couldn't live like that. It was pretty clear I didn't have the same pull afterwards. Not having hits was a huge disappointment, but I'd never taken the adulation seriously, so I didn't miss it."[20]

Joyce: "I hated to think that Marty might be unhappy because of me, but when my Marty makes up his mind, nothing can stop him. So we took the plunge. After all, you only fall really in love once, don't you?"[21]

The marriage coincided with the release of another hit single, the self-penned 'Bad Boy'. Marty felt frustrated that he wasn't getting the songs he wanted, and decided to write his own – which was unusual for rock'n'roll singers at that time. He'd written songs since he was young, so felt he could do it. The inspiration behind 'Bad Boy' was meeting Joyce and listening to Buddy Holly's band The Crickets' debut album, *The 'Chirping' Crickets*. The single reached No.7 in the UK singles chart and No.45 in the USA.

Marty: "When I first came in the industry they were putting songs in front of me and some of them were very good, but then the sources seemed to dry up so I wrote 'Bad Boy', which was my first hit in 1959. My frustration was the mother of invention, because it made me start writing my own songs."[22]

This American success prompted a recording session in New York, where Marty laid down a rendition of the 1947 Nat King Cole hit 'Little Girl', with 17-year-old Carole King on backing vocals. He also recorded 'Stop The World (My Baby's Gone)', 'Angry', 'Your Seventeenth Spring' and 'Little Miss Happiness'.

When 1960 started, Marty signed a contract worth more than £100,000 with impresario Harold Fielding, who wanted to develop Marty's career and get him beyond the pull of teenage fans and become a star for all age groups. It meant cutting down on TV performances and moving towards movie and musical projects.[23]

However, tragedy struck when Marty's Dad passed away in 1960.

Marty: "I was 21 when my father died suddenly at 48. He'd been ill with a heart problem, but you automatically think your father is indestructible, that he'd survive anything. It took the wind out of my sails. I don't think I've ever got over his death."[24]

In 1960, Marty enjoyed three more chart hits: 'Johnny Rocco', 'The Fight' and 'Little Girl'. None of those reached the top 10, however, causing press speculation. While 'Bad Boy' sold over 500,000 copies, 'Johnny Rocco' sold 45,000 and 'The Fight' 36,000 copies. Marty worried about this, but ultimately believed in himself.

Marty: "I was very, very bitter at first, but I realised that would get me nowhere. The only thing is to bury yourself in your work and really believe you will come out trumps again in the end. It is no good sitting around crying about it ... You can't retire at 21."[25]

CHAPTER 1: BEGINNINGS

Meanwhile, Joyce became pregnant and on 18 November 1960, their daughter was born at Chiswick Maternity Hospital. Kim Smith weighed 8 lbs 10 ozs. Elvis Presley, the artist who changed Marty's life, was No.1 in the UK charts at the time with 'It's Now or Never', and would soon greatly influence the couple's new-born baby girl.

CHAPTER 2:
CHILDHOOD

The year 1961 started with Marty's last top-10 hit: 'Rubber Ball'. It reached No.9 in the UK singles chart in February, with arranger Wally Stott's wife, daughter and friends providing backing vocals.

Marty: "The only time I think I felt possibly unsure was when the children started to arrive, because then it wasn't just me, I had a family to support. I had to take in as much work and do as many things as possible."[1]

Marty was signed for the musical *Bye Bye Birdie* in January 1961, the Edward Padula production running at Her Majesty's Theatre in Haymarket that summer. The story was inspired by the phenomenon of Elvis Presley and how he was drafted into the Army in 1957. Marty took on the title role, Conrad Birdie, the character's name a play on the name Conway Twitty, one of Presley's rock'n'roll rivals at that time. The original 1960–1961 Broadway production won a Tony Award, with the London production one of several major revivals, alongside a sequel, a 1963 film, and a 1995 television production. The show ran for 268 performances from June 1961, with a recording available as an album of the same name.

And with the movie *Jet Storm* under his belt, acting seemed to be a good alternative to his singing career, Marty going on to star in the films *The Hellions* and *What A Crazy World*, the latter with Joe Brown.

Marty: "Kim was nine months old when I took a role in the film *The Hellions*, shot in South Africa. I insisted that my wife and baby came too."[2]

The Hellions was directed by Ken Annakin, but the production didn't go entirely smoothly. Annakin had to stay in a nursing home in Pretoria for a while with suspected polio, which turned out to be dehydration. Furthermore, of the actors, James Uys caught a yeast virus, Lionel Jeffries fell from his horse, and Marty suffered from conjunctivitis, having to stay in a darkened room for 48 hours.[3]

In the movie, law enforcement officer Sam Hargis (Richard Todd) is battling criminals in South Africa when Luke Billings (Lionel Jeffries) and his four sons, including Marty as John Billings, ride into town to take revenge on Hargis for a previous clash, when he ran Luke Billings out of town, and trouble ensues. Again, Marty provided the title song, which appeared on the B-side of 'Tomorrow's Clown', which peaked at No.33 in the UK singles chart in November 1961.

The movie *What A Crazy World* was directed by Michael Carreras from a script co-written with Alan Klein, with unemployed working-class lad Alf Hitchens (Joe

CHAPTER 2: CHILDHOOD

Brown) dreaming of breaking into the music business and making it big with a song he has written, Marty playing Herbie Shadbolt.

On 6 November 1961, Marty and Joyce's second child, Richard James Reginald Steven Smith, was born. Just under a year younger than Kim, the two would grow up together. Living in Watchfield Court, Chiswick for the first two years, the family then moved to Eastbrook Road, Blackheath, where they remained until 1969.

Kim: "The first home I recall was in Eastbrook Road, Blackheath, south-east London. It was a semi-detached house, with a garden Ricky and I loved to play in and where we learnt to ride bikes. I remember collecting rose petals and making perfume in Coke bottles, attempting to sell them to the neighbours. I also remember planting my first bulb and my total amazement as the green shoot appeared a few months later."

Kim: "I vividly remember the winter of '63 when the snow fell heavily just before Christmas, I've loved the snow ever since."[4]

In 1962, Marty enjoyed his last two hit singles - 'Jezebel', a cover of Frankie Laine's classic song (No.19 in June) and 'Ever Since You Said Goodbye' (No.31 in November).

While the hits dried up, he started writing for other artists, both solo and together with Mike Hawker. They wrote 'My Heart Is Free' and 'I Wanted Everything' for Tony Allen. The former also appeared on the B-side of Jimmy Gilmer & the Playboys' US hit single 'Sugar Shack' in 1963 and, in a French adaptation, 'Mon Coeur Est Libre' by Gemma Barra in 1964.

Marty: "The pop thing, that lifestyle, you can't live that forever. It was time for me to move on." [5]

However, when Marty started writing songs, he decided to retain his publishing rights.

Marty: "It was offered to me to sign to a publishing company, and they were going to give us a large amount of money in advance, and it would have bought the house of my dreams almost outright. We were saving desperately to try and get this house, but Joyce said no to the advance, figuring my songwriting was worth much more... She was right, and a phenomenal guide. (...) It paid huge dividends once Kim's career started, because I was free as a writer, and we started our own publishing company."[6]

Marty's backing band The Wildcats moved on to work with Eddie Cochran and Gene Vincent. After his contract with Philips ended, Marty signed with EMI's label Columbia Records and released a string of singles. The first, 'Lonely Avenue', written by Doc Pomus, was originally a hit for Ray Charles in 1956, with Marty's version arranged and conducted by John Barry. The next single was 'Save Your Love For Me', composed by Alan Klein. 'When Day Is Done' and 'Kiss Me' were the last two singles for Columbia, after which Marty released one solo single on the Decca label, 'The Mexican Boy', written by himself and produced by Andrew Loog Oldham.

While still signed to Decca, Marty formed the Wilde Three in 1965. Harmony singing had become the new thing, and Marty and Joyce placed an advert to find a third musician. Answering the advert in the *Melody Maker* was a young Justin Hayward. He came to their house in Eastbrook Road, Blackheath and was surprised to find Marty Wilde open the door. He was accepted as the third member, and together they performed for the armed forces and on the UK club circuit. Two singles were released, 'Since You're Gone' in April 1965 and 'I Cried' in September of that year. Neither single charted though, and the trio soon ended their collaboration. But Justin credits Marty as the person who first encouraged him to write his own songs.

Justin Hayward: "Not many people know that Marty was one of the first real big rock stars before The Beatles to write his own material. I remember him saying that to survive in this business you have to write your own songs. That led to me writing a song called 'Nights in White Satin.'"[7]

When Justin joined the Moody Blues in 1966, Marty signed with Philips for the second time and released 'I've Got So Used to Loving You'. Two years later, the single 'By the Time I Get to Phoenix' was released, made famous by Glen Campbell a year earlier.

The family had a big scare when Kim suffered from meningitis at age five. Marty and Joyce were performing in Liverpool. A friend of Joyce's, Marian, took care of the children at home. She recognised the symptoms and had her rushed to hospital right away. When Marty and Joyce received the call from Marian, they were in a state of panic, knowing all too well that the disease could be deadly. They had to drive home, which took them around six hours. Two hours into the journey, Marty suddenly realised Kim would be alright. Joyce didn't understand and told him he'd gone mad. But it was this kind of clairvoyance that his grandmother also possessed. Eventually, they arrived at the hospital. Doctors explained that Kim's life had been saved by a matter of minutes, a few hours earlier. They had given her a lumbar puncture just in time, taking off the deadly fluid before it reached her brain.

Marty: "She only once caused me real anxiety: at the age of five she became very ill with meningitis. Joyce and I were touring, and Kim was at home in London, being cared for by a friend of Joyce's called Marian, to whom I'll always be grateful, because she recognised the symptoms and rushed Kim straight to hospital. After driving through the night from Liverpool to Kim's bedside, we found she had passed the crisis. She opened her eyes, looked at Joyce, whose stage make-up was smudged with tears, and whispered,

CHAPTER 2: CHILDHOOD

'Mummy, you look beautiful'. Thankfully there were no after-effects." [8]
Kim: "One of my earliest memories is of being really ill when I was five. I had meningitis, which in those days was pretty dangerous. I remember having a terrible headache, and great difficulty looking at light, being rushed to the hospital in an ambulance and having the lumbar puncture. I awoke to find my Mum, her mascara-streaked face from crying looked so beautiful, and I told her so."

Joyce and Marty decided to send Kim and Ricky to Oakfield School in Dulwich, a boarding school, in 1968. The couple had to be away from home a lot of the time and thought it would be the best thing to do. But it wasn't a pleasant experience for the children.

Kim: "It was awful. We hated it. We were so unhappy and miserable and wanted to be at home with Mum and Dad. My best memory is of the piano at one end of the common room, I'd place small pieces of paper on my favourite notes so as not to forget them. Looking back, I think music came to my rescue on those long and lonely days - music and Hans Christian Andersen."

Kim: "I remember watching [*Top of the Pops*] as a child, particularly when I spent a year or so of my eight-year-old life in a very strict boarding school. The only highlight was being able to watch *Top of the Pops* before being packed off to bed. Whenever a particularly 'noisy' or 'hairy' looking band came on, the old dear who ran the place would slap her hand over my eyes so I couldn't see!"[9]

In the meantime, Marty continued to write songs for other artists. His first production was a single for the Marionettes, providing both sides - 'Whirlpool of Love' backed with 'Nobody But You'. Other songs he wrote were 'How Many Times' (Judi Johnson and the Perfections), 'Your Kind of Love' (The Breakaways), 'Your Friend' and 'Give Me a Chance' (The Roemans), 'Hide All Emotion' (Sandie Shaw), 'Daddy What'll Happen to Me' (Adam Faith), 'Your Loving Touch' (Joe Brown), 'The Moment of Truth' (Three Good Reasons) and 'All I Can Say is Goodbye' (Tom Jones).

Later he teamed up with pop music promoter, group manager and songwriter Ronnie Scott (not to be confused with Ronnie Scott OBE, the jazz saxophonist and club owner), who worked for the George Cooper Agency, whose artists roster included the Bystanders and Marty himself. Together they wrote 'Have I Offended the Girl' and 'Jezamine' for the Bystanders. The songs didn't become chart hits until the Casuals covered the latter in 1968 and had a worldwide hit. By that time, Marty and his co-writer started using the pseudonyms Frere Manston and Jack Gellar, writing for Status Quo ('Ice in the Sun', 'Paradise Flat' and 'Elizabeth Dreams') and Lulu ('I'm a Tiger').

Marty filming his baby daughter Kim. © Wilde Productions

Kim, Joyce and Ricky posing for dad Marty. © Wilde Productions

Kim, Ricky and Joyce in the early 1960's. © Wilde Productions

I Am An Astronaut German 7" single

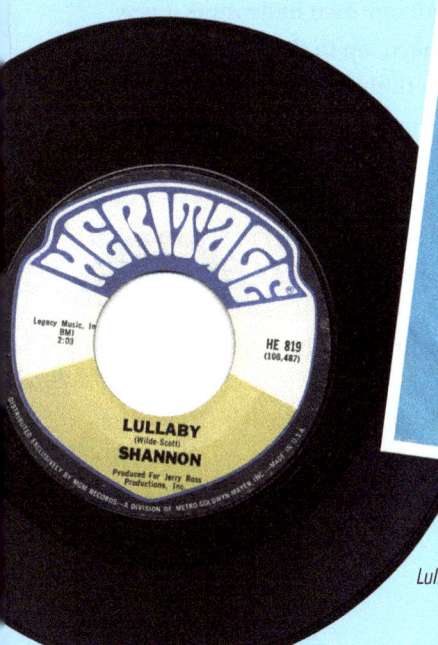

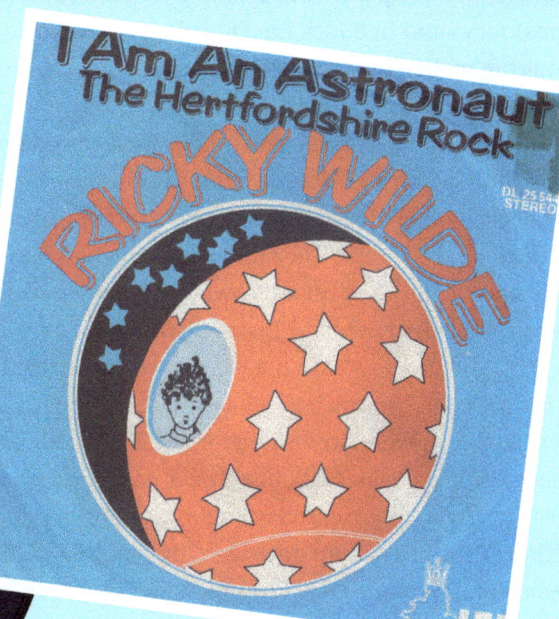

Lullaby - USA 7" single

Marty: "As songwriters, Ronnie Scott and I would write a song, then I would sing on the demo's, and then later, they would be sent to the A&R department of the artiste we chose. The only musicians I got involved with were Status Quo. I sang one of the top harmonies on 'Ice in the Sun', their big hit."[10]

In 1968 Marty participated in the 10th annual Knokke Festival in Belgium. Together with Freyday Braun, Allun Davies, Wayne Fontana and Brenda Marsh he represented the United Kingdom. The appearance helped to make his single 'Abergavenny', written with Ronnie Scott, a hit in Europe. In the Netherlands, it became his first and only hit single, peaking at No.5. In Belgium, the single reached No.6. A year later, the song was released in the USA, Marty using the pseudonym Shannon and reaching No.47 in the Billboard Hot 100.[11]

Privately, things were going well, and in spring 1969, Marty and Joyce were finally able to buy the home they were after, a beautiful thatched house in the Hertfordshire countryside.

Marty: "I got up to the door and felt the way I feel every time I come into this house. It's that same feeling. Sometimes it's quite intense and sometimes it's quite emotional. It was one of those things. I adore this place. And I love the area. I love Hertfordshire to bits."[12]

Kim: "I lived in that house [in Blackheath] from the time of my earliest memories until I was about eight, when we moved to an idyllic thatched house in the Hertfordshire countryside. One minute we were living in an ordinary semi in South East London, the next we were in paradise. It was like waking up in a fairy story, with forests on our doorstep, and beautiful flowers everywhere."[13]

Kim: "For the first time in our lives Ricky and I had our own bedrooms. I was a big music fan so I would spend a lot of time in there, up in the attic, listening to records and dreaming. My parents were only in their late 20s when we moved to the house. They knew nothing about gardening, but we inherited this paradise from the previous owners. We arrived there in June, when the garden was full of vivid colour. I instantly fell in love with country life."[14]

Kim and Ricky went to the village primary school, whilst both taking classical piano lessons, in which they reached Grade Seven. Kim also met Clare Smith, who would become her best friend for life. The fact that Kim and Ricky's Dad was a successful 'pop singer' didn't always go down well with their classmates though, causing them to be teased from time to time.

Kim: "Primary school days were the happiest school days of my life. There was some teasing about our famous Dad, especially for Ricky, but our parents were very involved at the school and everyone soon got to realise they were just two very down to earth people."

CHAPTER 2: CHILDHOOD

In 1969, Marty released the album *Diversions* (released in Australia as *Abergavenny*), a beautiful collection of 14 songs written with Ronnie Scott. It included Marty's own versions of 'Ice in the Sun' and 'Jesamine', as well as a re-recording of 'The Mexican Boy', now entitled 'Juan the Mexican Boy'. The song 'Lullaby', also included, was written especially for Kim and Ricky. However, while *Diversions* sounded sophisticated and mature, it didn't manage to persuade the record-buying public, the album failing to chart, disappearing for decades until it was finally re-released on CD in Australia in 2018.

Marty decided to go back to his roots for his next album in 1970. *Rock'n'Roll*, as it was simply called, featured 12 versions of well-known songs, including 'Hound Dog', 'Wake Up Little Susie' and The Beatles' 'Paperback Writer'.

The song 'I Still Believe in Tomorrow', written with Scott, became a hit in America for British duo Anne and John Ryder, reaching No.17 in the Adult Contemporary chart. In Sweden it was a hit for the Hootenanny Singers, the four-piece band including future Abba member Björn Ulvaeus. Stig Anderson wrote the Swedish translation, 'Om Jag Kunde Skriva En Visa'. The song's international appeal was underscored by versions in Dutch as 'Wij Blijven Geloven In Morgen' by Saskia & Serge, in Finnish by Danny as 'Yhä Virta Venhettä Kantaa' and in Portuguese as 'Eu Ainda Acredito No Amanha' on an album by Os Caçulas in Brazil.

'No Trams to Lime Street' was written for an Alun Owen play broadcast by the BBC. As a stage musical it also ran in Liverpool and at the Richmond Theatre, near London. Marty also recorded the song for a single, released in 1970, while another song from the production, 'Liverpool Hello', was recorded by the group Capricorn (produced by Marty) and became a hit in Japan. Marty's last single for Philips was 'The Busker', produced by John Franz.

Kim, meanwhile, went to Presdales School in Ware, an all-girl grammar school where she developed a love for writing poetry and had great interest in creative subjects like drama, dance, art, English and music.

In 1972, Marty Wilde wrote a song called 'I Am an Astronaut', aimed mainly at a young audience. Ricky, now 11 years old, recorded the song almost as an experiment. His mother Joyce and sister Kim added backing vocals, and for Ricky, the recording session was slightly overawing.

Ricky: "All I remember is sitting in this black chair and they put the earphones on my head and then played it through and asked me which key was best for me to sing in. And when it was all decided I just sang away. It took about half an hour in all."[15]

Children's magazine *Look-in* featured him on the cover of their June 1973 issue, alongside Donny Osmond, thus creating a certain rivalry. Although the single didn't chart in the UK, it was a big hit in Sweden. Weekly radio programme *Tio I*

Topp, which featured the top-10 best-selling singles, featured the song for a five-week run from 31 March 1973, 'I Am an Astronaut' peaking at No.3.[16]

In the summer of 1973, Ricky appeared with his father alongside 11-year-old pop rival Darren Burn in BBC TV's *Man Alive* documentary programme *Twinkle Twinkle Little Star*. The singles 'April Love' – a cover of a song written by Sammy Fain and Paul Francis Webster for the 1957 film of the same name – and 'Do It Again, A Little Bit Slower' – a cover of a song recorded by Jon & Robin and the In Crowd in 1957 – followed. Although the singles didn't chart, Ricky found himself the centre of attention during an appearance at Harlequin record shop in Oxford Street, London.

Ricky: "I only expected a hundred girls to turn up, but there were about 600. I had two bodyguards to help me, and both the buckles on my white jacket were ripped off!"[17]

Kim: "Ricky was about 11-years-old when he first started recording Dad's songs. I was happy for him but also a little envious at the same time. I'd already made up my mind by the age of 12 that I wanted music to be my life too."[18]

Ricky recorded three more singles on the UK label: 'Mrs. Malinski', 'I Wanna Go to a Disco' and 'Teen Wave', all written and produced by his Dad. As time progressed, Ricky experienced problems at school through his semi-star status, his classmates making fun of him. When none of the singles charted in the UK, the project was abandoned.

Marty: "That was a mistake that I made in a way, on reflection, although I didn't push him into it, he was a young kid and he loved music. When Rick recorded one of the songs I wrote, 'I Am an Astronaut', I never saw the big picture. The media saw it as The Osmonds. But very quickly Ricky stopped enjoying all the attention. I was glad when that part of his life ended, and I think he was as well."[19]

In 1973, Marty was touring in Australia, with his family following in his tracks, and even joining him on stage.

Kim: "My first memories of Australia are of staying in Sydney's Kings Cross area, where my Dad was performing. It was 1973 and I was 13 years old. Now, here we were the other side of the world – this was a great adventure! We loved the big clear-blue Australian skies; the rainbow-tinted opals sparkling in the shop windows, Bondi Beach, and we marvelled at the incredible Sydney Opera House, which had only just been completed."[20]

Marty also wrote songs with Peter Shelley from 1972 onwards, releasing singles anonymously as Scrumpy 'n Dumpy ('When You Wish Upon A Star', a novelty cover version of the song written by Leigh Harline and Ned Washington for Disney's 1940 adaptation of *Pinocchio*) and as Cold Fly ('Caterpillar' backed with 'Yesterday Started For Judy').

CHAPTER 2: CHILDHOOD

In 1973, Magnet Records was founded by Michael Levy (later Baron Levy) and Peter Shelley. A highly-successful independent label, the company is probably best known for hit singles by Alvin Stardust, Matchbox, Guys 'n' Dolls, Darts, Kissing the Pink, Bad Manners, Chris Rea, and Shelley himself, who scored with 'Gee Baby' and 'Love Me, Love My Dog'. The latter was written together with Marty, and became an evergreen in Europe. Dutch singers André van Duin, Ernst Daniël Smid, Andy de Witt, Peter van Bugnum and Rudi Carrell, and Belgian singer Luc Steeno recorded the song as 'Samen Een Straatje Om', Danish singer Bjørn Tidmand translated it into 'Gennem Sol Og Regn', the Norwegian band Yankee translated it into 'Lev Vel, Lev Ditt Liv', and Swedish bands Ola, Frukt & Flinger and The Schytts recorded it in their native language as 'Lev Väl, Lev Ditt Liv'.

The company also provided a home for some of the artists from Jonathan King's stable, after the collapse of his own UK Records around 1976.

Pete Shelley wrote, produced and sang 'My Coo Ca Choo', Magnet's first single. Since Shelley had no desire to front the project himself, he offered it to Marty, who turned it down. Accordingly, Shelley then headhunted Bernard William Jewry, then professionally known as Shane Fenton, who became known as Alvin Stardust.

The immediate success of 'My Coo Ca Choo' took Shelley and Levy by surprise, with the pair keen to capitalise. Teaming up with Marty, Shelley wrote and produced a handful of singles. And so, the second single release on the label was 'Rock 'n Roll Crazy' by Zappo, who was actually Marty, dressed in Superman-like attire in the hope of attracting a glam-rock fanbase. Other Shelley/Wilde collaborations included '20 Fantastic Bands' by the Dazzling All Night Rock Show, fronted by Marty as a studio-only band; 'The Shang-a-lang Song' by Ruby Pearl and the Dreamboats, with Marty impersonating a female doo-wop group, 'Come Back & Love Me' by Shannon, another pseudonym for Marty, and two singles under his own name, 'All Night Girl' and 'I Love You'. None of these attempts to pitch him into the glam-rock field worked, and he and Magnet soon parted company.

However, in February 1974, Marty and Billy Fury headlined a 20-day tour promoted by Hal Carter. Fury became a friend as well, visiting Marty's house in Hertfordshire regularly.

Kim: "Billy Fury used to turn up quite a lot in the early days... (...) He was a great wildlife fanatic and used to come and save deer and put them in our shed. Billy was a kind and gentle man, and him and Dad loved talking about music late into the night." [21]

Also in 1974, Marty played the part of Colin Day in the film *Stardust*, directed by Michael Apted and starring David Essex and Adam Faith. The story of a British musician (continuing a tale begun in 1973 film *That'll Be the Day*), Essex's main role mixed elements of Paul McCartney, Bob Dylan and Jim Morrison into a personality ill-suited to the demands of superstardom. Premiered on 24 October 1975 in the UK and 12 November 1975 in the USA, the film earned profits of more than £525,000.

In the meantime, Kim was growing up. At the age of 16, she started to flourish, and by 18 had passed her driving test and would often drive around in her Mum's car, going to the pub and to parties with a close-knit group of friends, many of whom she has to this day. During the summer she had a job disbudding carnations in a local greenhouse, and cleaning for her piano teacher. Kim stayed on at Presdales to do A-level art in the sixth form after her O-levels.

Kim: "I remember my art lessons best of all, and my teacher Miss Gallon, who helped me look at the world in a different way. She was very inspiring and opened my eyes and helped me see the beauty that exists everywhere."[22]

With a grade B in her A-level art, she was accepted for a year-long foundation course at Hertfordshire College of Art and Design in St. Albans.

Kim: "I think deep down I was hoping I'd meet some cool art students and form a band, and although I loved the arts, I knew the music world was where I wanted to be. Little did I know that the musicians I was searching for were living with me at home!"

Meanwhile, on 24 July 1979, Joyce gave birth to Roxanne Elisabeth Jessica Smith, the first name suggested by Kim, inspired by The Police song of the same name. And Roxanne's birth was followed in 1983 by the birth of Marty Jr., this 'second wave' of children a source of great joy for the whole family.

I AM AN ASTRONAUT
Written by Marty Wilde & Peter Shelley
Produced by Marty Wilde & Peter Shelley

Marty wrote 'I Am an Astronaut' for son Ricky. Aimed at a market of so-called teenyboppers – young stars like Donny Osmond and the Jackson Five were all the rage at the time – it was an unusually arranged song, with an almost psychedelic instrumental midsection. The single was also the recording debut of Ricky's sister Kim, who provided backing vocals.

Released in several European countries as well as the UK, it was an unexpected hit in Scandinavia, where anonymous cover versions kept popping up on LPs aimed at children, with titles like 'Barnens Bästa Bitar' and 'Barnens Bästisar' in 1973 and 1974. Scandinavian children like Linus Wahlgren and Anne Mette Torp subsequently covered the song, translated into Swedish as 'Jag Är En Astronaut' and in Norwegian as 'Jeg Er En Astronaut'.

Dutch child star Little Rockin' Rudy recorded the song in Dutch as 'Ik Ben Een Astronaut', in an arrangement by Jacques Zwart, who also used his translation for children's choir De Waagzangertjes.

In 1976 Czechoslovakian singer Jaromír Mayer released his version, entitled 'Nemám Se Zkrátka Prát'. The rock band Charta 77 recorded an English-language cover version in 1988, and the Swedish band Highway Stars followed in 1993.

Swedish child star Linus Wahlgren recorded 'Jag Är En Astronaut' in 1985, his nephew Benjamin Wahlgren following suit in 2007.

It was also covered by Snow Patrol, recorded for charity compilation album 'Colours Are Brighter', a selection of songs recorded by various artists to raise funds for Save The Children in 2006.

Benji and the Astronauts recorded a version in 2014, featuring contributions by Jeff Wayne and Alan Parsons, and remixed versions by Martyn Ware from Heaven 17 and Vince Clarke from Erasure. Ricky's version of the song was sampled by British electronic music composer Luke Vibert on his 2011 track 'Starchild'. And in 2017, Marty recorded the song himself on his album *Songs for your Children & Grandchildren*.

LULLABY
Written by Marty Wilde

Marty wrote 'Lullaby' especially for his children. The lines '*When you get lonely, don't you feel sad / Don't you feel bad, 'cos Daddy loves you*' sums up what the song is about.

Kim: "It's one of my most favourite songs ever, and I feel so privileged that Dad wrote it for Ricky and me. It was obviously written during a time he was away a lot. It meant a lot then and it means a lot now."[23]

In the USA, 'Lullaby' appeared on the B-side of the single 'Jesamine' – Marty's own recording of that song – in 1969. The single was released under Marty's pseudonym Shannon, since he'd reached No.47 with the song 'Abergavenny' using that name. Unfortunately, 'Jesamine' did not chart.

Marty re-recorded 'Lullaby' on his 2017 mini-album *Songs for your Children and Grandchildren*, a collection of songs for, and inspired by, children.

Abergavenny, Dutch
7" single

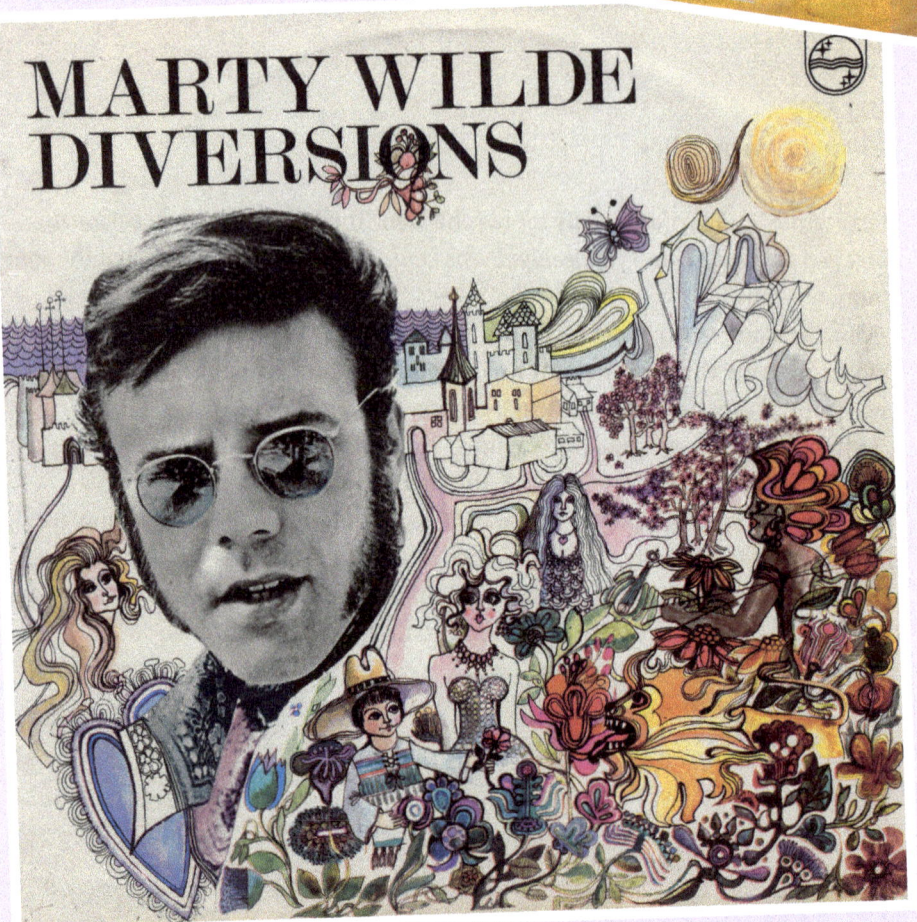

Endless Sleep Danish 7" single

Diversions, Marty's 1968 album

Marty Wilde, CC-BY-SA 4.0

CHAPTER 3:
KIDS IN AMERICA

Ricky Wilde had left school at 15 and went to play in his father's band. Marty was constantly gigging up and down the UK, and Ricky had more than enough music talent to support him during the live shows. But Ricky also wanted to write and produce songs and perhaps form his own band. In 1980, he felt he had a couple of songs that he was happy with, and on the advice of his father, Ricky arranged a meeting with Mickie Most at RAK studios. Mickie listened to the songs and was instantly impressed with this young writer/musician, inviting Ricky to record them at RAK. Ricky wanted backing vocals on the tracks, and proposed to have Kim sing them. Mickie agreed without meeting her, and so Kim came to the studio along with Ricky for the first time.

Ricky: "While she was singing, Mickie came in halfway through the session, saw Kim and heard her. He reached over to writer/producer Steve [Glen], had a quiet word in his ear, and said: 'She looks great, and she certainly can sing, let's get her in the studio and try out some new songs with her'." [1]

Kim: "Mickie also wanted me to work with Mike Chapman and Nicky Chinn, who had an awesome reputation for creating great hit records for The Sweet, Suzi Quatro and Mud. But Ricky was determined it was going to be him to write and produce me, went home that weekend and wrote 'Kids in America', with (Dad) Marty coming up with the title and writing the lyrics".

Ricky used his Wasp synthesizer to come up with the sound that eventually became the intro of the song, inspired by the basslines in Gary Numan's early work and the melody of OMD's 'Messages'.

Ricky: "It had this synth line, the very first thing you hear, and behind that you'd have the beautiful chords, and that's what made the whole riff so hypnotic. When I went into the studio and started to record 'Kids in America', before I knew it the backing track was down, the bass was down, the drums were kicking away and I just felt it needed something in that second verse to give it another little new element, so I just started mucking about with the little Minimoog and straight away that suddenly tapped in. It finished up being quite a major part of that verse. But without Andy McCluskey and Paul Humphreys that would not have happened. As simple as it was, it was perfect for that moment." [2]

Marty: "I like telling stories as a lyricist. I had the title and Rick was working on this little baby computer (Wasp). I listened to this melody for a while, and said,

CHAPTER 3: KIDS IN AMERICA

I can see this girl's face, skyscrapers and this girl's face behind it. It's going be about a girl, and she's going to be calling the shots.'"[3]

Marty: "I'd seen this TV show about teenagers in America, which frightened the life out of me. It was like an X-rated movie. They didn't seem to have any heart. I thought: 'My God, what are they going to grow into?' It was probably how the older generation had looked on me and all the other early rock'n'rollers. The lyrics tell the story of these kids' lives: *'Kind hearts don't make a new story/Kind hearts don't grab any glory'*. A lyricist's job is a bit like a screenwriter's: you're painting pictures with words. So I imagined this gutsy girl *'looking out a dirty old window'* in a dangerous city and deciding to take control of her own destiny."[4]

Ricky: "I booked the studio, The Enid's studio, which was based in Hertford, in a cellar. It was the nearest studio to where we all lived. I phoned them up, said, 'Have you got any downtime?' They said, 'Yes, we've got a day'. We recorded 'Kids in America' within two days, all the vocals, did a rough mix, went up to RAK Studios and played it to Mickie, and straight away, he heard it and said 'It's a No.1 hit'."[5]

Kim: "We recorded it in a studio in Hertfordshire owned by prog rock band The Enid. It was full of reptiles and snakes in glass boxes, like stepping into an underworld. The finished song sounded really exciting, but took a frustrating year to get released, during which time I worked in a local pub, wondering what was going to happen."[6]

With all the attention on Kim, Ricky was happy just to be involved, not having to play the star himself. He'd done that in the 70's and it wasn't for him. They recorded the track as a demo and presented it to Mickie. He immediately recognised it as a smash hit, but felt it needed remixing. They got to work and after several attempts got it right.

Then there was the question of Kim's name. It was actually Mickie Most who decided Kim should follow in her father's footsteps.

Kim: "My best memories of RAK include Mickie discussing my professional name in his usual blunt, no-nonsense style. Our family name was Smith: 'Kim Smith?', he said, 'Doesn't sound great, does it. Kim Wilde sounds much better, don't you think?', and I had to agree."[7]

The song 'Kids in America' was to be released as Kim's debut single, but it would need a B-side. In the summer of 1980, Ricky came up with another track, which became 'Tuning In Tuning On'.

Marty: "Rick gave it such a fantastic riff that it sounded sort of freaky. I said, "Oh, you must finish it off, it sounds a very eerie kind of track". I wasn't sure what kind of lyric I'd write, but in about an hour I had the title and then thought of a theory I had about sound being alive and not dead. So I wrote the lyrics around this pet theory of mine and later discovered there's an actual sect of yogis in the East who genuinely believe that sounds are alive and live on, so basically I'd like to think that's true."[8]

Kim had to wait around for a while, because her debut single wouldn't be released until after the Christmas rush. Planned for January, preparations were being made. A photo session with Terry Walker yielded 'the' shot that was used for the sleeve of Kim's first single. Although Kim would confess years later that she wasn't too enamoured by the photo.

In the first week of January, Kim received the first pressing of the single and went to RAK with Ricky to plan the promotion of the record. TV adverts, newspaper articles and visiting radio stations was all on the cards. One of the first interviews was with Judith Simons from the *Daily Express* over the telephone, for a small article published in the 12 January 1981 issue. It included a quote from Mickie Most.

Mickie Most: "When Ricky sent me a tape of Kim singing his song, I was impressed with her technique. She is ideal for a contemporary singer. Very hip girls will identify with her, and she'll appeal to boys."[9]

On the same day, she spoke with Nick Kent, whose article appeared on 14 January 1981 in the *Daily Mirror*.

Kim: "I grew up with music. It was all around me. Now it's going to be my life."[10]

On 13 January 1981, Kim did her first radio interview for *Newsbeat* on BBC Radio 1.

A music video was to be made for the single. At the time the medium was still young, but it was an easy way for artists to promote their singles - instead of flying around, having to appear on every imaginable TV programme, a recorded video could be sent out and broadcast everywhere. For Kim, it was a new experience. She appeared on the set at St. John's Wood Studios, wearing her own clothes, and seemed very shy. She asked director Brian Grant what she had to do, to which he replied she should just sing the song. When she confessed she'd never done this before, Brian panicked straight away.

Kim: "Of course I'd never made a video before, but found a connection with the camera very quickly, helped of course by the director Brian Grant, who I hit it off with instantly. I was so amazed to arrive with a huge wall mural painted especially for my video, featuring two of my all-time American heroes, Elvis and Phil Silvers of *Sgt Bilko* fame. This gave me a huge amount of confidence straight away. I knew this was going to be a very special video."

Mickie Most: "It was one of the first videos to be used on MTV, really in its infancy then. I remember being in some cities in America where half the city

was cabled up with MTV and the other half wasn't. So they say to me, 'Oh Kim, she's great!'. She was No.3 in the charts on the east side of the city and the west side of the city didn't know her from a bar of soap. It just shows how the power of MTV was even in those early times. It was that video that helped her break in America."[11]

Kim wore a black and white stripey top that was to become iconic, belonging to a friend who bought it at a jumble sale. She nicked her Mum's skinny blue jeans, and wore her Dad's old dinner jacket, that she'd pulled out of the attic. Mickie Most bought a pile of green Army shirts in his office ready for Kim to try, but was more than happy with Kim's individual tomboy style.

Kim's styling was her own from the beginning. The early press articles would describe her preference for wearing second-hand clothes, bought at jumble sales and Oxfam shops.

The single ´Kids in America´ was finally released on 26 January 1981. Initially, the single entered the UK singles chart at No.62 on 21 February 1981. After climbing to No.43, Kim and her band appeared on *Top of the Pops* and suddenly the single jumped to No.18, then No.6, then No.3, finally peaking at No.2 after six weeks, held off the top spot by Shakin' Stevens' 'This Ole House'.

Despite the music video doing its work in several territories, Kim still had to promote her debut single in Europe. Mickie Most didn't waste any time and sent her off to Germany, France and the Netherlands in March and April. Kim made her first appearances on the TV shows *Bananas*, *Musikladen* and *Toppop*. She didn't know that she would return to these shows multiple times. Her pop career had taken off instantly.

TEARAWAY
Written by Ricky & Marty Wilde

Although 'Tearaway' was never released officially, the track did end up on an unofficial Austrian CD, featuring tracks from various artists in 2002. It is widely assumed that this track was recorded at RAK Studios in London, after which Kim was 'discovered' by Mickie Most. The song fits the 'new wave' sound of the early 1980s very well. Musically it sounds a little rough, as if it really wouldn't have been out of place on Kim's debut album. The track was never submitted to RAK Records in the end, and as such it will probably remain unreleased.

KIDS IN AMERICA
Written by Ricky & Marty Wilde
Produced by Ricky Wilde
Released: 26 January 1981
Chart positions: 2 (UK), 12 (Austria), 4 (Belgium), 5 (Germany, New Zealand, Switzerland), 9 (Norway), 2 (Sweden), 25 (USA)

'Kids in America' starts with city sounds, horns blaring, traffic noise, and that pulsating rhythm from the Wasp synthesizer. After several mixes of the song, Mickie Most was finally satisfied with the track and released it as a single on his RAK label in January 1981.

From the very first lines (*'Looking out a dirty old window / Down below the cars in the city go rushing by'*) the listener is drawn into the imagery of a young woman looking for fun on a boring Friday night.

The single was released all over the world, but only in Europe did the public also get a 12" single. While it contained the same two songs as the 7" single, it wasn't unusual for record companies at the time to release a track this way. There was a lot of demand for these so-called maxi singles, nicknamed 'super sound singles' for the presumed better quality of a 'wider groove'.

Without a doubt, 'Kids in America' has taken on a life of its own, with more than 100 acts covering the song, both on record and during live performances. The many different versions span all genres, from slow, moody ballads, via country and punk to death metal. The best-known artists to have covered the song are Atomic Kitten, Bloodhound Gang, Sophie Ellis-Bextor, Foo Fighters, One Direction, and Tiffany.

Dutch singer Kim-Lian van der Meij had a hit with a cover of the song in the Netherlands in 2004.

Various translations of the song also exist, most notably the Finnish version, 'Kaupungin Lapset', recorded by Mona Carita in 1981, Jonna in 1986, Make Lentonen in 1993, and all-female band TikTak in 2001. Kim actually joined the latter act on stage to sing the track in English during a televised performance in January 2002.

Kim's favourite cover version of 'Kids in America' was recorded by the band Lawnmower Deth in 1991.

The song has also prompted several acts through the years to rewrite the lyrics. And so, on the melody of 'Kids in America', you can also hear songs like 'Fragen Sie Tante Erika' (Sensational Knecht Ruprecht Band), 'Generika' (QL), 'Kids de France' (Oi Banner), 'Kids in Australia' (Game Over), 'Kids in Quarantine' (Joe Trey), 'Kids in Tyne & Wear' (Toy Dolls), 'Kids in West Germany' (The Maniacs),

'Kids on Alcohol' (Anal Thunder), 'Kids of the Future' (Jonas Brothers), 'Loonies in the Bus Station' (Bus Station Loonies), and 'Verliebt in Veronika' (Robert Haag).

TUNING IN TUNING ON
Written by Ricky & Marty Wilde
Produced by Ricky Wilde

Originally recorded as the B-side for 'Kids in America', 'Tuning In Tuning On' was also used as the closing track of Kim's debut album. The existence of a separate master confirms that the track was probably tweaked for the album, but the difference is hard to discern. Still, both versions appear on the 2020 reissue of 'Kim Wilde', straight from the master tapes.

The song was performed live during Kim's first two tours, and in 2007 during the Perfect Girl tour.

RAK Studios, 42-48 Charlbert Street, St John's Wood, London. Photo: Simon Harriyott CC-BY-2.0

Vintage Kim Wilde sew-on patches from the early 1980's

CHAPTER 4:
DEBUT ALBUM

Kim Wilde
Released: 29 June 1981
Chart position: 3 (UK), 25 (Australia), 42 (Canada), 3 (Finland), 1 (Germany), 2 (Netherlands), 39 (New Zealand), 1 (Sweden), 86 (USA)

Kim Wilde made her debut in the singles charts at an interesting time in music. The 1970s had just ended, the 1980s just starting. And it showed, with old bands like Roxy Music, The Who and Status Quo battling with newcomers like Duran Duran, Bucks Fizz and Heaven 17. The fact that 'Kids in America' was held off the top spot by Shakin Stevens' 'This Ole House' was just as baffling as Ultravox's 'Vienna' being stopped from reaching No.1 by Joe Dolce's 'Shaddap You Face' a month earlier. Punk had just done its thing and new wave seemed to be the next big thing, but early appearances by Landscape and Visage in the charts already signalled that the 1980s would be full of synthesizer-driven pop tunes. In this transitional music landscape, making a successful follow-up for 'Kids in America' was not the easiest task in the world.

The pressure was on for Marty and Ricky. They had to come up with a worthy successor. They wrote several songs together and Ricky took them to Mickie Most on three or four occasions, bringing four songs each time. Mickie, the boss of the record label, famous for his scathing criticism on TV talent show *New Faces* in the 1970s, rejected them all. 'Chequered Love', the final song from Ricky's last trip, close to the deadline, was the track eventually selected as Kim's second single. The song was recorded in two days and mixed in the first week of April.

While promoting 'Chequered Love' in Europe, recording sessions for Kim's debut album took place. The LP came together with the involvement of The Enid, the band that owned The Lodge studio in Hertford where 'Kids in America' was recorded. All the tracks were written by Ricky and Marty, with the exception of 'Falling Out', written and composed by Ricky, one of the tracks Mickie Most heard during Ricky's first visit to RAK in St John's Wood. After Kim's career took off, it was decided that she would also record this track on her debut album.

Kim Wilde was released on 29 June 1981. For the album sleeve, a session with famed photographer Gered Mankowitz was arranged. The band that accompanied Kim during TV performances appeared alongside her on the cover: drummer Calvin Hayes, guitarist James Stevenson and brother Ricky, who played guitar, bass and keyboards on the record.

Although they travelled together, it was up to Kim to do all the interviews and promotional appearances. She seemed shy at first but comparing those first

CHAPTER 4: DEBUT ALBUM

TV interviews with those towards the end of 1981 already showed a growing confidence. There was a certain repetitiveness about the interviews: Kim explaining many times why she hadn't performed live yet, and why she was working with her father and brother.

The release of the album was supported by a nationwide flyposting campaign, large posters featuring the LP's front cover. Shop window displays were also made available, using a larger than lifesize Kim cut-out, also from the cover.

Reviews were favourable around the world. UK pop magazine *Smash Hits* wrote: "Kim is an able enough singer in a delightfully off-hand way and young Ricky is no slouch when it comes to reproducing the sound of the moment."[1] *Top* in Belgium proclaimed: "A good melody, original ideas in the music, a good story that makes for an impressive video. The collection of songs by Kim Wilde meets these criteria perfectly". [2] And Australian newspaper The Age concluded: "She has a young voice but, if this album is any guide, should do very well with her own brand of smart pop."[3]

The record peaked at No.3 in the UK albums chart and topped the chart in Germany and Sweden. Its appeal was immediate and broad: in the post-punk era 'new wave' was the new buzzword and this album fitted the bill perfectly: the guitars were prominent on most of the tracks, with Ricky's synth keyboards providing a very contemporary sound. In an age where most pop stars were clad by stylists, Kim went to charity stores to seek out her own clothing.

With the debut LP doing as well as it did, the family business had to go through some changes. Joyce, who had managed Marty's career since the early 1960s, took on the duty of managing her daughter as well.

After some initial doubts, a fan club was also set up. The Official Kim Wilde Fan Club started in the second half of 1981, with quarterly magazines detailing several aspects of Kim's life and career, lavishly illustrated with often-exclusive photography. In the early issues, Kim would write down and illustrate song lyrics, and she continued to write a letter to her fans in every issue until the fan club folded at the end of 1997. Various people were involved, but Kim's close friend Edwina Smith, who joined the team in the early 1980s, was the head administrator from 1985 to 1995.

And with the phenomenal success of Kim's first hits, especially 'Kids in America', there were soon plans for the family to create their own recording studio, Select Sound, in Knebworth, Hertfordshire – although that would take a couple of years to materialise.

With all these changes in motion, a friend of Kim's named Nick Boyles was employed by the family at Big M Productions in the summer of 1981. It was becoming increasingly obvious that the amount of work caused by Kim's popularity wasn't going to decrease any time soon – quite the opposite. Nick had just graduated from business school and Joyce invited him to take on the role of co-managing Kim's career, and he agreed. Little did he know that his involvement would span decades...

Nick Boyles: "She's incredibly industrious, she's very hard-working, she's very accommodating, and I see my job as basically trying to make what is a very difficult job sometimes as comfortable and as easy as I possibly can."[4]

Kim's promotion schedule was extensive and hectic: within months she was flying around the world, always accompanied by Sonja Hardie, an experienced employee at RAK who represented the label but also looked out for Kim during the first three years of her career. Whenever Kim returned to the UK, there was always a TV appearance on the schedule: in 1981 alone, she appeared on *Top Of The Pops* five times.

Although there wasn´t much time for pop stars to hang around and get to know one another, Kim and Ricky started hanging out with Kirsty MacColl. Like Kim, she was a young singer in a flourishing pop world. She was involved with a member of Tenpole Tudor, while Kim hung out with the band's guitarist Bob Kingston. Kim later credited Kirsty for encouraging her to get into songwriting.

Kim: "I remember thinking 'Wow! She's so young, she's 20 years old, she's writing these great songs, she's on the radio, she's so positive, so gutsy. I wanted really to be more like Kirsty MacColl. It was Kirsty who encouraged me to start songwriting myself, although it took a few years for me to find the time and the confidence. I subsequently got to know her, and in fact for a while we were both dating guys in the same band, Tenpole Tudor, which was great fun! She came to the very first rehearsals I did in North London for my very first tour. I've got lovely photographs that I've taken of her from that time."[5]

Another artist around at the time was Clare Grogan from Altered Images. There was a certain rivalry between the two, Kim later conceded, as Clare kept appearing on magazine covers that Kim also wanted to be on, but there were no lingering hard feelings.

Clare Grogan: "I think I've always had a sort of... I was going to say crush!... on Kim, ever since I was a wee Altered Images girl, and she always seemed so sophisticated, and she's so beautiful... and our paths crossed – we weren't pals or anything like that, but she always seemed such a supportive girl, and she is!"[6]

By September 1981, Kim's debut album had attained gold status. She returned from extensive promotional visits abroad to start work on new material, the single ´Water On Glass´ and her LP still in the UK charts, but with the record company and record-buying public already expecting a new album.

WATER ON GLASS
Written by Marty & Ricky Wilde
Produced by Ricky Wilde
Released: 17 July 1981
Chart position: 11 (UK), 10 (Ireland)

The opening track of Kim Wilde's debut album was not your average pop song. The crystalline sounds of the intro are interrupted by stabs of electric guitar, and when Kim starts to sing, she sings about '*a sound in my head that I feel / and it shuts me in a prison*'. In the chorus, it's a 'sound of running water'. The song references tinnitus, a symptom that causes the perception of sound within the human ear in the absence of corresponding external sound. A common cause is noise-induced hearing loss – which is why many pop musicians suffer from it. The subject may have come up because Marty experienced it, or else he had heard about it from fellow rock'n'roll stars. And Kim started to suffer from tinnitus in later years, although coping successfully with it.

The song was released as Kim's third single in the UK and Ireland, with that version a remix of the album track. Most notably, the left and right channels were switched. Remarkably, 'Water on Glass' was also the first Kim Wilde track listed in a US Billboard chart, reaching No.52 in the Top 60 Rock Tracks on 15 May 1982. It was unreleased elsewhere as by the time 'Chequered Love' had left the charts in those countries, new single 'Cambodia' was already available.

The single version appeared on various compilation albums in the 1990s and also featured in remastered form in re-releases of Kim's debut album in 2009 and 2020. The 2020 release also featured new remixes of the track by Project K. and Eddie Said & Luke Nutley.

Peruvian band Mache recorded a Spanish-language version called 'Vuelve Otra Vez' in 1984, while in 2003, Greek-Swedish DJ Steve Angello created the track 'Voices' around a sample of 'Water on Glass'.

Kim has always performed the song live, from her first tour in 1982 until the Here Come the Aliens tours in 2018 and 2019. It has become a live favourite for band and fans alike.

OUR TOWN
Written by Marty & Ricky Wilde
Produced by Ricky Wilde

Ricky composed the music for this song, and when Marty heard the backing track, he latched on to the idea of a 'city song', saying, 'It's written for the kid who lives in an area he should really get out of'.

Kim's young voice, bordering on the shrill, sounds almost desperate in the bridge, as she proclaims: *'No prospects, just projects / Don't try to tell me we're living / There's no real need to try / Can't you see this town's gonna die'*. A glorious, short instrumental break follows, embellished with synthesizers and soaring guitars. The sound of the first album is definitely 'new wave'.

EVERYTHING WE KNOW
Written by Marty & Ricky Wilde
Produced by Ricky Wilde

After the first two songs of Kim's debut album, 'Everything We Know' is a bit of a curveball. Suddenly there's a reggae rhythm and a very relaxed, almost sleepy vocal to take in. Described by Marty as 'a lazy reggae summer song', it is also a sad song when you listen to lyrics like *'Don't bring your gun 'round here / Don't need you mouthing off your fear / It touches all, you can build a wall / We all have tasted tears'*.

In an interview, Kim explained the use of this very different style: "We're not about doing only one style of song, one type of music. Our musical influences and tastes are very different and very wide, we want our music to reflect that. Ricky and I love 'The Police'; this track is very influenced by them."

The song became the B-side of 'Chequered Love' when it was released in the USA in 1982, but has only ever been performed live during Kim's debut tour in 1982.

YOUNG HEROES
Written by Marty & Ricky Wilde
Produced by Ricky Wilde

Just like 'Our Town', Marty wrote 'Young Heroes' specifically for young people. According to him, 'It's a kind of light rebellious song. The kids today are like the kids of any young generation: they are the young heroes, and we think the song celebrates that.'

Remarkably, the song ended up on a 7" single in Peru, appropriately paired with 'Our Town'.

She didn't perform the song during her debut tour in 1982, but it was included in the setlists during 1985's Rage to Rock Tour.

The song was eventually performed in the American TV series 'Fame', during its fourth season. In the episode 'Spontaneous Combustion', originally broadcast on 13 October 1984, pupils rebel against strict school rules, put in place after a teacher ends up in hospital during an incident involving pupils dancing and carrying on in the school corridors. When the injured teacher returns from hospital, she starts playing the piano in the canteen, and the characters Nicole Chapman (performed by Nia Peeples) and Doris Schwartz (Valerie Landsburg) sing 'Young Heroes'.

CHEQUERED LOVE
Written by Marty & Ricky Wilde
Produced by Ricky Wilde
Released: 27 April 1981
Chart positions: 4 (UK), 16 (Austria), 2 (Belgium), 2 (Germany), 4 (Ireland), 2 (Netherlands), 1 (South Africa), 6 (Sweden), 2 (Switzerland), 6 (Australia)

After the success of 'Kids in America', Marty and Ricky had to come up with an equally catchy hit single, so the pressure was on. They wrote several songs, Ricky going back to Mickie Most time and again with possibilities, but unable to convince the label boss there was a winner among them. During the final trip, 'Chequered Love' was the last song played, and Mickie decided that was the one. The song was recorded in two days, but like 'Kids in America' before it, it took several mixing sessions before it was ready for release. The final mix was made on 6 April and released three weeks later. Kim's involvement in the process was limited at this point, but she did suggest the title.

Kim: "Dad wrote [the song], but he didn't have a title. He just wrote a song about two people who are so different from one another, but they somehow needed to be together, something like the opposite poles of a magnet. I instantly said, 'Chequered Love.'"[7]

The video was again directed by Brian Grant and filmed at St. John's Wood Studios. Grant had the idea of putting Kim in the shower, setting the video in a bathroom.

Mickie Most: "I liked that. I think the shower idea went on to be used a couple of times after that. Olivia Newton-John used the same idea for 'Physical', and it set off a little pattern of girls in showers ... which had probably started with *Psycho...* (1960)."[8]

The song was released as Kim's second single and again as a 12" single in Europe. In 1982, a Columbian 12" single also appeared, on yellow vinyl, as well as a promotional 12" single in the USA. Like 'Kids in America' before it, none of these 12" singles featured a remix. The track was remixed by Matt Pop for the deluxe edition of 'Kim Wilde' in 2020.

East German singer Petra Zieger recorded a cover version for the state-run Amiga label within months of the single's release for the record-buying public in the German Democratic Republic. The recording appeared on a four-track

EP with three tracks by other artists. Zieger went on to become a popular singer across Germany after the Berlin Wall fell in 1989, and in 2011 met Kim when both performed live in Landsberg.

Other cover versions were recorded by rock band Human Hamster Hybrids, German orchestra leader James Last and UK band The Shields, whose acoustic take impressed Kim so much that she performed that arrangement herself during live concerts in 2016.

'Chequered Love' appeared on almost all Kim's live sets throughout her career, often at the beginning of the show.

2 6 5 8 0
Written by Marty & Ricky Wilde
Produced by Ricky Wilde

'2 6 5 8 0', is a bright and bouncy ska-influenced song. The song underscored the diversity of the album, sounding like nothing else on the LP. The lyrics were quite different too.

Kim: "I totally trusted my Dad's lyrics, a fantasy world we shared somehow, although we rarely discussed his lyrics in any great depth, it was left to me to interpret them in my own way." [9]

The song was performed live during Kim's first two tours, but hasn't appeared since.

Estonian band Kontor recorded a cover version in their native language (written by Peep Liblik), entitled 'Nõnda Uut Ei Loo', in 1990.

YOU'LL NEVER BE SO WRONG
Written by Marty & Ricky Wilde
Produced by Ricky Wilde

After 'Kids in America' and 'Tuning In Tuning On', this was the third song to be recorded. It was mixed a few times in March 1981, and originally intended as a B-side for the single, 'Chequered Love'. However, when Mickie heard the track, he thought it was too good for a B-side and said he would like Hot Chocolate to record it as their new single. The single charted when it was released in May 1981, but only reached No.52 in the UK, although it did become a big hit in Continental Europe.

Kim's version became a favourite, and it was decided it would be included on the debut album. She performed the song live during her first two tours in 1982 and 1983, and again in 1992, 2007 and 2017.

CHAPTER 4: DEBUT ALBUM

Marty: "We then wrote 'You'll Never Be So Wrong' and it came in about an hour and a half, so we recorded it and it turned out pretty good. We took the track to Mickie and after he'd listened to it a couple of times, he said it was too good to be a B-side and would like to have a crack at it with Hot Chocolate. He did a fabulous job with the song and Errol [Brown] sang it beautifully. We also thought Kim did a pretty nifty job on the old vocals. We thought it was the best track she'd ever sung."[10]

FALLING OUT
Written by Ricky Wilde
Produced by Ricky Wilde

'Falling Out' was the first song Ricky ever wrote. He recorded it in 1980, when Marty had booked studio time in Luton to record an album, but had to go to London to record a TV show instead. Ricky used the studio time to record his track. Upon hearing it, Marty was suitably impressed. Ricky's solo version never saw the light of day, but the song was used on Kim's debut LP.

The song's lyrics are about a love affair gone sour: "*So now it's over and there's nothing left to say / The flame that burned within my heart now slowly fades away*".

'Falling Out' was sampled by Un Kasa on their 2006 track 'Death Is the Only Escape'. Kim performed the track live during her debut tour, but after 1982 it was never performed again.

SHANE (B-side)
Written by Marty & Ricky Wilde
Produced by Ricky Wilde

The song 'Shane' was inspired by the classic 1953 Western movie of the same name, starring Alan Ladd and directed by George Stevens, adapted from the Jack Schaefer novel. The story involves the eponymous, mysterious stranger arriving in Wyoming, being hired as a farmhand on an isolated ranch, where the family have been hounded by a neighbouring rancher, his brother, cowhands and a vicious hired gunman out to steal land. Shane becomes attached to the family and tries everything to stop the neighbours stealing land.

Marty: "One night I was watching *Shane* on TV, and suddenly it dawned on me that I was watching a cinematic masterpiece. The film contains some of the finest acting performances in the history of celluloid. The understated way in which Alan Ladd played Shane was an inspiration to me - as, I'm sure, it has been to millions of others over the years. I wrote the lyrics to the song to Alan Ladd and the spirit he leaves behind - a tenderness and gentlemanliness that sometimes seems to have passed us by."[11]

'Shane' appeared on the B-side of 'Chequered Love', and was unreleased on CD until 1995, when EMI France released 'Un Bouquet Du Rock', a promotional sampler also featuring one track each by Joe Cocker and Tina Turner.

In 1994, Marty recorded his own version on the album 'Solid Gold'. That remains the only other recording of this remarkable track.

BOYS (B-side)
Written by Marty & Ricky Wilde
Produced by Ricky Wilde

When all the tracks of the album were recorded and it was being prepared for release, one final track was recorded and mixed that June. 'Boys' was issued on the B-side of Kim's third single, 'Water On Glass'. The style is similar to other tracks on the album, with synths and guitars in perfect harmony.

'Boys' also appeared on the first Kim Wilde compilation album, 1984's *The Very Best Of Kim Wilde*, first appearing on CD in 1987 as part of that compilation.

The song was performed live during Kim's first tour in 1982 and during the Catch Tour in 1983.

A selection of Kim Wilde badges sold during the 1980's © Marcel Rijs

CHAPTER 5:
SELECT

Released: 10 May 1982
Chart positions: 19 (UK), 8 (Australia), 20 (Austria), 1 (Finland), 3 (France), 4 (Germany), 5 (Netherlands), 12 (Norway), 2 (Sweden)

One of the most written about aspects of Kim's early career was that she had a handful of hits before she ever performed live. This was unusual at the time: most artists had to claw their way to a recording contract via live gigs in small clubs, before being noticed by a talent scout or record company representative. The assumption was that Kim was a 'manufactured pop star' – whatever that means – and that she couldn't sing without the aid of recording studio trickery.

Plans for Kim's first tour were initially made near the end of 1981, while the team was recording the second album. Apparently, Mickie Most wasn't too enthusiastic about the idea – he preferred the Wildes to concentrate on releasing hit singles – but the family pressed on.

Kim: "Of course I wanted to see who was buying my records and I wanted to meet my audience and have contact with them. Every performer who makes music wants to sing live, and up to that point I was beginning to be perceived as a video pop star, so I wanted to change that. It was in fact one of the main areas of disagreement between RAK Records, my first record company, and me. Luckily, I had my own family team to back me up, and we put a tour together and I went out and found my audience, and I've never looked back."[1]

But before Kim could go on tour, there was a second album to be made. Recording sessions started as early as August 1981, just after the release of her debut LP. The first track to come out of these sessions was 'Words Fell Down', with the first rough mixes being made near the end of the month. Work continued with 'Just a Feeling' and 'Action City' (for which an instrumental backing track was laid down by Ricky) in September, and then the Wilde team moved on to 'Cambodia'.

Originally meant for inclusion on Kim's second album, the team thought the song was strong enough to be a single release before the end of the year. So 'Cambodia' was put forward to RAK and they released the single on 2 November 1981. The single entered the UK chart on 14 November 1981 and slowly climbed to its peak position at No.12 four weeks later, Kim appearing on the *Top of the Pops* stage solo this time.

Kim celebrated her 21st birthday at Knebworth House. The setting was idyllic, suits of armour lining the walls and some of the guests dressed in medieval clothing. Part of the reason for having the party was to surprise Marty and Joyce. Kim told them it was just going to be a small do with a handful of friends. The party ended up lasting all night and featured three bands. It was Kim's way to thank her parents for all they had done for her.[2]

Kim: "I wanted something really out of the ordinary. It was at Knebworth House, which is very stately. There were 300 guests and three bands, and it was a surprise for Mum and Dad. I told them it was just going to be a small party with a handful of close friends. You should have seen their faces. They were stunned. I was glad because I felt I owed them so much. They've done a lot for me and I wanted to do something for them in return."[3]

In December 1981, Kim promoted 'Chequered Love' and 'Cambodia' in France, Spain, Portugal, Italy and Germany. She got home in time for Christmas, to celebrate with the family. It was time for a short break before the start of another successful year.

At the beginning of 1982, Kim visited America, despite the fact that her music hadn't yet been released there. She did promotion in America for the second time when EMI finally released 'Kids in America' in the summer of 1982. The single entered the Billboard Hot 100 chart on 14 August 1982. During four days in New York, she did radio and press interviews, accompanied by Sonja Hardie, head of International at RAK. There was also time to see a Broadway show starring Kim's idol Lauren Bacall, and a quick visit to the Statue of Liberty. From there, they travelled to Tokyo, Japan, staying for two weeks, doing exhaustive promotion.

Mickie Most: "I remember taking her to Los Angeles and she was just breaking through then, but the media and the record company and all the people that she met while she was there treated her as if she was already a star. She had that kind of stuff."[4]

Besides all the hard work, Kim did occasionally find the time to hang out with her colleagues. The press were always hunting for love stories, so according to the media folk every date with a pop star was an indication of love in the air for them. So, when Visage's Steve Strange went to a restaurant with Kim in January 1982 – and secretly tipped off the press – the tabloids were all over that. Amusingly, some of them reported that Kim wore no makeup while Steve wore hair lacquer and heavy mascara.

Kim: "Steve took me out on a date to the iconic Langan's Brasserie in Mayfair right at the beginning of my career in 1981, I was very in awe, having just met him, but we quickly became friends and laughed at ourselves ordering sausage and mash with champagne! As we left, the press descended on us and took some fabulous pictures, we both pouted furiously and headed off to The Blitz club, where we bumped into Marilyn and a host of exotic, beautiful New Romantics, drank vodka and crashed out at his apartment in Notting Hill.

CHAPTER 5: SELECT

When I woke up in the spare room the next morning, I wandered through his elegant apartment to find him asleep, with his eye mask on. I guess he didn't get to be that flawless without a beauty regime, and he certainly looked far more glamorous than I did the previous evening!"[5]

Steve Strange: "(...) I had a call from my PR Tony Brainsby to say the paparazzi were after me because they had heard I was having a whirlwind romance with Kim Wilde and we were going to get married. I found it all highly amusing, since all that had happened was that the previous night we had dinner together. It was probably Tony Brainsby himself who leaked the story, to get some publicity for my new club, The Playground."[6]

Kim also dated Adam Ant briefly. He sent Kim roses for her 21st birthday, although they'd never met in person. At first, she contacted his record company to thank him for her, because she was 'too embarrassed to ring him personally'.[7] But eventually, according to Kim, their managers arranged a date.[8]

Kim: "He took great care of me. He took me to very expensive restaurants. I was still living at home at that point. He would always make sure chocolate mousse was on the menu, even if it wasn't, because he knew I liked it."[9]

Kim: "I did have a few delicious dates with Adam Ant. I say delicious because the thought of it now, me, Kim Wilde at that time, and him, Adam Ant at that time, and both of us sitting in a restaurant eating chocolate mousse is a delicious memory. He looked after me for a little bit, took me out for some lovely meals in very swanky restaurants."[10]

There were occasional 'arranged dates' as well, such as a photoshoot for the UK's *Flexipop* magazine. Photographs of Kim with Duran Duran's Simon Le Bon went around the world. And in France, Kim paired up with French rock'n'roll legend Johnny Hallyday. In the TV programme *Formule 1+1*, broadcast on 24 May 1982, they performed a version of the Elvis Presley song 'Teddy Bear' together. The choice seemed surprising to Kim's fans, but in the Wilde household, Elvis was an idol. Marty was always a fan and even made his daughter Roxanne a member of his fan club when she was just a baby.[11]

On 10 May 1982, *Select* was released, just ten months after Kim's debut album. It was a conscious decision to write small stories for the album, as became apparent in an interview with Kim at the time.

Kim: "My father, who writes the lyrics, has said that he wanted to make stage plays of each of the songs. Well, he certainly succeeded, especially with 'View From A Bridge' and 'Cambodia'."[12]

Photographer Gered Mankowitz may have picked up on the two faces of this album when he created the iconic sleeve. While Kim looks the same on both sides, the background is white on one side and black on the other. There are some bright, positive songs on this album, like 'Just A Feeling', 'Take Me Tonight' and

Kim live at Muziekcentrum Vredenburg, Utrecht (Netherlands), 14 November 1982 © Robert Hoetink

RAK
Trade Mark of RAK RECORDS LTD
CAMBODIA
(R. Wilde / M. Wilde)
RAK 336
RAK 336A 45
Rickim Music Ltd. / RAK Publ. Ltd.
Produced by Ricky Wilde
KIM WILDE
℗1981 Original sound recording made by RAK Records Ltd.
CARBON FIBRE

'Can You Come Over', but there is certainly a dark quality to most of the other tracks.

Reviews of the album were, again, largely favourable. Dutch magazine *Popfoto* said: "Musically it has become a piece of work that finds a middle ground between recognisable and innovative. The lyrics are also outstanding."[13] *Top* in Belgium wrote: "Her new record answers questions like: How do I make a good song? How do I make an interesting lyric? How to combine music that has an impact with trends and sounding original?"[14] *Sounds* in Germany thought *Select* was 'better than Blondie and the equally good counterpart to the light-hearted, equally necessary Altered Images."[15]

Ricky's production work hadn't gone unnoticed. Having produced Kim's first two albums, he was in demand by other artists. On 25 June 1982, the single 'Sensitive' by Japan's Mick Karn was released, with both sides of the single produced and mixed by Mick Karn and Ricky Wilde.

Although Kim was often referred to as a passing pop phenomenon, the 'serious' music press couldn't ignore her for long. By the end of 1981 she appeared on the cover of the *NME (New Musical Express)*, and the March 1982 issue of *The Face* magazine also featured her on the cover.

Kim: "I remember at that time being pretty chuffed to be on the cover of *The Face*. It was all about style. I didn't really feel I had a lot and in retrospect I didn't. I was great at wearing jackets and jeans and being a tomboy, which I was at school and to a degree still am; a 55-year-old woman's version. I just wasn't a very stylish person and that kind of shows it. Even the cover of *The Face* couldn't make me look stylish."[16]

Kim's first live tour happened in the second half of 1982. Introducing Kim to a live audience was something that was carefully planned. A six-date tour in Denmark in September preceded an impressive 19-date UK tour in October, audiences in small Danish towns like Slagelse, Abenra and Vejle acting as a testing ground.

A band was put together through auditions and recommendations. Trevor Murrell (drums) and Gary Barnacle (saxophone) were involved in the recording of the first album and were obvious choices. Graham Pleath was recruited for keyboards and guitar, Mark Heyward Chaplin on bass, and Lynne Jones and Gaynor Wild would provide backing vocals. Then there was a young man named Steve Byrd. Born on 25 September 1955, he'd already worked with the bands Zzebra and Gillan. In the summer of 1982, he auditioned for a spot in the band.

Steve Byrd: "Rick showed me the chords to 'Chequered Love' and 'Kids in America', and we were off. Kim was not present and of course I was slightly disappointed, as I love to show my skills to a beautiful girl and she was one of the hottest at the time. We got through the songs with no problems as they are

not technically demanding, relying more on energy and vibe, and I had both in abundance. They thanked me for coming and said they would call me later."[17]

Two weeks of rehearsals followed, led by Ricky and under the watchful eye of Marty, who sometimes offered his advice. The final production rehearsals happened in the presence of family, promoters and a film crew, who produced a 25-minute special for Thames Television, *First Time Out*, and RAK boss, Mickie Most. The documentary went 'behind the scenes', giving fans a sneak peek into those rehearsals.

Then it was off to Denmark… The interest in Kim's live debut was there: media from all over Europe and the UK travelled to Slagelse to see her first show. One writer remarked that the audience 'wasn't exactly a difficult crowd to face - just 1,800 local children, who had never seen a rock show before and who would probably have clapped if Kim had stood stone still and recited a nursery rhyme.'[18] But the Danish had a reputation of being hard to win over, so if Kim was to have success on those stages, she would be equally successful – or even more – on stage in the UK and the rest of Europe.

Kim: "I was extremely nervous before doing my first live shows. I had no idea what to expect. But the audience reaction was overwhelming."[19]

During the tour, Kim stayed true to her philosophy of wearing 'normal' clothes. Dressed in jeans and a white t-shirt, plus a black leather jacket during the first few songs, she was instantly recognisable from all the photographs taken of her during the two preceding years. For Kim, her boots were also very important. For some years, she'd worn black boots with studs around the ankle, and even though they were almost worn out, she made sure she had them on for her first Danish concert.[20] For the UK tour, she had them copied.

Kim: "I had a beautiful pair of black boots made for the tour, a copy of some older boots I've always worn. I spent the morning throwing them around the room, kicking them, and everyone was asking, 'What are you doing? They cost you all that money!' But they looked too new!"[21]

The UK tour started in Bristol on 5 October 1982 and stopped by in Wolverhampton, Scarborough, Newcastle, Glasgow, Aberdeen, Dundee, Edinburgh, Southport, Sheffield, Manchester, Birmingham, Leicester, Gloucester, Paignton, Bournemouth and Brighton, finishing with two dates in London on 26 and 27 October.

Then it was off to Europe, where the group visited Nice, Lyon, Strasbourg, Lille, Paris and Annecy in France, Deinze in Belgium, Groningen and Utrecht in the Netherlands, then finally Brussels and Antwerp in Belgium.

The whole tour was met with enthusiastic audiences, screaming for Kim, and mostly favourable reviews. The *Daily Express* wrote: "She did give rousing treatments to numbers like 'Chequered Love', 'Kids in America' and 'Our Town', which in their way are marvellous anthems of teenage life. On a slower ballad she also proved she has a strong voice which can be stretched even further in the future."[22] German magazine *Popcorn* added: "Kim's voice fascinates throughout, she sings exactly as strong as on record."[23] Some papers were more critical, such as the Dutch *Utrechts Nieuwsblad*: "Kim played, beside songs from her two albums, all the hits, including the new single 'Child Come Away'. A great atmosphere was reserved for the slow 'I Really Can't Explain', which had a great sax solo. The celebratory 'Kids in America' ended a concert that didn't have the quality of Kim's records, but during which she was able to present herself well with her band."[24]

The year 1982 ended with another treat for Kim Wilde fans: the film crew who followed Kim during her tour in the UK had edited down hours of footage to create the *First Time Out* documentary, which was broadcast on ITV on New Year's Eve. For the first time in two years, Kim went on a holiday to the Caribbean in December. It was a brief respite from her hard work.

Kim: "I really needed that holiday. It has been such a hectic few years, and I'd become pretty run down before I left. The tour really took it out of me!" [25]

EGO
Written by Marty & Ricky Wilde
Produced by Ricky Wilde

From the first moments of 'Ego', it is obvious that the rock edge of the debut album has made way for a more electronic, synth-driven sound. Kim's vocals cut through the backing track with accusatory lines: '*All the time I try to reason with you / But I just can't seem to make you understand / Nothing seems to ever really get through / Can't you feel emotions like any other man?*'.

Marty: "The lyrics of 'Ego' were based on a particular person I know of, whose outlook to life is very narrow, basically because of his extreme self-centredness, and I hoped that if he heard the song he might change his ways. I feel that all of us at one time or another go through a very self-centred time, but how much nicer we are when we think of other people." [26]

Although the track wasn't released as a single, a promotional 7" was actually made in Australia, coupling 'Ego' with the next track on *Select*: 'Words Fell Down'. A rough mix of the track, created in March 1982, appeared on the 2020 deluxe release of 'Select'.

Kim performed the track on TV once, for French programme *Video Cracks* on 17 September 1982.

WORDS FELL DOWN
Written by Marty & Ricky Wilde
Produced by Ricky Wilde

'Words Fell Down' was one of the first songs to come together for 'Select'. Mixing started as early as August 1981, although several versions were needed to come to the final version in early 1982.

The song became a firm live favourite, performed until 1985 and from 2011 onwards. A live version was included on Kim's live album *Aliens Live* in 2019. One of the original mixes from August 1981 appeared on the 2020 deluxe release of *Select*.

UK-based DJ and producer John B created an unofficial remix of this track called 'Helpless', eventually released as a free download in 2016.

ACTION CITY
Written by Marty & Ricky Wilde
Produced by Ricky Wilde

In September 1981, Ricky recorded an instrumental backing track – ultimately included on the 2020 deluxe release of *Select* – that inspired Marty to write a song about his perception of the world around him.

Marty: "Action City was written at a time when our country, I felt, was in an extremely dangerous position. This was basically because of the great social unrest that was taking place."[27]

In 1983, Czech vocalist Marie Rottrová recorded a cover version in a Czech translation by Zdenek Mašta, titled 'Já Tvé Sny Znám' ('I Know Your Dreams').

VIEW FROM A BRIDGE
Written by Marty & Ricky Wilde
Produced by Ricky Wilde
Released: 5 April 1982
Chart positions: 16 (UK), 7 (Australia), 10 (Austria), 4 (Belgium, Sweden), 7 (Netherlands), 2 (Switzerland)

The lyrics of 'View From a Bridge' seem to be about suicide, but as with other lyrics penned by Marty, they are open to interpretation.

Kim: "It's mainly about someone looking at her own reflection in the water and who is coming to terms with herself. Indirectly it could be me."[28]

The song was selected as Kim's fifth single, following up 'Cambodia' after months of success for that single all over Europe. By comparison, 'View From a Bridge' had a more modest chart performance, but remains a strong favourite among fans.

Reviews were favourable. *Smash Hits* raved: "Have you ever noticed how clever the Wilde intros are? This is one of the best yet"[29], whereas the *Daily Mail* commented: "I'm not sure who impresses me most - Kim Wilde or her brother, Ricky, who has come up with an excellent production."[30]

Featuring a stunning cover created by Dutch photographer Anton Corbijn and graphic designer Simon Halfon, the single confirmed the new sound of Kim Wilde once more. The synth-driven song had a driving rhythm and a catchy chorus. The music video was again directed by Brian Grant and filmed at St John's Wood Studios – it was his fourth and last video with Kim.

Kim: "I remember when I first saw it, I didn't like the video at all. I remember turning around to the director, saying, 'This is a bit of a disappointment'. There you go, I was completely wrong. It was a very good video. I was just very self-critical in those days. I guess when you're 20-something that's what you do all the time, isn't it?"[31]

A 12" single was released in Europe, featuring the regular A and B-sides, but in Japan, a promotional 12" single featured 'Abracadabra' by the Steve Miller Band on the B-side.

Although the song was not remixed at the time, it was given the remix treatment in 2001 when EMI released *The Very Best Of Kim Wilde*. The 'RAW remix' was created by Johan Strandkvist especially for this release. In 2020, a remix by Luke Mornay was released on the 2020 deluxe release of *Select*.

The song has been covered by Chekov & Gagarin, Industrial Zoo, Ken, Leæther Strip, Lynn Sweet and the Top of the Poppers. A Finnish translation, 'Kuin Roskakertomus', was released by Meiju Suvas in 1982.

JUST A FEELING
Written by Marty & Ricky Wilde
Produced by Ricky Wilde

After 'Words Fell Down', 'Just A Feeling' was the next track for *Select* to be developed in August and September 1981. Marty called it 'just a simple love song'.

The rough mix that was included in the 2020 deluxe release of 'Select' revealed some alternative lyrics. The second verse starts, '*Feeling so bad, I just walk on my own / I go through the streets of the city I know / I just gotta find you and see you again / I look for the places, the places we'd go*'. The final version is an improvement for sure: '*Now all I see is the trace of a smile / Memories forgotten a long time ago / Never believed I could see you this way / I don't know what changed you, I'll just never know*'. Also, the early version didn't feature the guitar solo that ended up on the album.

In November 2015, Swedish singer Måns Wieslander recorded a cover version of 'Just A Feeling'.

CHAOS AT THE AIRPORT
Written by Marty & Ricky Wilde
Produced by Ricky Wilde

One of the more controversial tracks in Kim's repertoire is 'Chaos at the Airport', appearing on side two of *Select*. The menacing backing track added to the atmosphere of fear and paranoia, opening the second side in style.

Marty: "This stems from my own crazy, distorted opinion of flying and most of the chaos at the airport takes place in my own mind, since I'm rather scared of flying and I had this vision of all these jets trying to land at the same time and crashing." [32]

TAKE ME TONIGHT
Written by Marty & Ricky Wilde
Produced by Ricky Wilde

The first mixes of 'Take Me Tonight' were made in November 1981, with one included on the 2020 deluxe edition of *Select*.

The song became the B-side for 'View From A Bridge' and ended up being an A-side in Japan, where it was included on the soundtrack of the movie *Shadow* (aka *Tenebrae*), directed by Dario Argento. The film was originally released in America as *Unsane*, with around 10 minutes of footage cut, but 'Take Me Tonight' was added over the closing credits, without Argento's knowledge.

Kim performed the song live during her debut tour in 1982 and the Catch Tour in 1983.

CAN YOU COME OVER
Written by Marty & Ricky Wilde
Produced by Ricky Wilde

As the deadline for the album was approaching, there was a certain amount of urgency to record the last track. Hence the Blondie-inspired 'Can You Come Over' was recorded at the Wilde family home in Hertfordshire, using the RAK Mobile studio. It was parked in the bottom of the garden and all the cables ran into the house. Parts of the song were recorded in the hallway, in Kim's bedroom and in the dining room, at very odd hours in the morning. Backing vocals were provided by Kim and her mother Joyce.

The song has never been performed live.

WENDY SADD
Written by Marty & Ricky Wilde
Produced by Ricky Wilde

Marty: "This was based on the kind of police brutality you see in certain sections of America. I saw the song, like I see most of the others, as a mini-film, with a sad and vulnerable girl falling into the hands of a very powerful authority. The actual name comes from *Top of the Pops*, where there used to be a girl - she may still work there for all I know - called Wendy Sadd. When Ricky came home and said he had met a girl by that name, I said that's an incredible name and should be a title of a song. So, Wendy Sadd is actually a real name."[33]

Marty didn't hold back on the lyrics: it is surely the most dramatic story on the album, although other songs already put the listener through heartbreak, suicide, social unrest and airplanes crashing. The lyrics are underscored by Ricky's backing track, that has an increasingly haunting quality.

The song has never been performed live.

CAMBODIA
Written by Marty & Ricky Wilde
Produced by Ricky Wilde
Released: 2 November 1981
Chart positions: 1 (Denmark, France, Sweden, Switzerland), 2 (Belgium, Germany, Netherlands), 4 (Austria), 12 (UK)

Marty and Ricky heard a track with two bass notes repeating one after the other, and both thought it would be a great introduction to a song. Ricky recorded a track with Eastern percussion sounds on it, which inspired Marty to write a song about Cambodia, influenced by Michael Herr's *Dispatches*, one of many books about the war in Vietnam that Marty read at the time.

Marty: "I didn't want to turn the song into a political essay, I tried in my own way to show what I believe most people felt about South Vietnam and the terrible tragedies that occurred there."[34]

Kim: "My father and brother wrote the song. At the time the war was always in the news, which inspired them to write a love story in the midst of this terrible conflict." [35]

CHAPTER 5: SELECT

Kim had the lyrics of the song changed slightly, so she could sing it in the third person. She explained this while she was promoting the song in Europe.

Kim: "It's about a wife of an American pilot, who ends up being killed in the Cambodian war. The lyric was originally written in the first person. But while I could really identify with the woman in question, I changed it, so I now sing it in third person."[36]

The story hints at dramatic things happening but doesn't really explain. But it seemed that this was the whole idea of 'Cambodia', and indeed other tracks on the album.

Kim: "Cambodia is open to all kinds of interpretations like most of our songs, really. I prefer listeners to make their own interpretations."

The single, released on 2 November 1981, came in a remarkable sleeve, featuring a drawn story at the front (by an uncredited artist) and a photograph of Kim at the back (resulting from a session with Gered Mankowitz). There were a lot of variations internationally, probably because local record companies thought it was risky not to see the name 'Kim Wilde' appear on the single's sleeve — or a picture of the singer herself. So, while the 'real' front cover was used for UK and German pressings, record companies in France, Italy, Portugal and Spain all used variations on the back cover instead.

The music video was recorded in one day at Shepperton Film Studios, directed by Brian Grant. He would later admit he 'watched *Apocalypse Now* too many times and had delusions of being a movie director'.

Kim: "Doing 'Cambodia' was pretty scary because I was lying on the floor and had a huge boa constrictor snake slithering all over me. It scared the life out of me, and that's before they told me about the tarantulas! – but I was up for the challenge!"

The success of 'Cambodia' was major in Europe. The single topped the charts in Sweden, Denmark, Switzerland and France. It made the top five almost everywhere else. In France, the single sold over a million copies.

'Cambodia' was eventually remixed by Paul Oakenfold for the 2006 album *Never Say Never* and by Matt Pop and Luke Mornay for the 2020 deluxe edition of *Select*.

When EMI released several compilation albums during the 1990s, there was a strange mix-up with 'Cambodia' and its reprise. While the track listings of *The Gold Collection*, *The Best of Kim Wilde* and several repackages of that compilation listed 'Cambodia – Reprise', only the instrumental reprise appeared on these albums, confusing many listeners expecting to hear the hit, getting an instrumental version instead.

Just like Kim Wilde's debut single 'Kids in America', 'Cambodia' was subsequently covered by many other bands and artists. Where 'Kids in America' was recorded mainly (although not exclusively) by rock and punk-oriented bands, 'Cambodia' was recorded by a more varied group: starting with electronic bands such as Norwegian outfit Apoptygma Berzerk and German DJ Pulsedriver, there were also hardcore techno acts like Vorwerk and Marco V, as well as Swedish death metal band Hearse. Greek DJ and producer Zac F created the track 'Lover's Come' on the basis of the melody of 'Cambodia'. Swiss duo Letris made a rather innocent pop cover. And then there were some translations: German singer Jacqueline released 'Verloren in der Einsamkeit' ('Lost in Loneliness') in 2010, while Finnish singer Satu Pentikäinen released 'Matka Tuntemattomaan' in 1982.

BITTER IS BETTER
Written by Masami Tsuchiya & Bill Crunchfield
Produced by Ricky Wilde

Recording sessions for *Select* were interrupted in early 1982, because Kim had to record a single especially for the Japanese market. Masami Tsuchiya from the band Ippu-Do produced an advert for B&L Bitter Lemon. The advertising company wanted to bring together Ippu Do's music and Kim's image. So, the song 'Bitter Is Better' came together. Written by Tsuchiya with lyricist Bill Crunchfield, musically the song takes some cues from 'Words Fell Down', unreleased at that time.

Kim was persuaded to get involved in the campaign because it would bring extra exposure in Japan – many artists before her took the advertising route for promotional reasons – and she would be presented as a serious artist.

No less than 15 people were flown over from Japan to film the advert, which happened at the RAK Studios. The commercial was made in 15-second and 30-second versions. The single 'Bitter Is Better' was released in March 1982 to coincide with the launch of the ad campaign, but only in Japan. This sparked outrage among European fans, with the single very hard to get hold of elsewhere.

A Japanese promotional 12" single featured 'Bitter Is Better' on the A-side and Leo Sayer's 'Tuxedo Body' on the B-side. It is still a highly sought-after record. The song was also included on the Japanese version of *Select* instead of the reprise of 'Cambodia'. It was eventually released in France in 1984, to coincide with compilation albums released by EMI.

'Bitter Is Better' appeared on CD in 1989 on the Japanese release of *The Very Best of Kim Wilde* and in 2006 on UK compilation album *The Hits Collection*. The remastered versions of *Select* in 2009 and 2020 also included the song. On the 2020 edition of *Select*, the instrumental version appeared for the very first time.

WATCHING FOR SHAPES (B-side)
Written by Marty & Ricky Wilde
Produced by Ricky Wilde

Originally developed under the working title 'Shapes That Grow', Ricky originally laid down a backing track with a soft synth backing and a loud guitar solo. Marty's lyrics are mysterious on this track, with verses like '*In my mind there's a space that's full of painted pictures / Things I did that I went through but can't recall / Now and then there's a flash of the unknown*'.

With double-tracked voice loops and guitar playing throughout, the song contrasted well with the synth-driven A-side 'Cambodia'.

The song was performed live during Kim's first tour in 1982 and the Catch Tour in 1983, but has disappeared from setlists since.

CHILD COME AWAY
Written by Marty & Ricky Wilde
Produced by Ricky Wilde
Released: 4 October 1982
Chart positions: 43 (UK), 25 (Belgium), 36 (Germany), 10 (Sweden), 6 (Switzerland)

Although many would argue there was enough 'single material' on *Select* ('Ego' and 'Words Fell Down' come to mind), Mickie Most opted for a non-album single to be released around the time of Kim's first live tour. It was up to Marty and Ricky to come up with a song that warranted such a release.

Having written small stories like 'Wendy Sadd' and 'Cambodia' for the album, a similar approach was used for 'Child Come Away', recorded in August 1982, telling the story of a girl with a mark on the side of her face, found at the beach at night. Early mixes of the song have Kim singing harmonies in the verses, but the harmonies were eventually dropped from the final mix.

Dutch photographer Anton Corbijn provided the stunning shot for the sleeve, which was again designed by Simon Halfon. The 12" single, released in Europe, was pressed for the last time with the same versions as the 7".

The music video was directed by Tony van den Ende and recorded on a beach in Cornwall the day before Kim's debut tour started.

Kim: "We went down to a beautiful beach in Perranporth, Cornwall for the weekend, we were very lucky with the weather, as before we arrived it had been terrible, and it was essential we made the video that particular weekend as there was no other time to do it before the tour started."[37]

Kim: "Mickie Most arranged for an American police car to be parked on the beach and also a helicopter. The video featured members of the local

community, who gamely joined in as extras. At the end of the video a mysterious bright light dazzles the crowd, who cover their eyes. I think Mickie was suggesting that maybe something 'other worldly' was going on, and in a way it was!"[38]

The record-buying public didn't seem interested, as it was the first Kim Wilde single to stall just outside the UK top 40.

Although the song was never remixed originally, fans were treated to Matt Pop versions – both vocal and instrumental – in 2020, when the deluxe edition of *Select* was released by Cherry Pop.

JUST ANOTHER GUY (B-side)
Written by Marty & Ricky Wilde
Produced by Ricky Wilde

Released on the B-side of 'Child Come Away', 'Just Another Guy' is an overlooked gem in the Kim Wilde catalogue. The track speeds along like a fast train, appropriate since the lyrics mention '*Gotta say goodbye / Gonna catch a train to nowhere*'. Ricky provides backing vocals.

The song was released on CD for the first time in 1998, on Australian compilation double-CD *Collection*.

HE WILL BE THERE
Written by Marty & Ricky Wilde
Produced by Ricky Wilde

Informed mainly by Marty's preference for country-tinged ballads, this song was eventually dropped from the album, but rescued from the archives in 2020, when *Select* was released as a deluxe version by Cherry Pop. 'He Will Be There' delivers what the title promises: a song about a woman longing for the return of her love interest, with lines like '*Seven o'clock and he's late / Nevertheless, I guess I'll wait*' and '*Maybe there's something wrong / Maybe his work just took too long*'.
With Kim's image being the strong, young, independent girl, the song was probably deemed unsuitable. Listening back almost four decades later, it seems a bit old-fashioned, but charming nonetheless.

WHEN THE BOY'S HAPPY (THE GIRL'S HAPPY TOO) (live performance)
Written by Jeff Barry & Ellie Greenwich

'When the Boy's Happy (The Girl's Happy Too)' was originally released in 1963 as a single by the Four Pennies, an American girl group originating from the Bronx,

New York City. The single was a minor hit, stalling at No.95 in the Billboard Hot 100. As the Chiffons they recorded 'He's So Fine' that same year, and that single reached No.1, the band continuing to release singles under that name throughout the 1960s, with varying success.

During her debut tour, Kim performed this song – a personal favourite of hers – live, giving Gary Barnacle on saxophone and Steve Byrd on bass guitar a chance to shine during their respective solos. Kim introduced the song as one of her favourites, giving fans a chance to listen to a song from 1963 – which for many of them may have been a first encounter.

No official recordings of Kim's performance of this song exist. Audience recordings reveal that Kim and her band turn it into an upbeat, bouncy little number that is a joy to listen to.

INTERVIEW: ANTON CORBIJN

What was it like to work with Kim back in 1982? And do you remember how many sessions you did with her?

I believe I did two shoots with her - the first one for the *NME* and I reckon because of that shoot I was asked to do a shoot for her to be used for a calendar and a single sleeve.

What struck you most about her from a photographic point of view?

She was an interesting and very attractive mix between a 'babe' and the girl next door, if that doesn't sound insulting, because it isn't meant that way at all. Very likeable person.

You are probably best known for your images in black and white, but a lot of your photographs of Kim were actually made (and printed) in colour. Was this an artistic decision at the time, or were there other reasons?

Well, the *NME* shoot and the single sleeve for 'View From A Bridge' were in black and white. I guess the calendar had to be mostly colour as it was a very commercial enterprise, and not a great shoot from my end, I think.

Your photographs were used on the sleeves of the singles 'View From a Bridge' and 'Child Come Away'. Did you work with Simon Halfon (who designed them), or was it just a case of submitting the photographs?

No, he did his design on the photos once these were taken.

Is there any one photograph of Kim that you're particularly proud of?

Yes, my first shot with her, that is also published in my book *1-2-3-4*. It has a hint of sexuality to it, which was rare for me as I was quite shy then.

Do you have a favourite Kim Wilde track?

I still think that 'Kids in America' is a track you put the volume up for, so that would be my choice as fave track.

KIM WILDE

What do you admire most about Kim as an artist and/or person?
She is very down to earth, I always liked that about her. She interviewed me once for a TV show in 1985, and I was so chuffed to be invited by her for her show. She can do no wrong in my eyes obviously...

Kim live at Volksbelang, Mechelen (Belgium), 25 November 1983 © Bart Moons

CHAPTER 6:

CATCH AS CATCH CAN

Released: 24 October 1983
Chart positions: 90 (UK), 97 (Australia), 1 (Finland), 23 (Germany), 21 (Netherlands), 17 (Sweden), 6 (Switzerland)

In January 1983 Kim and her band performed four songs at the Midem Festival in Cannes, France. Industry chronicle *Music Week* wrote: "The immense European popularity of Kim Wilde was obvious from the wild applause at the mere mention of her name. While her striking good looks have helped to launch her, she proved in a sensational show that silenced the cynics that her simple, delightfully dated sound has great magnetism. Her tight, impressive backing musicians helped Kim score with immaculate versions of her hits 'Kids in America', 'Chequered Love' and View From a Bridge."[1]

Another event was the BPI Awards, now known as 'The Brits'. The event was held at Grosvenor House Hotel on 8 February 1983. Having survived the snowstorm outside, artists and representatives were treated to a dinner. Then, at 10pm, it was time to get down to business. Although many people surrounding her were aware that she was there to pick up the award for Best Female Artist, Kim was kept in the dark.

Kim: "I wasn't used to being around famous people at all, so when we got to the awards and sat at a table right next to Paul McCartney and his wife, Linda, I was very star-struck. I remember holding Ricky's hand under the table when the nominations were read out. I didn't think I'd be in with a chance of winning, and when I heard my name announced as Best British Female Solo Artist, I stood up in a blur. My head was completely spinning with the whole thing. I remember Paul McCartney looking up at me from his table, saying in his Scouse accent, 'Well done, luv!' It didn't seem real."[2]

Kim: "When Angela Rippon read out my name I nearly fell through the floor. By the time I got to the stage to pick up my award, I was so overcome I couldn't say a word. It was the most emotional experience of my life. I got Angela to say a few words of thanks to everyone there, but especially to the three most important people, my Mum and Dad and Ricky."[3]

Several group photos were taken during the night, with all the award-winners (Yazoo, John Williams, Michael Jackson, Kid Creole, Paul McCartney and Kim) appearing together, and in separate groups. One of the most iconic photographs from that night shows Kim alongside Michael Jackson, Pete Townshend and Paul McCartney.

Kim: "I didn't get to speak much with anyone on the night. I think we were all a bit shy of each other, in truth. But this photograph turned out to be incredibly prophetic, because a few years later, in 1988, I did the Bad tour with Michael Jackson. That tour was a game-changer for me, in terms of my career and as a live performer, watching him at the height of his potency as an artist. Then, in 1996, I was Mrs Walker in Pete Townshend's musical, *Tommy*, **in the West End, and that's where I met my husband, Hal [Fowler], who was one of my co-stars. I'm quite superstitious about these things, and when I look at the photograph, I think Paul McCartney is the only one who hasn't affected my life personally, although he has as a musician, for sure."**[4]

Kim was invited to appear on the 1,000[th] edition of *Top of the Pops*, along with many other pop acts. In between performances by Blancmange and Fun Boy Three, she and Barbara Dickson were briefly interviewed by Mike Read. Besides an hour-long show there was a big after-show party for all the stars present.

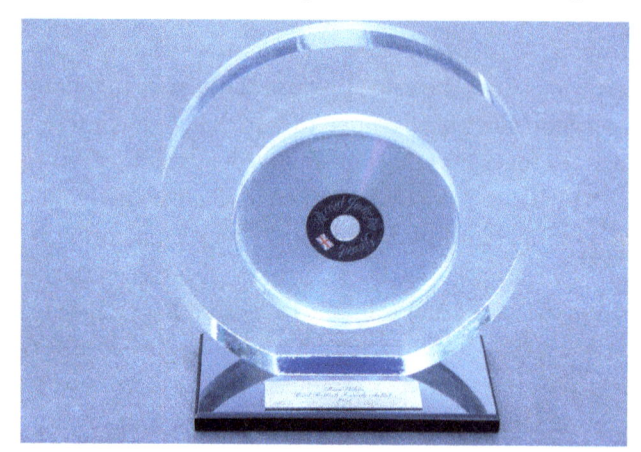

Kim Wilde's BPI Award from 1983 © Marcel Rijs

During the first half of 1983, most of the new album came together in demo form. The first demo of 'Shoot to Disable' was made in February, but it took a few months to be completed. Still, in July Kim said in an interview with pop magazine *No. 1*: "I think the new album will be called 'Shoot to Disable', which is the name of one of the tracks. It's a very strong song and title."[5] In the end Kim decided to name the album *Catch as Catch Can*, after a quote in the song 'Caroline Says' by Lou Reed.

On 24 October 1983, *Catch as Catch Can* was released. Reviews were favourable. *Record Mirror* in the UK wrote: "There's something for everyone on this album, from the toe-tapping ex-single 'Love Blonde', to the exotic and eastern-flavoured 'House of Salome'."[6] Dutch pop weekly *Hitkrant* wrote: "The blonde singer has matured and her live concerts have been good for her, apparently. She sings more fluently and with more conviction."[7] The German *Hamburger Morgenpost* wrote:

CHAPTER 6: CATCH AS CATCH CAN

"All the tempos are being used - there's something for every mood and every taste."[8]

Rather surprisingly, the album didn't do well in the UK, only reaching No.90. But in Europe, the LP fared better, staying in various charts for three months. A few months after its release, it was also the first of Kim's albums to be released on compact disc, just over a year after the commercial introduction of the format in Japan. Japanese company Toshiba EMI created a CD version that became one of the most collectable Kim Wilde items for over a decade, until it was finally released on CD in Europe as part of a limited-edition boxset.

A live tour started in November. Ricky stayed at home this time, but Kim was supported by a solid band consisting of Mark Heyward Chaplin (bass), Steve Byrd (guitar), Richard Blanshard (saxophone), Kevin McAlea (keyboards) and Boris Williams (drums). Prior to the tour Kim and the band rehearsed for three weeks in a small rehearsal studio in London, followed by four days of production rehearsals in the Golddiggers club in Chippenham. The tour took Kim and her band through Belgium, France, Switzerland, Austria, Netherlands, Germany, Denmark, Sweden and Finland within three weeks. They rode around in a 12m-long red bus with 15 bunks, each with its own stereo installation. A second bus transported the roadies and crew.[9]

Most artists talk about the dreaded second album, the one that either makes or breaks an act. For Kim, it was album number three. In various interviews she reflected that all the hard work from the past few years had taken its toll on Ricky and Marty as songwriters, and Kim was determined to start writing songs herself. So for Kim, that third album was a turning point.

Kim: "When my third album didn't do so well, I finally had time to sit down and assess what was going on in my career for the first time. I also had time to start concentrating on my writing, which I think has been the crucial area of improvement for me in the last year. Up until now, all my hit records have been written by my brother, Ricky, and my father, Marty, and I felt it was important to be saying something myself, to have an input in the material I was performing."[10]

HOUSE OF SALOME
Written by Ricky & Marty Wilde
Produced by Ricky Wilde
Released: March 1984
Chart position: 36 (Belgium)

The first track on *Catch as Catch Can* was released as a single in Europe and South Africa around the time that Kim's contract with RAK Records ended. The third

Kim live at Volksbelang, Mechelen (Belgium), 25 November 1983 © Bart Moons

© Sheila Rock

and final single taken from the album was not a chart success, probably because Kim did not promote the single at all, and there was no music video to support the release.

The track itself is strong enough, with thundering drums supplied by Trevor Murrell and backing vocals by band members Steve Byrd and Mark Hayward Chaplin. Of course, Ricky performed most of the instruments, having developed the track in the studio on his own.

Marty supplied the lyrics, which mention the biblical figure of Princess Salome, whose portrayal owes more to Oscar Wilde than the Gospels.

In Oscar Wilde's version, Salome falls in love with her stepfather's prisoner, John the Baptist, who rejects her attempted seduction. After her seductive dance of the seven veils, Herod offers her whatever she might wish for, and to his shock she demands the head of John the Baptist on a silver plate. Kim spoke about the song in a French interview and called Salome "a biblical figure, a seductress, a tease, a ruthless woman".[11]

The song was performed live during the Catch Tour in 1983.

In 2020, an instrumental version and an early rough mix of the track were released on the deluxe edition of *Catch as Catch Can*.

BACK STREET JOE
Written by Ricky & Marty Wilde
Produced by Ricky Wilde

The first lines of 'Back Street Joe' set the scene: '*Dancing with Back Street Joe / That was a time I loved / When we were kids so young / So long ago*'. It is a song that describes a longing for the past. Although Marty had worked with a few Joes in his time – Joe Dolan and Joe Brown come to mind – the song does not refer to them. The nostalgia remains unexplained, and in interviews there is no back story. What remains is an enjoyable song with a quirky intro.

STAY AWHILE
Written by Ricky & Marty Wilde
Produced by Ricky Wilde

A bit of a space age ballad, 'Stay Awhile' starts quietly with electronic sounds and a restrained electric guitar, but soon bursts into a powerful chorus. Back in 1983, Kim declared: "My favourite is 'Stay Awhile', it's a ballad, very beautiful."[12]

Kim performed the song live during the Catch Tour in 1983 and during a tour in the Netherlands in November 2017.

CHAPTER 6: CATCH AS CATCH CAN

The melody of 'Stay Awhile' reappeared near the end of the track 'Numinous', released in 2020.

Italian singer Sabrina Salermo – best known for her summer hit 'Boys' – recorded a cover version of the track in Italian in 1995: 'Alice Rivivra'. In 2008 she also recorded an English version for her compilation album *Erase/Rewind*.

LOVE BLONDE
Written by Ricky & Marty Wilde
Produced by Ricky Wilde
Released: 18 July 1983
Chart positions: 23 (UK), 34 (Australia), 7 (Belgium), 3 (Finland), 26 (Germany), 29 (Ireland), 10 (Netherlands), 7 (Sweden), 11 (Switzerland)

In March 1983, members of the band that accompanied Kim Wilde live on stage in the months before gathered at RAK Studios in London to record what was to become her next single. Trevor Murrell, Mark Hayward Chaplin, Gary Barnacle and Steve Byrd were playing a swing/rock song called 'Love Blonde'. The song was quite a departure from Kim's earlier work. It sounded nothing like previous tracks, and certainly wouldn't sound anything like other tracks on the new album. As for the lyrics, well...

Kim: "I had kind of a problem with ['Love Blonde'] at the time. Should I really be singing this song about me? I asked Dad, 'Is it about me?' And he said, 'No, it's about the mythology of the blonde sex symbol.' I said, 'Yes, but that's how everyone's perceiving me,' so he told me to just send the whole thing up and enjoy it, and I did and he was right. Most people have fun playing about with my image, often objectifying me, so I thought, 'Why not do it myself?'"[13]

Some reviewers made comparisons with the Stray Cats for its rockabilly style, while *No. 1* magazine´s Karen Swayne wrote: "'Love Blonde' is a lazy, strutting, almost jazzy workout, sung in superbly understated style. A must for all lovers of smoky nightclubs."[14]

Kim decided to give the song the performance it needed and went out to buy the most outlandish dress she could find. She bought the black leather dress at Joseph in Soho for a reported £500.

Kim: "So I went out and bought the most over-the-top dress I could find, and I send it up as much as I dare because I'm not really that much of an extrovert performer in that way."[15]

Kim: "It's the most expensive dress I've ever bought in my life. I certainly wouldn't have worn it when I was younger, but now I feel confident enough to [wear] it."[16]

The dress was certainly an eye-catcher, and Kim flaunted it in a big way on TV shows at the time. On 19 July 1983, she appeared on the ITV show *Razzmatazz* and the BBC's *Top of the Pops*. The single duly shot up the charts, finally peaking at No.23 in August.

'Love Blonde' was the first single to also be released in 12" format in the UK, featuring an extended remix. A limited quantity of 12" records also contained a colour poster to add to the collectability.

A music video to promote the single was directed by Mike Mansfield, who'd directed many music videos for the likes of Queen, Elton John, Electric Light Orchestra and Adam Ant. Originally it was to be used solely for Channel 4 TV programme *Hot For Dogs*, but it was so good that the Wilde team decided to keep using it.

For the first time, there was also an extended remix of 'Love Blonde', created by Ricky Wilde for the 12". Most of Kim's singles had been released in 12" vinyl format in Europe, but always replicating the tracks that were available on the 7" format. With the first 12" single also released in the UK, this changed.

In 2020, two more remixes of 'Love Blonde' were released on the deluxe version of *Catch as Catch Can*: a vocal and instrumental version of a remix by Popfidelity Allstars.

'Love Blonde' made an appearance on most of the setlists of Kim's live tours since 1983. A special mention has to be made for the version she performed with her band during the Another Step Tour in 1986, when she coupled the song with a cover version of the song 'Fever', composed by Eddie Cooley and Otis Blackwell in 1956, made famous by Peggy Lee two years later.

A Swedish cover version, 'Hon Går Rakt Fram' ('She Goes Straight Forward') was recorded by the band Cotton Club in 1984. Band member Lisa Ottosson supplied the Swedish lyrics. A 7" single was released but credited to the band's lead singer Leyla Yilbar Norgren.

DREAM SEQUENCE
Written by Ricky & Marty Wilde
Produced by Ricky Wilde

Ricky was clearly enjoying playing around with the newest synth gear, and started experimenting for the track that became 'Dream Sequence'. He managed to pull out the strangest sounds and the most beautiful soundscapes.

Ricky: "I was really just experimenting with a new synth I had just acquired, a Roland Jupiter 8, and it all came amazingly quickly. I wanted it to sound as different to a Kim Wilde track as possible, so it kind of turned out to be a little 'out there', but we loved writing and recording it."

CHAPTER 6: CATCH AS CATCH CAN

Several demos in the archives are testament to Ricky's experimentation at the time, with the first version sounding rather primitive, later morphing into the version that ended up on the album. An 'In Reverse' version, released on the 2020 deluxe edition of *Catch as Catch Can*, introduces a lengthy take on the intro. The final version has Ricky playing keyboards, bass, guitar, synclavier and singing backing vocals, with added drums by Trevor Murrell.

Lyrics were provided by Marty as usual, who employed a fragmented writing style. Starting with the words '*Goodnight Rox, I'll see you in the morning*', the song seems to describe the dreams of a young girl – after all, young Roxanne (also mentioned later in the song) was just four years old when the album was released – but also mentions historic figures like Cochise, leader of the Chihuicahui local group of the Chokonen and principal chief of the Chokonen band of Chiricahua Apache Indians. He led an uprising against the US government which began in 1861, persisting until a peace treaty in 1872.

The experimental track remains a favourite among fans, but was never performed live. The intro was used for the opening of the Snapshots & Greatest Hits Tour in 2012, with filmed images of a young Kim and Ricky shown on the video screens.

The Finnish band 1in10/Varia created the track 'Shadows Across the Floor' using samples of 'Dream Sequence' in 2012.

DANCING IN THE DARK
Written by Nicky Chinn & Adrian Gurvitz
Produced by Ricky Wilde
Released: 24 October 1983
Chart positions: 67 (UK), 11 (Belgium), 3 (Denmark), 9 (Finland), 26 (Germany), 9 (Switzerland)

Although Marty and Ricky supplied almost all the songs on *Catch as Catch Can*, one song was delivered by the songwriting team of Nicky Chinn and Adrian Gurvitz, perhaps on the suggestion of Mickie Most, who felt other writers might deliver a track that could conquer the clubs at the time. After the original recording failed to impress, the track was sent to Nile Rodgers, who added his particular brand of magic. He created a handful of versions, including an extended remix and an instrumental version, both released on the 12" single, and a 'full instrumental version' finally released on the deluxe version of *Catch as Catch Can* in 2020.

In Australia, a promotional 7" single of 'Dancing in the Dark' was released in an extremely rare picture sleeve. When this single appeared on the collectors' market in the early 1980s, it was selling for upwards of £50. It remains high on the wishlist of Kim Wilde collectors.[17]

The music video to accompany the single release was directed by Tim Pope. Best known for his work with Talk Talk, The The and The Cure, the video was appropriately dark, with shadows moving across the screen and Kim barely visible in the shadows. It became a bit of a rarity, the only video from the RAK era not to be included in a video EP that Picture Music International released in 1984.

There were high expectations for this release, but they weren't met.

Kim: "Every Monday I'd wake up feeling anxious, waiting to get the call about whether we'd made the charts or not from my record company, this time I knew it wasn't going to be good."

The poor performance of the single proved to be a happy accident, because it encouraged Kim to start writing songs herself.

Kim: "After 'Dancing in the Dark', I knew I had to get my songwriting together. Not just because the single was a flop but because I wasn't happy with it as a song and I wasn't happy wasting my time promoting it when I could be writing."[18]

Dutch singer Tony Sherman released the song as a single in 1983. His version was released on 7" and 12" but failed to chart. American singer Stacey Q recorded a version in 1985 and included it on her debut, a limited-edition five-track cassette that has become a rare collector's item. Another version was recorded by Dutch singer and presenter Patty Brard on her third album *Red Light*.

SHOOT TO DISABLE
Written by Ricky & Marty Wilde
Produced by Ricky Wilde

Initially a potential album title too, 'Shoot to Disable', musically, is dominated by Ricky's synclavier and keyboards, but also prominently features bass by Mark Hayward Chaplin and drums by Trevor Murrell. Lyrically, it is a very short song, with just two verses that don't explain much. By the end of the song Kim, exclaims, '*Oh what a fool I was to love*', followed by a lengthy instrumental break.

A rough mix, released in 2020, unveils an even longer instrumental break at the end.

CAN YOU HEAR IT
Written by Ricky & Marty Wilde
Produced by Ricky Wilde

'Can You Hear It' was first released as the B-side of 'Love Blonde'. Compared to the album version, released a few months later, the single version has more echo on the drums and features a more pronounced guitar solo at the end. Indeed, the album version was mixed four months later.

The earliest version, recorded at the beginning of 1983, reveals that the lyrics of the song changed slightly. While Kim sings '*You could be gone / You could be far away / Soon you must fly free*' on the released version, the original lyrics were '*Soon you'll be gone / You could be far away / Now you must fly free*'.

In 2020, a remix by Project K was released on the deluxe edition of *Catch as Catch Can*.

SPARKS
Written by Ricky & Marty Wilde
Produced by Ricky Wilde

The drums in 'Sparks' bang and crash around, while Kim sings one of the few overtly optimistic lines on the album: '*We've only one life / And we've got a lot to give / There's only one time / And we've got to make or break it*'. It is a remarkable standout track on an album full of melancholy and longing.

Although 'Sparks' was not released as a single, it was picked up by American DJ service Disconet. Members of the service received extended remixes and exclusive tracks, with Disconet able to attract the services of renowned names like John 'Jellybean' Benitez and Patrick Cowley. 'Sparks' was remixed by Glenn Howard, who basically took the album track and doubled the length by cutting and pasting pieces of the song. This version was eventually released on the deluxe edition of *Catch as Catch Can* in 2020.

SING IT OUT FOR LOVE
Written by Ricky & Marty Wilde
Produced by Ricky Wilde

Ending the album with more melancholy, 'Sing It Out for Love' is a description of a lonely female singer going through the motions in bars filled with drunks and truckers. It's no secret that Marty originally didn't want his daughter to be in the music industry. During his career in the 1950s and 1960s he saw many female singers in a desperate state. "I didn't want her to be tied to the road like I was", he said in 2019. "But she found her way." In 1983, he'd already made peace with the way things turned out, but 'Sing It Out for Love' still spells out his fears for other women in the industry.

BACK SEAT DRIVER (B-side)
Written by Ricky & Marty Wilde
Produced by Ricky Wilde

Originally developed under the working title 'Just wanna be near you', 'Back Seat driver' has a driving beat and simple 'oh oh oh' chorus. In the song, Kim sings, *'Any time you're gone, I get so blue / Any time I have I wanna spend with you'*. What follows is an almost manic journey towards the unnamed lover, with lines like *'Hitch a ride, I take a train / Any road just means the same / Anywhere you are, I'll get to you'*.

The track was recorded in September 1983 especially for the B-side of single 'Dancing In The Dark'.

The track was actually known as 'Back Street Driver', until it was discovered in 2019 that the original master-tape has the title 'Back Seat Driver' on it. The title was corrected for the 2020 deluxe edition of *Catch as Catch Can*.

SAIL ON
Written by Ricky & Marty Wilde
Produced by Ricky Wilde

RAIN ON
Written by Ricky & Marty Wilde
Produced by Ricky Wilde

In May 1983, Kim recorded 'Sail On'. In the song, Kim dramatically sings *'I'm standing on the edge of my life / When I thought I could see the lights at home tonight'*.

Three months later, the song was recorded with the same basic melody, but with different lyrics: *'I'm looking for the one in my life / But I guess I'll see those clouds again tonight'*.

Both versions never made it onto the album, but they were finally released in 2020 on the deluxe edition.

CHAPTER 7:
TEASES & DARES

Released: 12 November 1984
Chart positions: 66 (UK), 24 (Finland), 22 (Germany), 31 (Netherlands), 35 (Sweden), 10 (Switzerland), 84 (USA)

Kim Wilde's contract with RAK Records had come to an end. A few more releases from RAK went by quite silently: they released 'House of Salome' as a single in early 1984, without a music video or any promotion from Kim on TV programmes. And later in the year, when Kim's first album for MCA was about to come out, they released a compilation album, *The Very Best Of Kim Wilde*, as well as others for the French market: *Disque d'Or*, *Top 16* and *1 Heure de Musique*.

In 1982, Kim had bought an apartment at Grove Court in St John's Wood in London. She wouldn't move in until over a year later, having redecorated the place in the few spare moments she had, as it was 'in a bit of a state'.[1] In the apartment, she installed a small four-track studio, armed with a Yamaha DX7 synthesizer and small rhythm box. It enabled her to record demos and write songs herself, a desire that she had for some time but only materialised when she left home.

Kim: "I found a place to live, left home and started teaching myself how to write a song. The most difficult thing was after a day of getting absolutely no ideas at all having to go back and try all over again. It took me a long time to get to the point where I was actually pleased with anything I did, but my biggest enemy was my own lack of self-confidence. I started by learning other people's songs, analysing their song structure and reproducing them on a four-track I'd installed in my new flat, I was especially inspired by Todd Rundgren songs."[2]

In the summer of 1983, the Wildes started building their own recording studio in Knebworth, giving them the freedom to work whenever they felt like it. Select Sound Studios, as it was called, was used to record new material from the end of 1983 onwards. An 'in house' engineer was employed: Nigel Mills, who started his career as a recording engineer for Island Records, working with Joe Jackson (*Beat Crazy*), Modern Romance (*Adventures in Clubland*) Killing Joke (*Fire Dances*) and Bow Wow Wow (*When the Going Gets Tough, the Tough Get Going*). He was the sound engineer for one Kim Wilde album, the forthcoming *Teases & Dares*.

In 1984, Kim signed with MCA Records for the next batch of albums. Recording sessions for the new album had already started, and there were plenty of surprises in store. Kim worked on the song 'Thought It Was Goodbye' together with Ricky and Marty, and also composed songs on her own, two of which would end up on the album: 'Shangri-la' and 'Fit In'.

© Richard Blanshard

© Richard Blanshard

Kim: "The two songs I wrote which appeared on *Teases & Dares* were in fact the first two I'd ever written. I think they worked as songs and importantly to me they marked the beginning of my own songwriting contribution to my albums."[3]

The re-launch of Kim Wilde was taken on with ambition by her new record company. At the time, the company of artists and designers called XL Design were making waves with their work and were employed for the 'visual identity' of the new single, Kim's first for MCA. 'The Second Time' was an energetic pop song, with all the bombast and force typical for chart hits at that time.

XL Design was founded by Tom Watkins and Royston Edwards in the early 1980s. Initially designing music graphics and marketing campaigns, they started designing record sleeves in 1982. A year later, the British record label ZTT became their client and they designed sleeves for Art of Noise, Frankie Goes to Hollywood and Grace Jones. MCA felt they could do their thing for Kim Wilde as well, and they came up with the storyboard for the music video for 'The Second Time'.

In a video directed by Andy Morahan, Kim appears as a cross between a dominatrix and Barbarella in a post-apocalyptic world, fighting with mummies. In this setting, the phrases '*Go for it*' and '*Just go for the second time*' take on a new meaning besides the overt sexual innuendo of the song.

Tom Watkins: "Kim was initially open-minded and wanted someone to 'look objectively' at her image. She came into XL and we talked excitedly about the 'Kim Wilde reinvention'. She was lovely sweet, intelligent and grounded, and liked a cocktail or two, particularly Sex on the Beach. We got a bit carried away. Well, MCA had put up £10,000 and we were drinking Sex on the Beach, so why wouldn't we? The hairspray cans came out in full force. We made leather dresses. Suddenly Kim Wilde, the poster-pretty innocent of 'Kids in America', was a Barbarella-style supervixen. It wasn't so much girl-next-door as Wonder Woman crashing into Ann Summers. (...) It was only supposed to be a one-off sex-up for this particular single anyway. It was all a bit like a drunken one-night stand. And now she'd woken up and come to her senses. It just wasn't 'her.'"[4]

On 12 November 1984, the album 'Teases & Dares' was released. The press quickly picked up on the fact that Kim had written two songs and co-written one, the other seven written and composed by Marty and Ricky. The album's chart performance was slightly disappointing, as it only reached No.66 in the UK chart during a two-week run. It did slightly better in Sweden and the Netherlands (peaking at No.35 and No.31 respectively), and most successful in Germany, where it stayed in the chart for 23 weeks, peaking at No.22.

Despite being very proud of the album musically, Kim was not happy with the artwork and – in retrospect – the entire project with XL.

CHAPTER 7: TEASES & DARES

Kim: "One of the ones I was least happy with [was] the cover of *Teases & Dares*. I never actually liked it as an album cover. It was actually part of a video we made, and the record company said, 'We like this picture so much, we're going to have it as your album sleeve'. I phoned them up and said, 'I don't like it'. But I got overruled. I was never happy about that being a statement as to my style, because it wasn't."[5]

Tom Watkins: "The problem was the record company had forked out for this vampy revamp and they were going to milk it. To her dismay, a shot from the single became the cover of the album. (...) The moral of the tale? Sometimes all the inspired ideas and ludicrous excesses result in a great pop moment. Other times you jump the shark. Kim's time with XL didn't work out and she was gone by the end of the year."[6]

The sci-fi clothing lasted until the end of 1984. Kim did several TV appearances dressed in these colourful suits, in programmes like *Wogan*, *Top of the Pops*, *WWF Club* in Germany, and *Formule 1+1* in France. The biggest TV show was Germany's *Thommy's Popshow*, recorded at the Westfalenhalle in Dortmund before a few thousand enthusiastic fans. She performed 'The Second Time' and 'Suburbs of Moscow'. With performances by artists like Laura Branigan, Depeche Mode, Chris de Burgh, Limahl, Billy Idol, Duran Duran, Spandau Ballet, Talk Talk, Howard Jones and several German acts, this show was one of the highlights of the year in Central Europe. It may have helped her get the Golden Otto from German pop magazine *Bravo* in January 1985, a result of the fact that 32.9% of the readers voted her the most popular female pop star.

Kim was guest presenter on the UK's *Oxford Road Show*, broadcast on 18 January 1985. She performed 'Rage To Love', then proceeded to interview Glenn Gregory from Heaven 17 and photographer Anton Corbijn.

With the Rage to Rock Tour starting in early 1985, Kim ditched all the glamour and contrived imaging and went for a more conventional 'rock'n'roll' look. Kim's band consisted of John Edwards (bass), Preston Heyman (drums), Richard Blanchard (saxophone), Jeff Hammer (keyboards) and Steve Byrd (guitar). Starting in Hamburg (Germany) on 15 March 1985 and finishing on 2 April 1985 in Copenhagen (Denmark), the tour consisted of 16 dates, nine of which were in Germany.

During the concerts, Kim played keyboards during 'Fit In', while 'Putty In Your Hands', recorded for the B-side of the single 'Rage To Love', also got an outing.

In August, Kim did a short tour in France with the bands Cinema and Telephone. The dates in Béziers, Nîmes, Fréjus and Dax provided an opportunity for French fans to see Kim at open-air concerts in arenas in the South of France. Initially there were plans for a UK tour, but when those plans fell through, this mini-tour was an attractive alternative.

Two collaborations happened during the year 1985. She appeared in the song 'Les Nuits Sans Kim Wilde', recorded by French singer Laurent Voulzy and released as a single in France, and she provided backing vocals on a song by Stephen Bishop, that song remaining unreleased.

Kim: "I did backing vocals on a Stephen Bishop album which was never released. This was in 1985, and all I have is a cassette. I bumped into him a year later while promoting in L.A. and he told me the project was shelved. A song called 'Separate Lives' was released by Phil Collins and Marilyn Martin in conjunction with a film (of that name), and I remember telling Stephen how much I preferred his version. Well, at least one of the songs got heard – what a tragedy!"[7]

Also in 1985, Kim got a taste of the fickle nature of fame. While *Teases & Dares* performed reasonably well and 'Rage to Love' was a relatively successful single, she wasn't quite top of the bill at that point. There were new stars around, stars that seemed to replace her as the most popular female singer.

Kim: "I saw a bunch of journalists heading towards me, and just assumed they were after a photo. Then I realised they weren't going to stop; they ran past me heading for Jennifer Rush instead. I was heartbroken and mortified and cried all the way to the airport. I can laugh about it now, but I'm sure the feelings would come flooding back if I saw Jennifer Rush again... my first taste of the fickle nature of fame!"[8]

But, to end the year on a high note, Kim performed on 7 December 1985 at Le Bourget as part of an anti-racism concert. Unfortunately, most of her fans missed this performance following poor promotion for the event. But that didn't prevent her from giving a superb hour and a half show.[9]

THE TOUCH
Written by Ricky & Marty Wilde
Produced by Ricky & Marty Wilde
Released: 26 November 1984
Chart positions: 56 (UK), 20 (Belgium, Netherlands), 29 (Germany)

With Chris North on drums and Steve Byrd playing a Gibson Les Paul custom guitar, Ricky provided the synth tones that opened the first track on the album. The working title was 'So Right'; the phrase used in the chorus repeatedly.

This powerful pop song was chosen to be the second single to be taken from the album, and MCA released it on 7", 12" and a shaped picture disc with a picture of a smiling Kim.

Andy Morahan directed the music video for 'The Touch', based on a Cinderella theme. In it, Kim appears as a victim of two drag queen sisters who leave her at home, having to clean up. She gets help from a fairy godmother, then gets invited to a ball by four handsome dancers. In retrospect, Kim didn't like the video and felt it totally misinterpreted the song.

In 1985, 'The Touch' appeared in teen romantic comedy movie *Secret Admirer*, directed by David Greenwall.

IS IT OVER
Written by Ricky & Marty Wilde
Produced by Ricky & Marty Wilde

With its catchy refrain and danceable rhythm, 'Is It Over' is the single that never was. The lyrics seem to wonder whether a romance is over or just starting, but there is no resolution: In the last verse Kim sings: '*When you're reaching out / Do I still wanna hold you?*' There's no answer as the refrain keeps repeating, '*Is it over / or has it just begun*'.

In 1985, 'Is It Over' ended up on the soundtrack of the movie *Fletch*, starring Chevy Chase.

SUBURBS OF MOSCOW
Written by Ricky & Marty Wilde
Produced by Ricky & Marty Wilde

This was Cold War Europe, before the Berlin Wall came down. Moscow was an even more mysterious place than in today's world. At the time, Marty, who wrote the lyrics, was fascinated by Russian culture, while also a bit scared of it.
Kim: "It's about the life of young people in Eastern Europe, being in a cultural conflict on a daily basis. They are living with a dictatorial regime, which doesn't leave any space for their personal development, but the jeans they wear and music they listen to shows a bond with the Western world."[10]

It would seem that 'Suburbs of Moscow' was considered for a single release, as Kim performed the song at a handful of European TV shows. In the end, they went for 'The Touch' instead.

FIT IN
Written by Kim Wilde
Produced by Kim, Ricky & Marty Wilde

Kim wrote and arranged this track, producing it together with Ricky and Marty. She plays the Yamaha DX7 and Solina as well, backed by Steve Byrd on Fender Stratocaster, Gary Twigg on Fender Jazz bass and Chris North on drums. It is in fact the only track on the album on which Ricky doesn't play and only has an involvement as a producer.

'Fit In' was one of the first songs written by Kim, inspired by her experience of fame and success: *'I'm getting bored of the way they expect me to be'.*

Kim: 'Fit In' was one of the first songs and that showed how confused I was, in a way. I didn't feel like I fitted in at all for the conventional 'being a pop-star person'. I didn't like hanging out at the place to be, I wasn't into fashion and being an icon or anything like that. It didn't interest me. The only thing I was interested in was music."[11]

The song was only performed live during the Rage to Rock tour in 1985.

RAGE TO LOVE
Written by Ricky & Marty Wilde
Produced by Ricky & Marty Wilde
Released: 15 April 1985
Chart positions: 19 (UK), 45 (Germany), 94 (Australia)

'Rage to Love' has an altogether different style than all the other songs on the album, with clear rock'n'roll influences. Ricky prepared a backing track using an upright bass and drum track, and Steve Byrd added his guitar magic, using some of Marty´s guitars. He picked out a ´55 Gibson Scotty Moore, a ´61 Gibson Barney Kessell, and a ´57 Fender Stratocaster.

Steve Byrd: "I played through a Yamaha E1010 echo unit and had a tremolo pedal set to a fast speed. There were lots of gaps in the track and as I sat there, I came up with a little riff. The song is in F sharp, not a good key for guitar, so I cheated by leaving the top E-string open, so every chord had a drone in it. I came up with that little riff – 'dooby dooby bop bop' - on the guitar and it became the vocal hook too. When Marty and Rick heard me playing that, they were very excited. 'Whose riff is that?', they said eagerly. 'I just made it up', I replied. 'Quick! Record it, record it!' they shouted. So we put it down so as not to forget it."[12]

For the single version, a remix was made by Dave Edmunds, whose musical tendencies were always focused on rock'n'roll. The 12" remix was, as usual, delivered by Ricky. MCA supported the release with a shaped picture disc, featuring an image of Kim cropped from the picture sleeve of the single.

The music video was recorded at Camden's Electric Ballroom in North London. Directed by Pete Cornish, the video included a lot of Kim's friends and a cameo by Justin Hayward, playing a compere. Shooting started at 8am and lasted 16 hours. Kim herself was more involved with this video than any of her previous ones.

Kim: "With 'Rage to Love' I insisted it be a 'live' video because it suited the song, and even watched while they edited it down, which I've never had time to do before."[13]

Steve Byrd: "It was a baking hot day and the stage was illuminated with many kilowatts of lighting. So of course, we all wore leather and ran around like lunatics. There was so much energy expended in that video, and after a 7am call we still were filming at 10pm. So we're all exhausted and Marty wants one final scene. When the guitar solo starts, he wants me to run across the stage and slide on my knees. Don't try this at home - it HURTS LIKE HELL! I had to do it over and over until they filmed it right or I didn't fall over. The next day my knees were skinned and black and blue with bruising. Sometimes you have to suffer for your art!"[14]

In 1995, Swedish band Sneaky Pete & Cool Cats recorded a rockabilly-style version of 'Rage To Love' on their album *Refuse To Loose*.

THE SECOND TIME
Written by Ricky & Marty Wilde
Produced by Ricky & Marty Wilde
Released: 29 September 1984
Chart positions: 29 (UK), 15 (Belgium), 9 (Denmark, Germany), 24 (Netherlands), 7 (Switzerland)

GO FOR IT
Released: 16 January 1985
Chart position: 65 (USA)

When you listen to 'The Second Time', it is not immediately apparent that you're effectively listening to a one-man band. But that's what it is: Ricky Wilde plays all the instruments on this track and also provides the loud 'Go!' backing vocals. Created entirely on synthesizers (listed as a Yamaha DX7, a Roland Jupiter 8, the Synclavier II and a Mini Moog) and a '57 Fender Stratocaster, It is an extremely rousing track, with a rhythm that will lift you from your seat once you hear it.

As for the lyrics, they were bordering on the explicit. Even while Kim was singing: '*There's such an urgency in everything I need from you / Stop giving up – you know you can't refuse me / I've every reason to believe there's still a man in you / You done it once – so come on go again*', nobody seemed to notice that the exclamation '*Just go for the second time*' was all about sex.

'The Second Time' was released as a regular 7" single, a picture disc 7", and a 12" single featuring extended versions of the A-side and its B-side, 'Lovers

On A Beach'. Ricky Wilde invested quite some time in the extended version of 'The Second Time': several different versions were made, although only one was released.

The music video, directed by Andy Morahan, was developed with the aid of XL Design, the design company led by Tom Watkins that propelled the likes of Frankie Goes To Hollywood, Grace Jones, Duran Duran and the Pet Shop Boys into the public eye. They designed the image of a Barbarella-type warrior woman for Kim, and the video for 'The Second Time' sees her arriving in the room of a cheap motel, which starts to fall apart when something or someone starts to tear down the walls. Kim looks appropriately terrified as she's trying to keep the appearing holes closed, while singing the lines of her song. And then there are some fighting scenes...

The single was promoted by MCA with magazine ads and a flurry of TV performances, with a good response: the single certainly performed better in the charts than the previous year's RAK releases. Kim Wilde was back, and she was enjoying it.

In January 1985 MCA released the single in the US with a catchier title – 'Go For It' – and a poster sleeve. The 12" single featured two new remixes: an extended dance version and dub version. These were later re-edited for a 'US Remix' that appeared on the European 12" single of 'Rage To Love'. For the first time since 'Kids in America', Kim appeared in the Billboard Hot 100 singles charts, peaking at No.65.

A cover version of 'The Second Time' in Croatian was recorded by Elvira Voca as 'Drugo Vrijeme' for an album on which she covered many contemporary hits.

BLADERUNNER
Written by Ricky & Marty Wilde
Produced by Ricky & Marty Wilde

Like the title suggests, this song was inspired by the movie 'Bladerunner', the 1982 science fiction film directed by Ridley Scott, starring Harrison Ford, Rutger Hauer, Sean Young and Edward James Olmos. The track on the album even includes samples from the movie, while the lyrics describe some of the scenes, with lines like '*I watched her falling to the ground / and saw the glass go flying*'.

'Bladerunner' was performed live during the 'Rage to Rock' tour in 1985, and during the 'Here Come The Aliens' tour in 2018 and 2019.

JANINE
Written by Ricky & Marty Wilde
Produced by Ricky & Marty Wilde

The identity of the titular Janine remains unknown, but it's likely that, like Wendy Sadd, this is all about a fictional character. It is an up-tempo rock/pop tune that fits well in the album.

SHANGRI-LA
Written by Kim Wilde
Produced by Ricky & Marty Wilde

The second of two songs penned by Kim Wilde independently on this album, 'Shangri-la' explores a darker side to a relationship: '*Got my fingers burned and cut into the wire*', whilst searching for paradise.

Kim seems to long for this herself during a spoken passage: '*I take a look behind me / And the sun shines brighter there / And the people are much more beautiful / in a place without a care / And I'm wondering if there'll ever be room for me / in Shangri-la*'.

An early version appeared on the magazine/LP *Debut* in November 1984, around the same time as the release of the single 'The Touch', a new version of 'Shangri-la' making its debut on the B-side. An extended remix, featuring a beautiful lengthy instrumental intro, appeared on the 12" version of 'The Touch'.

THOUGHT IT WAS GOODBYE
Written by Ricky, Marty & Kim Wilde
Produced by Ricky & Marty Wilde

Marking the first-ever collaboration of the three Wildes, 'Thought It Was Goodbye' is a beautiful song to end the album. With percussion by Andy Duncan opening the track, Fender Jazz Bass by Gary Twigg and the Yamaha DX7, Roland Jupiter 8 and Synclavier II provided by Ricky, Kim sings lyrics that are markedly different from the other songs: '*The memories drift out of time / The face I used to kiss a million ways / The love I truly thought was mine*' before confessing '*I want to stay inside your life again / To fall apart just seems a crime*'.

Kim performed the song live during the Rage to Rock Tour and again in an acoustic version during the Come Out and Play Tour in 2011.

'Thought It Was Goodbye' was sampled by 1in10/Varia for the track 'A Million Ways', released in 2012.

LOVERS ON A BEACH (B-side)
Written by Ricky & Marty Wilde
Produced by Ricky & Marty Wilde

The B-side of 'The Second Time' was a beautiful up-tempo track that starts with a lengthy instrumental then paints a picture of someone reminiscing, thinking back to a summer romance.

The 12" single of 'The Second Time' included an extended version, in which instrumental breaks are extended to great effect.

The track was given a club remix treatment in 2009, featuring new vocals by Kim, but that version remains unreleased.

PUTTY IN YOUR HANDS (B-side)
Written by John Patton & Kay Rogers
Produced by Ricky & Marty Wilde

Originally recorded by the Shirelles in 1962, 'Putty in Your Hands' was subsequently covered by Jean and the Statesides, and the Yardbirds, but Kim Wilde's version is certainly informed by the original version. Included on the B-side of 'Rage to Love', it serves as a companion piece to the rock'n'roll flavour of the A-side. The song was performed live during the Rage to Rock Tour in 1985.

TURN IT ON
Written by Mike Chapman & Holly Knight
Produced by Ricky & Marty Wilde

The song 'Turn It On' was written for the 1985 movie *Weird Science*, the film written and directed by John Hughes and starring Anthony Michael Hall, Ilan Mitchell-Smith and Kelly LeBrock. Using a computer, nerdy social outcasts Gary Wallace and Wyatt Donnelly decide to create the perfect dream woman. After a power surge, their creation turns out to be not only stunningly beautiful but also in the possession of special powers.

The song is played in the background during one scene, and was recorded by Kim Wilde as part of her new association with the MCA label. Originally released solely on the *Weird Science* soundtrack LP, it finally appeared on CD when Cherry Pop released a deluxe edition of *Teases & Dares* in 2010.

American singer Marilyn Martin recorded the song on her self-titled debut album in 1986.

CHAPTER 7: TEASES & DARES

LES NUITS SANS KIM WILDE
Written by Alain Souchon & Laurent Voulzy
Produced by Laurent Voulzy & Michel Coeuriot

France always had a special place in Kim's heart. But even Kim couldn't foresee that a French singer would write a song about her. French singer Laurent Voulzy was born in Paris on 18 December 1948. His career in music started when he joined the band Le Temple de Vénus in 1969. His solo success started in 1977 with the hit single 'Rockollection', a song about typical adolescence illustrated with parts of songs originally performed by The Beatles, Bob Dylan and the Beach Boys. Several hit singles followed, all composed with friend and colleague Alain Souchon. A French TV regular, he eventually met Kim when they were both appearing in the same show. By that time, Laurent had become a bit of a fan, recording her TV appearances and showing them to Souchon.

Laurent Voulzy: "One day, while I was working with Alain Souchon on a song, I showed him this famous cassette. He understood immediately why she fascinated me. And it was this famous sentence: 'Since the time you've been telling me about it, we should make a song 'Les nuits sans Kim Wilde'. I could only consent. At first it was called 'Les Nuits sans Kim Wilde, je Joue au Flipper' ('The nights without Kim Wilde, I play pinball') (he chokes with laughter)."[15]

Laurent Voulzy and Alain Souchon wrote the song and sent it to Kim, who was curious to hear it.

Laurent Voulzy: "Through her record company, I offered her to appear in the song. At first, she was very embarrassed, and I was paralysed! She was getting off the poster! And then she accepted. Afterwards, we became friends. She's a delicious girl who didn't like being a star."[16]

Kim: "In 1986, I received a phone call from Laurent's record company informing me that a song had been written about me and its author wanted me to participate in one way or another in recording the disc. I have to admit I was flattered and amused because I had never heard of Laurent Voulzy. (...) I was intrigued to know who this French singer was. (...) The song arrived at our family studio one day. (...) We were surprised to find that it was a great pop record, with a catchy rhythm endowed with an irresistible energy. We immediately contacted the record company and a few weeks later Laurent was in our studio in Hertfordshire. I remember his excitement, like that of a child let loose in a candy store or a puppy happy to see you waking up in the morning. We all fell in love with Laurent and (after) a few minutes and, very quickly, while he was doing his vocalisations, my father had the idea of asking him to remove his glasses ... Brilliant!"[17]

A music video was filmed to accompany the release. Kim agreed to appear and flew out to Paris for a weekend. Her part was shot in six scenes in one day under the direction of Bernard Malige. In the video, a beautiful pinball machine with Kim's face on it appeared. According to Voulzy, it remained in his studio decades later.

'Les Nuits sans Kim Wilde' was released as a 7" single in June 1985. A 12" single with an extended version was also released. Surprisingly, the single did not chart. The record company decided to switch sides, releasing the B-side 'Belle-ile-en-mer Marie-Galante' as the A-side in September 1986. That version of the single peaked at No.20 in the French Top 50.

Voulzy proceeded to perform the song live during his tours. A recording from the Zenith in Paris appears on his 1993 album *Voulzy Tour*. Kim and Laurent actually performed the song live together on a few occasions, most notably during French TV programme *Vivement Dimanche* on 1 October 2006 and during the Night of the Proms concert at the Spiroudome in Charleroi (Belgium) on 24 April 2010.

'Les Nuits sans Kim Wilde' was covered by Marcel Wave in 2018.

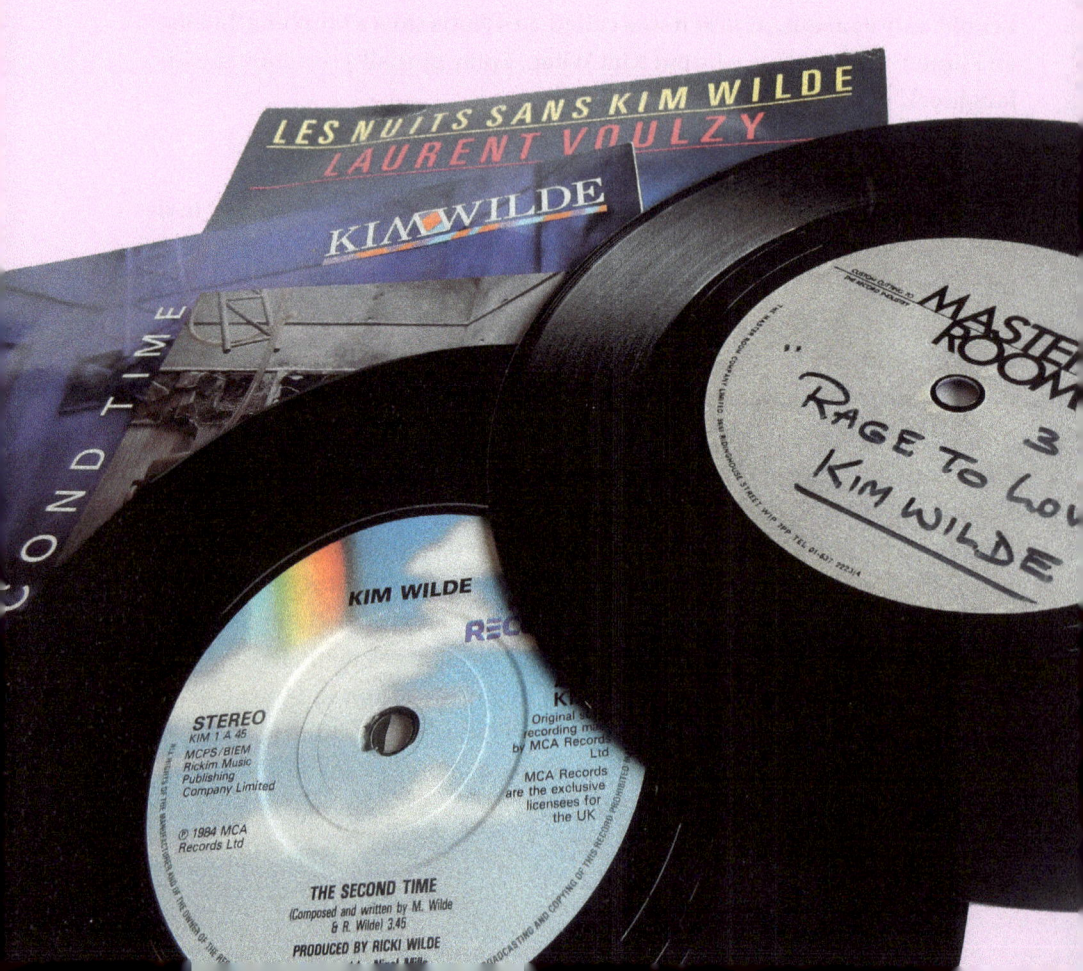

CHAPTER 8:
ANOTHER STEP

Released: 3 October 1986
Chart positions: 73 (UK), 31 (Australia), 12 (Canada), 41 (Germany), 52 (Netherlands), 2 (Norway), 49 (Sweden), 5 (Switzerland), 40 (USA)

During the second half of the 1980s, there seemed to be an increasing focus on the US by British artists. The Live Aid spectacle in July 1985 had given many of them a worldwide stage thanks to live television, and record companies were aware that reaching America would generate more revenue. In 1985 alone, Phil Collins, George Michael, Tears for Fears, Simple Minds and Paul Young managed to reach the top spot in the Billboard Hot 100 chart.

In order to cater to the US taste, artists were encouraged to work with American producers and/or songwriters. And with MCA being an American record company, it was inevitable that Kim and her team also received 'persuasion' to work with Americans. But at the same time, the Wilde team wanted to work in a similar way as before. Kim was developing her songwriting skills and Select Sound Studios had become a hub of inspired experimentation. Some middle ground had to be found.

Right after the mini-tour in France in the summer of 1985 Kim went at it. In 1985 and 1986 she was very productive, writing many more songs than would end up on the next album.

Together with Steve Byrd, Kim wrote a lot of songs for the next album. The experience of writing 'Fit In' and 'Shangri-la' for *Teases & Dares* under her belt, she felt that working with others could be a stimulating experience, although the prospect was certainly daunting as well.

Kim: "These days, I have been writing with my guitarist, Steve, as you know. He usually arrives around midday with his guitar and I make him a cup of tea (skimmed milk, no sugar). I play him any of the ideas I have been working on, including any lyrics I have written. I sit at the keyboards and he plugs his guitar in and off we go! We don't usually stop for lunch, we might grab a snack as we work." [1]

Steve Byrd: "I used to go over to her apartment in St Johns Wood and we'd jam around with a drum machine, I'd play guitar and bass and Kim is a pretty good keyboard player. We worked on a four-track Tascam portastudio. Kim would engineer, then we would take those ideas to a 12-track writing room in Knebworth to re-record and add harmony vocals and overdubs. Then

these demos could be presented to the family. If they liked any, Ricky would come into their 24-track studio with us and we would try them out properly. If they still sounded good, Rick would work on them until they were finished and propose them to the record company. I remember 'The Thrill of It' and 'Missing' from early on." [2]

MCA also wanted Kim to connect with American songwriters. Their reasoning was simple: MCA was based both in the UK and the USA, and had strong ties with the Universal film company. Various songs from *Teases & Dares* appeared in movies and there seemed to be an opportunity to use more of Kim's music in films, as long as the material was friendly on American ears.

And so, in early 1986, Kim flew to Los Angeles together with Steve Byrd and Nick Boyles to work with Richard Burgess. During a three-week stay, the sessions yielded one important new track: 'Say You Really Want Me', written by Danny Sembello, Dick Rudolph and Donnell Spencer Jr. The track was included in the soundtrack for the movie *Running Scared*, directed by Peter Hyams and starring Gregory Hines and Billy Crystal. Released in June 1986, the movie earned over $38 millon in the USA.

Almost at the same time, Europe and Australia released a new single by Kim, entitled 'Schoolgirl', produced by Reinhold Heil. Born in 1954, Heil started his music career as a member of the Nina Hagen Band in the 1970s. When Hagen went solo, the members of her band formed Spliff, one of many bands to form the 'Neue Deutsche Welle' ('New German Wave') in the early 1980s. Heil became widely regarded as one of the best keyboard players in Europe. He moved on to production work for Nena and Cosa Rosa.

While on the promotion trail again, Kim appeared in several European TV programmes. One notable programme was *Countdown* in the Netherlands, which became a European phenomenon thanks to satellite channel Europa TV. She was interviewed during a one-hour special by Adam Curry, who went on to become a VJ for MTV in America.

Kim's fifth studio album, *Another Step* was released in October 1986. The sleeve design showed Kim before a map of the world, coloured in pink and light green – although later pressings would have a different sleeve with red and dark green. Kim wore a crop top in the photograph, which caused comparisons with a new star on the horizon – American singer Madonna, who had taken the world by storm over the past two years. And so, some of the focus in the press was on the sleeve of the album, not on the music that was pressed on the disc.

Smash Hits in the UK started their review with: "She's back! On the cover she bares her midriff - very Madonna."[3] Fortunately, *Melody Maker* did pick up on Kim's artistic growth: "Her voice is remarkably similar, in its timbre and pitch, to Marie Osmond's - both embody a tenderness and poignancy that has never

CHAPTER 8: ANOTHER STEP

been critically acknowledged."[4] And in Dutch magazine *Hitkrant* the reviewer concluded: "'Another Step' is a mature step in the right direction."[5]

The album only made it to No.88 in the UK chart in November 1986. It did better in other territories, certified gold in Canada, Norway and Switzerland.

A tour was planned, but when the dates were supposed to happen, the single 'You Keep Me Hangin' On' suddenly took off in a big way, and Kim had promotional appearances to attend to. And so, those tour dates were postponed. Kim went to various European countries to perform 'You Keep Me Hangin' On' for TV programmes – with occasional variations of performing other album tracks from time to time. So 'Victim' appeared in a Swedish TV programme and 'Don't Say Nothing's Changed' featured on two French TV shows.

When the Another Step tour happened, Kim visited various countries with a different band: Richard Blanchard on saxophone, Matthew Letley on drums, Gary Twigg on bass, Gerry Moffett on guitar and Jeff Hammer on keyboards. The 20-date tour featured 10 dates in Germany, seven in France and one each in the UK, Belgium and the Netherlands. The tour started on 5 November 1986 at Metropol in Berlin and ended on 8 December 1986 at the Forum in London.

More promotion followed in Japan and Australia, Kim appearing in a handful of TV programmes and doing extensive interviews for radio and printed press.

At the end of the year, Kim did a one-off concert at Golddiggers in Chippenham. Part of that concert – approximately 40 minutes – was broadcast on BBC TV during a special end of year edition of *The Old Grey Whistle Test*. After live renditions of 'Chequered Love', 'View From a Bridge', 'The Thrill of It', 'How Do You Want My Love', 'The Second Time' and a medley of 'Fever' (made famous by Peggy Lee in 1958) and 'Love Blonde', the band played 'Auld Lang Syne', after which the concert continued with 'You Keep Me Hangin' On' and 'I've Got So Much Love'. During that song, the concert continues off-screen while the show's presenters switched to other subjects. It is a memorable registration of a dynamic concert. Those who were able to see the concert – the BBC could also be received in parts of Europe – had a memorable start to the New Year, the concert circulating on copied VHS tapes among fans for years afterwards.

On 6 March 1987, the ferry *MS Herald of Free Enterprise* capsized while leaving the port of Zeebrugge, Belgium, killing 193 passengers and crew. Garry Bushell from *The Sun* newspaper organised the recording of a single, enlisting hit producers Stock, Aitken and Waterman. After Band Aid in 1984, charity singles became a regular occurrence, with USA for Africa, Artists United against Apartheid and Dance Aid other examples of getting artists together to sing a song, selling as many copies of the resulting single to raise maximum funds.

Between 14 and 16 March 1987, Boy George, Keren Woodward, Nick Kamen, Paul King, Mark King, Jaki Graham, Taffy, Mark Knopfler, Andy Bell, Pepsi &

Shirlie, Mel and Kim, Gary Moore, Kim Wilde, Nik Kershaw, Edwin Starr, Ben Volpelière-Pierrot, Ruby Turner and Kate Bush all recorded a few lines of the song 'Let It Be', with a chorus of a few dozen more artists to fill the final minutes of the recording. Paul McCartney contributed his part – and his video as well - from his own studio. The single, credited to Ferry Aid, was released on 23 March and reached No.1 in the UK, Norway and Switzerland, and peaked in the top 10 all over Europe. It was the 13th best-selling single of the year in the UK, certified gold for selling over 500,000 copies.

On 1 April 1987, Kim and Marty went on stage during the Action for AIDS concert at Wembley, singing 'Sorry Seems To Be the Hardest Word', with Ricky playing piano. It was the first time that father and daughter had appeared on stage together.

Then, in April 1987, 'You Keep Me Hangin' On' entered the US Billboard Hot 100 chart. Kim went to America for promotional duties, appearing in several radio programmes and occasional TV shows. Some of those radio interviews were a bit bizarre, for instance when she visited KPLZ in Seattle and had to answer car-related questions from people phoning in during their morning show.

Kim: "The promotional trip I went on across America before my single went to No. 1 was a hoot. I have some great memories, like sitting in a jacuzzi staring up at the stars in the middle of the desert. Or cruising through New York in a stretch limo with Ricky, gazing up at the skyscrapers, thinking: 'Wow, it doesn't get much better than this!'" [6]

Kim did a short live performance at The Palace Club in Los Angeles, but plans for a live tour in America – possibly with Junior (Giscombe) as support act – never materialized. However, this didn't stop 'You Keep Me Hangin' On' reaching the top spot in the US in July 1987.

Kim: "It was incredible. I was pretty young. In my twenties. I'd just come from the dentist when I got the news. That's what I remember - my mouth hurting. I didn't celebrate with champagne and a party. I think I had a cup of tea." [7]

Kim: "I was in my studio in Knebworth when I got the phone call from America. Because of the time difference the call came in the late afternoon to confirm I was definitely No.1. I still have the original poster of the Hot 100 Billboard chart framed at home." [8]

It was only the third time a British female solo singer had reached the top spot in the US singles chart, following Petula Clark with 'Downtown' in 1965 and Sheena Easton with 'Morning Train' in 1981. It would take 20 years for Leona Lewis to follow in Kim's footsteps with 2008's 'Bleeding Love'.

MCA seized the opportunity to release a third single from *Another Step* in the UK and Australia: 'Say You Really Want Me', remixed by Ricky Wilde. In July and

CHAPTER 8: ANOTHER STEP

August, Kim was back on UK TV screens with the music video for that single and various TV appearances. New chart show *The Roxy* made an attempt to attract the weekly viewing figures of the BBC's *Top of the Pops*, and on 8 August 1987 Kim appeared in the show, wearing a jaw-dropping red velvet dress.

Kim: "I bought it for four pounds at a rummage sale, and a friend and I share it to go to parties!" [9]

A two-hour TV special was recorded in the Midlands to mark the 10th anniversary of Elvis Presley's death. A remarkable amount of famous faces were there to perform his songs, backed by Elvis' original backing band - James Burton, Glen Harding, Jerry Scheff and Ronnie Tutt. Over 40 songs were performed by the likes of Boy George, Kiki Dee, Dave Edmunds, Jaki Graham, Meatloaf, Pet Shop Boys, Ruby Turner and many others. Kim performed two tracks on stage: 'Big Hunk O' Love' and 'Treat Me Nice', and filmed a sensual music video for her version of 'One Night With You'.

Kim: "Elvis was always 'King' in our family as I was growing up, no questions asked!"

The *Another Step* campaign was concluded by MCA with a re-release of the album. The new version featured three bonus tracks: the single versions of 'Another Step (Closer to You)' and 'Say You Really Want Me' and a megamix of these two songs plus 'You Keep Me Hangin' On'. A new sleeve featured a stylish photograph by Laurie Lewis. Although this version of the album only charted for two weeks, it did improve on that initial peak position, entering at No.73.

In September 1987, Kim appeared at the Fete de l'Humanité near Paris. Murray Head, Carmel and many French bands also played, to an audience of approximately 200,000.

Near the end of 1987, Kim bought a 16th century barn in Hertfordshire. After nearly a decade in London, she was ready to leave.

Kim: "When I was in my late twenties, I was working on an album in our studio at Knebworth in Hertfordshire and began to dread returning to London at the end of recording. I was tired of my city lifestyle and realised how much I wanted to get back to the countryside where I grew up. At the time, in the late 1980s, the local papers were advertising lots of barns for sale, including one at a farm. I fell in love with the place and decided to have a go at converting it into my home." [10]

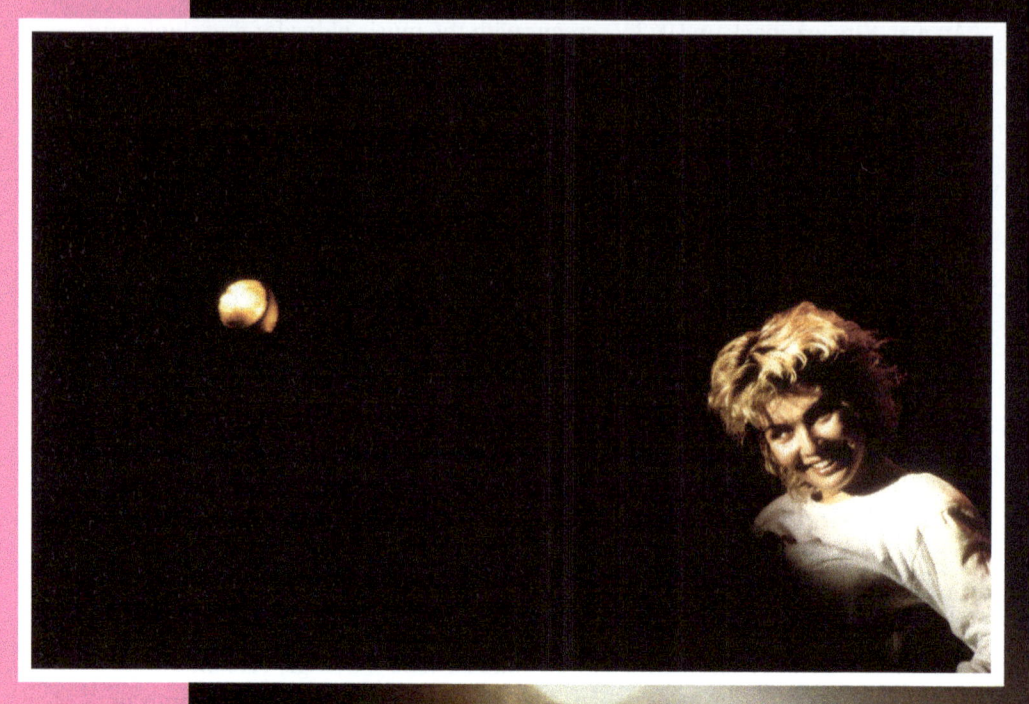

Kim live at Hof Ter Loo, Antwerp (Belgium), 2 December 1986
© Bart Moons

© Sheila Rock

© Sheila Rock

Kim live at Hof Ter Loo, Antwerp (Belgium), 2 December 1986 © Bart Moons

YOU KEEP ME HANGIN' ON
Written by Brian Holland, Lamont Dozier & Eddie Holland
Produced by Ricky Wilde
Released: 19 September 1986 (Europe) / 13 October 1986 (UK) / March 1987 (USA)
Chart positions: 2 (UK), 1 (Australia, Canada, Norway, USA), 2 (Ireland, Switzerland), 3 (Denmark), 8 (Germany), 12 (New Zealand), 16 (Belgium), 17 (Netherlands), 19 (France), 20 (Austria)

In September, Kim released the single 'You Keep Me Hangin' On' in Europe. The UK release followed a month later, on 13 October. Written by Lamont Dozier and the brothers Brian and Eddie Holland in 1966, it was a US No.1 hit for The Supremes, and reached No.8 in the UK singles chart. Ricky and Kim didn't originally intend to record a cover version but noticed a similarity in the chord structure with a new song composed by Ricky. They hadn't heard 'You Keep Me Hangin' On' for several years and decided to record the song as if it was a new composition, changing some of the lyrics in the process.

Kim: "My brother was writing for the album, was playing around with a chord progression and recognised it and realised it was 'You Keep Me Hangin' On'. At that point he was either going to write a song using the same chords or make a new backing track of "You Keep Me Hangin' On". He played it to me and asked me what I thought. I loved it. I remembered the song from a long time back on the radio. It wasn't a song I had in my collection, it wasn't a song I would play a lot. So when I went into the studio to record it was with a fresh approach, it wasn't paying homage to Diana Ross, although she was then, and remains my all-time favourite female vocalist."[11]

The music video was filmed at Albert Wharf in Battersea, South West London, directed by Gregg Masuak.

Two different extended versions of the song were made. In Europe, the 12" single featured the so-called WCH Club Mix, created by Ricky Wilde. The UK version of the 12" presented the longer WCH Mix, made by Ian Levine. This hi-energy version remained the best known remix, appearing on the mini-album 'You Keep Me Hangin' On', released by MCA in Japan in 1987.

HIT HIM
Written by Oscar Stewart Blandamer
Produced by Ricky Wilde

Many artists have used the services of the Kick Horns, and Kim Wilde is no exception. The trio, consisting of Simon Clarke, Roddy Lorimer and Tim Sanders, appear on this track, written by Oscar Stewart Blandamer, whose claims to fame include being a member of the Q-Tips and writing the song 'Darlin', a hit for Frankie Miller in 1978. Blandamer created the brass arrangement together with the Kick Horns for this track.

The song was performed live during the Another Step tour in 1986 and – unusually for an album track – also appeared on TV during a Cannon and Ball special on ITV in the UK on 27 December 1986.

ANOTHER STEP (CLOSER TO YOU)
Written by Kim Wilde & Steve Byrd
Produced by Ricky Wilde
Released: 16 March 1987
Chart positions: 6 (UK), 6 (Ireland)

One of the songs that came out of Kim's writing sessions with Steve Byrd, 'Another Step (Closer to You)' was conceived almost immediately as a duet.
Ricky: "When we did the demo of the track, Steve sang the duet with Kim, but we all felt it needed more of a soul feel, vocally. We chucked a few ideas around and came up with the idea of doing the duet with a great singer by the name of Junior (Giscombe). We phoned him and asked if he was up for it, and he said yes - thankfully. Junior came up to the studio and we recorded the song in about three days." [12]
Junior Giscombe: "I got a phone call from her brother saying she wanted to do a duet, and would I be up for it. They sent me the song. At the time Michael McDonald and Patti LaBelle had put out 'On My Own'. Everybody said to me that if I was going to do this, it had to be an R&B smooch record, and I was like, 'No, I'm not doing that kind of record. It makes no sense. That's what Americans do, and they do it better than us.' I wanted to do electronic pop – take people where they're not going to expect Junior to go. So we just decided to do what Kim does, but with more of a soulful approach." [13]

The first pressings of *Another Step* featured a different version of the (title) track than subsequent pressings. Although they are very similar, you can hear the difference in the first few seconds of the track.
Two more remixes appeared in 1987, when it was decided to release 'Another Step (Closer to You)' as a single.
Ricky: "When we recorded the track, none of us realised it was going to be the next single. When the decision came, I decided that for a single it needed to be 'beefed' up a bit. I kept the vocals and a couple of overdubs, but recorded all the rest using a Fairlight." [14]

Ricky created a 7" and 12" version, giving the track a fuller sound than the original album versions.

The music video was filmed in Paris under direction of Gregg Masuak. It features Kim arriving at the airport and walking through Paris to meet Junior Giscombe near the end of the video. The video concludes with them dancing together in a studio.

Kim: "There's a shot of me having to run up many, many steps In Paris. I had to do that shot about six times, and there was about a hundred steps. It was getting on my nerves. I wish I hadn't called it 'Another Step' after that." [15]

In 2000, Junior Giscombe recorded a solo version of 'Another Step (Closer To You)' on compilation album *His Very Best*.

THE THRILL OF IT
Written by Kim Wilde & Steve Byrd
Produced by Ricky Wilde

The second track on the album to be created by Kim with Steve Byrd during their writing sessions together was described by *The Sun*'s Helen Ballard as a 'shock rocker' in which Kim 'shows she can be as superficial about love as any macho on the mike'[16,] 'The Thrill Of It' certainly catches the ear instantly. The track brings to mind Kim's debut album with the male backing vocals in the choruses.

I'VE GOT SO MUCH LOVE
Written by Ricky, Marty & Kim Wilde
Produced by Ricky Wilde

A guitar cuts in while 'The Thrill of It' is still fading out on the album, and a rock-informed track starts. 'I've Got So Much Love' describes love and lust in equal measures, with lines like '*Now the cure is about to begin / I feel your fingers all over my skin*'. Steve Byrd contributes an impressive guitar solo and male backing vocals bring back memories of Kim's debut album, where this track wouldn't be entirely out of place.

'I've Got So Much Love' is the Kim Wilde single that never was. There were a few indications that the song was considered for a release: she performed the song on a French TV show and during the Midem conference in Cannes in early 1987. The song also made an impression on New Year's Eve in 1986 when *The Old Grey Whistle Test* broadcast part of her live concert at Golddiggers in Chippenham.

CHAPTER 8: ANOTHER STEP

VICTIM
Written by Ricky, Marty & Kim Wilde
Produced by Richard James Burgess

'Victim' was remixed by Ricky Wilde and Phill Brown for its release on the CD and cassette of *Another Step* in 1986. Despite this limited release, it was performed on Swedish TV programme *Kyss Karlsson* that year.

SCHOOLGIRL
Written by Ricky, Marty & Kim Wilde
Produced by Ricky Wilde & Reinhold Heil
Released: 8 June 1986
Chart positions: 7 (Denmark), 38 (Germany)

Although 'Schoolgirl' sounds like a catchy, upbeat pop song, Kim was inspired to write it after the disaster in the Chernobyl nuclear power station in Ukraine that happened on 26 April 1986.

   Released as a single in Europe and Australia, it was the first single of Wilde's career on which she was given co-writing credits. The 12" single featured the so-called 'Head-Mastermix', created by Ricky.

   The music video was directed by Peter Cornish and filmed on a playground. Kim performs the song while the camera crew circles around her, using the Steadicam. It allowed them to have a smooth shot, even while they were walking over a bumpy surface.

SAY YOU REALLY WANT ME
Written by David Sembello, Dick Rudolph & David Spencer Jr.
Produced by Rod Temperton, Dick Rudolph & Bruce Swedien
Released: July 1986 (USA, Canada), 3 August 1987 (UK), Ireland, Australia)
Chart positions: 29 (UK), 48 (Canada), 18 (Ireland), 44 (USA)

'Say You Really Want Me' was recorded in the USA with legendary producers Rod Temperton, Dick Rudolph and Bruce Swedien. The song was used in the film *Running Scared*, directed by Peter Hyams, starring Gregory Hines and Billy Crystal. According to Kim, the offer to record the song came directly from producer Rod Temperton.

   There is a definite American feel to the track, with its funky rhythm and catchy refrains, but it does miss that certain 'Wilde touch' that Ricky somehow adds to most of the other tracks on the album. Still, MCA had faith in the track. So much so, that they released several promotional singles and a host of different versions of the track.

Within weeks, no less than seven different edits appeared, all of them based on the *Running Scared* soundtrack version, but edited anywhere between 3'44 and 4'33 minutes. A video remix, just seconds short of 10 minutes, was created by Louil Silas Jr. (released in a shorter six-minute version as well) and a remix by David Todd appeared on one of the American 12" singles.

A year later, it was decided to release 'Say You Really Want Me' as a single in the UK, Ireland and Australia, but in a new remix by Ricky Wilde. He also created an extended version for the accompanying 12" single.

The video was directed by Gregg Masuak.

Kim: "I think the 'Say You Really Want Me' video was the most fun I've ever had making a video. I got to flirt mercilessly with three gorgeous guys, all at the same time with no-one asking any questions. Now how often does anyone get a chance to do that! (...) After the two-day shoot, the boys took me out to a club to dance the night away. We had so much fun making the video, we didn't want it to end." [17]

The video was not purposely made to shock, but when the ITV children's show *Get Fresh* banned it, stating that it was 'too saucy', MCA quickly made the most of it. Many UK newspapers reported that Kim's video was 'too sexy', and a promotional VHS video was circulated, with the cover stating 'The Banned Video – Complete Uncut Version Starring Kim Wilde; Certified Grown-Ups; The Ultimate Video Vinyl Experience, Twelve Inches of Pure Pleasure'. A photograph showing Kim with guest stars Brad Finkski, Wayne Johnson, Brett Synclairol and Matt Dellon must have raised a few eyebrows – although the video ultimately wasn't as saucy as suggested.

SHE HASN'T GOT TIME FOR YOU
Written by Ricky, Marty & Kim Wilde
Produced by Ricky Wilde

The concept of the album was to have a 'dance' side and a 'ballad' side. Although side two of the LP started with 'Say You Really Want Me', second track 'She Hasn't Got Time For You' was the first of five ballads on the album.

Two years later, Kim re-recorded the track in an up-tempo version for the B-side of 'Four Letter Word', called 'She Hasn't Got Time for You '88'.

BROTHERS
Written by Ricky & Marty Wilde
Produced by Ricky Wilde

This song talks about the difference between loving someone as you would a brother, but not as a lover, the eternal romantic conundrum! The musical backing on this track is subtle and beautiful, but it remains one of the lesser-known tracks in Kim's catalogue. It was only performed live during the Another Step tour in 1986.

MISSING
Written by Kim Wilde & Steve Byrd
Produced by Ricky & Kim Wilde

The third and final song on the album written by Kim and Steve Byrd. Using a TASCAM Portastudio, the world's first four-track recorder based on a standard compact audio cassette tape, they would work out songs which, if they were deemed good enough, were taken to the studio in Knebworth to re-record and add harmony vocals and overdubs.

'Missing' was one of the earliest songs to come out of these sessions. Steve provides a beautiful acoustic flamenco-tinged guitar intro, after which the story of a missing girl unfolds. '*Somebody help her*', Kim exclaims, and you can almost feel the desperation in her vocals. It is certainly one of the more moving tracks on the album.

HOW DO YOU WANT MY LOVE
Written by Ricky & Kim Wilde
Produced by Richard James Burgess

In an interview in 1987, Kim said she was really proud of this song.[18] It is certainly one of the most accomplished ballads on the album, with a sultry sound and affecting lyrics.

DON'T SAY NOTHING'S CHANGED
Written by Kim Wilde
Produced by Ricky Wilde

Although 'Don't Say Nothing's Changed' was never released as a single, Kim performed it on French television a few times. This self-penned number was a sign of Kim's growing confidence as a songwriter. It provided a perfect, if somewhat reflective, end to the album.

SONGS ABOUT LOVE (B-side)
Written by Kim Wilde
Produced by Kim Wilde

This song has the distinction of being the only track that was written, composed and produced solely by Kim. The song is a comment on love songs. Kim sings: '*So don't believe they're writing all those songs for you / 'cos you know they're only lies you're listening to / Those songs about love*'.

The song ends in a free form ad lib outro, with a brass section that sounds a lot like the Kick Horns (who were employed on the track 'Hit Him') and backing vocals provided by Kim herself. Released only on the B-side of 'Schoolgirl', it was finally released on CD in 2009 when Cherry Pop released an expanded deluxe edition of *Another Step*.

LOVING YOU (B-side)
Written by Kim & Ricky Wilde
Produced by Ricky Wilde

'Loving You' started out as an instrumental backing track – as was often the case when Ricky was developing songs – called 'Without You'. Ricky recorded a wordless vocal track to go with the instrumental, featuring only a few words for the chorus: '*What do I have to do / 'cos it's never the same without you*'.

Some of the melody lines played on keyboards on his demo were dropped in resulting track, 'Loving You'. The new lyrics, presumably written by Kim, included the lines '*I wanna be loved by you / Is there anything else I can do*'. It seemed to fit the mood of the song better.

Released as the B-side of 'You Keep Me Hangin' On', it became a suitable counterpart to the more up-tempo A-side, countering a longing for independence with a yearning for a real, lasting relationship.

HOLD BACK (B-side)
Written by Ricky & Marty Wilde
Produced by Ricky Wilde

'Hold Back' has the distinction of being the only Kim Wilde B-side performed on television. In Swedish programme *Ölandssommar* in the summer of 1986, Kim performed 'Schoolgirl', 'Cambodia' and 'Hold Back'. It was an exclusive premiere for the Swedish audience, since the track only appeared months later (in March 1987) as the B-side of 'Another Step (Closer to You)'.

CHAPTER 8: ANOTHER STEP

LIVE-IN WORLD
SOMETHING BETTER
Written by Charley Foskett
Produced by Charley Foskett

Kim Wilde, Daryl Pandy, Bobby Whitlock, Precious Wilson and Finchley's Children's Choir all appear on this 1986 track, recorded for the Anti-Heroin Project, a group of musical artists who contributed their talents to benefit the Phoenix House charity's recovery centres throughout the UK to battle heroin addiction. The Anti-Heroin Project, as it was called, released a compilation album, *Live-In World*, and a single with the same title. 'Something Better' appeared on the B-side and on the compilation album. The track was recorded at Abbey Road Studios, where promotional photos for the project were also made.

'Live In World' was a collaborative track, with no solo vocal for Kim. She does, however, appear briefly in the music video.

TURN BACK THE CLOCK (with Johnny Hates Jazz)
Written by Clark Datchler
Produced by Calvin Hayes & Mike Nocito
Released: November 1987
Chart positions: 12 (UK), 9 (Belgium), 12 (Finland), 1 (Iceland), 5 (Netherlands), 3 (New Zealand), 20 (Sweden), 19 (Germany)

Calvin Hayes was the drummer in Kim's first band and appeared with her on various TV shows in 1981 and 1982. Together with Clark Datchler and Mike Nocito he formed the band Johnny Hates Jazz in 1986, releasing their debut single 'Me and my Foolish Heart' on RAK Records. They were signed to Virgin next, and released the singles 'Shattered Dreams' and 'I Don't Want To Be A Hero', both big hits in the UK and Europe. They had already recorded a version of 'Turn Back the Clock', but decided to re-record the track before it was released as their third single. And then Calvin ran into Kim in the launderette around the corner from RAK Studios. She congratulated him on the success of those two singles, adding that she preferred the second one. Calvin then asked if she wanted to sing on the third.[19]

Kim agreed, and recorded beautiful backing vocals that featured more prominently on the extended version, released on the 12" single and CD-single.

Although Kim didn't appear in the music video for 'Turn Back the Clock', coincidentally directed by Brian Grant, she did perform the song together with Johnny Hates Jazz on BBC TV's *Wogan* on 21 December 1987.

ROCKIN' AROUND THE CHRISTMAS TREE (Mel & Kim)
Written by Johnny Marks
Produced by Stuart Colman
Released: 23 November 1986
Chart positions: 3 (UK), 16 (Denmark), 9 (Norway)

The UK's annual Comic Relief charity fundraising campaign was helped by some very funny single releases during the 1980s. Teaming up the comedians of the TV series *The Young Ones* with Cliff Richard for a rendition of 'Living Doll' proved a big success in 1986, and the following year they wanted to follow this up with another pairing of comedy and music.

As luck would have it, the duo Mel & Kim (Appleby) had just swept the nation with their hat-trick of hit singles, so comedian Mel Smith – usually working with comedy partner Griff Rhys-Jones – teamed up with Kim Wilde. They recorded seasonal song 'Rockin' Around The Christmas Tree' (originally a hit for Brenda Lee in the UK in 1962) with added comedy elements.

On 20 October 1987, Kim Wilde and Mel Smith recorded the music video for their Comic Relief single. The video featured a comedy intro by Mel Smith and Griff Rhys-Jones in the style of their comedy series *Alas Smith & Jones*, with guest appearances by Curiosity Killed The Cat and puppets from popular TV programme *Spitting Image* depicting Bette Midler and Tina Turner.

Mel Smith: "Comic Relief said to us, 'Would it be a fun idea to do a Mel & Kim single, rather than a Griff & Kim single, because it doesn't have the same ring to it. We were both very keen to become the Pearl Carr & Teddy Johnson of the Eighties." [20]

Kim: "It should bring a smile to people's faces this Christmas. Mel is such a funny person, and incredibly sweet. We were up until 3am making the video, but I was amazed that he had the energy to take part since only last week he was rushed off to hospital with a peptic ulcer!" [21]

The video met with a little controversy. In one scene, Kim opens a fridge to find Mel inside. The video was shown on Terry Wogan's evening talk show, after which the BBC received complaints from parents, claiming the BBC was irresponsible because the shot would encourage youngsters to climb into the fridge - with dangerous consequences. The scene was cut from later broadcasts.

The single entered the UK singles chart on 5 December 1987 and peaked at No.3 for two weeks on 26 December and 2 January 1988. It raised a total of £78,000.

Like many Christmas songs, 'Rockin' Around the Christmas Tree' continued to chart every year, and be played on the radio in December in the UK and Europe.

CHAPTER 8: ANOTHER STEP

Kim: "That was a great moment in my career in retrospect. I never thought the song would carry on being a hit every Christmas after that, and I absolutely love singing it, especially with an audience."

EVERYONE'S SWEETHEART (Demo)
Written by Kim Wilde & Steve Byrd

This jazzy track, probably created during sessions in 1986, was never officially released, but the demo appeared on the website kimwildetv.com for a few weeks in 2004. The recording was one of many owned by Steve Byrd on a collection of cassettes, and offered to the website's owner, Pierre Mathis, as an exclusive.

The recording is a significant one, because the song ended up being recorded by Belgian singer Muriel Dacq. Her biggest hit was 'Tropique' in 1986. In the five years that followed, she released several more singles, without much success. In 1995 she attempted to revive her career with the album 'Ohé du Vasseau', on which the song 'Ces Moments Là' appeared. Dacq wrote the French lyrics herself, the melody based on 'Everyone's Sweetheart'.

TIME TO LIVE YOUR LIFE (Demo)
Written by Kim Wilde & Steve Byrd

Just like 'Everyone's Sweetheart', this track appeared on kimwildetv.com for a few weeks in 2004. Another demo taken from Steve Byrd's cassette collection, the lyrics could be deemed a consolation for those with broken hearts, encouraging them to start taking fate into their own hands.

'*It's time to live your life / You've got to make it right / You better start planning your future / Be your own best friend tonight*', sings Kim in double-tracked vocals. The track sounds almost fully formed, despite only being a demo.

PREMIÈRE RENCONTRE (Live performance)
Written by Michel Berger

French singer Françoise Hardy recorded 'Première Rencontre' on 14th album *Message Personnel* (1973). Although Hardy wasn't particularly fond of the album, she felt 'Première Rencontre' was a beautiful song. [22] Kim Wilde sang the song live on two occasions: on 12 September 1987 at La Courneuve during a concert for the Fête de l'Humanité, and on 27 June 1988 when Kim was the support act during Michael Jackson's Bad Tour. Two decades later, she revealed why this was one of her favourite French songs.

Kim: "I love the song 'Première Rencontre'. I learned the song in French as I love the language, and the words by Michel Berger are pure poetry." [23]

INTERVIEW: RICHARD BLANSHARD

When did you first meet Kim Wilde?
It's funny, I was at an event, Kim was here and I thought to myself, one day I will be working with you, and it happened!

How did you become a member of her band?
I was in a band called Voice and we had spent four years putting an album together. The album was on MCA in America and we got totally ripped off. I decided it was time to put my energy in other places. I formed the Q Tips with Paul Young. I then joined Russ Ballard's Barnet Dogs and did the backing vocals on three albums. I got a call to step in for the sax player/vocalist for Barbara Dickson and her keyboard player Bias Boshell, who also played with Kiki Dee and Barclay James Harvest and was a friend of Ricky's, suggested me. I can't say it felt like an audition. It went well. We just got on personally and musically, and off we went.

Were you a fan of Kim's music before you joined?
I had worked in producing music videos and Brian Grant, who I worked with, directed the 'Kids in America' and 'Cambodia' videos, and I always thought she was great.

You toured as part of Kim's band between 1983 and 1986. What were they like to work with?
The touring was always great, the musicianship was polished. Kim has such great loyal fans and we always prepared really well before touring. You become like a family on the road, and we shared many funny moments, and the first tour took us on some pretty scary road journeys. I was given one of the first copies of the *Spinal Tap* video, and that gave us hours of laughter on tour. There was always competition on playing pranks and I remember one night going back to my room after a few drinks, opened the door and all the furniture had been removed - the only thing in the room was a plastic red nose on the carpet. I went to the reception and told them, and said, 'Come with me'. We went up to my room, I opened the door, and all the furniture was back in place!'

You've also taken several beautiful photographs of Kim. What struck you most about her from a photographic point of view?
Firstly, I discovered it is impossible to take a bad photograph of Kim. The camera loves her. One evening Marty invited us to see him play in a club. We were sitting at the table and a guy was going around the tables with a Polaroid camera, then putting the photos onto keyrings. He took a photo of Kim. He came back with

CHAPTER 8: ANOTHER STEP

it in a keyring. Well... it could have been an album cover. So my job was made very easy when I was asked to photograph her. Great photographs are all about connection with the person. I think because we had spent so much time together, it helped achieve some really special and beautiful images. Kim feels the camera, and it's a special gift. I am lucky to have worked with and shot some of our biggest celebrities and stars, and Kim's photos are still some of my best.

What do you admire most about Kim as an artist and/or person?
Well to start, let's forget music. Kim is a very special human being. She is kind, thoughtful, caring and generous. She is also a true professional and incredibly hard working and I admire her for that, and she is committed to her fans on a personal level. She is also someone you just want to spend time with. So as far as a musician and performer once again, she is totally professional and dedicated, she is a great songwriter and she always delivers 100 percent. I think because of Marty and the family's musical history, she is grounded, and that goes for all the Wilde family. The only thing I have to add is Kim, if you ever want to use a sax player/vocalist again, I am ready....

Richard Blanshard live with Kim Wilde, Palais de Sports, Montpellier (France), 27 March 1985
© Richard Blanshard

CHAPTER 9:
CLOSE

Released: 13 May 1988
Chart positions: 8 (UK), 82 (Australia), 7 (Austria), 11 (Finland), 17 (France), 10 (Germany), 20 (Italy), 7 (Netherlands), 6 (Norway), 11 (Sweden), 8 (Switzerland), 114 (USA)

1987 was a successful year for Kim, with a No.1 in America and various hit singles in the UK and Europe. While the Wilde team was working on the next album, the record company started to push them towards an even more 'America-oriented' repertoire. They wanted Kim to work with other producers – preferably American ones.

Kim: "After our No.1 in America the focus of my record company changed. There was talk of other producers, other management; let's get Kim to conquer USA! I had worked closely with my family; moreover, I had a thriving career this side of the pond and wasn't particularly ambitious about my career in the USA, although of course my record company was. It was obvious to me that I would have to live there to have any real chance of success, and that wasn't an option for me."

The Wildes decided they would bring in a producer, but one they were familiar with: Tony Swain. Swain had worked successfully with Imagination, Spandau Ballet, Alison Moyet and Bananarama, and brought something to the table that the record company could eventually live with: some of the tracks he'd produced charted in America, with Bananarama's 'Cruel Summer' and Spandau Ballet's 'True' top-10 hits across the Atlantic.

Ricky: "Up until that point, I hadn't worked with anybody else as a producer, so it was an interesting experience for me, and something I really wanted to embrace." [1]

The album almost got lost at the very last minute though.

**Rick: "We spent the best part of a year recording this album, and were all really pleased with it and everything was done, it was mastered, it was all great. But then the very final stage of that is you need to cut it in the cutting room in London. At that time we were working with Steve Streeter, who was our tape op. So we get in the car, he's got all the master tapes in a briefcase, so I said: 'Stick it in the boot and then it will be safe.' It was all on DAT tape, there was only one copy. We put it in the boot of my BMW, slammed the boot

CHAPTER 9: CLOSE

shut. We're driving up there, feeling a bit peckish, so I said, 'Fancy a Maccy D?'. So we got out of the car, locked it, Steve said, 'We're not leaving those tapes in that car, we're taking them with us.' He got it out of the boot, we go into McDonald's, and a Big Mac and fries and a chocolate milkshake later, get in the car and we drive to the cutting room. I say, 'Steve, you got the masters?' He looked at me and he's gone white. And he says, 'I left it in McDonald's!'. We dash back to McDonald's and thank Christ it was still sitting there, exactly where we left it. If anybody had picked it up, that was it, the album gone. A whole album gone!" [2]

Close was released on 13 May 1988. As for the title, Kim explained:
Kim: "I like intimate words. This is a very intimate album for me, especially since I wrote so many of the lyrics." [3]

Reviews were mixed. There was the usual snarling from the 'serious' music press, and a review in *Smash Hits* that slags off three tracks on the album, before continuing: "There's the brilliant single 'Hey Mister Heartache', the rather steamy 'Love In A Natural Way' and 'You'll Be The One Who'll Lose', which are perkier by far and *much* more the 'ticket'!"[4] The Boston Globe in America recognised: "*Close* is Kim Wilde's strongest album to date. She has matured as both singer and songwriter."[5] Most European reviews dwelled on the fact that the album featured more compositions by Kim, and that the album would profit from a certain tour that was just starting.

Close marks the first time Kim co-wrote all but one of the tracks on an album, while also featuring the last four co-writes of Marty. Tony Swain co-produced nine out of 10 tracks, while Steve Byrd only co-wrote one this time. He'd gone on to form Heartbeat UK together with Steve Lambert, Mark Heyward-Chaplin and Culture Club drummer Jon Moss. Their single 'Jump To It' wasn't the success it was expected to be, and the band became a short-lived project.

Steve Byrd: "Heartbeat UK didn't have much success and I was wondering what to do next when I had a call from Nick Boyles, Kim's manager. He asked if I would be interested in a tour lasting up to nine months, opening for a very large act. I said that I would be. "Who is it with?" I asked. "I can't tell you", said Nick, "I'll get back to you"." [6]

In early 1988, Kim's management was contacted by Michael Jackson's management. Perhaps Michael had heard No.1 hit 'You Keep Me Hangin' On', prompting him to invite Kim on tour with him as he embarked on the European leg of his 'Bad' tour.

Kim: "When the possibility of supporting Michael Jackson first arose, it was something I didn't dare think about. My first reaction was 'I can't do that!', to which my Mum replied, 'Why on earth not?!'. 'But I can't!' I screamed. 'He's

the greatest performer on earth, he's in a different league'. My Mum kept on and my Dad joined in, then the entire family jumped on the bandwagon until I started to think, 'Actually...why can't I?'. It's a challenge, I thought. I could fall flat on my face, or I could succeed and be brilliant and have something to be really proud of. I knew it would be sink or swim, and I decided to swim for England." [7]

A tour with Michael Jackson would prove to be an essential boost for Kim's album *Close*. The European tour started on 23 May 1988 at the Stadio Flaminio in Rome. It wasn't an immediate success. The gates were closed when Kim started her set and the few fans that turned up when they were finally opened were not too friendly: they started throwing things at the stage.

Kim: "I remember a very difficult evening in Italy, when they threw things at me. It was at the very start of the tour! I told my management: "It's a crazy idea, to do this tour. No-one is interested in Kim Wilde. I'm going home!". But in other parts of Europe it went a lot better than that. I got standing ovations, so the American entourage started wondering, "Who is this Kim Wilde?". But I knew in my heart that my fans wouldn't let me down." [8]

Subsequent dates were indeed more successful, with audiences highly appreciating Kim's hit-laden set. It was hard to resist songs like 'Chequered Love', 'You Came', 'View From a Bridge', 'Never Trust a Stranger', 'Cambodia' and 'Kids in America', which were in the charts around the same time as Jackson's biggest hits.

Kim: "I had a brilliant time, obviously having had so many hits in Europe for so long. The audience were behind me. I think they wanted me to succeed. They didn't want me to fail. And I felt very supported by them." [9]

The press in the UK were obsessed with one thing: did Kim meet Michael? Did they spend a lot of time together? When it turned out, after a few days, that they didn't, the media decided Michael had 'snubbed' Kim. Adding to this, the story got out that Michael actually met Kim's younger brother and sister.

Kim: "He heard my little sister Roxanne and brother Marty were on the tour with me at the start and made a special request to meet them. Everyone was green with envy. They were taken to his dressing room, and they stayed with him for quite a while, chatting and joking. When they got back, we all fell upon them with questions, but you know what kids are like - they didn't remember anything. Roxanne told me later that he said to her, 'You're every bit as cute as your sister.'" [10]

Of course, they did eventually meet, albeit briefly.

Kim: "One night in Munich, I came off the Olympic Stadium stage pretty worn out from the tour and looking forward to a nice bath and a bit of a rest. Then my manager, Nick, asked if I could be ready at nine o'clock to do something.

CHAPTER 9: CLOSE

He was very mysterious. I was really tired, so I told him I didn't want to do anything except relax. 'But Michael wants to meet you', Nick said. So of course I was ready! When I met him, photographs were quickly taken of the two of us, and he told me how great he thought my show was. I just said thank you and it was a great honour and that his show was brilliant, too!" [11]

Kim: "Michael was so nice, and he had the sweetest smile I've ever seen in my life. My heart just melted! I thanked him for having me on his tour, and then he was off to do the show. I watched from the wings, and he was pure magic. Today was one of the best days of the tour." [12]

Kim: "I only met him briefly in the two months I toured with him. In a subdued lighting scenario, he put his arm around me and I thought, 'That's sweet' and then he turned his head to a waiting camera... the only reason I was there. I told him to take care of himself because he looked like he needed a good meal. He looked at me as if to say, 'You've caught me out.'" [13]

Kim: "I only met him once to do a publicity photograph. I got taken into his dressing room and there he was with the lights dimmed and then his 'uncles' as I called them – these older men who seemed to control a lot of what was going on around him – they positioned me so I was looking in the right direction for the camera. We had our photograph taken, then I was gently persuaded to leave."

During the dates in the UK, Junior Giscombe made a guest appearance on stage to sing 'Another Step (Closer To You)' together with Kim.

The music video for 'You Came', released as a single during the tour, featured footage of Kim on stage and backstage. Viewers caught a glimpse of all the things that were going on while Kim was travelling Europe.

Kim: "I love the 'You Came' video, because it captures a moment in my career when everything was just perfect. It's beautiful." [14]

Being on tour with Michael Jackson had its perks. On many nights, Kim and Michael's entourage were escorted in and out of the stadiums with police escorts. Police would go ahead with motorcycles and cars with flashing lights and clear the junctions and traffic signals ahead. The tour buses would follow through the red lights and closed junctions. This privilege is usually reserved for world leaders, so the band and artists would enjoy this a lot, waving to confused drivers being held up.

But it wasn't just a fairytale: touring with Michael Jackson also meant hard work. In between live dates, Kim would fly back to England for TV performances or a few days doing press interviews, and the pressure of performing before thousands of people took its toll from time to time. The loneliness that fame seemed to have brought to Michael made a big impression on Kim.

Kim: "He was very gentle and sweet. He always had a lot of people around him – it was a complete circus and he just seemed this lonely figure in the middle. I was the one hanging out with his band, having a drink after the gig, and he was nowhere to be seen. You could see the level of isolation, and he paid the price with his life. I got to see up close what fame can take from a person." [15]

Kim: "Well, there was a time when, I think shortly after I was opening for Michael Jackson, when I seriously thought about giving up being a pop star really. I got very disillusioned with fame. I seemed to have a lot of success, but I wasn't happy. I thought 'What's the point of being famous if you're not happy?'" [16]

After the Michael Jackson tour, Kim went to America together with Ricky and Nick Boyles for promotional duties. In Los Angeles and Minneapolis, Kim personally delivered her album *Close* to competition winners who phoned in at radio stations. In December, Kim went to Japan and Australia. *Close* was a big success in Japan, aided by a beautiful LP release with four bonus posters inside.

On 10 March 1989, Comic Relief organised its second ever annual 'Red Nose Day', a fantastic night of television on the BBC featuring everyone from Lenny Henry to Billy Connolly, and from Griff Rhys-Jones to the cast of Australian soap opera *Neighbours*. During the night, Kim appeared in a sketch called 'The Last Waltz' alongside Wendy Craig, Nerys Hughes, Felicity Kendal, Linda McCartney, Jean Boht, Polly James and Caroline Blakiston. The charity raised £27 million that day.

A day earlier, Ricky's wife Mandy gave birth to a baby girl, Scarlett Lillian, a sister for Marty III. Scarlett would go on to become an integral member of Kim's touring band.

In April, Marty celebrated his 50th birthday. Joyce organised a big party at their house, and a lot of old music friends were present. Marty sang loads of old rock'n'roll songs with Bruce Welch and Brian Bennett from the Shadows and his old band The Wildcats. There were also guest performances by Tim Rice, Elaine Page, and Kim. During the evening a gigantic cake in the shape of a guitar was cut.[17]

At the end of the month, Kim performed 'You Keep Me Hangin' On' in a special 'Review Of The 80s' edition of *Top of the Pops*, rounding off an incredibly successful decade.

CHAPTER 9: CLOSE

HEY MISTER HEARTACHE
Written by Kim Wilde & Steve Byrd
Produced by Ricky Wilde & Tony Swain
Released: 18 April 1988
Chart positions: 31 (UK), 96 (Australia), 14 (Denmark), 13 (Germany), 22 (Ireland), 7 (Italy), 37 (Netherlands), 3 (Norway), 6 (Sweden), 12 (Switzerland)

The first track on the album *Close* was also the lead single in most territories: 'Hey Mister Heartache', written by Kim with Steve Byrd.
Kim: "I wrote this song with my then guitarist Steve Byrd. Together we had already penned a number of songs for my previous album, including 'Another Step (Closer to You)', a duet with Junior Giscombe. This dance-inspired groove was one of the first songs written for the album, motivated (as so often) by one of my several broken hearts! Growing up in public had its pros and cons, but at least I could pour my emotion into songwriting, which became a sort of therapy." [18]
Kim: "'Hey Mister Heartache' is really about someone who you're with and is just messing you around, and you say, 'Well I've had enough of this, it's time to say goodbye." [19]

The single version was considerably shorter than the album take, so fans were quite surprised to hear it on the album. Two separate 12" singles were released, each with a different remix. The extended remix, clocking it at eight minutes, was created by Ricky, whereas the so-called Kilo Watt Remix, at 6 minutes, was made by Timmy Regisford. A 'Bonus Beats' version and an 'Acapella with Percussion' version were released in 2013, when Universal released a 25th anniversary version of *Close* on a double-CD. 'Hey Mister Heartache' was also the first Kim Wilde single released in the relatively new CD-single format, the European division of MCA opting for the attractive 3-inch version – supplied with a free adapter for players that couldn't handle the smaller discs.

The music video, directed by Brian Ward, was shot over two days, the first day taking place in Kim's London flat with actor Jesse Birdsall.

In France, 'Hey Mister Heartache' was not released as a single. The French division of MCA opted for 'You Came' instead.

YOU CAME
Written by Ricky & Kim Wilde
Produced by Ricky Wilde & Tony Swain
Released: 4 July 1988
Chart positions: 3 (UK), 35 (Australia), 8 (Austria), 10 (Belgium), 42 (Canada), 1 (Denmark), 5 (France), 5 (Germany), 3 (Ireland), 4 (Italy), 13 (Netherlands), 4 (Norway), 7 (Sweden), 3 (Switzerland), 41 (USA)

When the album was almost complete, Ricky felt it needed one more track in order to be able to present a fully-formed collection of songs.
Ricky: "I had the weekend off and wanted to think about it calmly. At that time, I had a large studio and locked myself in there. I had sent my sound engineers home so I could fiddle around all by myself." [20]
Ricky: "We had a weekend before MCA were going to come back to the studio to have a live final playback of the album. I had just the weekend to sort out another track. I went into the studio on my own and turned all the gear on, got a couple of synths up, got a little groove going and started listening to a bit of Human League. The reason for that was *Dare* - I adored that album, it's one of my favourite albums, beautiful songs, every single track is just an absolute stunner. I just felt that there was one more track for our album. I wanted it to be like our *Dare*. There's a track The Human League released quite a few years ago, 'Life On Your Own'. It had very similar chords to 'You Came'. Then the melody came very quickly, and the lyric came very quickly. That was about my little boy, who was very young at the time, I think he was only a few months old. The whole chorus was written about him. But I wanted the rest of the lyric to sound more global, so I wanted it to mean that it could be anything to do with what changes your life. Whether it be religion, a best friend, a new situation or something that's affected your life in a life-changing way. So then I just phoned up Kimmy, and said, 'Look, I've come up with this, what do you think?' She loved it and finished off the lyrics." [21]
Kim: "This song was inspired by the birth of Ricky and Mandy's first child, Marty. Being an older sister, it felt really strange and yet wonderful for my little brother to become a father, and together we captured the joy of a new life." [22]
Kim: "Even though I wasn't a mother at the time, I was still able to put myself in his position. I saw how happy my brother was then." [23]

As it turned out, 'You Came' became one of the key tracks on the album. Although written about the arrival of a new life, Kim cleverly rewrote the lyrics in a way that they could also be interpreted as a love song.

'You Came' was released as a single in the summer of 1988, again with two different 12" singles: one featuring an extended remix by Ricky and one with a

CHAPTER 9: CLOSE

remix by Shep Pettibone. In the US, fans got an edit of that remix on the single, plus two dub mixes on a 12" single. The European CD-single was again released on 3-inch format. A handful were mispressed: some copies of A-ha's CD-single for 'Touchy!' featured the label print of both A-ha's 'Touchy!' and Kim Wilde's 'You Came', but played Kim's three tracks.

The music video was directed by Gregg Masuak and featured many scenes from Kim backstage and on stage during the tour with Michael Jackson. A separate studio session was also filmed, in which Kim performed the track together with her band, her hair tied together in a short ponytail.

Through the years, many acts have tried their hand at this song, with cover versions recorded by Estonia's Hylene, Portuguese girl group Maxgirls, German DJ Mario Lopez, Italo disco outfit Anigeer, DJ Project featuring Katla, and Danish duo Camilot. Greek singer Bessy Argyraki recorded a Greek version ('Eisai Oti Agapo'), Finnish band Hausmylly recorded a Finnish version ('Niin Tein'), and German girl duo Lollipops recorded a German-language birthday song to the tune of 'You Came', entitled 'Dein Tag'.

During Kim's live shows, 'You Came' always makes an appearance, audiences clapping along joyfully.

FOUR LETTER WORD
Written by Ricky & Marty Wilde
Produced by Ricky Wilde & Tony Swain
Released: 21 November 1988
Chart positions: 6 (UK), 23 (Austria), 9 (Belgium), 27 (Germany), 5 (Ireland), 8 (Netherlands), 18 (Switzerland)

According to Kim, Marty was strumming his guitar when he came up with the idea for this disconsolate, clever love song. With guitar by Ricky and Steve Byrd and keyboards again by Ricky and Tony Swain, not a lot of instruments were used, but in the vocal department it was a challenge for Kim.

Kim: "Tony Swain wanted more from my singing than ever before. He encouraged me to sing higher notes than I'd ever sung. I got an enormous kick out of it. Next to singing techniques he demanded everything from my emotions as well. The melancholy on 'Four Letter Word' is the result of that. I matured as a singer with that song." [24]

Eventually released as the fourth single from the album, it was a departure from previous singles, because despite its mid-tempo rhythm, it was a sad love song. The song was nominated for an Ivor Novello award.

An extended version appeared on the 12" single and CD-single, and the 12" single contained an additional 'Late Night Mix'. That version appeared on CD

Kim live during the 'Bad' tour with Michael Jackson at the Olympic Stadium, Munich (Germany), 8 July 1988. dpa picture alliance/ Alamy stock photo

© Robert Hoetink

for the first time in 1994 when MCA released *The Remix Collection* in Japan and Australia.

Having entered the UK chart on 3 December 1988 at No.51, it gradually climbed to its peak position of No.6 on 14 January 1989. The single had an impressive 12-week residence in the chart.

There were a couple of cover versions, both recorded in China. Fanny Cheng recorded a Chinese language version on her album *Be My Baby* in 1989, and Yvonne Lau followed suit in 1994 on her album *Lovelorn Restaurant*.

LOVE IN THE NATURAL WAY
Written by Kim, Ricky & Marty Wilde
Produced by Ricky Wilde & Tony Swain
Released: 20 February 1989
Chart positions: 32 (UK), 26 (Ireland)

Once rumoured to be the favourite track of Michael Jackson's manager Frank DiLeo, this love song was a classic melodic Kim Wilde pop tune.

Only two weeks after 'Four Letter Word' left the UK chart, single number five followed: 'Love in the Natural Way', a relatively low-key release with no new B-side and a short music video that contained elements of previous music videos. It was directed by Neil Thompson.

MCA supported the UK release with a 7" single in a poster sleeve and a beautiful picture disc CD-single. A miniature 3" CD-single in an equally small cardboard sleeve was produced for the European market.

Kim: "This was the fifth and final single from *Close* and one of my personal favourite love songs. I often still sing this today in an acoustic set at my concerts; the melody and sentiment still as potent as they were back in '88.... perhaps even more so." [25]

The extended version of 'Love in the Natural Way' appeared on the 12" single and CD-single. The shorter video version was released in 2013 on the 25th anniversary version of the *Close* CD.

LOVE'S A NO
Written by Ricky, Marty & Kim Wilde
Produced by Ricky Wilde & Tony Swain

Ending side one of the LP, this beautiful ballad started quietly, but took the listener on an emotional rollercoaster, courtesy of Kim's soaring vocals and an engaging melody.

CHAPTER 9: CLOSE

Kim: "My father and brother wrote this melancholy love song, probably without truly knowing how much the words resonated with me personally. Again, Ricky's incredible skill at crafting a beautiful melody comes to the fore, while my Dad's honest and sensitive lyrics speak directly to the heart." [26]

NEVER TRUST A STRANGER
Written by Kim & Ricky Wilde
Produced by Ricky Wilde
Released: 19 September 1988
Chart positions: 7 (UK), 2 (Austria), 6 (Belgium), 20 (France), 11 (Germany), 5 (Ireland), 4 (Netherlands), 12 (Sweden), 4 (Switzerland)

Opening side two of the album with a guitar chord, this track quickly explodes, revealing the most dramatic track of them all. '*My world is in pieces / You've stolen my pride / And I'm left defeated / And crushed by your lies*', sings Kim, adding the advice, '*Never trust a stranger with your heart*'. The track sounds aggressive and packs a mighty punch.

Kim: "I remember when Rick played me the backing track for 'Never Trust A Stranger'. I knew straight away it was a smash! There have only been a few songs in my career where I knew I was listening to a 'surefire' hit. 'Never Trust A Stranger' is one of my all-time favourite songs as a single that I released." [27]

Kim: "I remember Ricky playing this backing track to me one day as I was writing in the artist's accommodation at Select Sound Studios, Knebworth. We'd owned the studio for a few years, re-designing an old doctor's surgery into a state-of-the-art recording facility in the heart of Hertfordshire. I often stayed there whilst recording, rather than drive back to my flat in London after a long day in the studio. The 'hit you hard in the chest' backing track pulled no punches, and off I went to finish the lyrics. Some songs on *Close* are autobiographical and personal, while others immerse themselves in a world of fantasy... this song was a bit of both." [28]

Ricky provided a remix for the single release, and an extended version for the 12" single. Another remix was provided by the Sanjazz team, consisting of Emilio Sanchez IV and Jimmy Jazz, who were working at Select Sound at the time. Their remix included snippets from an interview with Kim.

'Never Trust A Stranger' was covered by British singer Belle Lawrence in 2005 and American singer Felicia Punzo in 2014. In 2020, Spanish singer Mónica Naranjo released a version called 'Hoy No!' ('Not Today!') in her native language.

YOU'LL BE THE ONE WHO'LL LOSE
Written by Ricky, Kim & Marty Wilde
Produced by Ricky Wilde & Tony Swain

The ominous title signals that this song is a message for someone. But 'You'll Be the One Who'll Lose' was mainly a way for Kim to cope with a broken heart.
Kim: "I wrote a song called 'You'll Be the One Who'll Lose' about a relationship that went nowhere with somebody that I cared about very much at the time. That song perfectly describes that situation. For me, songwriting has been a great therapy and a great way of working out the heartache of life." [29]
Kim: "This song describes how it feels to fall in love with the idea of falling in love. The atmospheric and reflective music dictated the subject matter, and once again a song came along to help ease the pain of growing up in public." [30]

'You'll Be the One Who'll Lose' was released as the B-side of 'Love in the Natural Way'. Kim performed it live during her performance in Sopot in August 1988, but it didn't get a live performance after that.

EUROPEAN SOUL
Written by Ricky & Kim Wilde
Produced by Ricky Wilde & Tony Swain

A keen admirer of French painter Marc Chagall, Kim studied his work while creating the album. It was almost inevitable that she would write a song about his work. '*Images dance, translucent colours seem to shine / They're a ghostly recollection / of another space and time*'.
Kim: "That song is about the painter Marc Chagall, of whom I'm a big fan. I'd locked myself into the studio for a few months for the recording of this album. I also read a lot of books about artists, such as Chagall. I knew something of him, since I studied art history in Art College, but I never studied his work properly. I was more into Degas and Toulouse-Lautrec then. When I saw Chagall's work, I went to the Tate Gallery to see his paintings. I am touched by his use of colours and his compositions. The feeling of wonder is consistent with the song." [31]
Kim: "Recently I read a book about Marc Chagall's life. When I was flicking through it, my mouth fell open, seeing all that beautiful work. I went to the Tate Gallery immediately and stood before one of his beautiful paintings for a while. Then I remembered suddenly that someone once asked me what I felt was closest to perfection. I suddenly knew the answer when I was there. I'm sad that Marc Chagall doesn't live anymore. I would have loved to play my song to him..." [32]

Kim: "Hands down one of my all-time KW favourite songs. I remember writing the lyrics as I recovered from a broken collarbone acquired at a rather hilarious party in Dorset! Inspired by the exquisite paintings of Chagall, whose work I have always loved, we tried to capture some of the magic of his art that still beguiles me today." [33]

An acoustic version of 'European Soul' was recorded on the CD-single of 'Perfect Girl' in 2006. The song was performed live during a German tour in 1992, the Hits Tour in 1994 and during live gigs in 2015 and 2016.

STONE
Written by Ricky, Kim & Marty Wilde
Produced by Ricky Wilde & Tony Swain

The song 'Stone' touched on the environmental theme, like 'Schoolgirl' before it. Shocked by the repeated violation of man against our planet, Kim became a keen supporter of Greenpeace and wrote songs like this to make people aware of what was going on in the world.

Kim: "This song was written with two big environmental disaster events in mind, but of course also with my more general growing unease as to the damage humans continue to inflict on our fragile planet in the name of 'progress'. The Chernobyl nuclear power plant in Ukraine exploded in April 1986. At the time it was the worst nuclear power plant accident in history, and it has left a huge area with a radius of 30km from the site of the explosion completely uninhabitable now and for thousands of years to come. Also in 1986, the River Rhine was poisoned by chemical firm Sandoz, contaminating the entire Rhine to the North Sea and reversing 10 years of work to clean up the river."

'Stone' appeared on the B-side of the single 'You Came'. It was incorporated in a remix of 'You Came' by American DJ service Razormaid, created by Joseph Watt.

Since its release, 'Stone' has remained an important track during Kim's live gigs. First performed during a German tour in 1992, it's re-appeared for most tours since.

LUCKY GUY
Written by Todd Rundgren
Produced by Ricky Wilde & Tony Swain

The album included one cover version. Kim wanted to pay tribute to one of her favourite songwriters, Todd Rundgren, and 'Lucky Guy', taken from his album *Hermit Of Mink Hollow* was the song she wanted to try and record.

Kim: "I've been a big fan of Todd Rundgren for some years now. He inspired me to write my own songs. I love the humour of his lyrics, his inventive melodies and, of course, his amazing voice. A genius in every sense of the word, a wizard." [34]

Kim: "Sometimes you wonder why destiny ever took you to a place, or to a person. I discovered this when I was introduced to the genius of Todd Rundgren by an old boyfriend. If the only reason I ever dated him was to discover Todd's remarkable talent, then destiny did her job extremely well! I had recently moved to London, and set up a writing room/studio in my spare bedroom, analysing his songs and recreating them in order to learn about the construction of songwriting. I am still a huge Todd Rundgren fan and recorded this as a tribute to his inspirational talent." [35]

Kim: "I think Tony and Rick both tried to talk me out of it, and I put my foot down, 'cause I wanted to have a Todd Rundgren song on the album. Mostly because I wanted to wake the world up to the glories of Todd Rundgren. I was on a one-woman mission to make everyone go, 'Who's he?', because too many people have never heard of him in the UK!" [36]

TELL ME WHERE YOU ARE (B-side)
Written by Ricky & Kim Wilde
Produced by Ricky Wilde

This track was released as the B-side of the single 'Hey Mister Heartache', except in France, where it was the B-side of 'You Came'. With its alluring rhythm and seductive melody, the song is a plea to a lover to open up his heart, *''Cause we seem so far apart'*. But: *'Honey, you're not in any danger / I'll never give up on what we've found'*.

WOTCHA GONNA DO (B-side)
Written by Ricky, Kim & Marty Wilde
Produced by Ricky Wilde

'Wotcha Gonna Do' could be seen as a sequel to 'Tell Me Where You Are', as the lover has gone and left a note behind, saying he needed to take some time to work out his life. *'Well, it's easy for you to just go off and do what you want / any time you please / Don't expect me to wait / If you leave it's too late / You're gonna have to crawl back on your knees'*, Kim sings, and it's a far cry from the soothing words in the other song.

'Wotcha Gonna Do' was released as the B-side of 'Never Trust a Stranger', and is the perfect addition to that song.

CHAPTER 9: CLOSE

BYE BYE LOVE (with Laurent Voulzy) (TV performance)
Written by Boudleaux and Felice Bryant

One of the first hits by the Everly Brothers, recorded in 1957, was performed by Laurent Voulzy and Kim Wilde for the French TV programme *Téléthon* on 3 December 1988. Kim sang the first verse in English, but they proceeded to sing the second in French, trading lines, a spontaneous performance, with Laurent on guitar, having the audience clapping along.

SPIRIT OF THE FOREST (Spirit Of The Forest)
Written by Kenny Young
Released: 5 June 1989
Chart position: 86 (UK)

English environmentalist band Gentlemen Without Weapons, who released the album *Transmissions* in 1988, wrote the song 'Spirit of the Forest' to support the Friends Of The Earth campaign charity's rainforest ball, a gala fundraiser held in London in November 1988. They pulled together over 50 international recording artists from around the world to record the song. After recording sessions in Los Angeles, New York, London, Rio de Janeiro and in the Brazilian forest with native Caraja Indians, the song was created entirely on the basis of natural sounds sampled into a Fairlight. A large proportion of sounds were of rainforest creatures facing extinction.

Two versions of the song appeared on the 7" single that was released on World Environment Day, 5 June 1989: with many artists singing one line of the verses. Kim Wilde appeared on the AA-side of the single, singing the second line of the song.

The project was endorsed by the United Nations Environment Programme (UNEP), with all proceeds going directly to organisations dedicated to rainforest preservation.

CHAPTER 10:
LOVE MOVES

Released: 14 May 1990
Chart positions: 37 (UK), 126 (Australia), 18 (Finland), 19 (France), 24 (Germany), 35 (Netherlands), 10 (Norway), 10 (Sweden), 12 (Switzerland)

During the first months of 1990 a lot of time was spent finishing a new Kim Wilde album.

Kim: "As soon as you stop writing, you start recording and when you finish recording you start promoting. And that pretty much takes you right through to when you start writing again. Which is basically what happened last year with *Close*. Then I did the tour with Michael Jackson and had about three weeks off then started writing again. But that's the great thing about being in music, you don't ever really want to be away from it for very long." [1]

Recording ended on 3 April, a few weeks after the release of the lead single. In between recording, Kim did a two-day photo session with photographer John Rutter. Kim made a tape of her favourite songs to take to the photo session, dancing throughout, resulting in some wonderful animated photographs, very different from ones taken previously. The photographs were used for the entire album campaign, including all the single sleeves. It was a significant change from previous years. During the 1980s, Kim did many photo sessions for magazines all over Europe. The demand for 'exclusive' photographs had decreased, with many magazines relying on what the record companies supplied to them, so Kim was determined these would be the best shots ever taken of her.

Before the release of the album, Kim promoted it all over Europe during the second half of April, visiting a lot of countries in the space of a couple of weeks. Kim visited Italy for a performance at the Azzurro festival at the Palazzo del Cinema in Venice. She also visited Florence to shoot the video for 'Time', the second single from the new album.

On 14 May 1990, Kim's sixth studio album *Love Moves* was released. Produced entirely by Ricky Wilde, it contained 10 tracks, all of which were co-written by Kim: six with Ricky and four with Tony Swain. The album was dedicated to Roxanne, Marty, M3 and Scarlett: Kim's younger sister and brother, and Ricky's two children.

As the 1990s began, there was the usual reshuffling of musical tastes. House and dance music had taken over the charts and there were more than a few anonymous acts and DJs who had no interest in becoming a 'pop star'. Being a pop star had fallen out of favour in some quarters, and some of the stars of the 1980s had trouble continuing their success stories into the new decade. And because the new music was grabbing so much attention, reviewers lazily called *Love Moves* 'predictable'. Dutch magazine *Hitkrant*, however, described it as 'a pop album that's pleasant to listen to'. [2]

MCA supported the release with large cardboard store displays and foldable cubes of the album sleeve, as well as a poster campaign and magazine ads. The album eventually went gold in France and Switzerland.

On 21 June, Kim was one of the artists performing live on a stage in front of the Eiffel Tower in Paris as part of the annual Fête de la Musique. She appeared in a tight black, glittering mini-dress, singing 'Can't Get Enough (Of Your Love)', supported by her band (Jeff Hammer, Simon Hill, Thomas Ribiero and Steve Byrd).

Kim also found time to participate in a programme about environmental concerns. In August, *Earth Dweller's Guide* broadcast an item about the plight of badgers threatened by hunters. Interviewing caretakers and a policeman, her appearance helped raise awareness of this problem. Incidentally, Kim modelled a knitted sweater with a badger on it in the book *Knitting Wildlife*, published by Pavilion Books and the WWF in 1989.

In August and September, Kim went on tour with David Bowie, the Sound and Vision tour, with Bowie delighting audiences with his greatest hits. Kim's band consisted of Steve Byrd on guitar, Jeff Hammer on keyboards, Simon Hill on drums, Pete Clarke on bass, Karlos Edwards on percussion and backing vocalists Jordan Bailey and Julie Moon.

Although the tour was shorter than that with Michael Jackson (21 dates compared to 36), Bowie was certainly more accessible.

Kim: "A couple of times he'd just pop his head in, wish me luck for the show. When I arrived, the first gig, there was a lovely bunch of flowers and a bottle of champagne. I know obviously his PA had done stuff like that, but it was nice. It didn't have to happen - and you know that he would have made sure it did. So, yeah, very down-to-earth, lovely bloke." [3]

Kim: "The last night of the tour I bought Bowie a present, it was a Marty Wilde T-shirt and album. He was in the middle of having his make-up done for his show, his eyes like insects, his bare chest pale and fragile. He held the t-shirt up to him and laughed as he said, 'It's Dad!'. Like most people around him, I was totally infatuated with Bowie, and was told he had fallen madly in love with a beautiful woman called Iman (whom he married soon after), I must confess on that tour I wish it had been me instead." [4]

Another highlight of the year was Kim's performance at the Diamond Awards in Antwerp, Belgium, the day before her birthday, with 18,000 people in the audience singing 'Happy Birthday' to her, and Kim performing 'Can't Get Enough

(Of Your Love)' and 'World In Perfect Harmony'. She was given a Diamond Award for 'Can't Get Enough'. After the show, she flew home in time for her birthday.

Kim: "I had to fly in and out of Antwerp in a small six-seater plane on the same day, as it was my party the next day. The band and I rehearsed songs on a small Casio keyboard so we wouldn't totally fall apart at the party, so we sang all the way there and back. The pilot said he'd never been serenaded so loudly before!" [5]

Kim was finally ready to move into her new home in Codicote. She celebrated her 30th birthday in her own new living room, with one of the highlights a live performance with her father.

Kim: "It was [part of the creative process] in the same way that moving out was eight years ago, moving back was as well and it was a very important step for me to find a home, because I was living in a flat in London that always felt like an extended hotel room. I'd never hang clothes up, they'd always be in suitcases and I felt constantly on the move. There was no stability and I was missing all my family growing up. There's lots of children in our family and I wanted to be part of their life, I didn't want to be a sort of transient pop star, Auntie who? I wanted them to know me as an individual, not someone they saw on the telly and in the newspapers." [6]

In December, Kim appeared on *Tonight with Jonathan Ross* to perform 'Santa Claus Is Coming To Town' and 'We Wish You A Merry Christmas' with the programme's house band.

At the turn of the year, Kim joined Vic Reeves on his *New Year's Eve Big Night Out* TV show. She participated in some comedy sketches and performed 'Oh! Mister Songwriter'. A few weeks later, the song was recorded by Reeves himself as the B-side for his debut single 'Born Free'.

Despite the tour and all the promotion for the album, *Love Moves* didn't emulate the commercial success *Close* achieved.

On 29 January 1991, Kim joined Midge Ure, Jools Holland and Nick Lowe for the first of three concerts at the Hackney Empire theatre in East London for Rock-a-Baby Week. The concerts were organised to raise funds for the Homerton Hospital's maternity and fertility units. She performed classic Motown songs 'Tracks Of My Tears', 'Wonderful World' and 'Dancing In The Street' before returning to close the show with Jools and his Big Band on a version of 'Shake, Rattle & Roll'.

CHAPTER 10: LOVE MOVES

IT'S HERE
Written by Ricky & Kim Wilde
Produced by Ricky Wilde
Released: 26 March 1990
Chart positions: 42 (UK), 32 (Belgium), 6 (Denmark), 4 (Finland), 21 (Germany), 27 (Italy), 44 (Japan), 6 (Norway), 12 (Poland), 13 (Sweden), 14 (Switzerland)

The opening track of *Love Moves* was a beautiful synth-laden track, created by Kim and Ricky with the aid of Steve Byrd on guitar. The lyrics are about trying to find something, whatever it is, and finally realising it's actually right in front of you. Hence, 'It's Here'.

Kim: 'It's Here' is really about rediscovering the good things that are very close to you that may have been overlooked. I see people rushing around, trying to find some truth, trying to find what is true in their life and finding out it's been right in front of them all the time. For me, that's how 'It's Here' developed as a song. It's about me and about how I see other people doing that too." [7]

Kim left London around this time to return home to Hertfordshire, where she grew up, and the song seems to reflect the reasons why.

The song was selected as the lead single for the album. MCA wanted to boost sales of the single by releasing a beautiful limited-edition boxset with the 7" single, featuring a poster and lyric sheet, with 7,500 copies of this edition produced. On the lyric sheet, Kim wrote a short introduction for her new offering.

Kim: "What is 'it'? Where is 'here'? Here is deep in my soul, it was there all the time – looking me in the eye. I hope I never lose it again..." [8]

The 12" single and CD-single featured an extended version of both sides of the single: 'It's Here' and 'Virtual World'. The music video was filmed partly in New Orleans by director Gregg Masuak, but the parts where Kim sang on camera were filmed in the UK, all edited down to one beautiful video.

Besides the music video, Kim also promoted the song in various TV programmes across Europe, most notably in Italy where she appeared at Festivalbar, a music event organised every summer between 1964 and 2007, and *Azzurro*, a TV programme that aired between 1982 and 1992. Austria, Germany, Denmark, Spain, Sweden and the Netherlands were also on the itinerary.

AF archive/Alamy stock photo

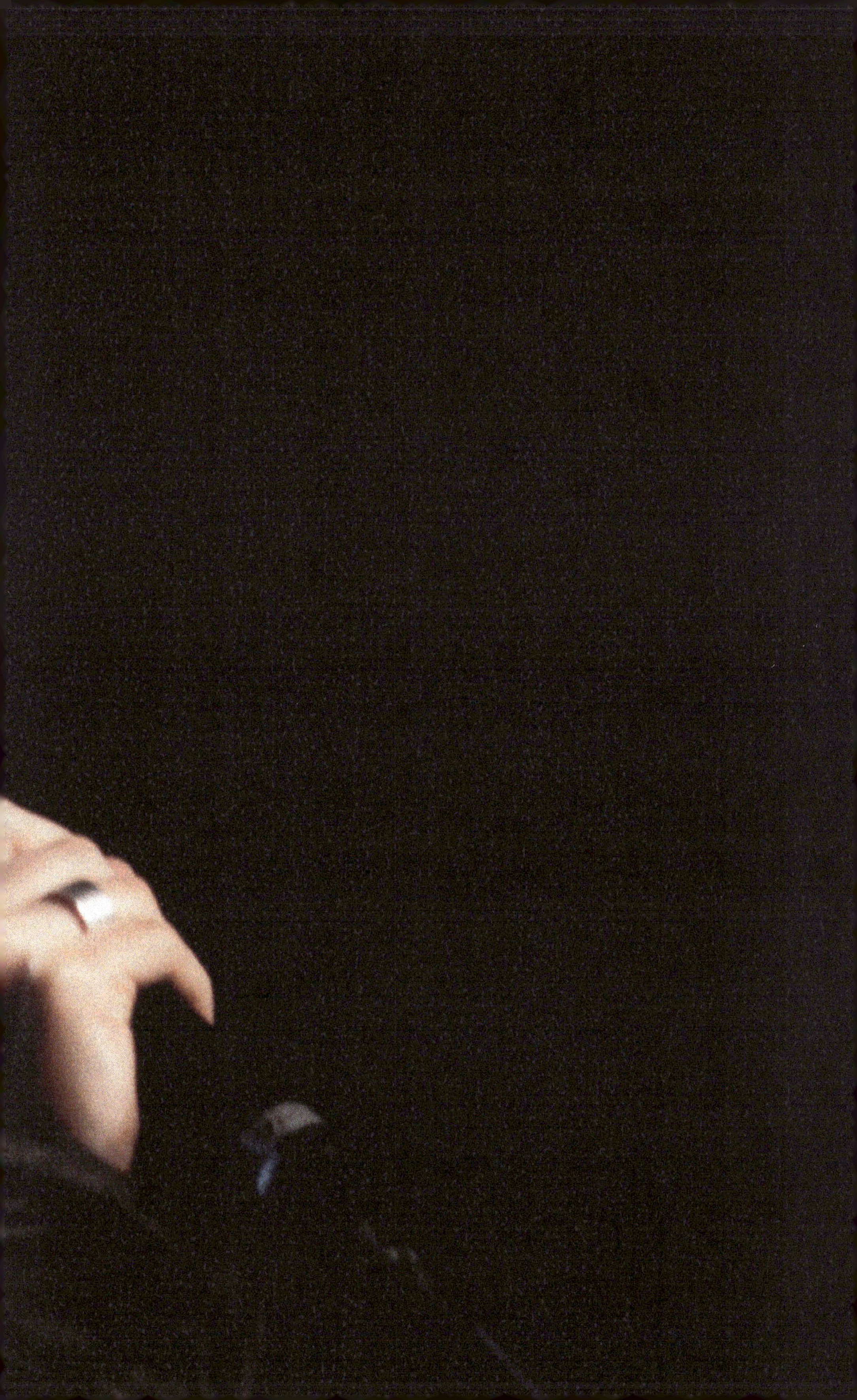

LOVE (SEND HIM BACK TO ME)
Written by Kim Wilde & Tony Swain
Produced by Ricky Wilde

Tony Swain and Ricky created a backing track using synthesizers and drum machines, and Kim provided the lyrics and melody on this danceable track.

Kim performed the track live during the tour with David Bowie, but not since then.

STORM IN OUR HEARTS
Written by Kim Wilde & Tony Swain
Produced by Ricky Wilde

The swooning 'Storm in Our Hearts' was one of Kim's favourite tracks on the album. It starts with the subtle sound of waves on the beach, underscoring the lyrics that mention storm, thunder, rain and crashing waves.

Kim and her band performed the track live at Camden Lock, London for a televised gig, broadcast in June 1990.

WORLD IN PERFECT HARMONY
Written by Ricky & Kim Wilde
Produced by Ricky Wilde
Released: 5 November 1990

The song 'World in Perfect Harmony' featured backing vocals by Jaki Graham and a guitar solo by Steve Byrd. It approaches the same theme as 'Who's to Blame', but from the optimistic side.

Kim: "It's a very idealistic song, and perhaps naive in so many ways, but I can't help but have positive feeling towards the future. When you're surrounded by children, I have an 11-year-old sister and nine-year-old brother, and plenty of us have children, you know you have to be positive about the future, you have to have an attitude that says, 'I'm going to make this work'. It's hard though, look around, there's not much to encourage you to be positive about sometimes. But there's a song on the album, 'Who's to Blame', which has probably a more realistic, much more melancholy, sad appraisal of the world's situation. I think that's why I put the two songs on the same album. I think it would have been wrong just to have one perspective on it, you know. It would have looked a bit naive, really." [9]

'World in Perfect Harmony' was released as a single in Europe. Steve Anderson created an extended version that was included on the 12" single and CD-single.

CHAPTER 10: LOVE MOVES

Although there was no music video, Kim supported the release by appearing on various TV programmes in Europe, including the Diamond Awards and *Lotterie Nationale* in Belgium, the *Holiday Show* and *Platen 10 Daagse* show in the Netherlands, and *Pero este que es?* and *Entre Amigos* in Spain.

SOMEDAY
Written by Ricky & Kim Wilde
Produced by Ricky Wilde

This delicate track was created almost entirely by Ricky on his synthesizers and keyboards. Kim's vocals shine throughout. It became one of the most touching tracks on the album. A slightly longer version ended up on the B-side of UK single 'Time' and the European release of 'Can't Get Enough (Of Your Love)'.
Kim: "When you are young, you create such perfect life situations: as you go along, disappointments start to happen. Life is never as perfect as in childhood dreams, since it is a sad song about growing up, facing reality. Me, I would say that I have my left foot in reality and my right foot in fantasies, and these are the two best places where they can be." [10]

'Someday' was performed live only once, during a concert in Paris on 20 February 2007 as part of the Perfect Girl tour.

TIME
Written by Ricky & Kim Wilde
Produced by Ricky Wilde
Released: 4 June 1990
Chart position: 71 (UK)

The second single from the album in the UK, 'Time' was an upbeat track in which Kim described the feeling of falling in love with someone after a long time just being friends. (*'It seems so long ago we were just friends / Different people with different faces / just getting on with our lives / Isn't it funny how fate is'*)

Although 'Time' wasn't released outside the UK, MCA still made an effort, releasing the single on 7", CD-single, cassette single and 12" single, and a limited edition 12" single with a poster sleeve with a shot from the sessions with John Rutter. The CD-single and 12" single featured an extended version of 'Time'.

The music video for 'Time' was filmed in Florence, with Gregg Masuak directing once again. The enchanting streets and squares accentuated her own beauty. In other scenes, a more sterile studio environment with a white background was used, with Kim and dancers.

Kim also performed the song on a handful of UK TV programmes, such as *Ghosttrain, Cannon & Ball's Casino*, the *Star Awards Gala* and, most notably, live at Camden Lock in London for a televised gig broadcast in June 1990.

WHO'S TO BLAME
Written by Kim Wilde & Tony Swain
Produced by Ricky Wilde

'Who's to Blame' returns to the theme of the environment, which is close to Kim's heart.
Kim: "'Who's to Blame?' [is] about environmental problems. Just like 'Stone': I'm really conscious of the fact that things are being destroyed before children have even had the chance to get to know them. It's very possible that by the time I have children of my own, elephants will have completely disappeared. That's the reason for writing that song." [11]

In the bridge, this song poses one of the most poignant questions: *'Don't you know that a day will come to everyone / When they'll ask us to explain / Are we going to say that we weren't to blame? / Who else could there be?'*.

CAN'T GET ENOUGH (OF YOUR LOVE)
Written by Kim & Ricky Wilde
Produced by Ricky Wilde
Released: 2 July 1990
Chart positions: 58 (Germany), 21 (France)

Described by *Q* magazine as 'stomping Eurobeat', 'Can't Get Enough (Of Your Love)' takes some cues from 'Never Trust A Stranger', featuring the same loud guitars and power vocals. A powerful guitar solo at the end of the track was delivered by Steve Byrd, making this one of the most memorable tracks on the album.
Kim: "My albums are always very varied, there are very real songs about real situations and there's songs like 'Can't Get Enough' which are just pure, positive energy, and give me a good excuse to strut my stuff around the stage!"

'Can't Get Enough' was released as the lead single in France instead of 'It's Here' and released as the album's second single in Europe and Australia. Although the 12" single and CD-single featured an extended version, a subsequent remix by Steve Anderson got the track from rock territory to the dancefloor. Three versions appeared on a promotional 12" single, and an edited version of this remix appeared on the B-side of 'World in Perfect Harmony', when that track was released as a single in Europe.

CHAPTER 10: LOVE MOVES

A remix for DJ service Hot Tracks by J.R. Clements was especially interesting for its inclusion of the melody of Abba's 'Lay Your Love On Me' in the mix.

The music video, directed by Pete Cornish, had Kim and her band on a spinning platform with burning candles and lovers on a bed in various shots. It was quite a dark video, and still regularly appears on various music channels.

Producer, arranger and composer Bernard Torelli recorded a synthesizer-based instrumental cover version of 'Can't Get Enough (Of Your Love)' on his 1990 album *Top Synthetiseur 2*, which included many more contemporary hits.

IN HOLLYWOOD
Written by Kim Wilde & Tony Swain
Produced by Ricky Wilde

'In Hollywood' starts with the sound of a radio being dialled, with snippets of news items about Mike Tyson and Robin Givens divorcing and the *'recent split between Donald Trump and his glamorous wife Ivana'*. It introduces a track that warns the listener against falling in love in Hollywood, because relationships do not last in the famed Los Angeles neighbourhood.

Kim: "'In Hollywood' was inspired by when I was in Japan and I was constantly watching CNN because I had a lot of time in my hotel room, you know, and there was all this stuff about Tyson and Givens, and they were in a battle around their divorce and their personal relationship, including a ridiculous scenario when Robin Givens' mother was interviewed, and I just thought - this can only happen in Hollywood, what a terrible place to have a relationship!" [12]

Backing vocals were provided by Jaki Graham. Also appearing on this track is percussionist David Cummings, who previously guested on albums by ABC, Black, Sam Brown, Clannad, Talk Talk, Paul Young, and George Michael.

I CAN'T SAY GOODBYE
Written by Kim & Ricky Wilde
Produced by Ricky Wilde
Released: 3 December 1990
Chart position: 51 (UK)

The soulful ballad 'I Can't Say Goodbye' ended the album 'Love Moves' in style. The song was originally an acoustic demo, recorded at Select Sound Studios by Kim and Ricky, but soon evolved into something more dramatic. Richard Niles, best known for his work with Grace Jones ('Slave to the Rhythm') and Pet Shop Boys ('Left to my Own Devices') arranged the strings and Jaki Graham provided backing vocals.

*Kim, Munich (Germany),
10 August 1990. dpa picture
alliance/Alamy stock photo*

CHAPTER 10: LOVE MOVES

Kim: "That woman's voice is something else, I'm such a huge fan. It was an honour to have her singing on it, especially as it was a song I wrote on my own called 'I Can't Say Goodbye' and then to be in the studio, I think it was Studio 3 at RAK Records, we had an orchestra doing a beautiful Richard Niles string arrangement and Jaki Graham singing backing vocals, it was an unforgettable moment for me".

Before the end of 1990, MCA released 'I Can't Say Goodbye' as the final single from the album. The track was remixed, with the 7" single and cassette single featuring an edit of that remix and the 12" single and CD-single containing the full-length version.

There was no music video for this single, but Kim did promote the song in a few television shows. She performed it on ITV's breakfast show *Good Morning Britain* and *Sunday Sunday* and the BBC's *Pebble Mill*. A limited edition of the 7" single featured a colour poster with a calendar for 1991 and a Christmas card.

The single entered the UK singles chart at No.55, rose to No.51 the next week, then fell to No.67.

VIRTUAL WORLD (B-side)
Written by Ricky & Kim Wilde
Produced by Ricky Wilde

When you hear the lyrics of this song (*'Images projected on a screen / Step into an artificial dream / Programme all the things you want to feel / Make a world where fantasies are real'*) it's fascinating to realise these words were written in 1989, when virtual reality was still in its infancy. A throbbing, pulsating soundtrack, provided by Ricky, makes this song an exciting ride into the future.

'Virtual World' appeared on the B-side of 7" single 'It's Here' and the Japanese CD-single. An extended version appeared on the 12" and CD single, adding extra instrumental parts to make the track even more exciting.

SANJAZZ MEGAMIX
Intro (Written by Ricky Wilde)
You Came (Written by Ricky & Kim Wilde)
You Keep Me Hangin' On (Written by Brian Holland, Lamont Dozier & Eddie Holland)
The Second Time (Written by Ricky & Marty Wilde)
Can't Get Enough (Of Your Love) (Written by Ricky & Kim Wilde)
Never Trust A Stranger (Written by Ricky & Kim Wilde)
Stone (Written by Ricky, Kim & Marty Wilde)

Officially presented as the 'double-A-side' of 'I Can't Say Goodbye', the Sanjazz Megamix of Kim's biggest hits and some favourites from the MCA era was created by Emilio Sanchez IV and Jimmy Jazz.

The full eight-and-a-half minute version appeared on the 12" and CD-single. It was also released on a promotional 12". A shorter five-minute version was released on the 7" single, this edit as yet unreleased digitally.

YOUR MISTAKE (with Johnny Hates Jazz)
Written by Phil Thornalley & Mike Nocito
Produced by Calvin Hayes & Mike Nocito

CLOSER (with Johnny Hates Jazz)
Written by Phil Thornalley & Chris Murrell
Produced by Calvin Hayes & Mike Nocito

Johnny Hates Jazz released their second album *Tall Stories* in 1991, three years after debut LP *Turn Back The Clock*. Lead singer Clark Datchler had left the band in the meantime, replaced by Phil Thornalley. The new album was produced by Mike Nocito and Calvin Hayes.

Having appeared on the title track of *Turn Back the Clock*, Kim made an appearance on two tracks of this second album, performing backing vocals on both.

When promotion for *Tall Stories* started, Thornalley had a bad car accident. As a result, the album did not have the desired success and the band disbanded the next year.

YOU DON'T KNOW ME (Charley)
Written by Kim Wilde & Tony Swain
Produced by Tony Swain

'You Don't Know Me' was recorded as an extra track on the 12" and CD-single 'The Best Thing' by Charley. Charley was the name of one of the characters played in popular BBC TV series *Byker Grove*, played by Michelle Charles. The single was a one-off project; Michelle did appear in other TV productions but didn't record music after this.

CHAPTER 10: LOVE MOVES

YOU HAVE TO LEARN TO LIVE ALONE (Live performance)
Written by Michel Berger, Luc Plamondon & Tim Rice

Having performed 'Première Rencontre', another Michel Berger composition in 1987 and 1988, Kim performed this song together with Berger in a French TV programme. She joined him for this duet after performing her single 'Can't Get Enough (Of Your Love)' on *Champs Elysées*, broadcast on 12 May 1990.

'You Have to Learn to Live Alone' was a translated version of the French song 'Les Uns Contre Les Autres'. It was written for Canadian-French cyberpunk rock opera *Starmania*. A studio recording of all the songs was released in 1978, before premiering as a stage musical in 1979. *Starmania* is considered one of the most famous rock operas in French history.

'You Have to Learn to Live Alone' was included in the musical *Tycoon*, which debuted on an album in 1992 and premiered in El Paso, Texas in 1996. Cyndi Lauper also recorded a version as a B-side for her 1992 single 'The World Is Stone'.

*Kim, Munich (Germany)
10 August 1990. dpa picture
alliance/Alamy stock photo*

CHAPTER 11:
LOVE IS

Released: 18 May 1992
Chart positions: 21 (UK), 95 (Australia), 22 (Austria), 7 (Denmark), 36 (France), 42 (Germany), 40 (Netherlands), 25 (Sweden), 7 (Switzerland)

After her 30th birthday, Kim finally moved into her house on the Hertfordshire countryside. After lengthy renovations it was finally ready to be lived in. Kim decorated the interior and set up a studio to work in. Crucially, the back garden with a pond remained untouched at first, because there was a lot of work to be done inside. There was still time.

Kim: "I did all the work and learned painting and decorating techniques. It was great. I lived in jeans and old clothes and it was wonderful. I even considered never making another record again and doing that instead." [1]

But not all was well. Having worked in the entertainment business almost non-stop for a decade, Kim started to realise her career had been very important, but it was blocking other important areas of her life. Living in a big house also meant it had to be filled with, for instance, a private life.

Kim: "I'd bought a 16th-century barn which I renovated and moved into on my 30th birthday. I had a great big party. My Dad got up and sang. I got up and sang. We had a great time, then when everyone left the next day I was all on my own – literally. I had a really tough time. I suppose I had a bit of a breakdown. It was pretty intense for me not having been down that dark tunnel before. I'd wake up and not be able to see any light at the end of it. I just remember being without motivation. I gave myself a hard time because I had everything I thought I wanted – to make music, be a pop star, travel the world – but had this gaping hole in my soul. I felt ungrateful because I had so much, and it wasn't enough." [2]

1991 was not an easy year for Kim. She had been feeling increasingly unhappy in her London apartment. It had become a substitute hotel room, where she just happened to be when she needed a change of clothes. But the move to Hertfordshire didn't solve everything at first. While her friends were all in relationships, she was still single, having just broken up with then-boyfriend Calvin Hayes.

Kim: "I found London a very lonely place. There was no feeling of community and I knew deep down I really didn't belong there." [3]

Kim: "I was doing everything in a half-baked way. I wasn't going to the gym,

I was eating and drinking too much, and I didn't feel good about my body. I think an element of allowing myself to gain weight was to put a barrier between the world and me. I wasn't trying to get attention anymore; I was trying to stop getting so much. I wanted to be anonymous. I'd been playing to 150,000 people at a time on the Michael Jackson tour and perhaps that pressure overwhelmed me more than I realised. Certainly, I was pretty naive to think I could take all that in my stride. I was much more fragile than I thought" [4]

Kim was suffering from depression. She dwelled on the fact that she was now 30 years old and was still alone with no one to share her life with. Perhaps 10 years of working hard for her music career had finally caught up with her: she felt tired all the time and couldn't think of any good reasons to get up in the morning. Knowing her father had suffered from a depression at some point in his life, she turned to him for advice.

Kim: "He was great really. I would go round to try and get a bit of pity from him, but he was really pragmatic. He'd say, 'Stop looking inward, look outward.' Gradually I began to understand." [5]

Kim: "When I was at an all-time low in my life, my Dad said: 'Kim, you've got to start pushing out on the world and stop letting it push in on you.' I heeded his advice and it worked." [6]

As 1991 drew to a close, Kim Wilde's fans didn't get a lot of news about their idol. Her appearance in a television programme to celebrate Amnesty International's 30th birthday was therefore a nice surprise. Together with Jason Donovan she sang a version of The Isley Brothers' 'Harvest for the World'. The video was pre-recorded since the two stars couldn't be in the studio where the party took place. Some hoped their recording would be released as a single, but this never happened.

Meanwhile, even Kim's fan club had fallen silent: the decision had been made to switch from quarterly magazines to just annual Christmas magazines, with newsletters to fill the long gap. But in 1991, no newsletters appeared, because there was simply no news to convey. So in December 1991 it was nice to get a little update in a new magazine.

Kim: "I started the year writing with Steve [Byrd], and both songs will be included on the album. These are, 'The Light of the Moon' and 'It's Too Late'. Then we met Rick Nowels (of Belinda Carlisle fame) and wrote 'A Miracle's Coming', an up-tempo rock track with a very catchy hook! Since then, Rick and I have written a ballad called 'I Won't Change the Way That I Feel'. Rick (my bro) has been writing some wonderful songs with myself and, for the first time, with Mick Silver (an old musician friend of his) – 'I Believe in You' and 'Touched by your Magic' among my favourites." [7]

CHAPTER 11: LOVE IS

Mick Silver was a new name for Kim's fans. Born in Nigeria on 6 August 1960, he was part of the band Kudos in the early 1980s. Together with David Mortimer, Marc Platt and Philip Fortescue Longden he recorded one album, *Kudos*, from which the singles 'No Reaction' and 'How Can This Be Love' were taken. When the band split, Silver released two solo singles, 'Everything You Need' (1985) and 'It's True' (1986). The two tracks he wrote with Ricky were his first productions since those releases.

Rick Nowels was indeed best known for work with Belinda Carlisle. Kim and Ricky met him for the first time in January 1991. They wrote 'A Miracle's Coming' within an hour of meeting. Nowels had to work on Belinda Carlisle's next album, *Live Your Life Be Free*, so Kim and Ricky worked on other songs. When Rick was free again later that year, he contacted Kim, asking how her album was coming along. They decided to work together some more, so he travelled to Select Sound Studios, where they wrote 'I Won't Change the Way That I Feel'. Then in January 1992 Kim flew to Los Angeles to record songs with Nowels and a live band. That's when she discovered 'Love is Holy'.

Kim: "I went to LA to do three tracks live with Rick Nowels, and when I got there he was very excited about the fact that I was there. He started playing me all these different songs, and one was 'Love is Holy' which he wrote with Ellen Shipley. He played it to me on guitar, and I just said to him, 'How long have you had that song?'. He said he'd had it a year. I said, 'You've had this song a year, do you think perhaps we should do it?', he said 'Oh yeah, definitely', so it was strange that the song had been around for a year, but I'm glad it had." [8]

The album *Love Is* was released on 18 May, four weeks after the release of lead single 'Love is Holy'. In various reviews, the focus was on the three Rick Nowels co-writes, drawing comparisons with Belinda Carlisle's material. The music on the album was certainly more organic, after the largely electronic sounds on *Love Moves*. With several guest musicians making an appearance, the 11 tracks sounded richer and fuller.

On the whole, the album was received rather well, although various music journalists seemed to be more interested in Kim's tour with Michael Jackson – now four years ago – and the state of her mental health, which she'd talked about in a few interviews. For some reason, Kim became more open-hearted about her private life as well, telling the story to various journalists. In retrospect Kim realised that interviews had become a sort of therapy for her, and sometimes said much more than she intended.

MCA supported the release of *Love Is* with a poster campaign, adverts in printed media and a promotional interview CD, from which radio stations could compile their own 'interview with Kim'. A collectable set of the CD and cassette was also released for promotional purposes, as well as a VHS video tape with an electronic press kit, subsequently broadcast on various TV channels across Europe.

On the sleeve of the album, Kim appeared in a floral dress that she would wear during several TV performances.

Kim: "I went out on to Melrose Avenue, and discovered this silky floral print dress, really subtle and it suddenly felt right." [9]

Positivity surrounded the promotion of the album. MCA's managing director Tony Powell remembered at the time:

Tony Powell: "When I arrived at MCA she was perceived as a hit singles pop star. Although she'd had the hits, her last album had only sold 30,000 units. I wanted her to be a serious artist. (…) *Love Is* sees Kim 'spreading her wings'. She needed to progress with the shifting music market, follow the path of Belinda Carlisle if you like. It's earnest, sophisticated, honest pop - what Kim has always been good at delivering." [10]

There was no shortage of TV performances this time. Kim performed 'Love is Holy' in an almost endless list of British and European programmes, including *Pebble Mill*, *Top of the Pops*, *Gloria* and *Wogan* in the UK, *Countdown* and *Fotofeestweek* in the Netherlands, *Tien Om Te Zien* in Belgium, *Zapper N'est Pas Jouer* and *Le Monde Est À Vous* in France, *Fernsehgarten* and *Gottschalk* in Germany, and *Ponte Las Pilas* and *Rockopop* in Spain.

In October, Kim went to Japan to promote *Love Is*. For a French television programme and magazine *Paris Match*, Kim Wilde went to Suzuka to meet Nigel Mansell, the British Formula One world champion, on 25 October. They spent some time together before the race. He gave her a tour around the compound, during which he insisted on Kim sitting in his car, which was quite unheard of. There are some beautiful photos of them together that day.

Another highlight was the *Frequenstar* special, broadcast on French channel M6 on 5 October 1992, in which Laurent Boyer interviewed Kim at her home. The hour-long special also showed Kim in the studio and short interviews with Ricky, Joyce and Nick Boyles. Another hour-long special happened the next month, when Patrick Willard interviewed her for the French music channel MCM.

In December Kim did a very short tour of four dates in Zurich, Switzerland (2 December), Oldenburg, Germany (4 and 5 December 1992) and Munich, Germany (7 December). The last of these, at the Nachtwerk Club, was filmed and televised on regional TV channel Bayerischer Rundfunk. The band consisted of Steve Byrd (guitar), Peter Clarke (bass), Simon Hill (drums), Steve Williams (percussion), Jordan Bailey (backing vocals) and Ricky Wilde (guitar, keyboards).

Work was progressing almost as normal, but Kim's state of mind had changed gradually. *Love Is* had performed better than *Love Moves*, but it didn't mean as much as it did before, and slowly but surely Kim felt herself disconnecting emotionally from her career.

LOVE IS HOLY
Written by Rick Nowels & Ellen Shipley
Produced by Rick Nowels
Released: 21 April 1992
Chart positions: 16 (UK), 29 (Australia), 28 (Austria), 23 (Belgium), 40 (France), 42 (Germany), 26 (Ireland), 18 (Netherlands), 39 (Sweden), 13 (Switzerland)

Kim discovered the song 'Love is Holy' when she visited Rick Nowels in January 1992.
Rick Nowels: "We were at the point of finishing the album and I was looking for another single for Kim. Ellen Shipley and I had an unfinished song called 'Love is Holy' and played it for Kim. She loved it straight away and said she thought it was a smash. We finished the lyrics and went in the studio the next day and cut it. The record is entirely live, with most of Kim's live vocal and just a few guitar overdubs." [11]

The track was released as the lead single from the album on 21 April 1992; Kim's first single release since December 1990. There were a wide variety of formats, all with their own sleeve art: a 7" single, 12" single, cassette single and CD-single were issued in the UK, with a so-called 'Ambient mix' on the 12" and CD-single. The cassette single format was short-lived in the Netherlands, so the one for 'Love is Holy' remains the only Dutch cassette-single by Kim Wilde. The photograph used on the UK 7" single was used for all other formats in Europe.
In Japan, a promotional 3" CD-single was issued, featuring 'Love is Holy' and 'Million Miles Away' by Kim and two tracks by Glenn Frey: 'I've Got Mine' and 'Strange Weather'.

The music video was shot with director Zanna, who presented Kim in the most stylish way possible. She wore a £4,000 dress designed by Jill Sanders, with video projections all around her. It was a stunning video that was picked up by various TV channels.
Kim: "I thought the 'Love is Holy' video was beautiful. Oh my God, that dress! The images, oh, I just love that video. It's interesting actually; the first time I saw it I loved it. Historically I'd looked at videos and been very critical, but I thought 'Love is Holy' was sublime. [12]

WHO DO YOU THINK YOU ARE?
Written by Ricky & Kim Wilde
Produced by Ricky Wilde
Released: 13 July 1992
Chart positions: 49 (UK), 58 (Germany)

The lyrics of 'Who Do You Think You Are' speak about fame and what it does to people's personalities. It was drawn from Kim's experiences and how people around her behaved sometimes.

Kim: "That was one of the early songs my brother and I came up with, and our confidence was quite low at the start of this album. We were throwing loads of ideas away and this was one that was just about to get put in the bin. I had this inspired idea for the lyric just at the last moment really and things just came together very quickly. I wrote the lyrics in a few hours and we recorded it very quickly. It's quite an angry little song, kind of encapsulates how I feel a lot about fame and how people handle it or don't. And it's not all together about one person or even a lot of people, or it doesn't even not include myself, so it's a sort of disenchanted view of fame." [13]

Kim: "'Who Do You Think You Are' is about fame and about how some people who are famous can become complete monsters and start believing fame makes them more special than they really are. So it's a quite cynical song. (...) The song is in part inspired by my own experience of fame, so I'm not just pointing fingers at others."

The track was released as a single in Europe at first, followed by the UK a few months later. An extended remix was provided by Ricky. The track was also remixed by Bruce Forest, released in a total of four different edits. The American DJ/producer previously supplied remixes for artists as diverse as Belouis Some, Donna Summer, Madonna and Orchestral Manoeuvres in the Dark.

The music video was directed by Gregg Masuak and featured Kim in various outfits, showing various aspects of being a diva.

Kim only performed the song live in December 1992, during a German tour.

I BELIEVE IN YOU
Written by Ricky Wilde & Mick Silver
Produced by Ricky Wilde

If 'Who Do You Think You Are' is a disenchanted view of fame, 'I Believe in You' could be perceived as a disenchanted view of love. Kim literally sings '*Some people believe in love / I'd rather believe in something real*'. But mostly, 'I Believe in You' describes an unfaltering faith in someone, saying '*I can't tell you I'm in love / But I can't stand to lose you*'.

Ricky Wilde and Mick Silver wrote this song, which was recorded at Select Sound Studio with contributions by guitarist Steve Byrd and drummer Geoff Dugmore.

TOUCHED BY YOUR MAGIC
Written by Ricky Wilde & Mick Silver
Produced by Ricky Wilde

Another collaboration by Ricky with Mick Silver, 'Touched by Your Magic' features backing vocals by Junior Giscombe, his most recent appearance on a Kim Wilde track. In a straightforward love song, Kim declares, '*I know that to lose your love would be more than I could bear / I would follow you anywhere*'.

Ricky created an extended version, which was included on the CD-single of 'Heart Over Mind'.

I WON'T CHANGE THE WAY THAT I FEEL
Written by Kim Wilde & Rick Nowels
Produced by Rick Nowels

Elton John fans will certainly like this track, because Davey Johnstone plays mandolin and sitar, and Paul Buckmaster arranged the string instruments. Both accompanied Elton for years. Guitarist Rusty Anderson, whose credentials include working with The Bangles, Neil Diamond and Paul McCartney, and keyboard wizard Charles Judge also made an appearance.

The song sounds like a statement of intent: Kim and the backing vocalists repeat the title 15 times within four minutes, while in the verses, undying love is promised.

Besides an impressive line-up of musicians, the song also benefits from a backing vocal group consisting of Ellen Shipley, Valerie Mayo Pinkston and Frances Ruffelle. Valerie previously worked with artists like Belinda Carlisle, Vanessa Williams, Jody Watley and Randy Crawford, while Frances Ruffelle had appeared in the musical *Les Miserables* and worked with Christopher Cross and Ian Dury. She would also go on to represent the UK at the 1994 Eurovision Song Contest.

MILLION MILES AWAY
Written by Ricky & Kim Wilde
Produced by Ricky Wilde
Released: 16 November 1992

Melodic pop songs had become Kim's trademark and 'Million Miles Away' is one of the best examples. It is hard to resist this melancholy tune, with its catchy rhythm and glorious keyboards. It was one of the songs that got this album started.

'Million Miles Away' was released as a single in Europe, Japan and Australia only. For this release, Ricky created a single version (slightly longer than the album version!) and a club mix – the latter together with James Richards. It was to be the last Kim Wilde single pressed on a European 7" vinyl, the format becoming obsolete. A cassette-single was released in France only, and a 12" single was made in the Netherlands. The CD-single format had taken over: versions from Austria, France, Japan and Australia exist.

The music video was directed by Zowie Broach, filmed at an airport hangar where Kim says goodbye to an unnamed handsome young man. For the first time in her career, the video was filmed entirely in black and white.

The track was covered by Estonian band Jam in their own language, entitled 'Kui Mõistad Mind' ('If You Understand Me').

THE LIGHT OF THE MOON (BELONGS TO ME)
Written by Steve Byrd, Ricky & Kim Wilde
Produced by Ricky Wilde

'The Light of the Moon (Belongs to Me)' included the first recording of Kim's younger sister Roxanne singing. She provided backing vocals at just 12 years old.

"Roxanne sings backing vocals on my new song 'The Light of the Moon (Belongs to Me)'. She acts like she isn't interested, like I did when I was her age. I didn't want people to notice how badly I wanted to become a singer. She does too, but she is such a natural. I can't imagine she hasn't got ambitions. She's a lot like me, and keeps her cards close to her chest!" [14]

This track was the B-side of the single 'Million Miles Away'. Kim performed the song live only once, during a performance at the Polish Sopot Festival in August 1992.

CHAPTER 11: LOVE IS

HEART OVER MIND
Written by David Munday, Sandy Stewart, John Hall & Nick Whitecross
Produced by Ricky Wilde
Released: 8 June 1992
Chart position: 34 (UK)

Although three songs on the album were co-written by Rick Nowels and the sound of those songs sounded a bit like Belinda Carlisle's, this song did as well – but Nowels himself was not involved in composing, although it was one of the songs he sent over to Kim. David Munday had written songs for Carlisle in the past, and often worked with Sandy Stewart in their group Blue Yonder. John Hall and Nick Whitecross, who were both in the band Kissing the Pink, were also involved, this beautiful, layered song coming to life with the aid of Ricky Wilde and Pete Schwier.

Kim: "'Heart Over Mind' was a song that was sent just as we thought we'd finished the album, hence 11 tracks. My brother and I were very happy the way the album was sounding, and then Rick Nowels sent over some songs and it was amongst those. It was written by Sandy Stewart, who I'd met in Los Angeles, and David Munday, who luckily for us was living in Hampstead in London. So he came and recreated what he had done on the demo, which was amazing - he's an incredible piano player, well just musician really, a very talented guy." [15]

Released as the second single from *Love Is* in the UK, 'Heart Over Mind' was not released on a 12" single the first time, but there were two different CD-singles – something many record companies were doing at the time. By releasing 'part one' on release day and 'part two' a week later, the aim was to push sales for a better chart placing. Part one featured extended remixes of 'Heart Over Mind' and 'Touched by your Magic', whereas part two – a beautiful picture disc CD - featured two old hits: 'You Keep Me Hangin' On' and 'Love is Holy'. The 7" single and cassette single both featured a new B-side – 'I've Found a Reason' – and the album version of 'Heart Over Mind'.

A club mix was created by Ricky with Stephen Streater, and appeared on the next CD-single release in the UK, 'Who Do You Think You Are'.

The track was covered by Anita Madigan in 1994.

A MIRACLE'S COMING
Written by Rick Nowels, Ricky & Kim Wilde
Produced by Rick Nowels

Written and recorded with Rick Nowels in Los Angeles, this dynamic track is the last up-tempo track on the album.

Kim: "Well, my brother, Rick and I sat down just prior to recording the album and decided we wanted to experiment writing with some other writers, which we haven't really done an awful lot before, and it actually coincided with an approach from Rick Nowels via MCA, whether we'd be interested in working with him. (…) He came and had a meeting with us and like within 14 minutes of actually meeting him in this room we started writing a song, 'A Miracle's Coming', which I ended up recording in Los Angeles." [16]

American studio drummer Curt Bisquera, who also did his thing on 'Love is Holy', makes his second appearance here. Backing vocals are provided by Ellen Shipley, Valerie Mayo Pinkston, Frances Ruffelle, and Kim herself.

TRY AGAIN
Written by Ricky & Kim Wilde
Produced by Ricky Wilde

The beautiful ballad 'Try Again' explores the feelings of a disrespected lover. *'You're the one who let me down / And now I find it hard to forgive / In my heart / But I'll try again',* Kim sings. Mick Karn makes an appearance, playing bass.

Ricky created a club mix of 'Try Again' which was included in the second UK CD-single of 'Who Do You Think You Are' and the European CD-single of 'Million Miles Away'.

TOO LATE
Written by Kim Wilde & Steve Byrd
Produced by Ricky Wilde

Ending the album on a quiet note, 'Too Late' is a slow song that reflects on the painful aspects of love. *'Hard to understand the reasons / Why love comes and goes'* (…) *'I know it's gonna be another lonely day / I can't find a reason I should stay'.*
Kim: "'Too Late' is a song that talks about life and love but also touches on my mental health problems. *'Hard to get a view of things through a broken window'.*"

BIRTHDAY SONG (B-side)
Written by Kim & Ricky Wilde
Produced by Ricky Wilde

Released on the B-side of 'Love is Holy', 'Birthday Song' was written after the birth of Ricky's daughter Scarlett on 9 March 1989. The multi-tracked backing vocals,

performed by Kim, mention her name several times in the chorus. Other than that, the song could be appropriate for any newborn child: '*The world looks bright today but one day you'll want to cry / And when your sky looks grey / there's one thing I hope you'll know / There's a place you can go*'.
Kim: "I wrote it for my little niece Scarlett, who is now nearly 18 and I think probably about to join us on stage quite soon. It's a song about finding strength within yourself when life gets really tough, and it's a strength we all have, but sometimes we forget it. It was a message to her as a child, to let her know that as she grew up, she could always rely on the voice inside her, to help get her through the tough times." [17]

Kim and her band performed 'Birthday Song' live during the Perfect Girl tour in February and March 2007.

I'VE FOUND A REASON (B-side)
Written by Ricky & Kim Wilde
Produced by Ricky Wilde

This song is bound to have a personal significance, with the lines '*Somewhere down the road I left a part of me behind / The girl you want to know left years ago / Before she lost her mind*'.

This track was released on the B-side of 'Heart Over Mind' in the UK, on the B-side of 'Who Do You Think You Are' in Europe and Australia, and as an extra track on the Japanese CD-single of 'Million Miles Away'.

BELLE-ILE-EN-MER MARIE-GALANTE (TV performance)
Written by Alain Souchon & Laurent Voulzy

Originally the B-side for Laurent Voulzy's 1985 single 'Les Nuits Sans Kim Wilde', this song became a hit when the record company swapped sides the next year.

The song takes its title from the islands of Marie-Galante in Guadeloupe and Belle-Île-en-Mer, an island off the coast of Brittany in North West France. By describing the island where Voulzy was born and the island where he was raised, the lyrics also subtly refer to being discriminated against because of the colour of one's skin, and being set apart – just like an island is separated from the mainland by water.
Laurent Voulzy: "The genius of Alain, I weigh my words, was to build a song about my life from these two islands which are my two attachments. I was made there and raised here. In the second line, he also talks about loneliness, isolation, my colour difference. There are two readings." [18]

On French TV programme *Sacrée Soirée* on 3 June 1992, Kim joined Laurent for an acoustic rendition of this song after she'd performed her own single, 'Love is Holy'.

INTERVIEW: GREGG MASUAK

Do you remember the first time you met Kim Wilde?
I didn't recognise her when she came into the office at the record company in our first meeting for 'You Keep Me Hangin' On' - I was looking over her shoulder thinking Kim Wilde was about to arrive, and that she must have been Kim's gorgeous assistant. Seriously! And realising how much more beautiful she was in real life than in the videos I'd seen before, every video to me was a mission to dismantle the old look she was known for and pull more of that beauty out of her.

What do you remember about shooting the music video for 'Another Step (Closer to You)'?
As far as I remember it was somewhere in the West End, I think a small studio in Mayfair. I kind of remember the general area but that's pretty much all I recall. I wanted to do a kind of Kim as Brigitte Bardot vibe, and you know Kim loves Paris, so that was fun and Junior (Giscombe) was just the sweetest guy. Whenever I would meet him for years and years afterwards, Kim's manager would say this was his favourite video of everything she'd done. It was the second video I did for her and I really wanted to capture how she looks in real life, so it wasn't like I was wanting her to look like Bardot, I wanted the natural Bardot part of Kim to be seen.

I guess you are aware that the music video for 'Say You Really Want Me' was deemed a 'saucy' video at the time. Did you set out to make it that, or was it just something that happened?
I believe it was 1986, I was still living in this warehouse space in Clapham Junction around the corner from where we shot - some photographer's home and studio right on Clapham Common. I guess it was intended to be 'steamy', but in a fun kind of way - I mean there's a shot of Kim laughing as she lies fully dressed on top of about four half-naked men in a floating kid's pool. Saucy, but with tongue firmly in cheek. Kim is game for a laugh and we had a ball filming it all. I did make a longer version of the video for the club mix and that was intentionally made to look steamier, which was also fun because we really didn't film it with that intention, so I used a lot of takes where the guys had to shake their chests and faces to make the fake sweat drip down, which ended up making them look like they were, uh, well, wanking. Haha!

Actually, as a result I was one of a trio of people pulled on to BETV in Washington, for a live call-in show talking about sex in music videos and censorship. There was me, another guy whose role I can't remember, and the head of the censorship board of America. It was clear that as a result of Kim's video I was being set up as the evil video director steering kids' morals in the wrong direction. The host was pretending to be nice on air but awful when the breaks came. About the third break she fired a question, I said, 'How interesting it is to watch a grown woman lie to her audience and pretend to be nice, while the minute the break comes, such hideous behaviour'. She was not expecting this live on air! In fact, the head of the censorship board took my side, defending the video (which after all is fun and a hell of a lot less negatively influential than a lot of violent videos shown at the time) and backed me up. When people calling in also supported me, she called the end of the show, wound things up quickly and I never saw her again. But it was a very satisfying moment … and all because of Kim Wilde taking a walk on the fun side of 'wild'.

How did the music video for 'You Came' come about? It was obviously shot during the Bad tour with Michael Jackson. Were you there during part of the tour?

I was there. My bestie Michael Reitz did Kim's hair for quite a while. He was living over here, flew to Switzerland and we did the filming over a short part of a day before she went on stage. She was incredible, I was like a proud papa. And Sophia Loren and her son were an arms-length in front of us in the VIP box, so it was memorable on a whole load of fronts.

Fun fact - the short hairdo at the end of the video was a result of Kim saying she wanted Michael Reitz's hair in the video, she loved the way it looked so much, so he gave Kim his exact hairdo. I was all about moving Kim away from the 'helmet hair' management insisted was 'her look' - you'll see that in all the videos I did with her, from the very first one I did, 'You Keep Me Hangin' On', when I realised the only way to get past that helmet look was an almighty blast of wind! It was great because the world saw just how stunning she is.

Part of the music video for 'It's Here' was shot in New Orleans, and Kim was filmed back home in the UK. How did you get the 'outdoors look' in the shots with her?

We filmed a ton of stuff in New Orleans and on the Bayou, then projected the Bayou on a screen within a simple set that had the textures and feeling of being back there. I can't recall why she couldn't make it to New Orleans. I was bummed, as I knew she would love it there.

Do you recall any details about filming 'Who Do You Think You Are'?

I only saw this video again recently and had to remind myself it was mine! I wish I remember who did the outfits and hate to guess - I worked as much with the same team as possible throughout my career, changing them out depending on the artist and availability. But my stylists were generally film stylists that also knew fashion, so working with that kind of stylist makes it easy because they are used to multiple characters and quick changes - and Kim is no diva, she dives into things with enthusiasm, so we got through a ton of characters. This was also me getting her to reveal more and more of herself and her fun side and her loving a laugh - which is why it's great when you get to work time and time again with one artist - the trust factor and the getting to know who they really are inspires stuff like this video.

CHAPTER 12:
THE SINGLES COLLECTION 1981-1993

Released: 6 September 1993
Chart positions: 11 (UK), 6 (Australia), 26 (Austria), 29 (Belgium), 1 (Denmark), 4 (Finland), 21 (Germany), 36 (Hungary), 5 (Netherlands), 11 (Sweden), 18 (Switzerland)

After 12 years in the pop business, the idea of a compilation album made sense. MCA realised the potential, and so after the relative success of *Love Is*, they proposed the idea and plans were made.

In fact, plans for this compilation had been made in 1992, but it took some time for the album to materialise. Then EMI released *Love Blonde: The Best Of Kim Wilde* that spring – featuring all the hits Kim recorded while signed to RAK Records – so MCA decided to postpone their own version until the autumn.

Kim took advantage of the postponement by going on holiday to Thailand for the first time, with her friend Sarah. They went backpacking for a couple of weeks, staying in the cheapest places they could find. On the last night, they reached an expensive hotel in Bangkok and had their first bath in weeks.

Kim: "An old girlfriend said, 'I'm going to Thailand, why don't you come?', so I just thought, 'Why not?' I scraped my hair back for a few weeks, ditched my celebrity persona and became anonymous. I absolutely loved it, and Thailand is the country I've revisited most over the decades. We took a boat from Koh Samui to Ko Pha Ngan for a full moon party and fell into the sea while wearing our rucksacks. We walked along this tiny jungle track and, all of a sudden, the trees cleared and this gorgeous beach opened up, filled with beautiful young people, all dressed up to the nines and as high as kites." [1]

'If I Can't Have You' was released as the lead single from the forthcoming compilation album. A cover of the Bee Gees-penned track, originally performed by Yvonne Elliman on the soundtrack of *Saturday Night Fever* in 1977, it was proposed by Ricky's wife Mandy after a desperate search for a song to record – a song that should become a surefire hit.

Kim: "We wanted to set it up properly. I didn't want to throw away 13 years of success with a No.75 record. So we worked really hard writing material, but quite frankly, we weren't coming up with the kind of material we felt would get us back into the charts. So we decided to do a cover... take a slightly less dangerous route. (...) We also tried several other songs, ones that if I told you

what they were, you'd say, 'What a great idea', but they just didn't work. Some songs certainly do not suit my voice, or suit being covered at all actually." [2]

The Singles Collection 1981-1993 was finally released on 6 September 1993 in Europe and on 13 September in the UK. In October, the rest of the world followed. September was filled with promotional appearances, Kim appearing on TV in the UK, Germany, Finland, Belgium and France. She also did some signing sessions at selected HMV stores in the UK, the store creating posters to be given away for free with the LP.

Kim: "The criteria for this album were the most successful singles from 1980 to 1993. There are a lot more singles I would have preferred to be on the collection, but this is an album the charts dictated first and foremost." [3]

In September, Kim went to Australia to promote the album, but also to present the Australian Music Awards. One of the promotional obligations was as the guest of honour to more than 100 people at Prahran's Continental Café. Presenting the Australian Music Awards was a flirtatious experience for Kim and co-host, Alex Dimitriades.

Alex Dimitriades: "Growing up, I loved the Kim Wilde song 'Kids in America'. I had a crush on her and years later, when I started in the acting business, about 24 years ago now, I got to meet her. She was older than me and took a liking to me. We hung out and nothing serious happened, but it was my first experience of the media picking up on something and spinning bullshit that Kim and I were dating. It's funny in hindsight. She was cool." [4]

Channel 4 breakfast show *The Big Breakfast* had started on 28 September 1992 and became one of the hottest new entertainment shows around. Presenters Chris Evans and Gaby Roslin managed to reach viewing figures of two million within a year, making it the highest-rated UK breakfast television programmes. Bob Geldof – who co-owned Planet 24, the production company responsible for the programme – presented a short-lived political interview slot in the show, and his wife Paula Yates interviewed celebrities whilst lying on a bed. Meanwhile, puppet characters Zig and Zag appeared in a segment with Evans called 'The Crunch'. It was a loud, lively and varied TV show.

When Gaby Roslin went on holiday, the show had to find a replacement. On previous occasions they'd hired several well-known women with varying experiences in presenting (some without any experience), but in September 1993 they decided to ask Kim Wilde. She did a screen-test on 17 September and was subsequently offered the job to co-host with Chris Evans for five mornings from 8 November, rehearsing with Chris and the crew on the 4th and 5th, and very nearly pulling out.

Kim: "After I agreed to do it, I became petrified. A few days before the first show, I decided to pull out. I couldn't cope with presenting a live programme.

CHAPTER 12: THE SINGLES COLLECTION 1981-1993

Fortunately, my Mum talked me round and told me to get out there and have a go. From the moment I arrived on set the team - and especially Chris - were fantastic. He helped me through it all." [5]

That week, Kim got up at 3am, presenting two hours of live TV between 7am and 9am. And during the week, a romance blossomed between the presenters. It started when they were doing a sequence in a tent in one of the shows.

Chris Evans: "I didn't care - I just had to do it, after all what's life for if not for kissing Kim Wilde in a one-man tent seconds before welcoming the world to a new day live on television? After no more than what was initially a nibble really on that famous full top lip of hers, Kim kissed me back. I took this as a green light to go for it - what followed next was the most memorable, fantasy-filled, nigh-on miraculous five-second snog any red-blooded male could ever experience. As the countdown ended and the director gave us our cue, the zipped-up door of the tent now filling the screen remained fastened for just that little bit longer than it should have done. And now you know why." [6]

Chris Evans: "I was very fortunate to have experienced that relationship. Kim Wilde is a pretty formidable woman. It would be wrong of me to go into why it ended but I can say it wasn't for any of the reasons that have been suggested so far. It wasn't because of our careers or a third party. Perhaps Kim and I would have been all right if people had left us alone, but we never had the chance to get on with it. We were always in the spotlight. A lot of people seemed to think it was a publicity stunt, but that's just rubbish. I don't have time for playing games like that. Our separation wasn't at all acrimonious and we're still the best of friends." [7]

Kim: "He was very important to me. We've kept in touch, but it doesn't necessarily mean we'll be together. However, we're good friends now and that means more to me than anything. Several of the songs on my album *Now and Forever* are about our short but intense time together."

At the beginning of 1994, Kim went skiing again with a group of friends, as had become tradition, this time in Tirol, Austria. She also brought along younger siblings Marty and Roxanne.[8] There was some speculation that she flew off to mend her broken heart, but the trip was already planned, even before Kim joined *The Big Breakfast*. A few months later, looking back, Kim would admit she'd had some busy months and was doing her best to keep up.

Kim: "I've been in the studio. And we had to have a photo session and make a video. These were intense experiences, because there was so much pressure on them to be won-der-ful. And then, I just went full on into massive promotion in the UK, and it's been full on all over Europe ever since. It's a full on lifestyle, but one I've grown accustomed to." [9]

Kim live at Salle Eden Club, Charleroi (Belgium), 28 June 1994 © Katrien Vercaigne

Kim live at Muziekcentrum Vredenburg, Utrecht (Netherlands), 3 February 1994 © Katrien Vercaigne

The interior of the office at Select Sound Studios, Knebworth, October 1993 © Marcel Rijs

After the holiday, the Hits Tour started, Kim supported by a band consisting of Steve Byrd (guitar), Pete Clarke (bass), Steve Williams (percussion), Trevor Thornton (drums) and Aileen McLaughlin (backing vocals). Support act for a lot of dates was Asian superstar Mari Hamada, who'd just released first international release *Introducing... Mari Hamada*. The tour started on 31 January 1994 with a concert at La Cigale, Paris, and after dates in Berne (Switzerland), Utrecht (Netherlands), and Hamburg (Germany), they were off to Japan for three dates and Australia for nine dates. After one gig in Bangkok, there was a break of two months. Kim used the time to travel around Australia with her friend Mark Stracey. They visited Perth and the Leeuwin Estate in Western Australia, the Daintree rainforest near Cairns, and Magnetic Island, both Queensland.

Kim: "I waved goodbye to the band at the airport, then a mate and I headed off with our rucksacks. The feeling of freedom was immense. We stayed in hostels and no one recognised me because I wasn't wearing make-up. We drank wine at the Leeuwin Estate in Western Australia, hiked through tropical rainforest near Cairns, snorkelled on the Great Barrier Reef, went whitewater-rafting on the Tully River and spent endless nights gazing up at the stars on Magnetic Island, off Townsville." [10]

In May, the Hits Tour resumed with dates in Scandinavia, the Baltic states, 15 shows in Germany and a few more in other European countries. The tour ended in Tilburg on the night of a World Cup football match, Morocco losing to the Netherlands. Understandably, there was a winning mood in the audience and Kim gleefully wrapped herself in a Dutch flag during the encore. This loud and lively gig would be the last proper Kim Wilde concert for quite some time.

Reviews of the tour were favourable. Germany's *Leipziger Volkszeitung* wrote: "Her fun during her appearance, and the almost familial atmosphere at the stage is credible, is infectious." [11] Dutch magazine *Oor* remarked: "After more than 13 years in the business she still can't believe that all the applause from the sold-out Vredenburg is meant for her. All the more reason to love Kim." [12]

In 1971, Mitch Murray founded the Society of Distinguished Songwriters (SODS). He invited some of the best songwriters, like Bill Martin, Roger Cook, Geoff Stephens and Tony Macauley, to celebrate their own brilliance. Members could only join if they'd had hit songs and if 75 percent of those present at a meeting voted for them, and in time Marty and Ricky duly became members. Each year, the society elects a King, who has to organise each of the meetings. In 1994, Ricky was elected, and organised the climax of his rule on 3 December 1994 at the Regent Hotel, London. During the night, the speech of the Queen SOD – Ricky's wife Mandy – was a highlight, as she showed footage from 1973 when Ricky was a child star. And the evening included a performance by fellow member Roy Wood with his 12-piece band, including a six-strong brass section. Kim joined them on stage for renditions of 'Rescue Me' (a hit for Fontella Bass in 1965) and Wood's own Wizzard hit, 'I Wish It Could Be Christmas Every Day'.

Kim reprised her appearance on 16 December 1994 when Roy Wood played the Symphony Hall in Birmingham, performing the same two songs with the band.

IF I CAN'T HAVE YOU
Written by Barry, Maurice & Robin Gibb
Produced by Ricky Wilde
Released: 28 June 1993
Chart positions: 12 (UK), 2 (Australia), 29 (Austria), 6 (Belgium), 52 (France), 51 (Germany), 9 (Ireland), 16 (Italy), 23 (Netherlands), 30 (Sweden), 18 (Switzerland)

'If I Can't Have You' was originally recorded for the movie *Saturday Night Fever* by Yvonne Elliman, and also by the song's writers, the Bee Gees. Elliman's version was released as a single in January 1978 and reached No.1 in the US Billboard Hot 100 chart and No.4 in the UK.

When it was decided to release a 'greatest hits' album, Kim really wanted to support it with a guaranteed hit single and feeling that she and Ricky couldn't come up with one, they decided to go for a cover version.

Kim: "Why a cover? I will be honest, we wanted to release a greatest hits album for a long time, but didn't feel confident after the mediocre success of 'Love is Holy'. To launch the project we needed a big hit. And when we talked about it, maybe half a year ago, Rick (her brother) and I didn't feel we had come up with something strong enough. So ultimately we decided to do a cover, one of my all-time favourite songs." [13]

It was Ricky's wife Mandy who suggested they would do this song from the *Saturday Night Fever* soundtrack.

Kim: "We went through the *Guinness Book of Hit Singles* and our record collection. Ricky had the relics of our 70s assortment, which was quite sweet - lots of things by Cat Stevens. But we were getting absolutely nowhere. Then his wife walked in and suggested 'If I Can't Have You'. I'd always thought it was one of the classier songs on that soundtrack. So we tried it and it worked!" [14]

The original version was never released: for the single and album the track was remixed by Phil Kelsey, a well-known remixer from the DMC remix service. Kelsey also contributed the 'Kelsey Mix' (a longer version). Ricky created an extended version and dub mix, and there was also a remix by John Robinson, originally released in Japan only, that finally appeared on the CD-single of follow-up single 'In My Life' as a bonus track. The instrumental version of that remix became a highly sought-after rarity, since it was only released on a Japanese promotional 12" single.

The music video for 'If I Can't Have You' had Kim walking up and down an apartment, smashing things and even going topless for a few seconds – albeit discreetly filmed from behind. Smashing things looked spectacular, but it didn't necessarily impress Kim.

Kim: "I think the people around me enjoyed it more than me. There was a lot of latent aggression there. I'm not a very aggressive person, so for me it wasn't a natural form of expression." [15]

'If I Can't Have You' became a considerable hit for Kim, most notably in Australia, where it spent 20 weeks in the singles charts, peaking at No.2.

IN MY LIFE
Written by Ricky & Kim Wilde
Produced by Ricky Wilde
Released: 25 October 1993
Chart position: 54 (UK), 78 (Germany)

Included on *The Singles Collection 1981-1993* as a bonus track, its release as a single was not originally planned. It was created for the album, but when it was decided to record a cover version to give the album a proper promotional push, this track was still included in order to please the fans. Its positive message was loud and clear, although when finally released as a single, that didn't convince the record-buying public, proving that releasing 'If I Can't Have You' was a smart move.

Kim: "It's a celebratory song about being in love with life. I know life is hard sometimes for people and everyone has bad times, but there's always one day in everybody's life where everything is going completely right, and this song is about that day in everyone's life." [16]

The release of the single was supported by lots of remixes. West End – an alias of British remixer and producer Eddie Gordon - contributed the single remix, but also a 12" remix, a 12" radio edit and the so-called D'Oomy Dub. A promotional 12" single featured a mix called 'Wilde Groovy', also created by West End. Other remixes were made by Ricky: the Rikkstyle Mix, the Lifestyle Mix, the Get A Life Mix, and a Dub Mix.

The video for 'In My Life' was directed by Zanna. In contrast to 'Love is Holy', this was a very simple video, Kim performing the song dressed in a silver suit, standing before a white background and playing around with a guitar.

"It's a mad video. I've always wanted to be a guitar hero, so I play one in the clip, with the strap really low. It's really cool, like the way my Dad does it. Quite funny too as there isn't even any guitar on the track!" [17]

NEVER FELT SO ALIVE (B-side)
Written by Kim & Ricky Wilde
Produced by Ricky Wilde

This track starts with a bang and presents a little story by Kim about the end of a relationship from the perspective of an independent woman, who clearly doesn't rely on any man to make her happy – and certainly the man she left behind. *'I don't feel broken-hearted / Don't feel that I should / I'm on my own again / Hard to believe but I never felt so alive'* sings Kim, with her delivery heartfelt.

The term 'B-side' doesn't necessarily mean a lot to young music fans who never collected 7" vinyl singles, but 'Never Felt So Alive' can be described as the last official B-side, because 'If I Can't Have You' was the penultimate Kim Wilde single to be released in that format (and 'In My Life', the last, only featured two versions of the track).

KIDS IN AMERICA 1994
Written by Ricky & Marty Wilde
Produced by Ricky Wilde
Remixed by Cappella
Released: 2 May 1994

In September 1993, MCA Germany released a promotional compact disc, *Employees Of The Month*, featuring new releases. One was the original version of 'Kids in America' with a proposed catalogue number KIM 19. However, when October came around, MCA changed their mind, that number given to a different Kim Wilde single: 'In My Life', a bonus track on *The Singles Collection 1981-1993*.

The change of plans was probably caused by the idea to remix 'Kids in America', and commissioning those remixes – and selecting the right one for a single release – would take time. In an interview with Dutch magazine *Hitkrant*, published in September, Kim hinted at these plans.

Kim: "At the moment it's being remixed. And after the album is released it will be released as a single. One mix is already done, by the Rupino Brothers. Really great! Kim Wilde on acid. Absolutely fantastic! I love house and dance music. You could say Kim Wilde crossed with 2 Unlimited, and this week another is being made. It's done by the Development Corps, who I believe have something to do with the Cookie Crew. When it's done, we'll choose the best one, and release it." [18]

In the end, 'Kids in America 1994' was a version remixed by Cappella, an Italian dance act that enjoyed two top-10 hits in the UK in 1993: 'U Got 2 Know' and 'U Got 2 Let The Music'. Producer Gianfranco Bortolotti of Media Records led the group, with contributions of other producers, which was fronted by vocalist Anna Ross and rapper MC Fixx It (aka Ricardo Overman). Their remix of 'Kids in America' was very different from the original and it was hoped this version would attract a new audience.

Besides Cappella, two other Italian dance acts contributed remixes: DJ Professor made the 'X Club Dub' and the 'X Cut Cut', whereas Bruno Guerrini created a remix called 'Plus Staples', named after the Italiance dance collective he was part of.

Other remixes of 'Kids in America' included a reggae remix by Naked Eyes, released on a Swedish promotional cassette only. Remixes by the Rapino Brothers and Development Corporation remained unreleased. Utah Saints were also reported to have made a remix, but these didn't happen in the end because of other commitments.

In May 1994, MCA finally released CD-singles of 'Kids in America 1994' in Europe, Japan and Australia. A 12" single was pressed in the Netherlands and a cassette-single was made in Australia. The single flopped, because it didn't bear any resemblance to the more rock-oriented live shows Kim and her band undertook in Europe, Australia and Japan – where the single was released – and in the UK the single wasn't even released, even if a design for a 7" single was made (with catalogue number KIM 20) and a promotional 12" single had been released.

That 12" single was an interesting release: not only did it contain unreleased remixes, there were also two notable errors. Cappella's 'Extension Mix' was included twice on the record (the second instance labelled 'House Mix') and the 'X Club Dub' was too (the 'X Cut Cut', intended as the last track on this 12" single, remained unreleased).

A music video for the re-release of 'Kids in America' had already been made in the summer of 1993.

Kim: "I have just made a video for 'Kids', last week. It was bizarre. We didn't even have the remixed version yet, so we had to work with the original." [19]

A short version of the video, with a three-minute edit of the original version of 'Kids in America', entitled 'Kids in America 1993' was produced, but never released. When the Cappella remix was finished and approved, the video was re-edited and released. The video was directed by Michael Geoghegan and featured Kim performing the song, and a lot of pictures and video from throughout her career. It was a stunning piece of work with a lot to please the eager fans' eyes.

With the right promotion and a marketing push, this remixed version of 'Kids in America' could have been a hit across Europe. But despite the long preparations, it didn't chart in any territory.

CHAPTER 12: THE SINGLES COLLECTION 1981-1993

REAL WILD CHILD (Live performance)
Written by David Owens, John Greenan & Johnny O'Keefe

'Wild One' was a rock'n'roll song, written in Australia and recorded by Johnny O'Keefe in 1958. The release of the single on 5 July 1958 is considered to mark the birth of Australian rock'n'roll.
Iggy Pop recorded a cover version on his 1986 album *Blah-Blah-Blah*, entitled 'Real Wild Child (Wild One)'. Released as a single, it reached No.10 in the UK chart in January 1987; his biggest UK hit.

During the Hits tour, Kim decided to do a version of the track with her band as an encore. It was a perfect song to 'rock out' on.
Kim: "I've always loved Iggy Pop's version, which I have in my collection, so I decided it was about time I did one myself. It was a song the whole band looked forward to and developed into quite a production by the end of the tour. Rick invariably broke a string, had blood pouring from his fingers, and occasionally whacked me on the head as he wielded his guitar in true ROCK fashion! Meanwhile, I had come across some illuminating red plastic 'devil' horns while spending a weekend in Utrecht early last year. These soon became a member of the band and resided on Trevor's drum kit. 'Wilde One' seemed a good time to wear them, and I did look ridiculous! But hell, I was having fun!" [20]

Kim performed the song live during 1994's Hits tour, and various gigs between 2003 and 2007.

CHAPTER 13:

NOW & FOREVER

Released: 30 October 1995
Chart position: 37 (Switzerland)

After the Hits Tour, Kim took some time to recover. She was certainly quiet for a few months, but didn't entirely sit still. It was time to work on another new album, after all the looking back of the previous two years. When asked about possible new material near the end of the Hits Tour in Denmark, Kim replied:
Kim: "I'm writing the songs at the moment. I hope it will come around the New Year. It's going to be a hardcore dance record. The melodies will still be there, but it's going to be more hard-pumped than what I've been doing before. Right now, I love dance." [1]

A good half-year of silence followed. Even her fan club fell silent. The traditional Christmas magazine didn't appear until February 1995. By then, Kim was able to give an update on the process, such as writing in New York in October 1994.
Kim: "I started writing four months ago and we've just about got all the songs ready to record. The feel of the album will be more 'soul' inspired. (...) I was recently in New York writing with some very vibey guys who write for Dina Carroll, Pointer Sisters, Celine Dion and Degrees of Motion. I went with Steve Wolfe (our A&R guy at MCA) who is involved with getting the songs together for this project. We had breakfast in a typical New York diner across from the hotel and walked to work at the 'Dream Factory' every day. Each of the 10 days I was there I was writing with a different writer on a different song. It was very intense, and I wrote songs there that I'll be proud of forever!" [2]

Kim appeared in the very last edition of Chris Evans' TV show *Don't Forget Your Toothbrush*, broadcast on Channel 4 in the UK on 25 February 1995. The programme started a year earlier as Chris' first major venture away from *The Big Breakfast*. During the second series, it was announced that there would be no third series, in order to allow the show to go out on a high. The last show contained elements of previous instalments, but sometimes with a twist. The Superfan quiz was held with Kim Wilde but she was not pitted against a superfan, but Chris Evans himself. He still managed to win, though. Kim performed energetic live versions of 'You Keep Me Hangin' On' and a cover of Stevie Wonder's 'Signed Sealed Delivered I'm Yours' with a house band led by Jools Holland, and at the end she and Chris gave away a £36,000 Ferrari 308GTS with a year's insurance (worth £5,000) – the biggest prize ever won on British TV at that point. [3]

CHAPTER 13: NOW & FOREVER

In March, Kim went back on holiday to Thailand with a girlfriend. They travelled across Krabi, getting lost on an island, swimming in waterfalls and getting caught in a rainstorm on a fishing boat. [4] It was another amazing experience in a country that Kim was getting increasingly fond of.

Upon her return, Kim turned her attention on the garden behind Select Sound Studios. It had always been a dull patch of grass, and she decided to brighten it up a bit. The little project foreshadowed Kim's activities in years to come...

Kim: "The planning and design took a few weeks and we started work back in March, just as the recording for the album began. The hard landscaping was done by Ray, a long-time friend and builder, whilst I did all the planting. It is now growing beautifully and is a welcome break from a claustrophobic studio." [5]

With recording sessions starting in March, work progressed on the new album. In July Kim and Ricky were joined in the studio by CJ Mackintosh, a club DJ at the Ministry of Sound in London. Having done remixes for acts like Lisa Stansfield, Yazz and Janet Jackson, he moved into production. For Kim, he produced four tracks on the album.

Kim: "For the first time I worked with other writers and producers. There were different singers for the backing vocals, which I used to do myself. The most important difference is that I have listened more to the soul girl within me. I do love pop music, but somehow I've always had a love affair with soul, so I followed my intuition." [6]

Promotion for the lead single 'Breakin' Away' started in August, a month ahead of the single's release. Kim made an appearance on a handful of roadshows: one organised by Birmingham's BRMB, one by BBC Radio One in Blackpool and one at the Live '95 computer and electronics exhibition at Earls Court as part of Capital Radio's roadshow. On all of these occasions she performed 'Breakin' Away' and one or two old hits.

Now & Forever was released on 30 October 1995. Its 14 tracks had a decidedly soul and R&B feel to them, which was probably a shock to her fans. But it was the music Kim wanted to make after looking back on her career for more than a year.

Kim: "The first song I wrote after I got back from the tour, after a short break, was 'Life & Soul', which I wrote with Tony Swain. And that, to me, dictated the style for the rest of the album." [7]

Kim: "I think this album is a mixture of personal and commercial interests. I would love to have a hit again. That is important. A hit record does open doors, but I will always love what I do whether I have a hit or not." [8]

Reviews were mixed. For some reviewers, Kim Wilde as a soul artist was not a believable proposition. *Beat* in Norway, for instance, offered: "*Now & Forever* is not Wilde's best moment - all too often she lets herself out into 'modern' machine pop without any warmth or finesse." [9] But *Q* in the UK, on the other hand, was complimentary: "*Now & Forever* sees her going all soulish. Like Kylie Minogue, Wilde has taken on the trappings of swing-beat, soft soul and jazziness; unlike the Australian, she's done so with convincing songs, invested with enough charisma to make them hers." [10]

Kim supported the release of the album with several radio and TV appearances. In the UK, she appeared on the usual breakfast shows like *GMTV* and *This Morning*, whereas abroad she had to appear in whatever entertainment programme was available. The disappearance of popular music programmes like *Countdown* and *Musikladen* had made the promotion of music more difficult for pop artists, and Kim was no exception.

Besides promoting her own music, she also appeared on BBC show *Showstoppers* singing 'They Can't Take That Away From Me', a song written by George and Ira Gershwin in 1937. Backed by a 70-piece orchestra and wearing a beautiful dress, she did a stunning performance of this classic song.

On 18 November 1995 Kim celebrated her birthday by doing a 40-minute club appearance, singing amongst others 'Heaven', 'Breakin' Away', 'This I Swear' and 'Kids in America'. This was a celebration for the fans who were there as well as Kim herself, who was presented with birthday cakes on stage.

It is fair to say *Now & Forever* never really got a chance to take off. MCA did all they could to promote the album at first, with large posters on the Underground, radio advertising and various magazine ads, but the audiences weren't enthusiastic about a soulful Kim Wilde album.

Kim: "At the time I recorded *Now & Forever*, I was listening a lot to Zhané, SWV, Aaliyah and Mary J. Blige. Inspired by their unique and incredible sounds, I found myself making an album Kim Wilde fans weren't ready for!" [11]

Many artists at some point want to express themselves in a different way. When Duran Duran split in the mid-1980s, one half of the band started rock outfit Power Station and the other half went off to do an art-rock album as Arcadia. Paul Young started a band called Los Pacaminos to record and perform Tex-Mex and Americana music. The fact that Kim decided to do something completely different under her own name was a challenge for MCA's marketing department and puzzled her fans. With the benefit of hindsight, given a second chance, *Now & Forever* could be seen as one of her best albums, if one was to let go of certain preconceived ideas of what kind of music Kim Wilde 'should' be recording.

By the time the single 'This I Swear' was released in January 1996, the press were more interested in Kim's new adventure: appearing in West End musical *Tommy*. But still, Kim did her best to promote this single while rehearsing for her role. She performed the song in TV shows like *Talking Telephone Numbers* and *Pebble Mill*.

CHAPTER 13: NOW & FOREVER

On 1 February 1996 she appeared on stage at Meadowhall, Sheffield with five dancers to perform a handful of songs as part of the *Biggest Ever Shopping Mall Show*, as it was called. [12]

In February 1996, Kim received the so-called RSH Gold Award for being the 'Klassikerin des Jahres' ('Classic of the Year') in Germany, an honour bestowed to Cliff Richard, Paul Young and Robert Palmer before her.

For the first time ever, a fan meeting was organised in March 1996. Fans from various European countries flocked together in the Dutch city of Breda to sell and swap items, watch exclusive video material from throughout Kim's career, and take part in a special charity auction to benefit Ataxia UK – an organisation Kim went on to support. Organised by fans in cooperation with the official Fan Club, the auction's prize piece was the dress worn by Kim on the cover of the album *Love Is*: this piece alone raised £910. With Melanie Almond from the Fan Club and Kim's younger sister Roxanne attending, the fan meeting was a unique event – but it was also the only fan meeting that was ever organised. It did result in an early version of the next big thing: somewhere in a corner of the so-called World Wide Web, a webpage dedicated to Kim Wilde was set up. This would grow into the spiritual successor of the Official Kim Wilde Fan Club in subsequent years.

BREAKIN' AWAY
Written by Mike Percy, Tim Lever & Tracy Ackerman
Produced by Ricky Wilde & Serious Rope
Released: 25 September 1995
Chart positions: 43 (UK), 79 (Germany)

Lead single from the album and opening track, 'Breakin' Away' starts uncharacteristically with backing vocalists Georgia Lewis, Melanie Lewis, Sarah Nelson and Richard Wayler, before Kim sings the first verse. The lyrics are forward-looking and optimistic.

Kim: "I think it contains a really good message: it's about someone who disconnects from the past and their own limits. It is about me in a way, because with this album in a different style I disconnect from the past as well. On top of that, it's a really great song, full of energy." [13]

The single version – entitled 'radio mix' - was slightly different from the original version, but the original version was only ever released on a promotional compilation CD, released by MCA. Promotional 12" singles featured remixes by Matt Darey and T'empo, as well as an 'Original 12" Mix' by Ricky Wilde. The DJ subscription service ACE also provided a remix on one of their compilations. The music video, directed by Gregg Masuak and shot in Los Angeles, saw Kim show off her rollerblading skills, picked up after she got rollerblades as a

Christmas present from her brother Ricky and wife Mandy in December 1994.
Gregg Masuak: "We shot this on a disused air-strip in the desert outside LA, so all the gang were locals to LA, strangers to begin with, friends at the end! The light was so strong throughout the day, it was actually hard to get a shot of Kim without her squinting in the glare, but she's a trooper - her eyeballs are probably still singed to this very day."

Kim: "Sometimes I go to a big parking lot with friends, in the weekend when there are no cars. There are also bunches of children skating around there too, learning tricks and having fun. One time there was this boy who came skating alongside me. I asked him, 'How old are you?' and he said 'Five!'. He went: 'How old are you?' And I (grumpy), '35'. That was so sweet. He didn't know who I was. All he knew was I was this crazy old woman who goes out rollerblading on a parking lot!'" [14]

HIGH ON YOU
Written by Ricky & Kim Wilde
Produced by Ricky Wilde & Serious Rope

The optimistic 'High on You' is one of Kim's favourites from the album, especially because of the amazing backing vocals provided by Beverley Skeete and Sylvia Mason-James.

   Kim: "This song was written by Rick and I, and produced by Ricky and Aron Friedman. The background vocalists really surpass themselves, especially at the end of the song." [15]

   Kim performed a short acapella version of this song during an interview on German music channel Viva, proving – as if it were still needed – her voice didn't need any studio trickery to reach the high notes.

THIS I SWEAR
Written by Tony Swain & Pam Sheyne
Produced by Ricky Wilde & Serious Rope
Released: 29 January 1996
Chart positions: 46 (UK), 91 (Germany)

Tony Swain wrote 'This I Swear' together with Pam Sheyne, an accomplished songwriter who had written songs for Sonia, MN8 and Sheena Easton, and went on to co-write 'Genie In A Bottle' for Christina Aguilera.

Kim Wilde: "Tony Swain played this to me in his studio and I loved it immediately. It is a very intimate song. I love it for its honesty and its simple message of unconditional love." [16]

CHAPTER 13: NOW & FOREVER

Kim recorded a beautiful version with backing vocals by British soul singers Chris Ballin and Hazel Fernandes. Aron Friedman provided the string arrangement, performed by Rosie Wetters (cello), Frances Illman (viola) and Prabjote Osahn (violin).

Although 'This I Swear' would have been a perfect single release for the Christmas season and Kim promoted the song both in the UK and in Europe (appearing on several different TV and radio shows), the single only reached the shops on 29 January 1996.

Two promotional 12" singles, released a few weeks earlier, included exciting remixes of 'Heaven' by Matt Darey and Eddie Fingers, and received an enthusiastic response in clubs.

The music video was shot at the Chelsea Hotel in New York in November, with Daniela Federici directing.

Kim: "We shot it at the Chelsea Hotel, an infamous rock'n'roll hang-out (Sid and Nancy set the place alight and Nancy died there). An incredible atmosphere, if a little spooky." [17]

It was while Kim was in New York that she learned from Pete Townshend she had been given the part of Mrs Walker in the musical 'Tommy' in London's West End.

'This I Swear' was covered by the Danish boyband Fortyfive Degrees in 1997.

C'MON LOVE ME
Written by Kim Wilde & George McFarlane
Produced by Ricky Wilde & CJ Mackintosh

One of the more sensual tracks on the album, 'C'mon Love Me' includes some sighing and breathing that wouldn't be entirely out of place on a track like 'Je T'Aime... Moi Non Plus'. In fact, Kim admitted as much when she spoke about the album.

Kim: "Written by George McFarlane and I. I've written with George for three years now and this is the first time I've recorded one of our songs. It is a sensual song and needs no explanation! I'd love to do a version in French with LOTS of heavy breathing. Look out Serge Gainsbourg and Jane Birkin!" [18]

Backing vocals were provided by Lance Ellington and Miriam Stockley.

TRUE TO YOU
Written by Kim Wilde & David James
Produced by Ricky Wilde & CJ Mackintosh

Starting with a 'scratchy' intro, the first thing that leaps out is the funky rhythm of this track. The lyrics may be a bit on the syrupy side for some, with lines like '*Love and honesty is what you're gonna get from me / Every step of the way / You can trust me, when I say / I'll be true*', but Kim's delivery on this track sounds sincere and impressive.
Kim: "David James is someone I've written with for two years, and this is the first time I've recorded one of our collaborations. Luckily for me, like Tony Swain, he only lives down the road. Dave has written for Michelle Gayle and Take That amongst others. He's always very busy and loves the same kind of music I do." [19]

HYPNOTISE
Written by Kim & Ricky Wilde
Produced by Ricky Wilde

Although several backing vocalists were drafted in for various tracks on *Now & Forever*, Kim sings all the vocals on 'Hypnotise' herself. It is an intimate, melodic song, supported only by Ricky's keyboards and programming.
Kim: "In the future if someone was to ask me to name my favourite song I've written with Ricky, I think this would jump straight into my mind. Ricky has composed one of the most beautiful melodies on the album. The words are from the heart of someone who felt hypnotised by someone. What more can I say?" [20]

In 1996, 'Hypnotise' became the B-side of 'Shame', Kim's last single of the 1990's.

HEAVEN
Written by Kim & Ricky Wilde
Produced by Ricky Wilde & Serious Rope

The ecstatic song 'Heaven' was originally produced by Ricky and the Serious Rope team. With keyboards and a steady beat, this track was supported by four backing vocalists (Georgia and Melanie Lewis, Sarah Nelson and Richard Wayler) and soaring vocals by Kim.

The track was given a new lease of life by Matt Darey, who created a powerful remix also included as a 7" edit on the CD-single for 'This I Swear'. Promotional

CHAPTER 13: NOW & FOREVER

12" singles featuring remixes by Matt Darey and T'empo became big hits on the UK club circuit.

DJ subscription services Razormaid, Rampage, Ace and Ultimix also released re-edits of the remixes.

SWEET INSPIRATION
Written by Steve Welton-Jaimes, Juliette & Mark Jaimes
Produced by Ricky Wilde

Georgia and Melanie Lewis, Sarah Nelson and Richard Wayler start this song with an uplifting chorus. It's a high energy track with simple, direct lyrics: '*I never needed nobody / Until you came along / And this feeling's so strong / I should be working on something / But I ain't got the time / I've got you on my mind*.' You could imagine the chant '*We got the love / Yeah got the love*' going down well live, but like most songs on this album, 'Sweet Inspiration' was never performed live.

WHERE DO YOU GO FROM HERE?
Written by Peter Zizzo, Rich Tancred, Kim & Ricky Wilde
Produced by Ricky Wilde

This song was written in New York by Kim with Peter Zizzo, who had written hits for Celine Dion, Donna Summer, Diana Ross and Cliff Richard, and Rich Tancred, who wrote and arranged songs for Taylor Dayne, Kym Mazelle and Mariah Carey. Back at Select Sound Studios, Kim and Ricky added their own ingredients to an upbeat, rhythmic song, one of the most accessible tracks on the album.

Backing vocals wee provided by Clive Griffin, a British vocalist best known for his duet with Celine Dion on a version of 'When I Fall In Love' for the *Sleepless in Seattle* soundtrack (1993). He also enjoyed some success with his own solo albums, released between 1988 and 1993.

HOLD ON
Written by Kim Wilde & Tony Swain
Produced by Ricky Wilde & Serious Rope

Without a doubt, lyrically speaking, 'Hold On' is the saddest song on *Now & Forever*. '*In the day I can smile though I wanna die / I hold on, hold on / I can keep it together for a little while / and be strong, so strong / But when the sun goes down and I'm all alone / I haven't the strength to fight / That's when my tears give into the night*.' Anyone who has struggled with depression or a love gone wrong will recognise the lyrics in this chorus.

Kim: "Tony Swain and I wrote this song late into the evening at his studio. It is a very sad song, but as they say, better to have loved and lost..." [21]

British soul singers Chris Ballin and Hazel Fernandes made another appearance on this track, and Aron Friedman's string arrangement was again performed by Rosie Wetters (cello), Frances Illman (viola) and Prabjote Osahn (violin).

YOU'RE ALL I WANNA DO
Written by Arnie Roman & Peter Zizzo
Produced by Ricky Wilde & Serious Rope

Another song written in New York by Peter Zizzo, this time with Arnie Roman, an American songwriter who wrote songs for Shannon, Taylor Dayne, Cher, Sheena Easton and Celine Dion.

Kim: "Peter Zizzo, a co-writer of this song, played it to me in New York, and I was blown away. I love the innocence of the lyric and melody. A classic soul/pop record." [22]

The song certainly has a strong melody, underscored by backing vocalists Beverley Skeete and Sylvia Mason-James. Lyrically, this is a love song that describes the preference for an intimate relationship instead of fame and fortune. It's easy to see why Kim related to this song at this point in her life. *'I could rise in a jet-black Benz / Movie stars could all be my friends / But I'd trade it in for the touch of your hand'*.

LIFE & SOUL
Written by Kim Wilde & Tony Swain
Produced by Ricky Wilde & CJ Mackintosh

'Life & Soul' was the song that got the album started. Kim wrote it with Tony Swain. The idea came during the Hits tour, in the first half of 1994.

Kim: "I was on tour, talking to the coach driver one morning whilst everyone else was asleep. I couldn't sleep and was feeling a bit down, sitting at the front of the bus driving past beautiful mountains, talking to the driver about life and everything. And we got talking about Ricky. 'You know it's so fantastic being on the road with my brother; I just love him so much. We don't see each other enough when I'm at home, just him and me'. I said, 'It's just so great being with him', and the driver said to me, 'Yeah, he really is the life and soul of this, isn't he?', and I said: 'Graham, I'm going to write a song and I'm calling it 'Life & Soul'. It really struck a chord with me. Life is an incredible gift, and Soul is just the essence of Life." [23]

The song actually turned into a love song, with lines like '*Pride is a wall that we can climb / Baby hold on together we'll find / Life and Soul*'. Ricky produced the track together with CJ Mackintosh, turning it into a funky track that fitted the style of the album very well.

NOW & FOREVER
Written by Kim & Ricky Wilde
Produced by Ricky Wilde & CJ Mackintosh

The title track of the album is a sad song, with lyrics like '*Time will never mend / This broken heart / Now and forever / I will always love you*'.
Kim: "'Now & Forever', a song influenced by soul and R&B, one of the songs on the album I'm most proud of. It is a good example of the new direction I have taken. On top of that I like the expression of eternity: things that will live on forever and that express magical energy, like music and love. [24]

BACK TO HEAVEN
Written by Kim & Ricky Wilde
Produced by Ricky Wilde & Serious Rope

'Back to Heaven' is a reprise of the track 'Heaven', the shortest track on the album at just 100 seconds. Kim sings the first verse and chorus, and the backing vocalists (Georgia and Melanie Lewis, Sarah Nelson and Richard Wayler) feature more prominently in this mix.
Kim: "I just adore Ricky's 'Back to Heaven' reprise featuring the excellent backing vocalists, literally sounding like angels from heaven!" [25]

STAYING WITH MY BABY (B-side)
Written by Ricky Wilde
Produced by Ricky Wilde

'Staying with My Baby' was released as an extra track on the CD-single of 'Breakin' Away'. Musically the track wouldn't be out of place on *Now & Forever*. In fact, in Japan it was added on the CD as a 15th track. The lyrics seem to be about an extramarital affair that is ending, the protagonist seeming to feel a responsibility for her family. In the bridge, Kim exclaims: '*Please understand / He's just a desperate man / who's doing all he can / So I'm going back*'.

INTERVIEW: MARTIN ZANDSTRA

How did you become a fan of Kim Wilde?

Right away in 1981 with the first single 'Kids in America'. She was a special appearance with a special voice and exciting music. In the end it took me eight years before I bought my first record…

Do you have a favorite track from Kim?

In 1989 I bought my first Kim Wilde record, the CD-single of 'Four Letter Word'. That's why it is my favourite track of hers, at least in part, but also because it is a beautiful song, beautifully sung. Other songs that come to mind are 'Dream Sequence', 'You Came', and 'Cambodia'.

How did you come up with the idea of organizing a fan meeting?

In the 1980s I went to a number of Beatles meetings in Amsterdam and in conversations with Marcel Rijs we agreed something like this should be organised for Kim, because that had really never been done.

What do you remember about the day?

The auction was a highlight, partly because of the high proceeds but also because of the items donated by Kim, Ricky and Marty, and the presence of sister Roxanne and Melanie from the fan club. The quiz was also a success, with nice candidates. It was also great to meet famous and unknown fans.

What do you admire most about Kim?

Particularly in her early days, she had a mystical atmosphere around her, both in appearance and music, and I find that special. During the 1990s I have regularly met her in person, and she came across as very 'down to earth'. I find that contrast very special. It is also fantastic that after 40 years she is still making records and performing!

Scenes from the fan meeting: Melanie Almond and Martin Zandstra leading the auction and fans looking at photographs with Melanie Almond and Roxanne Wilde (far right) © Marcel Rijs

CHAPTER 14:
TOMMY

In 1969, English rock legends The Who released their fourth album, *Tommy*. The album was almost entirely composed by lead guitarist Pete Townshend, and conceived as a rock opera. The album tells the story of Tommy Walker, a 'deaf, dumb and blind' boy, including his experiences with life and his relationship with his family. Tommy is neglected by his parents, tortured by sadistic cousin Kevin, molested by his uncle Ernie, and given LSD by the Acid Queen. After discovering he can play pinball purely on the basis of feeling vibrations, he becomes a 'Pinball Wizard' (one of the key tracks on the album). After losing his mental block he recovers his senses and becomes a powerful leader and becomes an idol, but ultimately retreats inward again.

The Who performed the album live during an extensive tour in 1969 and 1970, after which the concept piece took on a different life. The Seattle Opera produced a version in 1971, an orchestral version was staged by The Who with the London Symphony Orchestra in 1972, with a film directed by Ken Russell, starring Elton John and The Who's Roger Daltrey following in 1975, before in 1992 *Tommy* was turned into a musical, under the direction of Des McAnuff.

The musical initially ran at the La Jolla Playhouse in San Diego, California, starting on 1 July 1992. In April 1993 it moved to St James' Theatre on Broadway, closing on 17 June 1995 after 899 performances.

In November 1995, Kim received a copy of the Broadway musical CD of *Tommy* plus the script, with a question as to whether she was interested in auditioning for the part of Mrs Walker, Tommy's Mum, for a version of the musical in London's West End. She was immediately interested, having listened to The Who's album when it came out. So she went to audition before Pete Townshend and Des McAnuff.

Kim: "I was very nervous because I had never auditioned for anything in my life before. But I thought that, if I'd performed with Michael Jackson and presented *The Big Breakfast*, I could do anything! I'm not afraid of a challenge. Besides, it's not such a massive leap. It's not as if I'm taking up landscape gardening! Singing is after all something I know I can do." [1]

Kim: "It was at a studio in Covent Garden, Pete Townshend was there, and the director Des McAnuff. I basically had to sing the songs Mrs Walker sings. And I had to do some reading, dramatic reading, which I'd never done. It was pretty terrifying!" [2]

She performed Mrs Walker's songs and read out some lines, and within a few days Kim heard she'd got the part, whilst filming a video for 'This I Swear' in New

York. Rehearsals followed from 8 January 1996, six days a week in Acton, West London.[3] Paul Keating, a young actor, only 20, took the lead role – the same age as Kim when she started out. Except Keating had been involved in acting since he was 12, appearing in the musical *Les Miserables*, with *Tommy* his big break, the start of a career that would endure.

However, during rehearsals, Kim managed to freak out Pete Townshend.

Kim: "Alistair, who plays my husband, and myself were getting a bit fed up calling ourselves Mr and Mrs Walker, so gave ourselves first names too. He called himself Frank and I called myself Betty…the name of Pete's own Mum."[4]

The audience got their first taste of the West End version when Kim appeared on BBC television programme *Pebble Mill*. A large part of the programme was devoted to the new musical. Pete Townshend was interviewed, Nicola Hughes performed 'Acid Queen', Kim sang recent single 'This I Swear', and joined Alistair Robins in a performance of 'I Believe My Own Eyes', a new song written for the musical.

Previews of the musical started on 20 February at Shaftesbury Theatre, London, followed by opening night on 5 March 1996. Reviews were enthusiastic. 'It's the type of supercharged production that puts the show into show business. Rock along and marvel!' wrote the *News of the World*. 'Anyone who does not come away frothing at the mouth with excitement at this thrilling £3.5 million stage realisation of Pete Townshend's famous 1969 rock-opera must have taken leave of their senses', wrote the *Daily Express*. *The Sun* added: 'Kim Wilde makes her acting debut as Tommy's Mum, Mrs Walker, and - despite obvious first-night nerves - she was belting out the numbers by the second act.'[5] And Dutch newspaper *De Telegraaf* was quick to recognise *Tommy* was 'a turning point in the life of this pop star, who showed herself a true musical star in this role.'[6]

In April, Kim's hands were immortalised in the Wall of Hands at the Rock Circus in London's Piccadilly. Madame Tussaud's Rock Circus launched in August 1989 and showed the history of rock and pop music, featuring its major stars recreated in wax. Not only that: the attraction also featured moving dolls, with a stage show including, among others, the *Sgt Pepper*-era Beatles and Bruce Springsteen. The attraction was built in the top four floors of the London Pavilion building at Piccadilly Circus. The Wall of Hands featured hand-prints of artists such as All Saints, Tony Bennett and Alice Cooper. Kim's hands remained on the wall until the Rock Circus closed in September 2001. According to Madame Tussaud's, the item was removed from their collection after this.

Kim: "When I began *Tommy* in January, the last thing I intended to do was to get involved with anyone in the company. Falling in love with Hal was something I fought against, initially. I really put up all the barriers. But he persisted and in the end it was his honesty and the fact that he loved me so

CHAPTER 14: TOMMY

much that broke down the barriers. I know that we'll be laughing together and still loving each other the way we do now when we are well into our ripe old 80s."[7]

Hal Fowler played the role of Cousin Kevin. Until then he'd performed in various film, television and theatre productions. His film work included the lead role of Bunty in Terrance Ryan's *Brylcreem Boys*, and the lead role in Roy Oxlade's *Plato's Revenge* and *When in London*. On television he appeared in *The Bill*, *Alas Smith & Jones* (also featuring Kim's former duet partner, Mel Smith) and *For Valour*. Theatre productions included *Dorian Gray* at the Bloomsbury Theatre, *Aspects of Love* at the Prince of Wales in London and *Calamity Jane* at the Haymarket Theatre in Leicester. [8]

Hal: "I went out of my way to avoid her; only because everybody else was making it their job to be around her as much as possible. However, during rehearsals there was a limp conversation about who would have enough courage to ask Kim out for dinner. I'd spoken to her only three or four times but decided I'd go and ask her, rather than listen to all this talk. So I strutted over the stage: "Would you like to come out for dinner with me next week?" As bold as brass, even though I'd never done anything like that before. She made me squirm for about a minute, her revenge for how I'd treated her, until finally she agreed." [9]

The two went to The Ivy, a firm fixture on London's dining and social scene since its foundation in 1917. The dinner was a success, as rather than talking about work they spoke about their childhood, their interests and other things. They didn't want to leave, so in the end were 'booted out'.

Kim: "The first time we went out, he took me to The Ivy, hoping to impress me. He thought I went there all the time, but I'd never been in my life. I couldn't believe how glamorous it was. He'd got a wad of money from his agent because he obviously thought I was going to order champagne and caviar, and was ready for the worst, but I didn't go mad." [10]

Hal: "When I got back home, I wrote a little poem for her, which I thought I would give her as a thank you for a marvellous evening. I put it in my bag ready, then thought: 'What on earth are you doing that for? What a ridiculous thing to do.' So I got out of bed, ripped it to pieces, put it in the bin and went back to bed. Then I got up, wrote it out again, got into bed - and then ripped it up again. This happened three times until I finally thought, 'Right, that's enough', put it in a sealed envelope, wrote 'Kim', and gave it to the stagedoor man next day." [11]

Kim: "I've got [a poem] from our first date. When he gave it to me, I thought, 'Either this guy is taking the mickey or something really special is going on here.'" [12]

Legend had it that Hal didn't know anything about pop music and had no idea who Kim Wilde was. That turned out to be not completely true.

Kim: "I noticed he had a photo of Kylie [Minogue] on his fridge, which got taken off after about our fourth date. He knew who I was, he just hadn't paid much attention. I joked that he didn't know if I was Kim Wilde or Kim Carnes!" [13]

They continued to see each other, and romance blossomed. During rehearsals, Hal had a bad fall and smashed all the ligaments in his knee. He managed to get on with things for the opening night with the aid of carbon-fibre ski braces, but after four months had to have an operation and leave the show.

Kim, meanwhile, also had to deal with keeping the press at bay. While she was doing a feature for a magazine at her home, Hal was sent away with her brother Ricky.

Hal: "I had to leave because she didn't want me to be seen, so I went up to the pub with Rick. I kept ringing to see if she'd finished but it kept going on. Six pints later, Rick and I were slaughtered, so I said, 'Come on, we're going in there'. And not only that, I said, 'Let's take all our clothes off!' So me and Rick walked stark naked from the drive all the way to the front door, at which point Kim's Mum chased us out of view!" [14]

Kim: "My neighbour at the time sent a postcard expressing her disgust and asserting that she never again 'wished to see a naked man strolling down her drive'. I still have it pinned up in the kitchen — always makes me giggle." [15]

The secret was out, finally, during an interview on ITV's *This Morning* on 21 May. A few weeks later, Hal decided to 'pop the question', and the couple headed to France on a short break from the musical.

Hal: "After about six months we had a few days off and I persuaded a newly-qualified pilot friend to fly us over from Elstree airport to France for lunch. It was meant to be a surprise, but I had to tell Kim first in case she had any worries about going on the trip. The pilot left us in the little square in the middle of Calais." [16]

Kim: "Hal proposed to me in Calais, France, after we took a four-seater plane out there for lunch. After lunch we went shopping for engagement rings. We found one jeweller, but he only had two rings in stock, which Hal and I loved, and they fitted us both perfectly – it was destined to be!" [17]

The engagement was made public by various UK newspapers on 27 June. Interestingly, most of them illustrated the news with a photograph of Kim with co-star Alistair Robbins instead of Hal. Only *The Sun* got it right.

Kim and Hal decided to get married on 1 September, so there was only a short time to prepare the wedding. But one thing was already decided: the dress!

Kim: "I first saw my wedding dress in a shop in Covent Garden. I spotted it long before Hal proposed to me. I remember thinking, 'What a fabulous dress', because it was so simple. When he proposed, I thought - ding - 'I know the dress I'm going to have'. It teams up brilliantly with the shoes I got from Gamba." [18]

On 18 August 1996, Hal and Kim celebrated their hen and stag do's. Hal took all his mates to the Robin Hood & Little John pub in Codicote, whereas Kim met her girlfriends in a pub in the next village. They spent the day being taken by horse and cart from pub to pub until they eventually ended up with the boys at the Robin Hood & Little John.

Kim: "As we approached the pub, we were all singing songs so loudly that the boys could hear us halfway down the road. So they decided to greet us in a different manner – they sat on the fence next to the road with their trousers down! Or as *The Sun* newspaper put it, a '12 Bum Salute'! Very silly and very funny! We all had a wonderful hen/stag day, although we never dreamt it would all end up in a national newspaper – the price of fame!" [19]

The wedding took place as planned on 1 September 1996. The wedding, at St Giles' Church, Codicote, was attended by 150 guests. [20] Kim's younger sister Roxanne was chief bridesmaid, with Scarlett (Ricky's seven-year-old daughter) and Jasmine (Hal's three-year-old niece) the other bridesmaids. A lot of local people, as well as hardcore fans, turned up to see the happy couple. Kim and Marty drove to the church in a horse-drawn carriage, then went inside for the ceremony. Scarlett read the first reading, Penny-Belle (Hal's sister) sang a song in Latin written especially for the wedding by Hal's father Bob Fowler and composer Howard Goodall, and Roxanne sang 'So Wide Awake', written by Ricky and Marty – a song that was never heard by the general public until Marty included a version on his 2020 album *Running Together*. [21] After the service, Kim and Hal were driven to the reception in their white Land Rover. The reception was held at her parents' house in Tewin (five miles away). A large marquee was put up for the guests, who were treated to the sounds of a string quartet and a pianist. [22] Later there was a banquet for the guests, masterminded by top chef Antony Worrall Thompson. [23]

Kim: "Hal and I packed for our wedding night, which we spent at a local hotel, before a trip to the Lake District for our honeymoon the next day. Hal picked up the wrong bag and we ended up having to go down for breakfast the next day in our wedding clothes, much to everyone else's amusement!" [24]

After a four-day honeymoon in the Lakes, Kim returned to work. [25] The eight-performances-a-week schedule was tough, but she continued without failing.

Kim: "Nothing prepared me for how exhausting it was to perform night after night - it was relentless, but I really enjoyed it." [26]

She surprised her fans by releasing a new single in September 1996 too: 'Shame', a cover version of a song originally recorded by Evelyn 'Champagne' King in 1978. Kim noticed the song on the jukebox in the youth club scene of *Tommy* and was inspired to record it herself.

The Official Fan Club released colourful magazines regularly.
© Marcel Rijs

Between 1996 and 2006, many compilation albums were released.
© Marcel Rijs

After Hal moved into Kim's house, the pair sat down with their friend Ray, a builder and gardener, to start and design the garden behind the house.

Kim: "The three of us sat outside, around a garden table, and made plans - we still have the original sketches, long since marked with countless coffee stains and rain splashes. I wanted the garden to have some formality, but with a cottage garden feel - exuberant with lots of colour. The 400-year-old barn sits on top of a hill, so it can get very windy. I decided to put in lots of uprights and arches and climbers and pergolas to provide some shelter." [27]

According to co-producer Joop van den Ende, Tommy would have to run for 41 weeks to reach a break-even point. *Tommy* eventually closed on 8 February 1997, 48 weeks after its premiere. During the matinee performance, there were practical jokes on stage, but the last performance in the evening was a serious one. All the actors gave their all and went out with a bang.

A large group of fans waited outside the stage entrance for the stars to come out. Kim was handed a small 'Oscar' by one, and after giving out some autographs she left the scene together with Hal.

A week later, the Laurence Olivier Awards were announced. *Tommy* picked up a prize for best lighting design and the year's outstanding musical production, while director Des McAnuff picked up the award for best director. [28]

Kim and Hal went on holiday, visiting Phuket, Koh Phi Phi and Bangkok in Thailand over a three-week period as a belated honeymoon.

Kim: "*Tommy* was an album I'd listened to over and over again as a kid. My Dad had it on vinyl and I used to pour over that fascinating artwork and listen to that incredible music. Then all of a sudden I got handed this script and a chance to be a part of it, and I just couldn't turn it down. I remember at the time I had a record contract and the production just seemed more important to do, and as fate would have it, within six months I'd found the man that I married and we started a family. So it was a great decision, and, in a way, Pete Townshend is kind of like my fairy godmother." [29]

In December 1997, the Kim Wilde Official Fan Club published its final magazine. Melanie Almond, who had run the club during the last three years, was leaving to go and work in London at an advertising agency. An information service would provide an alternative, but in the absence of 'hard' news, there wasn't much to report during the next few years. But in October 1998 the website kimwilde.com started, the logical successor to the webpage that had started after the fan meeting in March 1996, and that would become the main source of information about Kim and her activities.

CHAPTER 14: TOMMY

SHAME
Written by John Henry Fitch & Reuben Cross
Produced by Tag Team
Released: 30 September 1996
Chart position: 86 (UK)

'Shame' was originally a hit for Evelyn 'Champagne' King in 1978. It reached No.9 in the US Billboard Hot 100 chart and No.39 in the UK singles chart.
Kim: "I've always loved the song and happened to notice it on the jukebox in the youth club scene of *Tommy*." [30]
Kim recorded her version in the first half of 1996. The original mix of Kim's version debuted in France on compilation album *The Singles Collection*, released that July. That version also appeared on a CD-single, released in France only.

Two months later, 'Shame' was released as a single in the UK, in a remixed version created by Jupiter, its production team consisting of Guy Phethean and Limahl. The latter was best known as the front-man of the band Kajagoogoo, best known for 'Too Shy', and as a solo artist, best known for 'The Never Ending Story'.

The single release was originally scheduled for 2 September 1996, but ultimately postponed until 30 September to accommodate Kim's busy schedule.

The music video was directed by Katie Bell. It featured Kim in various glamorous outfits, surrounded by dancers. The dancers were auditioned in the summer of 1996 and became the subject of a short film by Cerith Wyn Evans called *Kim Wilde Auditions*. In the video, two handsome men are asked to respond to the instructions of an off-screen director. They take up poses, follow the absent Kim with their eyes, peel off their shirts and walk the set. The actors are obviously nervous.

Although 'Shame' only got to No.86 in the UK singles chart, the promotional 12" singles featuring dance mixes by T'empo and Matt Darey were a big success in the club charts.

Since Kim didn't tour again until after the turn of the century, her version of 'Shame' made its first live appearance during the Snapshots & Greatest Hits tour in 2012.

I BELIEVE MY OWN EYES
Written by Pete Townshend

Pete Townshend wrote 'I Believe My Own Eyes' for the musical version of *Tommy*. A recording of the song first appeared on a CD-single included with the book *The Who's Tommy* (Pantheon Books, New York, 1993) on the occasion of the Broadway premiere of the musical. An original cast recording of that musical was released commercially in 1994. This version was performed by Jonathan Dokuchitz and Marcia Mitzman.

Alistair Robins and Kim Wilde performed the song in London's West End version of the musical, and also performed the song live on television on BBC's *Pebble Mill* on 2 February 1996 and again on ITV's *GMTV* in March 1996.

Kim receiving an 'Oscar' and leaving with Hal after the last performance of 'Tommy', 8 February 1997 © Marcel Rijs

CHAPTER 15:
BETTER GARDENS

According to all the stories about Kim that were published in the 21st century, Kim retreated from the public eye after *Tommy* to devote herself to her family. In truth, things weren't quite as black and white. KIm did disappear from the public eye, but that had happened before: in large parts of 1989, 1991 and 1994 little was heard from her in the press.

In reality, she started writing for her next album, while also working on her garden at home. Now that she was married, Kim could work on that part of her property together with Hal, and they made plans to design a garden for about half an acre of land behind her house.

Kim: "The first thing we did was to get a couple of truckloads of cow dung – great piles of the stuff – and let that rot down for a month. Now we've created an area for the beds and we're going to edge them with boarding." [1]

Not knowing too much about gardening, Kim decided to enrol at a college in Enfield to learn more.

Kim: "My introduction to Capel Manor Horticultural College was the single biggest influence upon the gradual change from my being interested in all things horticultural to being completely hooked! After a few short summer courses in planting and design, while I was pregnant with Harry in 1998, I felt like a born-again person who had discovered a new and enlightening path." [2]

Kim: "I went back to college and did some courses, after which I was obsessed. I would be driving along, trying to name trees and almost going into the backs of cars. I never thought anything other than music would have that effect." [3]

Kim: "Frustrated by my lack of plant knowledge, I enrolled for a two-year evening course in garden planting design. The most brilliant thing about the course was that for the first time I was a really good student. My first piece of work came back marked with a D. I was devastated. Then I was told that D was for distinction! It did wonders for my self-confidence." [4]

Work on the album progressed as well. Select Sound Studios was still the epicentre of creativity for Kim and Ricky, and they also involved other songwriters. Ricky also worked with a band called Fly, also featuring Mark Cummins and Roxanne. He produced a track for Luciana Caporaso's debut album *One More River*, and in 1998 wrote and produced the track 'Feel My Vibe' for the trio Blush, consisting of young singers Natalie Kington, Fran Chapman and Anna Williamson.

When Kim went into hospital for the birth of her first child, she was surprised to meet a fellow pop star there: Tracey Thorn from Everything But the Girl was about to give birth to twin girls Jean and Alfie. And on 3 January 1998, Harry Tristan Fowler was born, weighing 9lb 1oz. Hal was quoted as saying 'We are ecstatic'. [5] A rare interview was also published in April of the same year in the *Daily Mail*'s weekend magazine.

Ricky: "I've never seen her happier now she's got Hal and little Harry. She and my wife are constantly on the phone, swapping baby tips, passing on clothes and prams and all that stuff. We see each other two or three times a week - babies permitting." [6]

It seemed that Kim's new album was still being worked on, but at the same time, things were changing at MCA Records. Seagram had acquired Universal and MCA and in 1998 also paid $11 billion to acquire PolyGram Records and associated companies Island and Mercury. That acquisition was finalised on 10 December 1998. As a result, unprofitable artists were to be dropped and many members of staff sacked. A side-effect was that MCA and Universal were afraid to commit to new record deals, and existing deals were re-evaluated. In the midst of all that, Kim decided she didn't want to get into the merry-go-round of promoting a new album again, now she was focusing on her home life, causing some turmoil within the family. After all, Kim's career was also a family affair.

Kim: "My family maybe assumed everything would be the same as it had always been, but now I was married and had a family, nothing would ever be the same again. So it was a big decision to leave the family business, but all I really wanted to do was start a family of my own."

After a period of negotiations, Kim was relieved of her contract in 1999, with the new album never released. Entitled *The Promise*, its 12 tracks sounded a lot like a natural evolution of *Now & Forever*, still sounding soulful but with added influences like pop and drum & bass.

Kim's new project was something entirely different. Having been at Capel Manor for some time, she was spotted by a development team from ITV working on a series called *Better Gardens*, a spin-off from Carol Vorderman series *Better Homes*. The idea was that Kim would be one of five experts who would design gardens in a competition-based programme, executing a complete makeover of their back gardens. [7]

The news prompted a furious reaction from Dr Stefan Buczacki, a horticulturalist and one-time chairman of Radio 4's *Gardeners' Question Time*. In *The Garden*, journal of the Royal Horticultural Society, he growled: "On gardening pages, in gardening magazines and on television gardening programmes, I am frequently confronted by folk who are full of enthusiasm and good teeth but remarkably deficient in experience of horticulture". [8] The implication was that 'lifestyle' television would give viewers the impression that gardening was a quick

CHAPTER 15: BETTER GARDENS

fix, entertainment instead of years of dedication. Kim's response was, as always, calm and collected.

Kim: "I think it is wrong to be elitist about gardening. When I went down to the local allotments to ask for advice, no one gave me Latin names, they told me not to put manure on the carrots and to stagger the times you sow your beans, so they will come up throughout the whole season. Gardening is not something to get on your high horse about or be overwhelmed by. Either you enjoy it, or you don't." [9]

The first episode of *Better Gardens* was broadcast on Channel 4 on 9 January 2000. Each episode featured next-door neighbours who received £7,000 plus a garden designer each to create a better garden. Judges would decide who created the best garden. The owners of the best garden of the series would also win their very own cottage, 'Little Thatch', in the heart of the English countryside.

The series consisted of eight episodes, and Kim appeared in five. In the second episode, recorded in Northampton, Kim's design lost out to one by Ross Alan. A week later, she saw off designer Antony Henn. On 30 January, she was up against Ross Alan again, this time in Southampton. And he won again. In the episode broadcast on 6 February, she won with a garden inspired by Sri Lanka and India, beating designer Toby Musgrave. And finally, on 13 February Kim chalked up a third victory in Manchester, up against Toby Buckland. In the same episode, the series winner was announced. All the designers were interviewed in the episode, recorded just days before broadcast. And Carol Vorderman couldn't let the moment pass without asking if Kim would give up singing and get into gardening full-time.

Kim: "I don't know about giving up singing, I'm certainly going to be concentrating more on gardening. So singing can just take a backburner for a while. I'll keep my options open." [10]

Better Gardens was recorded in 1999, during Kim's second pregnancy. Kim was never afraid of hard work, but hard landscaping was rather tough at the time.

Kim: "I didn't want to tell them I was pregnant in case they thought I was a health and safety risk, so I made sure we'd done two or three episodes before they found out. Then I thought, they've got me now, they can't get rid of me." [11]

Kim: "I actually felt quite energised. I obviously needed help sometimes, lifting stuff. It was frustrating feeling a bit useless, but there were enough people on hand to help." [12]

Kim: "It was so emancipating. I was getting fat, and having babies, and not doing anything to my hair, and sweating a lot... I've walked into houses where it's obvious that the husband had a thing about me at some point in the Eighties. And I turn up looking very different to my Pop Star persona, totally

shattering their illusions - the slim figure, the lips, the hair all gone out the window, it always made me secretly chuckle to myself." [13]

On 14 January 2000, Rose Elisabeth Fowler was born at 9.30am, weighing 7lb 15oz (3.5kg), Hal reportedly revealing, "We are completely over the moon". [14] The next month, Kim and Hal appeared in *OK! Magazine* for a 10-page feature, showing off the new addition and her brother Harry.

With Kim settling into family life and a new gardening career, younger sister Roxanne seemed to be taking over. In the summer of 1999 she signed a contract with Polydor, one of four members of a band managed by Hilary Shaw, who previously looked after Bananarama. Roxanne had already sung on Kim's 1992 album *Love Is*, on the track 'The Light of the Moon (Belongs To Me)', and also on Marty's 1994 album *Solid Gold*, on the track 'I'm Leaving It All Up to You'.

Dimestars, as the band became known, featured Roxanne on vocals, Morgan Quaintance on guitar, Tom Hanna on bass and Joe Holweger on drums. On 30 October 2000, their first single was released, 'Solo So Long'. The band recorded an album and supported Kylie Minogue during her 'On A Night Like This' tour in the UK in March. They then released second single 'My Superstar' on 21 May 2001. It reached No.72 in the UK chart. The album *Living For The Weekend* was scheduled for release around the same time, but although copies were made for promotional use, it was ultimately shelved.

The album was produced by Terry Ronald, Lee Knott and Nick Bagnall, who wrote the majority of the songs in collaboration with Roxanne. Besides the two singles and nine further tracks there was a cover version of Martha & the Muffins' 'Echo Beach' – a live favourite of the band.

Roxanne: "I like to think that people will relate to our songs and lyrics. I used to listen to the lyrics of songs and think, that's exactly what's going on in my life, or interpret it that way. We want to appeal to our age group. It's all about being young and having a laugh." [15]

While Roxanne was hitting the music scene, Kim was at home, having distanced herself from it. What did Marty think of his oldest daughter turning her back on the pop scene? Kim actually offered an insight in April 2000.

Kim: "I think he wonders where my head is because his passion for rock'n'roll has never diminished, whereas my passion for pop has been replaced by a passion for my family and other things. We are different people. My Dad has just taken on a whole load of new gigs doing his rock'n'roll show, which he loves. His voice is stronger than it's ever been and there is a great demand for it. He does a great show and he still loves it." [16]

In the course of 2000, the family decided to sell Select Sound Studios. The studio was dismantled and the building sold. The move shocked fans, as news got around. Some of them even went to Knebworth to see the outside of the building

CHAPTER 15: BETTER GARDENS

one last time. It seemed to be a definite ending of music being produced by the Wilde family. The building was eventually sold and turned into Art Van Go, a shop for artist materials, as well as a venue for workshops.

But it didn't take long for Kim to be lured back into the music world. In January 2001, she was asked to perform live as a special guest of Abba tribute band Fabba during a concert at the Campus West Theatre, Welwyn Garden City. The concert raised funds for Codicote's Village Fun Day that July. Kim was on the organising committee, so it was hard to refuse....

Kim: "I was volunteering on our local village committee and met a guy who fronted an Abba tribute band. He persuaded me to do a concert of Abba and Kim Wilde songs. I hadn't been on stage for years. I had been too busy getting married and having babies. I thought that was really good fun and the timing was right. There's more of an appreciation of the Eighties now people are not so embarrassed to say they loved the music. It's a one-off way of celebrating the small part I played in the pop world." [17]

The concert took place on 13 January 2001. Many villagers turned up, but when Kim's fans got wind of the news, some flew in from the Netherlands and Germany to experience the event, snapping up the very last tickets, leaving many other fans disappointed.

Fabba, consisting of Caroline Illingworth (vocals), Laurie Briggs (vocals), Andy Skelton (guitar and vocals), Glenn Annett (keyboards, vocals) and backing musicians Kevin Cartwright (bass, vocals) and Bob Dalton (drums, vocals), played two sets of Abba songs during the concert. Kim appeared a few songs into the second set after the interval to sing 1977 Abba classic 'The Name of the Game'. A bouncy, rocking version of 'Rage to Love', one of Kim's own songs, followed. Kim was visibly enjoying herself on stage again. Mentioning that her family were in the audience, 'all of them', plus husband Hal, 'who's never seen me be a popstar on stage before', he replied with a loud, "I love it!". Then came a third and final song for Kim, 'You Keep Me Hangin' On'. She went offstage with tears in her eyes, clearly touched by the abundance of warmth and affection that could be felt in the theatre.

Kim returned during the encore for a full-on version of 'Kids in America' and an acapella rendition of Abba's 'Thank You For The Music'. [18]

After the concert, Kim did a signing session in the foyer, meeting all the fans and taking the time to speak with everyone who approached her.

Kim: "I had a great night. It gave me a taste for doing more concerts." [19]

Kim: "[When I was younger] I really wanted to be Agnetha from Abba. But actually I got a chance to be her a few months ago, because I did a fundraising show with a band called Fabba, who do Abba covers. And that´s what got me into thinking maybe I´d like to do more of this." [20]

In the meantime, Kim moved on to her next television project. In the last week of April 2001, the BBC started broadcasting new episodes of *Garden Invaders*, a gardening show with a twist. A team of gardeners and one designer created a garden makeover with materials the garden owners could win by answering questions from the show host correctly. The shows were presented in turn by Mark Evans and Nick Clark. Between April and June, Kim appeared in 22 episodes, each featuring a design by her.

Kim: "When they told me I had to do 20 gardens for the series I was terrified! But I think everyone was happy with what we did." [21]

Kim: "The prizes were things like gravel, sleepers, paving stones, paint and trellis, so it was quite hard to change the garden when the contestants hadn't won much. We just had to be imaginative and improvise with anything we could find. But it was great fun and I learnt a lot." [22]

In July, the RHS Tatton Flower Show took place on the Tatton Park estate in Cheshire. Kim Wilde and David Fountain designed a garden together for the show, All About Alice, inspired by Lewis Carroll's 'Alice In Wonderland'. The garden was built on two levels, with a large gnarled oak tree as its centrepiece, displaying a carving of the Cheshire Cat. The lower level of the garden contained a grotto, with tapered walls to give the impression of the room becoming smaller, like the rabbit hole down which Alice tumbled to her adventures. A maze of tall, clipped hornbeam-enclosed contorted mirrors added to the sense of distortion. Throughout the garden, scale was increased or decreased and the planting was wild and unkempt, in keeping with Alice's confusion during her strange experiences.

The upper level of the garden represented four stories from Alice's adventures. Old tree stumps were used by a chainsaw artist to become oversized teacups for a Mad Hatter's Tea Party, placed amongst wild woodland planting. The Queen's croquet lawn was set in a wildflower meadow. Figures of the Queen, King and a pawn stood on a chessboard of grass and water, surrounded by playing cards from the four suits, created from clipped box.

Kim: "We felt it was important to incorporate all the main elements of the story. So you enter the garden by descending into the dark rabbit warren before coming up into the maze (carpinus betulus) and the Hall of Mirrors. The Tea Party takes place in a woodland glade (betula utilis, betula jacquemontii and fagus sylvatica) and the playing cards are outlined in dwarf box. The main challenge was recreating Lewis Carroll's surreal atmosphere without 'Disneyfying' it. It's been six months of very hard work, including going round at 4.30am with a bucket of snails and placing them one by one, very carefully, in the nooks and crannies of a stone wall. The moment I knew it was all worth it came when the garden was finished, and suddenly the air

CHAPTER 15: BETTER GARDENS

came alive with dragonflies, bumble bees and beautiful butterflies - I felt that was a definite omen." [23]

The garden was awarded a gold medal – a first for a show garden at the RHS Flower Show at Tatton Park. Diarmuid Gavin announced this in a televised segment, causing both designers to stare in disbelief, Kim exclaiming, "I need a cup of tea".

The garden got a second life in October, with elements of it moved to the Warrington Peace Centre, built in memory of 12-year-old Tim Parry and three-year-old Johnathan Ball, victims of the 1993 Warrington bomb attacks. Various items from the Alice in Wonderland design at Tatton were brought to the Peace Centre, such as the giant wooden teacups and teapot from the Mad Hatter's tea party, the Mad Hatter's giant wooden hat, and the contorted mirrors.[24] The garden was officially opened by David Fountain and Kim on 24 October 2001.

During the year, Kim was dropping hints that she might return to the world of pop though. Having been asked by promoter Tony Denton, she considered taking part in the UK's Here & Now tour, consisting of eight dates up and down the country, also set to feature Carol Decker from T'Pau, Go West, Heaven 17, Nick Heyward, Ben Volpelière-Pierrot from Curiosity Killed The Cat, and Paul Young.

Kim: "The promoter got in touch and asked if I was interested and I got aboard the '80s rollercoaster. He had done a few and they'd done really well. They had approached me before, but it was at a time I was pregnant having babies, but I thought it would be a really good thing to aim for to get me back in shape." [25]

Indeed, in June 2001, a press presentation followed with all the artists, resulting in UK-wide press coverage and a very enthusiastic response. Press interest continued through the year, with Kim having to explain why she was combining a flourishing gardening career with a return to pop music.

Kim: "I always loved my pop career. Writing hit songs and performing music was just great. It wasn't like I walked away in disgust. I walked away because I was bored, and new opportunities were coming my way. I still think I wouldn't mind doing some more music and performing. I'm really pleased that the Eighties revival has ended up being so enthusiastically received." [26]

In September, Kim started a City and Guilds course in Plants and Planting Design, coinciding with rehearsals for the Here & Now tour, and the tour itself in November.

Opening on 8 November 2001 at the Telewest Arena in Newcastle, the tour went on to Sheffield (9 November), Birmingham (10 November), Brighton (14 November), London (15 November), Manchester (16 November) and Cardiff (17 November), ended at Butlins in Minehead (1 December). Carol Decker started each concert with a performance of 'Heart & Soul', 'Valentine' and 'China in Your Hand', backed by a band that would play for all the artists performing. Next up was Nick Heyward with his versions of Haircut 100's 'Love Plus One', 'Blue Hat for a Blue Day', 'Whistle Down the Wind' and 'Fantastic Day'. Go West performed 'Don't Look Down', 'Call Me', 'We Close Our Eyes' and 'King of Wishful Thinking', and Heaven 17 rocked the crowds with '(We Don't Need This) Fascist Groove Thang', 'Come Live With Me', 'Penthouse And Pavement' and 'Temptation'. Ben Volpelière-Pierrot from Curiosity Killed the Cat did lively versions of 'Name and Number', 'Misfit', 'Down To Earth' and 'Hang On In There Baby'. And then there was Kim Wilde...

Although Kim wasn't the last performer of the night, audiences and press soon concluded she should have been. Her set, consisting of 'Chequered Love', 'View From a Bridge', 'Never Trust a Stranger', 'Cambodia', 'You Came', 'You Keep Me Hangin' On' and finishing with 'Kids in America' was hard to beat. Paul Young did a decent job, however, with his hits 'Wherever I Lay My Hat', 'Come Back and Stay', 'Love of the Common People', 'I'm Gonna Tear Your Playhouse Down' and a crowd-pleasing 'Every Time You Go Away'. Each concert lasted around three hours, proving a great party for everyone.

On a more personal level, Kim enjoyed hanging out with her Eighties co-stars. They didn't really have the time to do this when they were younger, but now they were chatting away backstage, exchanging photographs of their children and making plans for visits later in the year. They had all grown up, and the chart rivalry was behind them. And professionally, it was a pleasant experience as well: Kim had a chance to be the pop star for a short period and not worry about the household for a change. And, contrary to what she might have thought, her fans hadn't forgotten about her at all.

Kim: "I was overwhelmed by the warmth people had for me. It was great fun, but I found I couldn't walk in high heels anymore. I'm more used to wellies these days!" [27]

Also, EMI decided to release a compilation album, *The Very Best Of Kim Wilde*, to coincide with the tour. Besides the biggest hits of her career, the album also contained new track 'Loved', written by Ricky Wilde and Terry Ronald, who also produced the track with Ian Masterson. It was recorded as a gift to her fans. To make things even better, the album also featured new remixes of 'View From a Bridge' by RAW and 'Kids in America' by Dave Cross and Andy Allder, aka. D-Bop. Kim listened to the remix before it was released in order to give it her blessing, but while playing it at home it caught the attention of her children. Before she knew it, she was made to play it every day...

Kim: "Harry knows I made records, because I've been playing the 'Kids in America' remix. The kids caught on to it and decided it would be good to jump up and down to. Now I have to put it on for that mad hour they have after their

CHAPTER 15: BETTER GARDENS

tea and before they go to bed. It's very embarrassing. The neighbours must think, 'Poor girl, she's lost in the Eighties, playing all her old records.'" [28]

To support the release, Kim undertook a small promotion tour. Just before the Here & Now tour she went to Denmark to appear on music programme *Musikbutikken*, singing 'Loved' and the remixed version of 'View From a Bridge'. She was also interviewed, along with Rick Astley, during which he sang some lines of 'Kids in America' and she did a part of 'Together Forever'. On 25 November she appeared on the Belgian version of *Big Brother* and went to Radio Donna for an interview. Two weeks later, she returned to Belgium to perform 'Loved' during the televised election of Miss Belgique and to do a five-song live performance at the nightclub Who's Who's Land in Brussels. This club performance was a solo appearance in the middle of the night, during which she sang 'Loved', 'You Came', 'View From a Bridge', 'You Keep Me Hangin' On' and 'Kids in America' to a pre-recorded backing track.

Promotion for 'Loved' extended into 2002, with a performance on Swedish TV programme *Bingolotto* on 19 January and in Finland, where she performed 'Loved' during *Fashion Night* on 25 January, as well as a version of 'Kids in America' together with Finnish band TikTak, who had covered the song in Finnish on their recent album. After this, Kim took a step back again.

During the summer of 2001, Kim had recorded new episodes of *Garden Invaders* for the BBC, and in January and February 2002, they were broadcast. In various episodes she teamed up with presenters Mark Evans, Nick Clark and Alistair Appleton to revamp gardens all over the UK. Her second season in the programme was also her last.

Kim also appeared in two-part programme *The Joy Of Gardening*, in which various celebrity gardeners talked about their passion. Starting on 12 March 2002, Kim became the resident gardener on popular UK daytime programme *This Morning* on ITV, with a 10-minute slot live in the studio every Tuesday.

But the music also kept pulling at Kim. She was asked to record 'Born to be Wild', a cover of the famous Steppenwolf track, as the theme song for the German Touring Car racing championships. She recorded the track in Germany, with Jeo Pard producing. During the presentation of the starting field on 30 June 2002 in Nuremberg, the song was introduced to the fans. Before the engines started, Kim sang 'Born To Be Wild' on the Norisring. Kim also got the chance to take a seat in Michael Bartels' Opel Astra V8 Coupé, the German racing driver chauffeuring her. [29]

In July, Kim and David Fountain participated in the RHS Flower Show at Tatton Park for a second time. After their successful creation All About Alice the previous year, they opted for a garden inspired by the Tolkien books. Entitled 'A Hobbit Garden', it features a round door, small leaded windows and large timber beams

*Kim live during Here & Now Tour, Minehead,
1 December 2001 © Katrien Vercaigne*

Kim live at the Diamond Awards Festival, 23 November 2002 © Katrien Vercaigne

and supports set into a wildflower grass hill planted with meadow foxtail, crested dogtail and oxeye daisies. The garden design was awarded a silver medal.

Like the 'All About Alice' garden before it, the garden was given a new home, this time at Little Haven Children's Hospice, Thundersley, which offers a warm, homely atmosphere in Essex and the Outer London boroughs for children affected by life-threatening illnesses. [30] [31]

Gardening had become the focus of Kim's career in the UK. Besides writing gardening pages for monthly magazine *Prima*, she also answered gardening questions sent in by readers of the respected newspaper *The Guardian* in June 2002. Entitled 'Wilde Side', the column ran every week on Saturday until 6 March 2004.

Kim: "Can you believe it? Kim Wilde writing about gardening in *The Guardian*!" [32]

During 2002 she also appeared twice on the celebrity version of ITV show *Stars in Their Eyes*. She dressed up as Doris Day for the episode broadcast in August, singing 'Que Sera Sera'. At the end of the year, she reappeared as Carly Simon, singing a beautiful version of 'Nobody Does It Better'. Astonishingly, she didn't win the contest both times. She was beaten by a slightly-weird Rolf Harris impersonation by Jarvis Cocker the first time, then Boy George performing as David Bowie.

On 23 November 2002, Kim was one of the performing artists during the Diamond Awards festival, 12 years after her last appearance at this annual event. It had gone through some changes in the meantime. Since the first Diamond Awards ceremony in 1986, artists played their recent hits, but after a few years it changed into a 'retro' event. In 2002, other acts performing during the night were T'Pau, Go West, Belinda Carlisle, ABC, and Spandau Ballet's Tony Hadley. All the artists performed their greatest hits from the Eighties, which delighted the audience.

In December, Kim went on the road with the Here & Now tour for a second time. A spring edition featured Tony Hadley, Steve Norman and John Keeble from Spandau Ballet, Belinda Carlisle, ABC, Howard Jones, Go West, Toyah and China Crisis. However, headliner Adam Ant was forced to pull out at the last minute after an incident at the beginning of the year. The third Here & Now tour featured Visage's Steve Strange, The Belle Stars, Dollar, Claire Grogan of Altered Images, Five Star, Kim Wilde and headliners The Human League.

Opening on 12 December 2002 at the Telewest Arena in Newcastle, the tour went to Sheffield (13 December), London Arena (14 December), Wembley Arena, also in London (15 December), Bournemouth (16 December), Cardiff (18 December), Brighton (20 December), Birmingham (21 December) and ended in Manchester on 22 December.

CHAPTER 15: BETTER GARDENS

Steve Strange started each concert, accompanied by two male dancers, singing 'Night Train', 'Pleasure Boys' and 'Fade to Grey'. Two members of the Belle Stars – Jenny Matthias and Lesley Shone – performed 'The Clapping Song', 'Iko Iko' and 'Sign of the Times'. Up next was Clare Grogan, who sang 'Happy Birthday' while climbing out of a huge birthday cake, 'Don't Talk to Me About Love', 'See Those Eyes' and 'I Could Be Happy'. David Van Day and Thereza Bazar reformed as Dollar for the tour, singing eight of their popular hits, although some were crammed into a medley: 'Videotheque', 'Shooting Star', 'Who Were You With in the Moonlight', 'Hand Held In Black And White', 'I Wanna Hold Your Hand', 'Mirror Mirror', 'Give Me Back My Heart' and 'Oh L'Amour'.

After an intermission, three members of Five Star (only Denise, Lorraine and Stedman Pearson appeared on stage) performed 'Can't Wait Another Minute', 'All Fall Down', 'Rain or Shine', 'The Slightest Touch', 'Stay Out of My Life' and 'System Addict'.

Next up was Kim, who at the start of the tour was recovering from a severe cold, causing her to cut a few songs out during the first few dates. The complete setlist, performed from 16 December onwards, consisted of 'Chequered Love', 'You Came', 'View From a Bridge', 'Never Trust a Stranger', 'Four Letter Word', 'You Keep Me Hangin' On' and 'Kids in America'.

Synth gods The Human League ended the proceedings as the only act not using the house band, relying on their own musicians. A strong 10-song set featured 'The Things That Dreams Are Made Of', 'Mirror Man', 'Love Action', 'All I Ever Wanted', 'Human', 'Fascination', 'Open Your Heart', 'Together in Electric Dreams', 'Tell Me When' and 'Don't You Want Me?'.

Reviews were scathing for some artists, but Kim got praise almost universally. "Kim Wilde was the night's highlight and the only singer who brought a bit of rock'n'roll to the arena," wrote *The Times*. [33] The Daily Telegraph added: "Wilde was a revelation, sending up her glamour puss 1980s persona while simultaneously showcasing the best voice of the tour." [34]

A rather different experience came at the expense of a TV station. Kim was sent to Thailand's Koh Samui by Channel Five for a programme about detoxing, together with ex-Boyzone member Keith Duffy, actor and presenter Richard Blackwood, and socialite Tamara Beckwith. In the autumn of 2002, the four had to undergo twice-daily, self-administered enemas with 18 litres of coffee solution, while also fasting, practising yoga, and enjoying spiritual relaxation. When the programme was finally broadcast in May 2003, *Celebrity Detox Camp*, as it was called, prompted disgusted reactions as well as a lot of admiration. For years afterwards, people contacted Kim Wilde's website to find out where exactly this detox camp took place.

Kim: "When Five asked me to take part in a celebrity detox programme in Thailand, along with Tamara Beckwith and Keith Duffy, I jumped at the chance. It was a fantastic experience, giving my vital organs a rest as well as a thorough cleanse. As a Mum it was lovely to be pampered for 10 days. I also lost a lot of the weight I hadn't been able to get rid of after giving birth to Harry, who's now five, and Rose, who's three. I was a bit worried about the colonic irrigation, but it didn't hurt and turned out fine - but I'm not sure it's something you should do very often..." [35]

Kim: "I had pain in my lower back for most of this year and was delighted when I was asked to go on a 10-day detox trip to the Koh Samui Health Spa in Thailand. When I was there, I fasted for seven days, only having detoxifying drinks. The detox really woke me up about looking after myself, although I still find it hard to prioritise my needs. I tend to focus on everyone else first. I did things like yoga, which really helps my lower back. After I got home, I had a sneaking suspicion I might be wheat and dairy intolerant, so I've almost completely cut them out. I eat loads more fresh fruit and vegetables and a lot less red meat. I feel much better and have kept off the weight I lost in Thailand." [36]

Kim: "Thailand, I love Thailand! It was fantastic, it changed my life. Of course, it was difficult to not drink or eat for seven days, but it was well worth it. Contrary to my three travelling mates, I had no problems with the abstinence, although I didn't like the colonic irrigations much. I really wanted to get into the programme, because the spiritual side of it was very appealing to me. I lost more than six kilos in seven days! I felt fantastic. I even went back there two years ago with my sister for the same treatment, that's how much I liked it. But I also really loved Thailand. I would love to live there with Hal once the children are all grown up. It would be great to be there a few months every year - the winter months of course." [37]

Another event in 2002 had its consequences in 2003. During a media conference in Berlin, Kim bumped into German singer Nena, who was busy putting together an album to celebrate 20 years in the pop business. They knew one another from the many pop programmes in Germany they appeared in during the 1980s at the height of their fame, and Nena thought it would be a great idea to have Kim sing one of the songs on her album.

Nena fronted one of the most popular bands in Germany during the 1980s. Their first two albums went platinum, their third gold. Soon after their fourth album became a relative failure, the band broke up and singer Nena Kerner continued as a solo artist, still using the name Nena. Her solo efforts couldn't match the spectacular success of the band's albums though, so the idea to celebrate 20

CHAPTER 15: BETTER GARDENS

years in the business by re-recording some of her biggest successes was as much inspired by necessity as nostalgia.

As it turned out, it wasn't a bad idea. *Nena Feat. Nena*, as the album was called, was released in October 2002. For the first time since 1985, Nena managed to top the albums chart in Germany. The album went triple platinum, while also reaching platinum status in Switzerland and Austria – a first for Nena. Five singles were taken from the album in the course of the following year, of which 'Anyplace, Anywhere, Anytime', the duet with Kim Wilde, which was released as the fourth single in May 2003, was undoubtedly the most successful. It reached No.3 in Germany, No.2 in Belgium and No.1 in Austria and the Netherlands. The music video, directed by Marcus Stenberg, was filmed in London in early 2003.

The pair also promoted the song on several German television programmes. Perhaps the most interesting one was an interview for Stephan Raab's popular programme *TV Total*, during which Nena was a bit drunk and Kim wore a red suit, chosen by Nena's stylist. The interview was conducted mostly in German, and in the end Kim sang part of 'Kids in America' with Stephan.

In later years, Kim repeatedly credited Nena for bringing her back into the music business. The success of 'Anyplace, Anywhere, Anytime' certainly played a part, as well as Nena's suggestion to re-record her old hits, as she had done with staggering success. There is no doubt that without this collaboration, Kim might never have considered recording new music. But eventually she did.

BECAUSE THE NIGHT
Written by Bruce Springsteen & Patricia Smith
Produced by Mike Batt

An unexpected release for Kim Wilde fans was the album *Philharmania* in 1998. Released in Germany only, the album might easily have been missed by various fans. It featured versions of classic songs performed by classic artists with the backing of the Royal Philharmonic Orchestra. Marc Almond sang 'Paint It Black', Lemmy from Motörhead sang 'Eve of Destruction', Colin Blunstone sang 'Owner of a Lonely Heart', and Kim delivered a version of 'Because the Night'.

The original song was recorded by Bruce Springsteen during sessions for his album *Darkness on the Edge of Town*. The Patti Smith Group was working on *Easter* in the studio next door, and the bands were exchanging tapes. The original version – a working man's lament – didn't end up on Springsteen's album. But Smith took the song and rewrote it to fit a female perspective, and included it on her own. Released as a single, it reached No.13 on the US Billboard Hot 100 and No.5 in the UK singles chart.

Oddly, 'Because The Night' was listed as one of the tracks on *The Singles Collection 1981-1993* on a French promotional folder for record shops back in 1993, instead of the song 'In My Life', which finally did end up on that album. Whether Kim recorded the song herself around that time is unknown.

The version on *Philharmania* starts quietly but soon reaches its crescendo during almost bombastic choruses.

LOVED
Written by Ricky Wilde & Terry Ronald
Produced by Ricky Wilde, Terry Ronald & Ian Masterson
Released: 5 November 2001
Chart positions: 7 (Belgium), 19 (Finland), 45 (Sweden), 68 (Switzerland)

'Loved' was recorded specifically for the compilation album *The Very Best of Kim Wilde*, released by EMI to coincide with the Here & Now tour in the UK. Terry Ronald and Ian Masterson produced the track together with Ricky, making the track sound a lot like the Trouser Enthusiasts remixes created by Masterson with David Green. This electronic treatment complemented Kim's voice very well.

Upon the release of the album in Europe it became a hit in various countries, even without a music video to support it. 'Loved' was played on several European radio stations, and on 24 November 2001 entered the Belgian singles chart. During a 12-week chart run, it reached No.7 there. Finland, Sweden and Switzerland also gave Kim a minor hit: 'Loved' peaked at No.'s 19, 45 and 68 respectively.

Kim: "EMI thought it was the ideal moment to release a 'best of' and asked whether I would like to contribute a new song. Ricky, my brother, had just written a song with Terry Ronald, and we decided to record it. It is entitled 'Loved', so we had a 'previously unreleased bonus track' on the album. In any case, we would never have imagined that this title would become a hit. What a great surprise!" [38]

'Loved' was remixed by DJ Slobodan Petrovic Jr., aka Pulsedriver, who had had a hit with a cover version of 'Cambodia' earlier in 2001, and Beam (real name Michael Urgacz), a producer from Cologne. Their 'Pulsedriver vs Beam remix' was released commercially in early 2002. Although the single didn't chart in Germany, it did help to get the single to chart in Switzerland.

No music video was made for 'Loved', but Kim did perform the song on various TV programmes in Europe, most notably on Danish programme *Musikbutikken* and the Belgian version of *Big Brother*, the reality TV show in which a group of Belgian civilians were locked in a house and filmed 24 hours a day, seven days a week. Kim's short visit to the house prompted some excited remarks from the contestants.

BORN TO BE WILD
Written by Mars Bonfire
Produced by Jeo Pard
Released: 14 October 2002
Chart positions: 84 (Germany), 71 (Switzerland)

Kim was asked to record 'Born to be Wild' as the theme song for the DTM races (German Touring Car championship races) in 2002.
Kim: "I never really liked the original song, 'Born to be Wild' by Steppenwolf. But in the end, I said: 'Okay, let's try it out. If it doesn't work out, we'll leave it at that.' Fortunately, I ended up really loving the result." [39]

A version with car noises was published on DTM's website in May 2002, but the single release a few months later disposed of these, featuring three mixes of the track as well as B-side 'All About Me'.

A music video was produced for this single, directed by Phil Griffin, featuring a group of break-dancers and even a leopard. Despite her chilling experiences with live animals during the filming of 'Cambodia' 20 years earlier, Kim still sat down near it during one or two shots.

Kim did just one TV performance of the song, during German TV programme *Was Passiert Wenn* on 12 October 2002. While never included in her live tour sets, she did perform the song at selected festival dates in Belgium, Germany, Denmark, Czech Republic and Poland in 2006 and 2008.

ALL ABOUT ME
Written by Ricky Wilde & Kim Wilde
Produced by Ricky Wilde
Released: 14 October 2002

Perhaps one of the most experimental Kim Wilde tracks since 'Dream Sequence', with Ricky working on his synths in a six-minute epic with lots of different sounds and rhythms. The first part of the track is rather slow, with a slightly meditative quality as Kim sings: '*The sun kisses my soul / and peace has taken hold*'. A stomping beat kicks in and the latter part of the song has Kim singing in distorted vocals, '*It's all about me / It's not about you / I need to be free / I've got to be true*'.

So what was this song? A farewell message to her fans? A sad love song? There was no shortage of speculation about these short and cryptic lyrics.

YOU AND ME (with Readymade)
Written by Zachary Johnson
Produced by Ian Grimble
Released: 22 July 2002

German rock band Readymade reached out to Kim for backing vocals on their track 'You and Me', one of the tracks on their third album, *The Feeling Modified*. On the track they also employed the Brilliant Strings Orchestra from London, to give it a more polished, fuller sound.

When it came to recording the duet, it was band member Zach Johnson who suggested Kim.

Zach Johnson: "That was my idea. Kim is a Mum with two kids and her own gardening show on British television, but back when she had a hit with 'Kids in America' I was 11 and had a huge crush on her, and most importantly, I love her voice. There was just nobody else who came into question for me." [40]

The release was a surprise for fans, who didn't expect her to record new music. The track wasn't released as a single – as one might have expected – and so it remained a hidden gem. Some reviewers picked up on her guest appearance: "Also nice, 'You and Me' with backing vocals by Kim Wilde (yes, *the* Kim Wilde), which may cause a little frown among the old fans. No matter. After all, it is not just a question of satisfying long-term fans with the tried and tested, but also of gaining a few new admirers. That should succeed." [41]

In 2004, the band announced they had gone their separate ways.

ANYPLACE, ANYWHERE, ANYTIME (with Nena)
Written by Uwe Fahrenkrog-Petersen, Carlo Karges and Lisa Dalbello.
Produced by Uwe Fahrenkrog-Petersen, Jeo Pard & Gena Wernick
Released: 19 May 2003
Chart position: 1 (Austria, Netherlands), 2 (Belgium), 3 (Germany), 9 (Switzerland), 19 (Denmark)

Back in 1984, German band Nena had a European hit with the song 'Irgendwie, Irgendwo, Irgendwann'. The song was released as the lead single for their third album, *Feuer und Flamme*. Prompted by the international success of earlier single '99 Red Balloons', the LP was simultaneously recorded in German and English, with translations provided by Lisa Dalbello. The English language album was called *It's All in the Game* and 'Irgendwie, Irgendwo, Irgendwann' became 'Anyplace, Anywhere, Anytime'.

The band broke up in April 1987, and lead singer Gabriele Kerner, whose nickname gave the band its name, continued as a solo artist, retaining the name.

CHAPTER 15: BETTER GARDENS

Her solo career was moderately successful in Germany but it was the LP *Nena feat. Nena* in 2002 that propelled her back into the top 10 across central Europe.

For the album, Nena reunited with former bandmate Uwe Fahrenkrog-Petersen, who produced the songs. The LP consisted of re-recordings of her biggest hits, including some by the old band. It also featured many guest stars. On the re-recording of 'Anyplace, Anywhere, Anytime', Nena sang with Kim Wilde, having met during a media event in Berlin in the summer of 2002. Nena sang in German while Kim added English lyrics into the recording, making this a bilingual version of the song.

Kim: "We met firstly in the Eighties, then again in Berlin during a promo party for a song I recorded for DTM ['Born To Be Wild']. She asked if I wanted to sing on her song 'Anyplace, Anywhere, Anytime.'" [42]

The song was released as the fourth single from the album and became its biggest hit. Over 150.000 copies were sold, and the single became a No.1 hit in Austria and the Netherlands. In Belgium and Germany it narrowly missed the top spot.

Kim and Nena promoted the song on various big TV shows, including the German and Dutch versions of *Top of the Pops*. The music video, directed by Marcus Sternberg, was filmed in the City of London, near the London Stock Exchange in early 2003.

Marcus Sternberg: "I studied and lived in London for many years, so when Nena sent me the song with Kim, I said, 'Let´s go film with Kim in London'. For the look of the video I was channelling the music video for 'Let Me Go' by Heaven 17. I was a bit nervous meeting Kim, a big fan of hers since the Eighties. I remember coming into the costume trailer early in the morning, Kim was already there and the first thing I said to her was, 'I am so, so sorry, but can´t shake your hand because I have the worst cold and you have to be in perfect shape today'. She was of course very sweet about it and got me a huge cup of very hot tea. We talked about some of the other bands having revivals, like Spandau Ballet, and of course her gardening show and how much fun she was having with Nena to record the song and performing it live with her.

"My choreographer friend Venol King came in to give some input on the performance of Kim and Nena. We tried some things out but pretty much stuck with my original idea to have the two of them sing right at each other while we circled around them with the camera on a Steadicam rig. The set-up was a bit of a challenge because we had five people (camera, focus puller, gaffer, make-up and me) run a tight circle around the girls without tripping over. After circling five rounds one way we had to reverse direction to unwind the electric cable again - before it strangled us like a python. Filmmaking is a silly job really.

"Apart from the great solo and duet performances with Kim and Nena I figured I needed a mini-story, just something small for the mood. We already had two strong women performing, so I thought let´s cast a young guy who explores the city and ends up going to a strange party with dancers and performance artists. Probably a bit like myself when I moved to London at 17. The creative process brings out some of your personal journeys, I suppose. We filmed Nena and Kim till about seven in the evening and then moved on to the Roundhouse, Camden to film the 'arty party'. We wrapped just after 1am.

"It was all shot on one long day - like many music videos. I had a lovely crew, but the most important credit really goes to Kim and Nena for delivering such charming and warm performance. I love the little gestures, the smiles, the shared laughs. I just looked at it again to refresh my memory - what a total delight to watch two artists at the top of their game."

Kim and Nena performed the song live on a handful of occasions. Kim has also included the song in her own concerts through the years, singing both the German and English parts – although usually she sings all the verses in English.

Czech power metal band Symphonity recorded a cover version of the song as a bonus track on the Japanese release of their 2016 album, *King Of Persia*.

IF THERE WAS LOVE

Nathan Moore became well-known as a member of boy bands Brother Beyond and Worlds Apart. Having worked with Ricky Wilde while in Worlds Apart, it was perhaps no surprise that he ended up recording a duet with Kim towards the end of the 1990s. It was, however, a surprise that he suddenly published the track on his website on 9 July 2002, the free music file coming with a short message from Nathan.

Nathan Moore: "This song is the solo project I've been talking about for months. Cal [Cooper, bandmate in Worlds Apart] was involved in it as well. Unfortunately, no record company is interested in having this song (neither in signing Worlds Apart). That's why I decided to put it on my website, so you can all enjoy it..." [43]

CHAPTER 16:
CUMBRIAN FELLSIDE GARDEN

Between 16 February and 6 April 2003, ITV broadcast eight episodes of *Great Garden Guide*, a programme devoted to showing the most beautiful gardens in the west of England. The programme was presented by leading garden history writer and garden consultant Toby Musgrave together with Kim, each visiting one picturesque location in every episode.

Gardening and music were competing for Kim's attention. For the moment she was enjoying her gardening career in the UK while slowly returning on the music scene in Europe. After two Here & Now tours, it seemed Kim was ready to perform on her own again. On 16 May 2003 she did her first solo concert at Copenhagen open-air amusement park Tivoli before 25,000 people. It was the only solo concert of the year, but Kim participated in various festivals in Germany, Switzerland and Denmark as well. "Would you like a new album?", she asked the Danish audience at Rock under Broen on 14 June 2003. It might as well have been a rhetoric question. Then in August, in an interview promoting the next UK Here & Now tour, Kim mentioned she was collecting songs for a new CD.

Kim: "It's going to be a real rock chick album." [1]

At that point, Kim had recorded a few demos, but it was still very early days. But fans had something to look forward to, especially when it was reported that she spent a few days writing and recording during the last week of September. It would take a lot of time for these songs to see daylight, but fans around the world were already hoping for the best.

Between 6 and 17 November, the Here & Now tour took place in Australia for the first time ever. Australian bands Mondo Rock and 1927 joined Go West, Belinda Carlisle, Paul Young, Kim Wilde and The Human League for five dates starting in Perth on 6 November, via Adelaide (8 November), Melbourne (10 November) and Brisbane (15 November) to finish in Sydney on 17 November.

Arriving in Australia in the middle of the night, things got off to a rocky start for promoter Tony Denton, when after a drinking session with all the artists he was carried to his bedroom by Paul Young and his wife Stacey. They didn't do very well: first the door got in the way, then the quilt was all over the floor and they tripped over that... Three days later Tony was in a hospital in Adelaide being told he had a cracked rib and bruised muscles. [2]

The tour certainly was a merry one. The five concerts spread across 12 days meant the artists and their entourage had spare time in between, and they made the most of it. Ricky and his wife Mandy went swimming with dolphins and stayed up late together with some of the other stars, while Belinda Carlisle and Kim spent a lot of time sleeping, cementing their status as the dormice of rock.

Kim: "Strolling along Surfers Paradise at 5.45am the day after we arrived was lovely, but I can assure all of you that was a one-off! Since then I've been catching rays, swimming in the hotel's sea water lagoon, and wondering just how cold it will be once we hit our beloved Blighty." [3]

The last show in Sydney happened the day after the English rugby team won A World Cup semi-final against France. They would go on to win the competition on 22 November. The match was watched by Ricky, Kim's manager Nick Boyles and Go West at the Telstra Stadium, Kim doing a national TV show straight after. The next night, the Here and Now tour lit up Sydney's Entertainment Centre.

Kim: "The mood at the venue was predictably frisky, especially as word got round that the very lads we'd been cheering the night before were coming to watch us - apparently they'd spotted the advert in the local paper when they arrived in Sydney the previous week!" [4]

In December, the Here & Now Greatest Hits tour took place in the UK. Starting on 12 December at the Hallam FM Arena in Sheffield, the tour went to Brighton (13 December), Cardiff (14 December), Newcastle (17 December), Manchester (18 December), London (19 December) and finally Birmingham (20 December). This time, the line-up was even more impressive, with 10 artists taking to the stage: China Crisis, T'Pau's Carol Decker, Curiosity Killed the Cat's Ben Volpeliere-Pierrot, Nick Heyward, Heaven 17, Howard Jones, Five Star, ABC's Martin Fry, Kim Wilde, and Paul Young.

The tour was a feast for the audiences. China Crisis opened with 'Christian', 'Black Man Ray' and 'Wishful Thinking'. Carol Decker belted out 'Heart & Soul', 'Sex Talk' and 'China in Your Hands', then Ben Volpeliere-Pierrot performed 'Name & Number', 'Misfit' and 'Hang on in There Baby'. Nick Heyward got the audiences on their feet with 'Favourite Shirts', 'Blue Hat For A Blue Day' and 'Fantastic Day', then Heaven 17 brought the house down with extended versions of 'Penthouse & Pavement', 'Come Live With Me' and 'Temptation'. The first part of the concert ended with Howard Jones performing 'Things Can Only Get Better', 'Like to Get to Know You Well', 'New Song' and 'What is Love'.

After the break, it was a welcome return for Denise, Lorraine and Stedman Pearson from Five Star with 'Can't Wait Another Minute', 'The Slightest Touch', 'Rain or Shine' and 'System Addict'. Martin Fry sang 'Poison Arrow', 'Tears Are Not Enough', 'When Smokey Sings' and 'The Look Of Love', then Kim Wilde performed six of her biggest hits: 'Chequered Love', 'Never Trust A Stranger', 'You Came', 'You Keep Me Hangin' On', 'Rockin' Around the Christmas Tree' and 'Kids in America'. Finally, evening headliner Paul Young sang 'Wherever I Lay My Hat', 'Love of the Common People', 'Come Back and Stay' and 'Everytime You Go Away'.

CHAPTER 16: CUMBRIAN FELLSIDE GARDEN

'She sent the crowd into raptures with her five songs,' said the Manchester Online website [5] The Evening Chronicle added: 'It was only when Kim Wilde took to the stage that things really took off'. [6]

Kim: "I still do a bit of singing, with the Eighties tours last year, but they were very much on my terms, just two or three weeks - not months on the road with schedules that leave you feeling half-dead. It has been fun meeting up with the old crew, but I'm not selling a record and there's no pressure of trying to prove myself to anyone." [7]

But gardening was very much still part of Kim's life. Together with Richard Lucas, Kim designed a garden called A Lifetime Ahead in Spalding, Lincolnshire, inspired by issues of global warming. Opening in spring 2004, it was one of five permanent show gardens at Springfields Festival Gardens. The gardens were completely redeveloped in conjunction with the local horticultural society, a charity dedicated to the improvement and growth of horticulture and floral design in the region.

They also worked together on a garden called Wonderland for the Garden Festival at Holker Hall, Barrow, Cumbria, in June 2004. Like All About Alice before it, Alice in Wonderland inspired this garden. The garden involved a 10m circle divided into quarters, each displaying different elements of the story: the Mad Hatters Tea Party, the Queen of Hearts, the Chess Match and Magic Mushroom Garden.

Then, on 20 June, Kim flew to Germany for a one-off concert in Gaisbach, part of a line-up with Dave Dee, Dozy, Beaky, Mick & Tich, and Bonnie Tyler. This time, Ricky wasn't on stage with Kim, as he was attending a wedding. Still, it was a 14-song set, the longest Kim Wilde concert of the year.

A one-off Here & Now show in Bournemouth took place on 31 July at the Fitness First Stadium. Go West, Paul Young, Belinda Carlisle, ABC and The Human League were also there, and Ricky joined not only Kim, but also Belinda Carlisle on stage, playing guitar.

In December, Kim participated in the Here & Now tour across the UK for the fourth time. This time they started in Sheffield on 10 December, going on to Birmingham (11 December), Newcastle (14 December), Manchester (15 December), London (16 December), Plymouth (17 December) and finally Brighton (18 December). Artists performing were Limahl, Living in a Box, Bucks Fizz, Nik Kershaw, Belinda Carlisle, Kim Wilde, and Midge Ure.

Limahl opened a three-hour show with Kajagoogoo hits 'Too Shy' and 'Ooh to Be Aah' then solo hit 'The NeverEnding Story'. Living in a Box performed 'Blow the House Down', 'Room in Your Heart' and 'Living in a Box'. The original line-up of Bucks Fizz performed 'New Beginning (Mamba Seyra)', 'My Camera Never Lies', 'Run For Your Life', 'Piece of the Action', 'If You Can't Stand the Heat', 'The Land of

Make Believe' and 'Making Your Mind Up', then it was time for Nik Kershaw with 'Wide Boy', 'The Riddle', 'I Won't Let the Sun Go Down On Me' and 'Wouldn't It Be Good'. Belinda Carlisle followed with 'Live Your Life Be Free', 'I Get Weak', '(We Want) The Same Thing', 'Circle in the Sand', 'Leave A Light On' and 'Heaven is a Place On Earth'.

Kim's set consisted of 'Chequered Love', 'Never Trust a Stranger', a medley of 'Cambodia' and 'If I Can't Have You', 'Rockin' Around the Christmas Tree', 'You Came', 'You Keep Me Hangin' On' and of course 'Kids in America'.
And then headliner Midge Ure performed 'Hymn', 'Fade To Grey', 'If I Was', 'No Regrets', 'Love's Great Adventure', 'Vienna' and 'Dancing With Tears In My Eyes', before all the artists reappeared on stage for finale 'Do They Know It's Christmas?', the audience singing along.

The reviews were, again, positive for Kim: in the *Manchester Evening News*, Gary Ryan wrote: "Kim Wilde emerges as the night's highlight, torpedoing around the stage in a leather catsuit. Entering to the dramatic sweep of 'Never Trust a Stranger', flanked by brother Ricky on guitar, she has nothing to prove, but with rousing tracks like 'You Came', somehow proves it anyway."[8] David Dunn and Graham Walker from *The Star* added: "Kim Wilde is better known to the younger generation as a gardener but for a few lively minutes last night the mum-of-two was back in pop and looking good on it." [9]

Kim: "My life is completely absurd. One minute I'm in front of thousands of people going mad in a top slashed to my navel, and the next I'm sitting in Wyevale Garden Centre signing autographs for people who want to know what's wrong with their Ficus benjamina, and there's a life-size Noddy scaring all the children. I sit there and think, my life is bizarre; sometimes like a black comedy. And everything I ever wanted." [10]

In November it was announced that Wyevale had signed up Kim Wilde as the face of their chain of garden centres. She was to open new and refurbished centres and feature in their biggest ad campaign: on TV, radio and in the written press. The campaign started in 2005, Wyevale also selling a plant named after her. The Sweet Pea Kim Wilde had pretty lavender blue flowers with frilled petal edges.

Kim: "I'm absolutely thrilled with the idea of having a plant named after me. I take this as a great compliment to my hard work in gardening over the last few years. The Kim Wilde Sweet Pea is a stunning flower and I now have it growing in my own garden." [11]

In 2005, intensity was increasing for Kim's gardening pursuits. During the first half of 2004 Kim had been writing her first book. The manuscript was sent to the publisher in August, after which corrections and proofing had to take place. The book was finally published on 4 April 2005 by Collins publishers as *Gardening with Children*. It featured photographs of her children as well as Nick Boyles'

CHAPTER 16: CUMBRIAN FELLSIDE GARDEN

daughters, and Kim. Promotion for the book started a couple of weeks before the official release date on 22 March, Kim's first book signing session at Ottakar's bookshop in Milton Keynes, followed by appearances in several Wyevale garden centres.

Kim: "It's full of ideas and information in simple terms. There is so much to absorb in the garden, it can be a time for parents and children to connect." [12]

Kim: "I wanted to share my passion with my children. Writing *Gardening with Children* was really a logical step. I wanted to talk about my children and make a book with beautiful pictures of them. This was a great opportunity. My children didn't like posing for pictures, by the way. I had to promise them they would never have to go through this again." [13]

During one book signing session in Birmingham, she met an old friend.

Kim: "Roy Wood, I used to have a picture of him on my wall in my bedroom. Funnily enough, when I was wearing my gardening hat, I did a signing for a book I had out about gardening with children, I was up near Birmingham, and I was at the garden centre and he turned up! The people at the garden centre said, 'We can't believe it, Roy Wood's just come in!'. He had his pink sunglasses on and his long hair and his waistcoat on, his jacket, I nearly fell through the floor! (...) He came to see me!" [14]

The book was eventually translated into Dutch, German, French, Danish and Spanish. Two educational 'spinoffs' were published in Collins' Big Cat series: *Harry's Garden* and *How to Make a Scarecrow*, both based on chapters in the book.

Kim Wilde and Richard Lucas had worked on a few gardens together but started their design for the 2005 edition of the RHS Chelsea Flower Show in the summer of 2004. They started with the idea of recreating the Lake District, where Kim's parents-in-law live and where Richard had lived and worked for years.

Richard: "Kim and I first hit Chelsea last year and we had a good look around. In the car, on the way back from Chelsea, Kim scratched a little design of a garden on her leg and said, 'What about that?'" [15]

From that first sketch the Cumbrian Fellside Garden took shape.

Kim: "We used anything we could lay our hands on when we were designing it - bricks, a child's chair, the dead branch of a tree to suggest the height of our hawthorn tree, a bucket for the slate urn, all to give us an idea of the space and scale of our garden." [16]

They gave their scale model to artist Judith Glover, in part because Wilde greatly admired her watercolour-filled notebooks when they followed the same Plants and Planting Design course at Capel Manor. With her impression of the garden, the design was submitted for the Chelsea Flower Show. By the end of 2004, it was accepted. Things started to come together.

Top to bottom: Gold medal, Richard Lucas, Kim in her own garden © Katrien Vercaigne

Top to bottom: Kim in her own garden, together with Jessica, the Cumbrian Fellside Garden
© Katrien Vercaigne

Portrait of Kim, 2005 and scenes from the Cumbrian Fellside Garden © Katrien Vercaigne

Scenes from the Cumbrian Fellside Garden © Katrien Vercaigne

In fact, it was an astonishing feat that Kim managed to combine her gardening ambitions with her musical career. During the Here & Now tour in December 2004, she switched effortlessly between the two. On 11 December she played live in Birmingham – the second date of the tour – and worked on her Chelsea garden with Richard Lucas in the dressing room.

Kim: "2004 has been a busy year for me with writing my first book, *Gardening with Children*, as well as music festivals and garden shows in the summer. It's an odd mix of activities that's for sure, one minute designing gardens, the next squeezing into my leather pants! In fact in Birmingham I was doing just that as Richard Lucas, friend and gardener, pitched up with the planting plans we're submitting to the RHS for Chelsea Flower Show 2005, and we worked on that for an hour in my dressing room!" [17]

Richard and Kim visited Honister Slate Mine in Borrowdale – the only working slate mine in England – to select the green slate that would be incorporated in the design. They worked with Cumbrian artists to have sculptures made from slate. A stretch of chestnut post-and-rail fencing was built by Knebworth's expert woodsman and deerkeeper, Lloyd Watkins. He also made the wooden stile leading out of the garden. A 'largish trickle' of water tumbled down a rill, in an imitation of a fellside rivulet. All the slate, timber and willow were produced from sustainable sources or reclaimed materials.

A mature hawthorn stood at one corner, a native elder at the other, both from civic trees in Hertfordshire. The rear of the garden was filled mainly with wildflowers, the front planted with a spread of mostly herbaceous perennials by Claire Austin Hardy Plants in Shropshire and British Wildflower Plants of Norfolk. These included plants native to Cumbria. Old slate flagstones were inset with a 10cm-wide strip of polished slate bearing engraved words from a line of William Wordsworth's 1802 poem 'A Farewell': "Our spirits carrying with them dreams of flowers". And on her first visit to his Grasmere home, Rydal Mount, Kim read those words.

The attention to detail even stretched to the tangled rusty barbed wire with Cumbrian sheep's wool hanging on it.

Kim: "Everywhere you drive [in Cumbria] you see a bit of barbed wire with a bit of sheep wool on it. So Richard stopped the car, I jumped out, got the wool, brought it all the way down, so that's genuine Cumbrian wool there on the barbed wire." [18]

It all had to come together in the final days before the 2005 edition of the Chelsea Flower Show had its first day. Some of the plants weren't fully in bloom, so Kim even employed a hairdryer to give them some extra warmth. All the efforts paid off: on press day, the garden looked spectacular. And when the general public was allowed in, people passed by the garden in droves, clearly in awe of what they were seeing.

Kim and Richard described the garden in a leaflet available at the Chelsea Flower Show:

"Majestic fells, ancient lakes, Beatrix Potter, Wordsworth...each provide inspiration for this romantic Cumbrian Garden. The garden has been carved from a gently sloping plot in the Lake District. A constant trickle of water is guided gently through the garden by a rill, providing a simple and relaxing feature. The rear of the garden is still mostly wild, with nature being held back in its attempt to reclaim its former territory. Wildflowers grow in the long grass and in crevices within the drystone walls. The front of the garden is romantically planted with Aquilegia, Geranium, Linaria and Astrantia. Natural Cumbrian slates are put to use, both as flagstones and to retain the wildflower bank while a narrow pathway leads out of the garden over a stile and on to the fellside.

A living willow arbour provides a place to rest among the flowers. A contemporary slate sculpture, opposite, creates a focal point. Cumbrian slate sphere provides a balance and are echoed by the planting of clipped box balls. The garden is dominated by a hawthorn tree, whilst a native elder provides structure, height and maturity. All materials used in the garden such as slate, timber and willow are produced from sustainable sources, or are reclaimed materials, 25 percent of the garden is planted with native trees and flowers enhancing biodiversity in the garden. The Cumbrian Fellside Garden sets out to both work with, yet contrast against, the indisputable influence of Mother Nature herself." [19]

The garden still survives to this day as a digitised web production. All the flowers and ornaments were meticulously photographed and placed on Kim's fansite, wilde-life.com.

Their effort was rewarded with a gold medal and the title of Best Courtyard Garden. They received a third award, too: the BBC RHS people's vote award. For Kim, achieving this was an amazing feat, and she insisted it trumped all the awards she'd received during her music career.

Kim: "This is genuinely as thrilling as any hit record. For our work to be recognised in this way by our peers is as good as it gets." [20]

Of course, her children were less impressed. After having been away from home for two weeks, Kim phoned her daughter Rose on 24 May and asked if she wanted to come and see her garden. The answer was emphatic: it was no. She was more interested in it being 'one more sleep till Mummy comes home'. [21]

Kim: "Making time for the family of course is the most important thing. So, I hopped back from Chelsea last night after 10, 12 days of just really... I didn't even speak to the kids because I couldn't bring myself to it, it was too painful. I've left Richard at the garden today looking after it with the public and I've come home with the children and… they might not make it to school today." [22]

© Katrien Vercaigne

CHAPTER 17:

NEVER SAY NEVER

Released: 8 September 2006
Chart positions: 22 (Austria), 32 (Belgium), 30 (Finland), 22 (France), 17 (Germany), 32 (Netherlands), 11 (Switzerland)

During the summer of 2005, Kim didn't exactly rest on her laurels. After *Gardening with Children,* Kim had agreed to write a second book, to be published by Collins in 2006. This time around, she wrote it with Richard Lucas.

Writing was becoming increasingly important for Kim: she also wrote weekly gardening columns, syndicated to local newspapers across the UK; monthly gardening columns for *Healthy,* a magazine distributed by Holland & Barrett in their shops; and a set of monthly gardening columns for the magazine *Period House.*

Work on the book progressed while she was also working on new music. A few demos were recorded in 2004, including early versions of 'Baby Obey Me', 'I Fly' and 'Maybe I'm Crazy'.

Kim: "We are currently talking with a German record label. I'm going to start writing and recording new material very soon, which will be published next year. I guess what really spurred me on was working with Nena, seeing how successful her comeback has been. (...) My instinct also tells me it would be a good thing for me to do. (...) Most of the time they lead me in the right direction." [1]

At the beginning of 2006, it was reported that Kim had signed a contract with EMI for the release of a new album. Fans rejoiced, but their patience was tested for a while yet.

Up first was the release of *First-time Gardener,* on 3 April 2006. The book was all about the basics: how to create a garden that is fun to be in and easy to work with. Kim took the reader through every step from garden design to planting and keeping the garden in shape, ideal for those taking on a garden for the very first time.

Kim: "The book is based on my own experience of jumping in at the deep end without making adequate preparation and planning, which is the natural response of anyone who gets really excited in the spring, finds themselves in a garden centre and falls in love with a beautiful spring-flowering kerria or forsythia, gets home, puts it in the garden, then wonders why it doesn't look as beautiful as it did in the garden centre. The reason is that because in the

garden centre there were 20 other forsythias looking fantastic at the same time. I have fumbled through, made mistakes and tried to put my experiences into some coherent manner." [2]

Although the book could be read either as an instruction manual or a bundle of top tips, Kim added her personal touch by writing about her own experiences and appearing in the book herself on various photographs. Like *Gardening with Children* before it, the book was translated into many languages: in this case French, Spanish, Dutch and Estonian. Collins published a paperback edition a year after the original hardback version in the UK.

Between the release of the book and a new album, Kim did some book signings at garden centres in the UK and played a festival in Poland and Denmark. The latter was for A Day in the 80s festival in Esbjerg, in some ways the closing statement of an era. Kim and her band played for a full hour and performed all her biggest hits.

Never Say Never was finally released in September 2006. EMI released two versions of the CD: a single CD and a limited edition with a free bonus DVD, featuring two music videos of 'You Came (2006)' and an interview with Kim. The process of making the album was a lengthy one, as Kim explained in several interviews.

Kim: "It's been quite a long time in the making, this album. We started recording I think probably at Jeo Park in Hamburg, where I recorded 'Born to be Wild', and did some recording in London at my old recording studio, where I was signed to Mickie Most's RAK Records. That was an emotional experience, going back to the studio where it all began. Even though Mickie Most wasn't there, I felt he was around, watching over us." [3]

Kim's first new studio album since *Now & Forever* in 1995 was a media event, promoted heavily in Germany and the Netherlands, with appearances on TV programmes and days of interviews for the written media. The lead single 'You Came (2006)' was released three weeks before, long enough to feed the curiosity of the audiences but short enough to the able to promote the single and album simultaneously.

Promotion started in August in Belgium, with appearances for Radio 2 in Westende, popular music programme *Tien Om Te Zien*, filmed in Blankenberge, and a special appearance in summer programme *Zomer 2006*, filmed at the Royal Galleries in Oostende. Kim also appeared on popular German show *The Dome*, then spent two days in Amsterdam for interviews with radio DJs and the written press. In September, Kim visited France for more interviews and went to Finland with Ricky for a live appearance during a charity concert to benefit university hospitals for children. This busy schedule was mostly planned during weekdays,

CHAPTER 17: NEVER SAY NEVER

so Kim could be home at weekends. Kim was the famous person everyone knew, but back home had a private life, and the two had to exist separately.

However, the title of the new album, *Never Say Never*, was a bold statement.

Kim: "After I stepped away from my career, I thought 'I'll never return, I'll never go back into the music industry, I'll never do an Eighties retro thing, I'll never sing 'Kids in America' again'. I left the music business, got married and had two amazing children. But after doing the Eighties tours and really loving it, enjoying it and getting such an incredible reaction from audiences, I thought actually saying never is really dull. You should never say never, because life has a way of surprising you sometimes. My life took an amazingly different course after I got married. I enrolled at Horticultural College, became completely obsessed with plants, became a journalist and an author, even a gold medal winner at the Chelsea Flower Show. If someone had told me all that was going to happen, I'm not sure I would have believed them. Now I know I'll never say never again!"

Some of the songs from the album were debuted at the Stars for Free concert in Berlin on 2 September 2006. Her set consisted of 'I Fly', 'You Came', 'Together We Belong', 'Forgive Me', 'Perfect Girl' and 'Kids in America', all of which would appear on the LP. Backing vocals were performed by Sabrina Winter, who had become Kim's friend. Originally a fan of Kim, following her around with a group of friends known as the Crazy Gang, she was there at every live concert and TV performance during the 1980s. And a visit in 1989 led to a friendship that lasted for decades.

Meanwhile, Kim's website, kimwilde.com, was claimed and re-designed by her record company, EMI Germany, so the fansite created in 1998 had to switch addresses. While kimwilde.com reported all the latest news about the new release, wilde-life.com was the new home of the 'old' website, which by then had grown into a veritable archive of Kim's entire career, with photographs, videos and occasional exclusive interviews. From then on, Kim had an official website and official fansite.

Never Say Never, released on 8 September 2006, was produced by Uwe Fahrenkrog-Petersen, whom Kim had met via Nena.

Kim: "I first met Uwe and Nena back in the Eighties, doing TV with them, then one time they came over to England, to our studio. I suppose Uwe for Nena was what Ricky was for me, the musical maestro, the one without whom it could never have happened, and obviously watching Nena's amazing re-emergence, along with Uwe's fantastic production and writing and the way he's worked with her... But actually it was after meeting him that I knew he was the right guy for this project. I was fairly sceptical about making another album at all for a long time, before we started doing it. It was really only when I met Uwe

and he told me why he wanted to make the record and the ideas he had for it, I just knew it was in safe hands." [4]

As with other Kim Wilde albums, there was family involvement as well. Uwe recognised that one of the greatest things about Kim was Ricky Wilde, so he was involved in writing new songs. Also, Roxanne delivered vocals on 'Forgive Me'.

In October, fans were treated to something very different: an album by Sonic Hub, Ricky's side-project. Together with Rob Berwick and Sean Vincent he created a 13-song set, with a handful of special guests. Martin Fry from ABC appeared on 'New Man', which was also released as a single, Loretta Heywood (previously on tracks by Bomb The Bass and Adamski) sang on 'Never Knowing', Roxanne appeared on 'Colours', and Scarlett on 'My Open Mind'. Meanwhile, Hal Fowler did a beautiful recreation of an old Churchill speech (albeit with changed words) in 'Fact Destruction', and Kim sang opera-style vocals on 'The Hunt for Zero Point'.

Kim: "I remember when I first met Hal, he used to play me lots of different kinds of music I never sat down and listened to before. One of the things he used to play a lot was this beautiful music by Górecki [Symphony of Sorrowful Songs]. (...) So when Ricky asked me to do that I did think of Górecki and thought I'd like to do more of that sort of singing. I've got the sort of physical power now to find notes from that place where opera singers sing. I'm not trained in that way. But my husband Hal is very interested and can sing opera very well. It does interest me." [5]

A special appearance on European television screens happened in November 2006, as 80 to 90 million people saw Kim perform two songs on live television event *Domino Day*, an attempt to topple 4.4 million domino stones at the WTC Expo in Leeuwarden in the Netherlands on 17 November 2006. Kim also pushed the first stone, starting a successful record attempt that saw 4,079,381 stones toppled, setting a new world record that would last for two years.

Kim: "I've got some friends who live here in Holland and they told me all about how special it was and how much they look forward to seeing it all, and I feel really nervous now, 'cause I can't believe how hard this team has worked to do this over such a long period of time. They must have had fun too, but there must have been some pretty terrifying moments." [6]

Even more special was a live performance in the German town of Kirchbrombach on 10 December 2006. Radio station FFH organised a series of Christmas concerts with several artists during the month to raise money for homes for children with disabilities. Kim appeared in a church for a special acoustic performance, together with her band, consisting of Perry ap Gwynnedd, Nick Beggs and Ricky. She played some of her hits, but also traditional Christmas songs 'Silent Night' and 'Have Yourself A Merry Little Christmas'.

CHAPTER 17: NEVER SAY NEVER

The Perfect Girl tour followed in February and March 2007, Kim on the road with a band consisting of Nick Beggs (bass), Perry ap Gwynnedd (guitar), Steve Power (keyboards), Jonathan Atkinson (drums) and her siblings Ricky (guitar) and Roxanne (backing vocals). Fans were delighted, some of them never dreaming a tour would ever happen again.

Throughout the tour, every concert started with a recorded intro with samples from 'Kids in America', 'You Came', 'Never Trust A Stranger' and 'I Fly'.

The first date was in Paris on 20 February. It was a special one, with the opening act Sonic Hub, while Dan Peters' DJ set included samples from the album. During Kim's performance she gave the only live rendition of 'Someday' from the album *Love Moves*. Also, Rick's daughter Scarlett joined Roxanne on backing vocals. In Brussels (21 February), Kim did various interviews for the written press and TV before her show, and afterwards she met prize-winners, while several fans took the opportunity to talk with Kim and get pictures and autographs. The next day in Amsterdam, Kim performed live at the legendary Paradiso for the first time. After the first song, she tripped over an uneven spot on the stage, but pulled herself together quickly to launch into 'Chequered Love'. The ghosts of this former church still had their wicked old ways.

On 24 February, Kim gave a short performance at the Opernball in Frankfurt, set to play a short six-song set. But due to technical difficulties she had to stop after just one song, an electric shock ending her performance prematurely. The tour resumed in Copenhagen, her Danish audience treated to a dynamic live show, Kim and her band serenaded as they chanted the familiar tune of 'Cambodia' for several minutes mid-song.

After a short break back home in the UK, the tour resumed a week later in Germany, visiting Munich (4 March), Cologne (5 March), Hamburg (6 March) and Berlin (7 March). The setlist was tweaked a little, and the band considered it an improvement. The faithful German fans obviously agreed: there was loud applause each night. A large group of Polish fans appeared in Germany for their first Kim Wilde concert experience, and enjoyed every minute - especially on getting to meet Kim after the concert.

On 11 March, Kim and her band performed at the cosy Den Atelier in Luxembourg, where there was time to meet fans before, and Kim did interviews with media. Scarlett, who turned 18 two days earlier, joined Roxanne on stage for backing vocals again, like she had in Paris.

The final show for the first leg took place in Kosice, Slovakia, at the Steel Arena, with an estimated audience of 5000 – easily the biggest audience of the tour.

Kim: "It's just been fantastic. One of the most enjoyable tours I've ever done in my life. It's been quite short and sweet. (...) The band has been amazing and the whole team has been incredible. The crew that we have - we travel in

a party of 13 - we're all after the same result each night, making a fantastic gig. I'm back in front of an audience I haven't seen for quite a few years. I'm amazed at the warmth and depth of feeling I get from the audience, it's quite overwhelming sometimes." [7]

After the first leg of the tour ended, it was announced that Kim would appear on television for a celebration of the 50th anniversary of the EU. *Stars of Europe* was a live event in Brussels, broadcast all over Europe on 24 March 2007. She performed 'You Came' and 'Together We Belong'. A more spontaneous appearance happened later in the evening, when she joined former UB40 frontman Ali Campbell on stage to sing 'I Got You Babe'.

Ali: "This is the first time I've sung with Kim. No rehearsals - Kim's a consummate professional. We just turned up and did it." [8]

With Kim's music career back on track, Marty was also making an impact again. In March 2007, Universal records released a compilation album, *Born To Rock'n'Roll: The Greatest Hits* to commemorate his 50th year as a performer. The album contained 25 tracks, including new recording 'Sorry Seems to be the Hardest Word', performed with Kim, their first studio recording together.

Kim: "I think it was really long overdue. It was to honour the fact that he had been in rock'n'roll for 50 years, which is quite phenomenal." [9]

On 24 June 2007, Kim appeared at Parkpop, Europe's largest free pop festival, in The Hague on the last Sunday of June every year. Over 175.000 people were there, treated to an hour-long set. Other festivals were graced with her presence too: including the Kieler Woche in Kiel (Germany), Bospop in Weert (Netherlands), the Baltic Beach Party in Liepaja (Latvia) and the Langelandsfestival in Langeland (Denmark).

Kim: "We got a lot of gigs coming up in the summer, which I'm really looking forward to. I love being on stage now, playing live in front of audiences. And I feel physically and mentally in the best place I've ever been to do that." [10]

The Perfect Girl tour picked up at the end of October with 10 dates in Germany, one date in Austria and two dates in the Netherlands. This time around, one new song was introduced, 'Lay Your Weapons Down', one highly appreciated by fans but never recorded in the studio.

The support act for this part of the tour was Sabrina Winter's band Stereoblonde, but they had to cancel after a handful of dates due to unforeseen circumstances. Instead, Nick Beggs performed a set of songs with his Chapman Stick, including a rousing instrumental version of the Ellis, Beggs & Howard hit from the 1980s, 'Big Bubbles, No Troubles'.

On November 23 and 25, Kim Wilde performed live in Moscow and St Petersburg, as one of the performers in a festival called Discoteka 80s. Kim and her band used the opportunity to roam around Moscow, visiting Red Square and

CHAPTER 17: NEVER SAY NEVER

enjoying the snow-covered surroundings. It was the only time Kim performed in Russia.

At the end of 2007 Kim participated in ITV programme *Britain Sings Christmas*, in which a choir of celebrities and members of the public was brought together to sing Britain's favourite Christmas songs. The show was in aid of the Prince's Trust, with viewers invited to vote for their favourite Christmas song. On the final episode she sang 'Santa Claus is Coming to Town' together with actor and singer Ray Quinn, the choir backing them up.

Then, 2008 started with the announcement that Kim's younger sister Roxanne was to be wed that September, with boyfriend Richard Rizzo.

Roxanne: "Richie took me to Bruges, Belgium, and I didn't know anything. He'd taken Mum and Dad out before to ask them, so even they knew. He took me on a horse and carriage and asked me by the Lake of Love. I was so shocked I asked if it was a joke. Then, after I realised what he'd said, I said yes, without hesitation!" [11]

Roxanne joined Kylie Minogue on tour in May 2008, which meant that she wouldn't be available for Kim's concerts during the summer. She had already shared backing vocal duties with her niece Scarlett on some concerts in 2007, so Scarlett joined Kim's live band from 2008 onwards.

On 3 April 2008 Kim made a surprise appearance during a concert by Ali Campbell at the Royal Albert Hall in London. They reprised their performance of 'I Got You Babe', which eventually ended up on a DVD released in 2011. Other guests were Beverley Knight, Lemar, and Pato Banton.

The festival season came with a couple of surprises. On 3 July, Kim opened the 12th edition of the Wilkinson American Movie Day with a free concert at the De Brouckère Square in Brussels. During the event, several summer blockbusters like *Hancock*, *Mamma Mia* and *Wall-E* premiered in Belgium. Kim's performance featured guest star Born Crain, a Belgian singer who enjoyed considerable success in his homeland with his debut album the previous year. He was Kim's opening act, but the two also did duets during Kim's set on 'If I Can't Have You' and 'I Drove All Night'. Born Crain would go on to record a cover version of 'Kids in America' on 2012 album *Born in the USA*, and recorded an original duet with Kim on 'Superstars' for his 2013 album *Identity*.

Kim also appeared at the Polish Sopot festival for a third time, the 2008 edition featuring a celebration of music from the 1980s on the second day, with special guests Shakin' Stevens, Sandra, Samantha Fox, Limahl, Sabrina, Thomas Anders from Modern Talking, and Kim – all performing three or four songs.[12]

A new endeavour was Kim's job as a presenter at Magic 105.4 FM Radio. In September 2008 she started the show *Secret Songs* every Sunday, presenting songs that had a special, usually secret meaning for listeners. She also chose one song herself in every show, often a 1970s pop song.

Kim: "I'm a presenter now at Magic FM and get to choose a favourite song each week. I love to choose something from the Seventies. That teenage period, up to the age of 20, is a defining decade for anyone, and those songs take me straight back to those days." [13]

On 19 October 2008, Kim and Ricky appeared on stage at Nachtleben in Frankfurt, Germany, as special guests at Sabrina Winter's band Stereoblonde's 10th anniversary gig.

Sabrina Winter: "Kim and Ricky (and let's not forget about dear Marty Wilde here) kick-started my passion for music, songwriting and singing. So, I naturally gravitated towards the Wilde camp and I asked them. Kim and Ricky readily accepted the invite. What an honour and privilege that was for me. We agreed on performing 'Kids in America' and 'Top of the World', Stereoblonde's first single. With zero time to rehearse, apart from a little soundcheck, we were flying by the seat of our pants throughout. The performance was a lot of fun and well received by the audience. I felt as if I was on top of the world whilst Kim and I sang about it in one of our duets."

In November and December, Kim went on tour with the Nokia Night of the Proms in Germany, together with Dennis DeYoung from Styx, Graham Gouldman from 10CC, Robin Gibb from the Bee Gees, and Tears for Fears. Igudesman and Joo, the Angels of Harlem Gospel Choir, and the orchestra Il Novecento completed the line-up.

Kim: "I have made friends with Igudesman and Joo, the mad and brilliant comedy duo, who tear around the stage, breathing new life into the classical concept. I am delighted too to be working with Trevor Murrell, who drummed on my very first album and toured with me from my first tour - we have a lot to catch up on!" [14]

While the tour was great fun and Kim certainly enjoyed the German Christmas markets and restaurants, it was also hard being separated from her family for a whole month. Three weeks into the tour, Hal and the children came over to Munich for a weekend, to the city where the tour stopped for four consecutive nights at the Olympiahalle, Harry and Rose came up on stage with all the other artists for the finale.

Kim: "They all really loved the show, and Rose and Harry got up on stage with us all for the finale, 'Imagine' and 'Give Peace a Chance'. Rose made me repeat the words to 'Give Peace a Chance' over and over again so she wouldn't get them wrong - what a professional!" [15]

In March 2009, Kim embarked on a new 14-date live tour, mostly in Germany and Denmark, but finishing with concerts in Amsterdam, Luxembourg and Paris.

CHAPTER 17: NEVER SAY NEVER

German newspapers had nothing but praise for Kim and her band. In a review of the first gig in Munich, the *Süddeutsche Zeitung* wrote: 'The fact that the whole never really comes into nostalgic waters lies on the one hand to the well-rehearsed band, but still more because of an obviously lighthearted, well-presented Kim, who is at ease with her age and her image.' [16] The *Mannheimer Morgen* wrote: 'The Capitol in Mannheim, almost sold out, is jubilant right at the beginning of the nearly two-hour show, and one has to look twice to believe the energy and enthusiasm that has become so rare during concerts these days.'[17] The *Allgemeine Zeitung* concluded: "It was certain that they would get their fans hopping with their classics, but the remaining repertoire caused excessive uncontrolled wriggle into the cosy world of sound, good humour, rock music." [18]

The Here and Now tour followed in May 2009. Headliner Boy George's legal problems meant he had to pull out a few months before, but he was replaced by Rick Astley. Together with Howard Jones, Kid Creole & the Coconuts, Clare Grogan, Brother Beyond and Hazel O'Connor, they toured the UK between 14 and 23 May, visiting Liverpool, Manchester, Nottingham, Cardiff, Newcastle, Birmingham and London.

And during the summer, there were a handful of festival concerts in Germany, Belgium and the Netherlands, before a return to the studio for work on a new album.

PERFECT GIRL
Written by Uwe Fahrenkrog-Petersen & Ricky Wilde
Produced by Uwe Fahrenkrog-Petersen & Gena Wernick
Released: 17 November 2006
Chart position: 52 (Germany)

Although Kim didn't write the song, she could certainly relate to its message. Not one to be narcissistic, she exclaims 'It's not me!' repeatedly during the course of this track. Just to underline that she saw herself as far from perfect.
Kim: "I am perfectly imperfect. I think there is too much pressure on women to be 'perfect', more than ever, especially with social media, and it affects young girls most of all. I'm flying the flag for all women to be themselves, and not try to conform to anyone else's concept of beauty!" [19]

The song was released as the second single from *Never Say Never* after fans declared it the best choice in a poll on her official website. Besides a shorter radio version, the CD-single came with two remixes. The 'Perfect Chill mix' was created by Groovenut, whereas the 'Elektrika mix' was created by Ian Finch.
Ian Finch: "What I attempted to capture in my remix was the power of the chorus and verses, such great lyrics and very meaningful at the same time.

By putting those warm synth strings behind the vocals, it elevates what she says, making it feel like she's belting it out. By putting the echo effects (delay) to the vocals, it gives them a huge atmospheric feel, which when played in a club, reverberates around the room... It sounds amazing if you are there." [20]

The video for 'Perfect Girl' was filmed in Germany and directed by Sandra Marschner. Shots of Kim and her band performing the track alternate with shots of Kim and a group of girls dressed in pink blouses and a white heart with the word 'perfect' on it.

YOU CAME (2006)
Written by Ricky & Kim Wilde
Produced by Uwe Fahrenkrog-Petersen & Derek von Krogh
Released: 18 August 2006
Chart positions: 24 (Austria), 33 (Belgium), 20 (Germany), 26 (Netherlands), 25 (Sweden), 19 (Switzerland)

In July, promotion for Kim's new album started with the release of 'You Came (2006)', a re-recording of her 1988 hit single, produced by Uwe Fahrenkrog-Petersen. Although the new LP consisted of eight new tracks and six re-recordings, EMI were very clear they wanted the lead single to be one of the re-recordings.

The video, directed by Phil Griffin, was full of references to Kim's career. In it, she's wearing different clothes, such as a black and white striped t-shirt (referring to Kim's first video, 'Kids in America'), a backless dress (emulating the leather dress worn for 'Love Blonde') and a long necklace (as seen in 'Say You Really Want Me'). Also, the microphone stand was embellished with a red scarf. Kim explained this in an interview at the time.

Kim: "When I was on Michael Jackson's Bad tour in 1988 it was my way of claiming the stage prior to him coming on. So although I was opening for Michael Jackson, it was just my way of coming on stage and I used to get my red scarf and tie it to the microphone. Just to say, 'It's me, now. If you don't like it: tough, I'm staying for the next half an hour. Get your heads around it." [21]
Kim: "It has references to the past, visual references. Small things, like the red scarf that I tie on the microphone, which I did during the Michael Jackson tour, then of course the stripy top I wore in the 'Kids in America' video. We make a reference to that as well, the dinner jacket, but it's very much Kim Wilde in the 21st century having some fun." [22]

At the end of the video, she is seen kissing her husband Hal. In interviews, she explained that 'You Came' was originally written for Ricky's first-born child, but this version was dedicated to Hal.

CHAPTER 17: NEVER SAY NEVER

Kim: "I think they say never work with animals, children and husbands (laughs). So actually it was a really fun experience and I couldn't have kissed anybody else like that. Well, I wouldn't have wanted to, and he's got a beautiful face, so I wanted to show him off really." [23]

TOGETHER WE BELONG
Written by Uwe Fahrenkrog-Petersen, Ricky & Kim Wilde
Produced by Uwe Fahrenkrog-Petersen, Derek von Krogh
Released: 30 March 2007

This song is a declaration of love, although it does come with the warning that even a long-term relationship is not without ups and downs. '*We know and we both understand / We hold the fire in our hands / But every fire's bound to have its sparks*'.

Released as the third single from the album, the radio edit was cut short by 30 seconds. There were no added remixes and no music video. Kim performed the song during two high-profile occasions on TV: on the *Domino Day* broadcast in November 2006 and *Stars of Europe* in March 2007.

FORGIVE ME
Written by Uwe Fahrenkrog-Petersen, Gena Wernik & Kim Wilde
Produced by Uwe Fahrenkrog-Petersen & Gena Wernik

'Forgive Me' is a song about the environment, a theme that cropped up on previous Kim Wilde albums. Kim's younger sister Roxanne contributed backing vocals, the repeated line '*What have you done to me*' representing the planet. The lyrics spell out '*The world is sending an SOS to us all / is sending an SOS, but her call / is lost in our greed for having it all*', and you can't help wonder why this fact is not more widely recognised.

Kim: "It's one of the saddest songs on the album. We must ask for forgiveness for all the devastation we have done to our beautiful planet. We have to take responsibility for global warming. It breaks my heart when I see the destruction mankind continually inflicts on our natural world." [24]

Kim: "So how do you find the voice for a planet? I would say there's an innocence to Roxanne's voice, a fragility, but strength as well. I felt she had the perfect voice for the part that talked back to humanity: '*What have you done to me, why don't you look after me?*'"

'Forgive Me' was performed live on only one occasion: during a concert in Berlin on 2 September 2006, when a selection of songs from the album were performed live for the first time.

Kim and Roxanne Wilde backstage at Den Atelier, Luxembourg, 11 March 2007 © Katrien Vercaigne

Kim live with Perry ap Gwynnedd, Luxembourg, 11 March 2007 © Marcel Rijs

Kim & band live at La Cigale, Paris (France), 8 April 2009 © Katrien Vercaigne

Kim live at Kulturbrauerei, Berlin (Germany), 7 March 2007
© Marcel Rijs

Kim backstage at Den Atelier, Luxembourg, 11 March 2007

FOUR LETTER WORD (2006)
Written by Ricky & Marty Wilde
Produced by Uwe Fahrenkrog-Petersen & Derek von Krogh

'Never Say Never' was criticised by some for its inclusion of remakes of songs that were already quite perfect in their original incarnations. 'Four Letter Word' was identified as the most obvious culprit: although the sound was updated, it was basically a repeat of the original version. There is nothing wrong with the recording, but it doesn't surprise the listener.

YOU KEEP ME HANGIN' ON (2006)
Written by Brian Holland, Lamont Dozier & Eddie Holland
Produced by Uwe Fahrenkrog-Petersen, Gena Wernik & Derek von Krogh

Kim Wilde appeared on the album *Nena Feat. Nena* for a re-recording of one of Nena's old hits and Nena returned the favour on a re-recording of 'You Keep Me Hangin' On'. The original version - a snippet of which sneaked out on a Swedish music website in 2006 - channelled the Eurythmics' 'Sweet Dreams (Are Made Of This)', but the final version that appears on the album was harder to pin down.

In 2007, another version – without Nena's vocals – appeared on an American promotional CD, featuring an intro similar to the original Supremes version and a rather funky music track.

BABY OBEY ME
Written by Robert Ellis Orrall, Jeff Coplan, Kim & Ricky Wilde
Produced by Jeff Coplan
Released: 3 August 2007

'Baby Obey Me' had gone through different versions, until It finally became a reggae-tinged track.
Kim: "It was one of the first songs we selected for the album. It passed by many versions and at the beginning was very different from what it is today. I really had fun with the words, sometimes funny but also serious, because I actually wrote it right after I married, 10 years ago."
Kim: "When my husband and I got married, we swore to do certain things for the rest of our lives. To say 'Baby Obey me' is my way to remind him of those oaths. The song is more playful, although I take my marriage seriously. My husband is very independent. I could never make him obey me, if he didn't want to himself." [26]

CHAPTER 17: NEVER SAY NEVER

Almost a year after the release of the album, 'Baby Obey Me' was released as the fourth single. On that version, there is a guest appearance by rapper Ill Inspecta (real name: Kahlil Lechelt), the release prompted by a TV appearance of the pair on German programme *Ballermann Hits*. Ill Inspecta's career was relatively short: a year after the release of 'Baby Obey Me' he announced his own 'death' via a Myspace page, finding a new career as a web developer in Stuttgart.

Although the single did not chart, the CD-single was notable for the inclusion of two live tracks – the first ever released officially by Kim. 'Enjoy the Silence', a cover version of the Depeche Mode hit, and 'Kids in America' were recorded at the Ancienne Belgique in Brussels on 21 February 2007.

KIDS IN AMERICA (2006)
Written by Ricky & Marty Wilde
Produced by Uwe Fahrenkrog-Petersen & Derek von Krogh

The re-recording of 'Kids in America' featured vocals and guitar by Charlotte Hatherley, a former member of the band Ash, whose debut solo album featured a track called 'Kim Wilde' in 2004. She also performed 'Kids in America' live during some of her concerts in 2005, and became a logical choice for an appearance on this track.

Kim: "We asked her to do guitar and she turned up in the studio and I, at the time, was having a bit of a problem with 'Kids in America', because I couldn't quite get my head around the fact that I was recording it again after all these years. (...) Charlotte was due to play guitar that day and I thought, 'You know what, 'Kids in America' would make sense for me if she sings it too'. So when she turned up, I said, 'Would you sing 'Kids in America'?' and she said, 'Sure, I'll do backing vocals'. And I said, 'No, no... not backing vocals - I want you to sing it'. She looked shocked... 'Oh God, you know, I would love to, but you are going to have to go shopping, because I'm not doing it with you in the studio.' So I went shopping that afternoon, instead of being there, and let her get on with it. When I got back and heard what she'd done, I was so happy. Charlotte had brought 'Kids in America' back to life for me again as a new recording." [27]

Kim appeared live on stage in Westende (Belgium) for Radio 2 in August 2006. While she was singing live on stage, the radio programme broadcast a solo version of 'Kids in America (2006)' in which Kim sings all the verses herself. That version was never released officially.

I FLY
Written by Robert Ellis Orrall & Jeff Coplan
Produced by Uwe Fahrenkrog-Petersen & Derek von Krogh

Kim's fans first heard a few lines of 'I Fly' on German TV programme *Blitz*, broadcast on 2 June 2006. They had to wait until the release of 'Never Say Never' two months later to hear the whole thing.

The lyrics are staccato, full of short words delivered on a high energy pop/rock track.

Kim: "I like 'I Fly' a lot. It's a very sexy pop song, and I think it contains lots of interesting ideas to make a good video." [28]

Kim did hope that 'I Fly' would become a single at some point, but that didn't happen. She performed the song live during the Perfect Girl tour in 2007.

GAME OVER
Written by Ricky Wilde & Steve DuBerry
Produced by Uwe Fahrenkrog-Petersen & Derek von Krogh

If 'I Fly' was high energy, 'Game Over' turns the beat up a notch and delivers quick drums and stabs of guitar chords. Fahrenkrog-Petersen created a sped-up version of Nena's old hit 'Nur Geträumt' ('Just a Dream'). The lyrics are about standing tall despite criticism from the outside world.

The song was performed live during the Perfect Girl tour in 2007 and summer festival performances in 2008.

LOST WITHOUT YOU
Written by Ricky Wilde & Steve DuBerry
Produced by Uwe Fahrenkrog-Petersen & Derek von Krogh

Easily the most dramatic song on the album, 'Lost Without You' has a beautiful melody and soaring vocals by Kim. According to Martin Schlögl in the *Frankfurther Neue Presse*, the song was 'filled with melodrama' and looked 'likely to be a single sooner or later'. [29]

VIEW FROM A BRIDGE (2006)
Written by Ricky & Marty Wilde
Produced by Uwe Fahrenkrog-Petersen & Gena Wernik

The last re-recording of the album is an updated version of 'View From a Bridge', with the music created entirely electronically, aside from guitar stabs performed by Jörg Sander, one of Germany's most sought-after session guitarists, who also played on 'Four Letter Word (2006)', 'Forgive Me' and 'Maybe I'm Crazy'.

MAYBE I'M CRAZY
Written by Ricky Wilde, Ken Thomas & Carolynne Good
Produced by Uwe Fahrenkrog-Petersen & Gena Wernik

With a chorus that sounds a bit like Kylie's 'On a Night Like This', 'Maybe I'm Crazy' is one of the poppiest tracks on the album. It was included on the CD-single for 'You Came (2006)', a few weeks before the release of 'Never Say Never'.

THE HUNT FOR ZERO POINT (with Sonic Hub)
Written by Sean Vincent & Ricky Wilde
Produced by Sean Vincent & Ricky Wilde

The song was written after Sean Vincent read the book of the same name, written by Nick Cook in 2002. The book details one man's journey to discover the truth behind the myth that is 'anti-gravity' propulsion and the associated technologies.

When it came to writing songs for Sonic Hub's 2006 album *Eye of the Storm*, Sean had already persuaded Ricky to read the book, and before long Sean had the basics of 'Zero Point' recorded. He wanted to create a piece that captured the mystery, underhand dealing and downright weirdness of the book's awesome story. With Ricky's help, Sean feels he captured exactly that.

When it came to adding a vocal, Sonic Hub knew they wanted to continue their theme of taking artists out of their comfort zone, which is why they asked Kim to do the opera-style vocal.

Sean actually met Nick Cook in January 2007. They talked about the book and Sean gave Nick a copy of the album. Nick Cook responded: "I was amazed when Sean first wrote to me to say that Sonic Hub had produced a track inspired by 'The Hunt for Zero Point', but, then again, the book does seem to have had an impact on people. I'd never have guessed that when I sat down to write it five years ago. I love the track, am very happy that Kim Wilde is featured on it, and think it captures the essence of the book - a mixture of the sense of wonder, mystery, threat and hope that I felt when I went out on the road to research it."

SORRY SEEMS TO BE THE HARDEST WORD (with Marty Wilde)
Written by Elton John & Bernie Taupin
Released: 5 March 2007

Recorded by Elton John in 1976 for his album *Blue Moves*, his version became a top-10 hit all over Europe and reached No.6 in the US Billboard Hot 100 singles chart. It was certified gold in Canada and the United States.

On 1 April 1987, Marty, Ricky and Kim took to the stage during the Action for AIDS concert at Wembley in London to perform this song live. Although they didn't record the song in the studio at that time, they did 20 years later, when Marty celebrated his 50th year in the music business. The song was included on the compilation *Born to Rock'n'Roll*. This album reached No.19 in the UK – Marty's first appearance in that chart.

Kim and Marty performed the song together on ITV's *GMTV* in the UK on 4 April 2007. When Marty did a concert at the London Palladium on 27 May 2007, Kim joined Marty on stage for another live performance of the song, that concert subsequently released on DVD.

CHASING CARS (live performance)
Written by Gary Lightbody, Nathan Connolly, Tom Simpson, Jonny Quinn & Paul Wilson.

Snow Patrol lead singer Gary Lightbody apparently wrote 'Chasing Cars' after becoming sober, following a binge of white wine, while sat in the garden of producer Jacknife Lee's cottage in Kent. The phrase 'Chasing Cars' was inspired by his father in reference to a girl he was infatuated with: "You're like a dog chasing a car. You'll never catch it and you wouldn't know what to do with it if you did." [30]

Kim and her band performed the song during 2007's Perfect Girl tour, the song made even more beautiful by Steve Power's keyboard parts and Ricky, Roxanne and Kim's harmonies on the chorus.

LAY YOUR WEAPONS DOWN (live performance)
Written by Curtis Richardson, Ella Soza & Ricky Wilde

'Lay Your Weapons Down' is one of just a few songs Kim performed live but never recorded in the studio. It was presented during the second leg of the Perfect Girl tour, in the autumn of 2007, and performed as an acoustic song by Kim and her entire band.

The lyrics can be taken literally as a quest for peace, but on a more personal level could refer to a truce within a relationship. '*Like a war that rages on and on / We're running on a path to nowhere / Lay your weapons down*'.

CHAPTER 17: NEVER SAY NEVER

ENJOY THE SILENCE (live performance)
Written by Martin L. Gore

One of Depeche Mode's main songwriters, Martin Gore, originally recorded 'Enjoy the Silence' as a ballad. When band member Alan Wilder insisted the song should be up-tempo, it was reworked and recorded for the album *Violator*, and released as the second single from that album. Supported by a remarkable music video directed by Anton Corbijn and several remixes, the song became a worldwide hit, going top 5 in most European countries, No.6 in the UK and No.8 in the US.

Kim and her band performed a version during the Perfect Girl tour in 2007 and subsequent tours in 2008, 2009 and 2012. A recording from Ancienne Belgique in Brussels on 21 February 2007 was released on the CD-single for 'Baby Obey Me' in August 2007.

RUN TO YOU (with Fibes Oh Fibes!)
Written by Christian Olsson, Mathias Nilsson & Linda Sundblad
Produced by Mathias Nilsson & Christian Olsson
Released: 2 September 2009
Chart position: 24 (Sweden)

An unexpected collaboration happened in the summer of 2009, Kim joining Swedish band Fibes Oh Fibes! for the song 'Run to You'. Frontman Christian Olsson explained that the album *1987* – on which the song appeared – was named after his favourite year in pop. The song was recorded in May at RAK Studios in London and released as a single (digital download only) in September.

Kim visited Sweden in September for a short promotional trip, during which she performed the song live during TV programme *Sommarkrysset*.

INTERVIEW: SABRINA WINTER

How did you first become a fan of Kim Wilde?
It was in 1981 and I was a 13-year-old, insecure teenager, living with nuns in a children's home, having to deal with the loss of both parents at such a tender age. Like most teens, I was in need of someone to look up to, someone to guide me through my youth and all the insecurities and changes that naturally come with it. I wanted to be different, but wanted to fit in at the same time. I had no clue of what or who I wanted to be, what I wanted to stand for, which routes to follow and what my style was or could be.

On one of our annual school trips, my friend Jagoda let me have use of her Walkman. On her cassette tape was a song called 'Kids in America'. When I heard Kim's unique voice for the first time I was totally hooked and couldn't stop rewinding and replaying the tune; until the batteries ran out. A few days later she gave me a *Bravo* poster with Kim on it and said, *"This is the singer of your new favourite song. I thought you might like to have this."* And there she was: a stunningly beautiful young woman. Strong. Confident. Rebellious. Different! Everything I wanted to be. My role model. My muse. And a 'Sweetest of all Darlings' to me in the years to come. Who would have thought back then? Certainly not my 13-year-old me.

You started seeing Kim live whenever she was in Germany. When did this start and what were those first concerts like for you?

My very first concert ever was Kim Wilde in 1983 in Offenbach on the Catch tour. For two years, Kim was this idea of a person I had created in my mind; fed by press articles, posters, video clips and TV performances. She was almost like a comic character. Barbarella and Wonder Woman morphed into one, refined by a rock'n'roll look. It hit me like a freight train wrapped up in cotton wool when I saw Kim in flesh and blood on stage only a few metres away from me in the second row. I couldn't believe that she was a real person. The first few songs I watched through a natural filter of joyful tears. What an amazing performer she was. But more importantly she seemed very sweet, funny and kind.

After the gig, I was told that Kim may meet a few of the fans backstage. To be allowed to go to the show I had to promise the nuns that I would make my way back home straight after the gig. Now I had to choose between sticking to my promise and possibly missing out on meeting Kim or facing some trouble back home if I stayed. Needless to say, I went for trouble. It was well rewarded, as I got to meet Kim for the very first time. She was so lovely, and I had my favourite live photo signed by her to take home and cherish. It went straight on to my bedroom wall, next to my blue Catch tour scarf I had purchased at the gig and uncountable posters. Oh, and yes, I was grounded for two weeks for coming home late. Sacrifices have to be made sometimes.

How did the group of fans known as the Crazy Gang come to be (and who were they)?

I not only met Kim for the first time back in 1983 but also Peter. Alongside Domenica (still my bestie), Sylka, Manu and myself, Peter was an early member of our fan group that we 'formed' in 1986. He is one of my dearest friends to this day and also Kim's trusted German press promoter, and has been for many, many years now.

Whenever Kim touched German soil to promote her latest releases or toured in Germany, our group, soon to be known as Crazy Gang, wasn't far away. Long car journeys, dodgy hotel rooms, car breakdowns and expensive car towing due to unauthorised parking - one was in a hurry - we did it all. TV shows were our

CHAPTER 17: NEVER SAY NEVER

favourites as they were so hard to get into. We loved a challenge! I even remember hiding in a toilet cabin for about an hour to join the Formel Eins after-show party... Uninvited, of course!

In 1988 an informer who shall remain anonymous, working for Kim's German record company, told us she would be coming to Cologne on a short promotional trip soon and she would be staying at the Ramada Hotel. So, there we were, sitting in the hotel bar, sipping on overprized soft drinks (well, there might have been the odd glass of wine involved) as Kim suddenly walked by. She´d already spotted us and laughed and shouted, 'You are such a crazy gang'. And there it was... our name.

One of my most treasured memories is when we were invited to her then-apartment (the one in the 'Hey Mister Heartache' video) on her birthday; and with a little help from our friend, Edwina (before she handed the 'dealing with that crazy lot' baton over to Mel). Over the years, a few more fans and friends such as Tommy, Angi, Eric, Bärbel, Carmen and Ian joined our gang. With most of them, I am still friends. Occasionally we get to see each other at Kim shows in Germany. But those days when we all travelled together to attend every single show are long gone. Blame this boring adult life! We had such a brilliant time, and all these memories will stay forever in my heart.

How did you eventually become friends?

It's hard to say when exactly Kim and I became friends, as it was a slow and sliding process. When Kim decided to focus on her gardening projects and spend more time with her family, she stopped performing throughout that period. In the meantime, I signed a record deal with my band, Stereoblonde, released an album and started a second career as a radio PR manager in the music industry.

If there ever was such a turning point, it could possibly be the day Kim performed at The Dome in Leipzig in 2006. My best friend, Reno and I were in a taxi on our way to the venue when a car crashed into the side of our taxi. I ended up in an ambulance, taking me to the nearest hospital. Thankfully I got away with my body covered in bruises, a massive headache and whiplash. It was quite painful, but as we already missed out on the TV show, Reno and I accepted a kind invitation to meet Kim and (ex-manager) Nick Boyles at the hotel bar for a drink (or two). So, we went straight from the hospital to the hotel bar. There obviously was still enough of the old craziness in me. We showed up at the bar, me wearing a rather unflattering cervical collar, my eye make-up smeary and not where it was supposed to be. I must have looked absolutely ridiculous. When Kim saw me, she released a little squeaky but shocked kind of sound. She said to me: "I can't believe this. You are the second friend of mine this week that had a car accident on the way to meet me." This is the first time I remember her saying my name and the word 'friend' in combination. I felt that was a very special moment.

*Kim live at Night of the Proms, TUI Arena Hannover (Germany), 18 December 2008.
© Katrien Vercaigne*

Badges sold during the Perfect Girl Tour in 2007 © Marcel Rijs

Kim live at Oosterpoort, Groningen (Netherlands), 15 November 2007 © Katrien Vercaigne

Kim live at Ancienne Belgique, Brussels (Belgium), 21 February 2007 © Katrien Vercaigne

You ended up singing backing vocals for Kim on a few occasions. What was that like?

Inspired by Kim, I started singing and songwriting when I was about 16. Whenever I had the chance, I played her my newest songs. She listened patiently and gave me her honest and very respectful feedback and advice. She taught me that it is more important how I feel about my music and not so much how others rate it. You can never please everyone, can you? But thankfully she liked most of the tunes I played to her. And that´s what mattered most to me.

One fine day in 2006, shortly after my taxi accident in Leipzig, Nick Boyles called me. Kim was booked for RTL Stars for Free, a big radio concert at the Wuhlheide in Berlin. She was looking for a backing vocalist at short notice, as neither Roxy nor Scarlett could do the gig. Kim and Nick were discussing the matter and came up with an idea. And the idea was me. OMG! Me joining Kim on stage to sing with her in front of 17,000 people? No pressure, eh? The show was so much fun, but I couldn't stop my mind from going around in circles. How did I end up here? Next to Kim. On Stage. Singing. Please don't let this show end! It did end, like all good things, but only to make space for more happy moments and performances with Kimmi, including Stereoblonde opening for her on the first part of 2007's Perfect Girl tour.

Your single 'Sweetest of all Darlings' was recorded with Steve Byrd and Roxanne. Can you tell me a bit about the idea and creation of this song?

For Kim's 50th birthday I wanted to come up with a special and personal gift. So, I decided to write a song for and about her and our friendship. I hadn't written a song for quite a while. But when I picked up my guitar and began strumming, the melody and lyrics came out naturally, unexpectedly, as if they were laying around me somewhere, waiting to be detected. Just the title and chorus were still missing. I asked my guitarist and bandmate Michael for help and inspiration. All he replied was: "I love the song. Now go and write the bloody chorus. You can do it." Great! That didn't help much, at first, but suddenly 'Sweetest of all Darlings' came to my mind. Kim and I often call each other 'Sweety Darling' in an *Ab Fab* kind of way. I finished writing the chorus and Michael kindly helped by producing and recording the backing track.

Kim was overwhelmed when I played the song on her birthday in Dresden. She even encouraged me to release it. So, she must have really liked it. Phew!

Steve Byrd, Kim's ex-guitarist and a very dear friend to me - who sadly passed away in 2016 - had just started his label Byrdsongs and wanted me to be involved. We always spoke about recording a song together but apart from some demos, the idea never went any further. When he asked if I had any new songs written, I told him about 'Sweetest of all Darlings'. He loved the tune and wanted to record it properly to release it. Kim's ex-keyboard player Steven Williams offered to produce it together with Steve, so Michael and I flew to London to record it in Steven's Capel Studios.

I suggested an additional version to be added to the CD-single and thought of a duet with Roxanne, Kim's sister. Roxy and I have been good friends for many years, and I adore her angelic voice. I am still so happy that she is part of a song that is so very close to my heart. Now, I look at it not only as an homage to Kim but also as an homage to all friendship, including my friendship to Steve Byrd, without whom this song possibly would never been released.

What do you admire most about Kim as an artist and/or person?

First and foremost, I admire her voice. It is unique, beautiful, and so very different from all other female voices. She is a powerhouse live performer and a great role model to her huge and loyal fan base. Kim never chases trends or hypes, stays true to herself, and her music and lyrics come straight from the heart. She is talented in so many ways and a great inspiration, creatively and artistically. Her fans, she treats with respect and she is very approachable. And her stunning beauty, both inside and out.

What I love most about Kim as a person is her empathy, her great sense of humour, her generosity, her big heart and her great instinct. She has very fine antennae when it comes to assessing people. I very rarely hear her say something negative about someone. And on the rare occasions when she does, she's always spot on. Well, at least from my personal experience. I admire her family spirit and that she turns into a lioness when it comes to protecting her family and friends. And throughout it all she still remains very sweet, funny and kind. Oh, and she does a damned fine Spiegelei.

CHAPTER 18:

COME OUT AND PLAY

Released: 27 August 2010
Chart positions: 24 (Austria), 156 (France), 10 (Germany), 9 (Switzerland)

Those who kept an eye on international media didn't see or hear much from Kim in the second half of 2009 and early 2010. She was working on new music, and not giving many interviews. But occasionally an interview turned up. In April 2010, she appeared in Virgin Trains' *Hotline* magazine, talking about the forthcoming new album.

Kim: "Turning 50, I want to write a really kick-ass rock'n'roll album - I'm not going out gracefully. I'm very excited about the project: it's coming on brilliantly and will be out later this year." [1]

While Kim was working on new music, her old tracks were very much in demand.

German duo Blank & Jones created a new remix of 'Kids in America', released on Volume 2 of their *So 80s* compilation albums. The duo, consisting of Piet Blank and René Runge (aka DJ Jaspa Jones) started releasing singles in 2006, but became better known as remixers, having created remixes for Sash!, Dario G, and Pet Shop Boys. Their *So 80s* compilations started in 2009, when they realised that many 12" singles from the 1980s were never released properly on CD. Occasionally they added new remixes, but always made in a way that they would sound like an extended version, as they were known back then. The first record Piet Blank ever bought was 'Kids in America', and he remained a huge fan. So it was something very special for them to get their hands on this classic song.

English singer Lemar also worked with an old Kim Wilde track for a compilation album with his own biggest hits, simply called *The Hits*, adding new track 'You Don't Love Me', which contained a sample of Kim's version of 'You Keep Me Hangin' On'.

One of the biggest concerts of 2010 for Kim was at the Donauinselfest in Vienna on 25 June 2010, when she rocked an audience of 10,000 people. Also on the bill was Billy Idol, and Scarlett grabbed the chance to sing backing vocals for him during his 'Mony Mony' cover.

In August 2010, Kim joined social networking site Twitter. The account had until then been used by her official fansite to inform fans about the latest news, but in a changing world, more artists were persuaded to do their own marketing. Microblogging on Twitter seemed to be the best way to keep in touch with

CHAPTER 18: COME OUT AND PLAY

fans, so Kim slowly started to give regular updates about her professional (and sometimes personal) life. She shared photographs as well, including when she met kickboxing champion Christine Theis for an Austrian TV report, while doing promotion in Cologne, during rehearsals.

On 13 August 2010, new single 'Lights Down Low' was released in Germany. The single, like the forthcoming album, was released by Columbia Music. The album *Come Out and Play* was released a few weeks later. There were some big names on the album. Glenn Gregory from Heaven 17 provided vocals on 'Greatest Journey', and Kim sang a duet with Nik Kershaw on 'Love Conquers All'. OMD's Paul Humphreys added programming on the latter track. It wasn't just a retro affair - young Scandinavian writers Fredrik Thomander and Anders Wikström were credited for co-writing 'King of the World', 'Hey! You!' and 'This Paranoia'.

The title was taken from a line in the song 'Hey! You!', one of the sexier cuts on the album. It encapsulated the idea of the album, that each and every track should be fit for live performance.

The album project was overseen by Henrik Gümoes, A&R freelancer for Starwatch Music, part-owner of the SevenOne label, a collaboration between Sony Music and German TV channel ProSieben, who invested in several TV productions featuring Kim during that summer.

Indeed, a lot of German TV programmes paid attention to Kim's new release. Sat1 broadcast a 25-minute 'Rockumentary', in which Kim was interviewed at home. She confessed to having cold feet about a new album project, but added that it was certainly worth doing.

Kim: "It felt like a scary decision to commit to such a big project - all that time again, all that pressure, all that stress, travel, all the expectations... All that scrutiny. I wasn't sure... it was scary and I thought, hang on, if this is starting to feel scary, it must be a good idea." [2]

Kim did a promotional tour with Ricky and guitarist Neil Jones, performing acoustic versions of 'Lights Down Low' and 'Real Life' on a handful of German TV programmes.

A special live performance followed at Shepherd's Bush Empire on 10 October 2010. A Concert for Kirsty was a tribute to Kirsty MacColl, 10 years after her tragic passing, on what would have been her 51st birthday. Kim was one of more than a dozen artists singing one of her songs. She chose 'They Don't Know'. Outtakes from the concert were eventually released on Salvo Records' *A Concert for Kirsty MacColl* CD in February 2013, unfortunately without Kim's song.

Kim: "The first time I heard Kirsty sing on Radio One, they back-announced that she'd written 'They Don't Know', a song I later covered on my *Snapshots* album. Kirsty inspired me to become a songwriter with that brilliant pop song." [3]

Kim and band live at Musical Dome, Cologne (Germany), 21 February 2011 © Marcel Rijs

Kim live at Tivoli, Utrecht (Netherlands), 20 March 2011 © Katrien Vercaigne

Kim at home, 2010 © Katrien Vercaigne

Kim celebrated her 50th birthday a day early at home, with her family giving her presents. Her daughter gave her a home-made birthday cake and self-made presents, parents Marty and Joyce gave her a bouquet of 50 roses.[4] Then, on 18 November, she flew to Dresden in Germany for a special live performance at Club Nero with 150 fans present.

Kim: "It is an occasion to reflect and I'm grateful for the most important thing. My family, my health..." [5]

The next morning, Kim appeared on Sat1 TV in Germany for an interview. In between acoustic performances of 'Get Out' and 'Kids in America', she was presented with a huge birthday cake, with candles to blow out live in the programme.

For her 50th birthday, Kim also got a tattoo on her right shoulder, in Berlin. She designed it herself, based on a necklace she got as a present. In the middle is a heart that reads 'Amor vincit omnia' ('Love conquers all' in Latin); around it are stars and flowers.[6] But the reaction from her daughter Rose when she got home was perhaps a little unexpected...

Rose: "When she came back from working in Germany last year, she lifted up her top and showed me a tattoo on her back made up of hearts and stars. I couldn't stop laughing." [7]

During the last weekend of November, Kim went to three German cities together with Scarlett, Ricky, John Atkinson and Neil Jones to perform acoustic sets for radio stations. On 27 November, she appeared at the Congress Center in Ulm for Radio 7's annual charity night. The next day they went to Frankfurt for radio station HR1's Live Lounge. Finally, on 29 November they played an exclusive acoustic concert in front of 100 lucky listeners on RPR1 radio.

The album release was followed by a tour in 2011, starting with a date in St Moritz, Switzerland, where Kim and her band performed for Art On Ice 2011, a spectacle in which ice skaters showed their stuff while live music was performed by several artists, including Kim.

Kim: "Art on Ice in St Moritz was a dream. Watching the skaters perform to our songs was truly breathtaking. The event was staged on the ice lake, with majestic, snow-covered mountains overlooking us. The full moon shone down that night - all in all a magical experience."

The Come Out and Play tour started for real on 19 February 2011 in Zurich, followed by 10 dates in Germany, one in Paris and finally one in Utrecht, in the Netherlands. The support act was Kellner, a German quartet who had just released fourth album *The Road Sessions*. Kim's band consisted of John Atkinson (drums), Steve Power (keyboards), Neil Jones (guitar), Nick Beggs (bass), Scarlett (backing vocals) and Ricky (guitar). The relatively short tour was made up for by the length of the gigs: each show clocked in at 120 minutes. Notable inclusions, besides a selection of tracks from the album and past hits, were the track 'Words Fell Down' (featuring a keytar solo by Steve Power and a 'hard rock' ending by the entire band), and a rendition of Alphaville's 'Forever Young'. Halfway through the show, Kim played 'Jessica' solo on keyboards, followed by a short acoustic set during which she was accompanied by Ricky and Scarlett. The pleasure they had during performing was evident for everyone who attended.

Favourable reviews appeared in many newspapers and on various websites. The *Gelnhäuser Tageblatt* wrote: "It's certain, however: Kimberley Wilde celebrated in Frankfurt a concert that is so great because she's a genuine, honest and authentic act in the best sense." [8] "Wilde sings the classics, indestructible and still crystal clear", added the *Berliner Zeitung*. [9] And the *Regiomusik* website in Germany concluded: "Overall, the live show by Kim Wilde is fast-paced as well as colourful musical fireworks with a journey through the past 30 years of music." [10]

And so, at 50, Kim reached a stage in her career where record sales and chart placings had become less important, and live performances increased in importance. The Come Out and Play tour was just the first of many tours that would follow during the next 10 years.

Kim: "In fact, my career has been mainly a series of performance videos and television, but it is only lately that I really discovered myself as an artist on stage. I felt new vibrations, and a relationship with the audience that I would like to develop further in the future. I never thought when I started at age 20, that when I was 50, I'd make a great tour!" [11]

KING OF THE WORLD
Written by Kim Wilde, Fredrik Thomander and Anders Wikström
Produced by John McLaughlin & Dave Thomas Jr.

On 15 April 2009, Kim's best friend Clare lost her partner Patrick Jordan very suddenly. They had two sons Sebastian and William. Soon after Clare met Patrick, Kim met Hal, and they all got on very well together, spending holidays in the summer with their children as they were growing up. It was hard to lose such a charismatic man, and Kim felt she should turn this tragic loss into a tribute. Many people could relate to the lyrics: '*Why do they leave the bad and take away the good? / You were no angel, but we all knew where we stood.*'
Kim: "I wanted to make a tribute for my friend Patrick, who died of heart failure, with this song."[12]
Kim: "The first song I wrote is called 'King Of The World', it also opens the album. It is a very personal track that I composed in Stockholm with Fredrick Thomander and Anders Wikström. I wrote it after the sudden death of a dear friend of mine, Patrick Olaf Jordan, in April 2009. In this song, I explain that

life would be much better if there were more people like him who attached more importance to positive things in life in general." [13]

Kim has performed the song live on most of her tours since.

LIGHTS DOWN LOW
Written by Anthony Galatis and Mark Frisch
Produced by Ricky Wilde & Andrew Murray
Released: 13 August 2010
Chart positions: 34 (Germany), 62 (Switzerland)

'Lights Down Low' was delivered by Kim's label Starwatch. Kim described it as a song about seduction, and it fitted well within the playful theme of the album.
Kim: "A typical Kim Wilde song, a strong hook and very sexy. This was a welcome gift of my new record label Starwatch, which has offered me this song. For that I'll always love them. Rarely have I got such a strong song from a label. Therefore, it is also our first single now." [14]

Although CD-singles were becoming a bit rare, they continued to be sold in Germany, so a two-track CD-single was released in that country, featuring 'Snakes and Ladders' as the second track. It was the only physical release of this single, although promotional CD-singles were also made in Germany and France.

The music video featured pole dancers in a dark setting. It was filmed in Germany on one day, with Kim and her band.
Kim: "The video is set in a pole-dancing club. A few years ago, I did a gig in a very famous one in London. That was a strange atmosphere of us and them, us observing them and them observing us. It was a very interesting experience, but a feeling of being at a bizarre zoo. I thought it would be visually strong to recreate that particular night. We needed to find a very big, empty industrial location big enough for us to set up a complex light system around a spinning turntable where me and the band performed... and pole dancers of course." [15]

REAL LIFE
Written by Alex Geringas, Erik Nyholm & Dimitri Ehrlich
Produced by Ricky Wilde & Andrew Murray

Vanessa Meisinger and Leonardo Ritzmann participated in German TV talent show *Popstars Du & Ich* (*Popstars You & Me*). After telephone voting, they won the show's eighth series. Calling themselves Some & Any, they released the album *First Shot* in December 2009. In April 2010 it was announced that their recording contract was terminated, going their separate ways. Leo recorded a handful of

CHAPTER 18: COME OUT AND PLAY

solo singles while Vanessa went on to present programmes on German television channel RTL.

One of the tracks on Some & Any's album was 'Story To Tell', an early version of 'Real Life', as recorded by Kim on *Come Out and Play*. The song was offered to Kim via Starwatch.

Kim: "Life should be like a wonderful book, full of unusual chapters, characters, challenges, and of course love. Honesty, romance and poetry - these are three of my favourite words. " [16]

Kim: "What would my final page be, that is a question I don't really want to think about. No one wants to think about the final pages of their life, but it's a fascinating thing to ponder on from time to time."

A small portion of the song was used in the German trailer for the movie *Love And Other Drugs*, starring Anne Hathaway and Jake Gyllenhaal. The movie premiered in Germany on 13 January 2011.

In September 2010, a single release was announced with a projected release date of 29 October 2010, but the record company pulled it at the last minute. The track was remixed by Bodybangers, consisting of producers Andreas Hinz and Michael Müller. This version was only available as a digital download.

GREATEST JOURNEY (with Glenn Gregory)
Written by Kim & Ricky Wilde
Produced by Ricky Wilde & Andrew Murray

This song starts with a chant, performed by Angie Brown, Glenn Gregory, Ricky, Scarlett and Kim. The intro was also used as the introduction theme for Kim's concerts during 2011's Come Out and Play tour.

Lyrically, it is the most spiritual track of the album, as it hints at whatever might happen after this life ends: '*We're learning to believe / In the things we can't see / A ticket for the greatest journey*'. Kim explained that the song was a result of a 'deep' discussion between Ricky and herself.

Kim: "I wrote the song together with Ricky, my brother. We have long talked about things like the universe, spirituality and the meaning of life, and came to the conclusion that this long journey cannot simply come to an end when one leaves the world. Glenn Gregory assisted us musically. Ricky and I are huge fans, we were ecstatic when he came into the studio to record the song." [17]

Kim: " Glenn's voice has always impressed me, since the early Eighties in Heaven 17. My brother and I are very honoured to have him on the album, we are huge fans of his rich and charismatic voice." [18]

253

Kim at home, 2010 © Katrien Vercaigne

Kim Wilde at home, 2010
© Katrien Vercaigne

I WANT WHAT I WANT
Written by Robert Habolm & Kim Wilde
Produced by John McLaughlin & Dave Thomas Jr.

Just like 'Real Life', 'I Want What I Want' was originally performed by two young singers on German TV programme *Popstars Du & Ich* in 2009, this time Jana and Manuela.

Before Kim recorded the song for *Come Out and Play*, she rewrote some of the verses. The basic message remained the same: to live life to the full.

Kim: "This song is meant to encourage everyone to make their lives as fantastic, as ambitious, as beautiful as they really want, to make the best of any situation and not be afraid to plunge into the unknown. I've met some people who have regretted not doing certain things at certain times in their lives." [19]

LOVE CONQUERS ALL (feat. Nik Kershaw)
Written by Kim Wilde & Rob Davis
Produced by Philip Larsen & Paul Humphreys

Although Nik Kershaw features on this track, his contribution is relatively modest: he provides backing vocals on this sweet, slow love ballad. The track was produced by Philip Larsen, together with Paul Humphreys from OMD. They also provided keyboards.

Kim: "Nik Kershaw is featured on this track. I collected his albums for years. It was incredibly exciting to work together with another of my musical heroes." [20]

HEY! YOU!
Written by Kim Wilde, Fredrik Thomander & Anders Wikström
Produced by Carsten Heller

The playful 'Hey! You' was written in Sweden together with Thomander and Wikström. It draws comparisons between children going out to play outside (hence *Come Out and Play*) and games that adults play (hence the lyrics *'I'm gonna wait on the corner of the street for ya / But I won't be responsible for the things that I do / When I'm with you'*). Danish mixer and producer Carsten Heller produced the track and played percussion. He also brought in associates Kristian Riis (guitar) and René Munk Thalund (keyboards).

Kim: "'Come out and play' is a line in this song, but also the backbone for the entire album, hence the title. I wanted, namely, that each and every song works live on stage." [21]

The song was played live during the Come Out and Play tour in 2011, but not since.

SUICIDE
Written by Kim Wilde, Andrew Murray, Stephen Jones & Neil Jones
Produced by Andrew Murray, Stephen Jones & Ricky Wilde

'*Having it all / Having it all / You better get ready to fall / Having it all is suicide*', says the chorus, and it tells you a lot about this song. 'Suicide' is a feisty track, tackling the subject of human greed. It was written in the midst of the financial crisis that happened towards the end of the first decade of this century, when financial institutions collapsed, several banks having to be supported by governments to avoid collapsing. But according to Kim, greed went further than just the financial world: it exists in most of us, humans.
Kim: "This song is about greed. How often do we want more than we need? Always and everywhere: too much sugar, too much pride, too much oil ... the list is endless. I fear, greed will be the final downfall of the human race, and there is little hope that this will change any day soon." [22]

THIS PARANOIA
Written by Kim & Ricky Wilde, Fredrik Thomander & Anders Wikström
Produced by Ricky Wilde & Andrew Murray

Kim and Ricky wrote this song with Fredrik Thomander and Anders Wikström. It features a guitar solo by Kim's son Harry.

Kim: "On this track I'm especially proud, because I persuaded my son Harry to play a guitar solo. He has been playing some really good electric guitar for years, and I thought this piece could be a great challenge for him. He took it all in his stride and did an impressive job." [23]

LOVING YOU MORE
Written by Ricky Wilde & Steve Hart
Produced by Philip Larsen

'Loving You More' got its first public airing during Kim's live tour in April 2009. The song was written by Ricky with ex-Worlds Apart band member Steve Hart, who also recorded his own version. Kim recorded her version for *Come Out and Play*.
Kim: "This is a wonderful song that my brother played to me a few years ago, which was not recorded until now. It has all the drama of a classic '60s ballad, with a beautiful melody and a lot of emotion." [24]

GET OUT
Written by Pete Kirtley, Erik Nyholm & Sacha Collisson
Produced by Pete Kirtley & Sacha Collisson

Pete Kirtley and Sacha Collisson, who co-wrote this track, also feature prominently on this track, performing drums, keyboards and backing vocals (Kirtley) and bass, guitars and keyboards (Collisson). They also jointly produced this album track.

During live concerts, the song always gets an audience response. It was performed during the Come Out and Play tour and many tours after that. In 2021, it also appeared on Kim's *Greatest Hits* album, despite not having been a single.
Kim: "I love a song where I get to strut around the stage and point a lot. 'Never Trust a Stranger' is perfect for that, and so is 'Get Out', always tongue-in-cheek of course!"

MY WISH IS YOUR COMMAND
Written by Ricky & Scarlett Wilde
Produced by Ricky Wilde & Andrew Murray

One of several tracks on this album to lean towards the rock genre, it features an impressive guitar solo by Perry ap Gwynedd, a member of Kim's live band in 2007 who moved on full time to the band Pendulum, having joined them the previous year.
Kim: "My brother and my niece Scarlett wrote 'My Wish'. I am particularly proud that my old guitarist Perry ap Gwynedd from Pendulum plays a divine rock solo." [25]

JESSICA
Written by Kim Wilde
Produced by Ricky Wilde, Andrew Murray & Kim Wilde

The song 'Jessica' is a tribute to Kim's Airedale terrier, who at that point had been in her house for six years. The short, cute song was added to the album as the final track.
Kim: "This is the name of our beloved beyond-all-measure dog. An Airedale terrier, seven years old, and beloved family member. I wrote this song in Stockholm in a single night. I could not sleep and suddenly I had the song in my head - and then on my iPhone."[26]

Kim performed 'Jessica' live on stage during the Come Out and Play tour in 2011, while playing keyboards.

CHAPTER 18: COME OUT AND PLAY

SNAKES AND LADDERS
Written by Kim Wilde, Fredrik Thomander and Anders Wikström
Produced by John McLaughlin & Dave Thomas Jr.

The title refers to an ancient Indian board game, the 'snakes and ladders' in the title seeming to refer to life's ups and downs. The track sounds a lot tougher than most Kim Wilde tracks. It was included as the B-side of the single 'Lights Down Low' and was added to the album in March 2011, when Columbia released a deluxe edition of *Come Out and Play* on digital platforms.

CARRY ME HOME
Written by Kim Wilde, Fredrik Thomander and Anders Wikström

Written in Sweden with Thomander and Wikström, Kim described her feelings about being away from home, counting her blessings. '*And I'm so many miles from home / I'm all alone, but I can feel you with me now*'.

The song was given a limited release as part of a deluxe edition of *Come Out and Play* on digital platforms in March 2011.

ADDICTED TO YOU
Written by Sean Vincent, Roxanne & Ricky Wilde

The dynamic track 'Addicted to You' first appeared on the deluxe edition of *Come Out and Play* on digital platforms in March 2011. This original version was produced by Andrew Murray and featured more electronic sounds than the version that would appear on 2018 album *Here Come the Aliens*.

PARTY ON THE BRINK
Written by Hayley Bonnick & Nick Beggs
Produced by Dave Thomas and John McLaughlin

The environment had been a subject of many previous Kim Wilde tracks, but was never described as sardonically as in 'Party on the Brink', contributed by Kim's bass player Nick Beggs. He originally wrote the song for Industrial Salt, a duo consisting of Hayley Bonnick and Alex Stamp. Their album *A Pocket Full of Magnetic Letters* was released by Sony Music in Japan in 2005 and featured their version. Bonnick left the band in November 2007, before the release of a second album. Kim recorded her version as an extra track on the digital deluxe edition of *Come Out and Play*.

'*You emptied the seas / So you bring the sushi / Between you and me / We're speeding to the brink of mass extinction*', Kim sings on a rocking backing track with an almost celebratory backing vocal by her sister Roxanne. For someone who has tried to convey the message more gently in songs like 'Schoolgirl', 'Stone' and 'Who's to Blame', this would bring home the message in the bluntest way possible.

ÇA PLANE POUR MOI (live performance)
Written by Yvan Lacomblez

'Ça Plane pour Moi' was released as a single by Plastic Bertrand in December 1977. An exponent of the punk movement, it was the first punk record in French that was also a success outside French-speaking countries. The song has been described as a parody of punk and new wave.

The lyrics are full of 1970s French slang, very difficult to translate exactly into English. Even native French speakers disagree on the exact meaning. The title in particular is ambiguous: 'Ça Plane Pour Moi' means 'It is gliding for me', which could imply that having his head in the clouds, or possibly being high on drugs, works for the singer. The basic theme is a chaotic, drunken sexual encounter with a girl, told in retrospect.

In 2010, Plastic Bertrand admitted he didn't actually sing the track in 1977. Instead, the track, and most of Bertrand's first four albums were sung by producer Lou Deprijck. Ironically, Bertrand won a lawsuit in 2006 against Deprijck, who wanted to acquire the rights to the song.

Kim performed the song live during her European tour in March/April 2009, subsequent festival performances in the summer of 2009 and 2010 and during the Come Out and Play tour in 2011. In her version, guitarist Neil Jones performed a great solo, audience participation becoming increasingly important during the repeated choruses, the song extended to almost five minutes.

OH LORI (with Laurent Voulzy) (live performance)
Written by Billy & Bobby Alessi

Identical twins Billy and Bobby Alessi enjoyed worldwide success with 'Oh Lori' in 1977, a top-10 hit in 18 countries, including the UK.

When Laurent Voulzy and Kim appeared on the Night of the Proms concert in Charleroi, Belgium on 24 April 2010, they performed the song together, changing the title in turn to 'Oh Laurent' and 'Oh Kim'.

CHAPTER 18: COME OUT AND PLAY

INTERVIEW: NICK BEGGS

When did you first meet Kim Wilde?
I first met Kim in 1983 when we both appeared on British TV panel show *Pop Quiz* along with Morrissey, Alvin Stardust, Phil Lynott and Derek Forbes.

How did you become a member of her live band?
After recording a later studio album with her I joined the Here & Now band, playing for all the Eighties acts. It was during that time that Kim asked me to join her band as a full member, sometime around 2003.

Were you a fan of Kim's music before you joined?
I thought she had some great tunes and clearly a fabulous career. A couple of my friends had been in her live band for years and told me what fun she was to work for. So I had more than a passing interest in her music. But I could not have imagined the path that ultimately led me to work with her so closely for so long. I guess I was just lucky.

As a bass player, is there a big difference between Kim's concerts and (even) more rock-oriented gigs like Steven Wilson and Steve Hackett?
Kim's music is more complex than may first appear to the layman. It has many trap doors that you can trip over if you don't pay close attention. But there's a little bit of Kim's music in everything I've done, including with Steven Wilson.

You toured as part of Kim's band between 2003 and 2015. What were they like to work with?
These were some of the most fun times of my career. Kim was like a sister to me. Always lovely and great fun to be around. Her brother Ricky used to make me cry with laughter. It was all together too much fun, if anything. I will cherish the memories forever.

Any particular anecdotes or standout gigs?
After one show in Vienna we celebrated Kim's birthday with invited friends and family. Ricky and I tried to join the guests after the show in the lift up to Kim's hotel room. However, it was full and we both agreed to walk up to the floor and meet everyone there. When we arrived ahead of the congregation, I had a brainwave and instructed Ricky to take his clothes off, which we both did in an instant. When the lift doors opened the guests were confronted with two naked men running around before them. The screaming could still be heard as the lift doors closed and went to another floor. One of my greatest moments!

How did the song 'Party on the Brink' (recorded by Kim in 2010) come about?

I wrote two albums for a girl band I put together. We were fortunate enough to have a hit in Japan with the group, but once the second album was completed the band broke up, so I used numbers of the songs for other projects. I played 'Party on the Brink' to Kim and she loved it.

What do you admire most about Kim as an artist and/or person?

I think her consistency and stamina are breath-taking. Her voice has stayed strong and her fanbase supportive. What more can an artist ask for?

Nick Beggs live with Kim at Tivoli, Utrecht (Netherlands), 20 March 2011. © Katrien Vercaigne

CHAPTER 19:
SNAPSHOTS

Released: 26 August 2011
Chart positions: 14 (Germany), 27 (Switzerland)

'Snapshots' was released exactly one year after *Come Out and Play*. The idea for Kim to record a selection of her favourite songs came up during the Come Out and Play tour, with the album recorded in a relatively short time after the record company proposed the idea.

Kim: "Last year my last album *Come Out and Play* was released, which also received good reviews. I hadn't thought about releasing another album so soon after. My record company heard me sing cover versions at the gigs and proposed this record to me to celebrate my 50th Birthday." [1]

After a few months of silence, Kim's official website presented a contest on 20 June 2011. Fans were invited to send in their photographs with Kim, which would be used for the booklet of the CD. Other photographs appeared from Kim's own archive, which had been sorted in the summer of 2010 with a little help from her friends. All these photographs were used for the album *Snapshots*, as it was called: a collection of cover versions of favourite songs from throughout Kim's life.

On 30 June 2011, Kim Wilde was at the Grand Hotel Kameha in Bonn to shoot videos for 'Sleeping Satellite' and 'It's Alright', the two songs selected from the forthcoming album as singles. [2]

A few songs on the album, which was released on 24 August, had been played during the Come Out and Play tour, with 'Sleeping Satellite' and 'Forever Young' going down well with audiences.

Kim: "Scarlett proposed 'Forever Young' and 'Sleeping Satellite'. 'Forever Young' became a favourite of mine to sing live, and so beautiful when the audience joined in with me."

So how did the selection of songs for *Snapshots* come about?

Kim: "A lot of it was just instinct. Some of it was history – the first song I ever remember listening to was 'Anyone Who Had A Heart' by Cilla Black in 1968 – that kind of chose itself in a way, because I was always going to choose the first song that made a big impression on me...I was only eight years old! Others are songs that I've just loved over the years, enjoyed singing along to on the radio. A few suggestions came from very close friends and from Ricky. It was Ricky who came up with the idea of calling it *Snapshots*". [3]

The album's release was preceded by a double-A single of 'Sleeping Satellite' and 'It's Alright'. A promotional CD was released around the same time, featuring rough demo mixes and 'mixed but not mastered' versions. The album only reached the charts in Germany and Switzerland, mostly because it wasn't released or promoted in other countries. Faithful fans were quick to get the album, however: in a changing world the internet was becoming the primary distribution for Kim's albums, with fans depending on online stores like Amazon instead of local record shops.

Other changes had also affected the music world: 'Sleeping Satellite / It's Alright' was to be the last Kim Wilde CD-single to be released commercially. Although two further singles were taken from the album ('To France' and 'Ever Fallen in Love' / 'Spirit In The Sky'), these were only released on digital platforms like iTunes and Google Play. Singles had always been a way to promote albums, but falling sales meant that artists and record companies were only releasing albums physically and live concerts were quickly becoming the main source of income for musicians.

The album would be supported by a European tour in 2012, but before that, Kim was a special guest during special gigs organised by Heaven 17 in October 2011. Martyn Ware and Glenn Gregory organised two concerts to celebrate the release of B.E.F. album *Music of Quality & Distinction Volume 3: Dark*. On 14 October, they played songs from Heaven 17's impressive back-catalogue, but 15 October was dedicated entirely to the new B.E.F. album, with guest artists appearing on stage for various songs. Kim Wilde sang 'There's a Ghost in my House', 'Everytime I See You I Go Wild' and 'You Keep Me Hangin' On'. Other artists appearing during the concert were Midge Ure, Scritti Politti's Green Gartside, Polly Scattergood, David J Roch, Kate Jackson, Shingai Shoniwa, Boy George, and Sandie Shaw, with one of her last live performances. For Kim, meeting Green Gartside was a highlight, having been a fan of Scritti Politti for a long time.

Kim: "Meeting Green was a highlight, having been such a huge fan. And I thought I'm going to seize the moment, I'm not going to let this go, because he's quite an elusive man and he darts in and out... so I grabbed hold of him, and said [goes completely gushy]: 'I just want to let you know how much your music meant to me – I know you probably get this all the time, and I know people say it to me and I try and be gracious, and I don't mean to embarrass you – but I just want to thank you so much for making such perfect music and inspiring me so much.' Thankfully, he looked quite pleased!" [4]

In December, Kim went on tour with Status Quo as part of the Quofestive tour. Both Kim and Roy Wood were special guests, promoting the tour with Quo's Francis Rossi and Rick Parfitt.

Kim: "For me, the Quo have been part of my extended family since I was a little girl. My Dad wrote their second single 'Ice in the Sun' in 1968. To be on tour with the Quo right now is so awesome!" [5]

CHAPTER 19: SNAPSHOTS

Kim played an eight-song set of her biggest hits. At the end of Status Quo's set, Roy Wood and Kim joined in on a medley of 'Winter Wonderland' and 'Santa Claus is Coming to Town' every night. The 11-date UK tour ran between 3 and 17 December 2011. A recording of the entire Status Quo set at London's O2 was released on a double-CD.

In the final hours of 2011, Kim performed live in Berlin near the Brandenburg Gate, celebrating the new year in front of a million people. Other artists performing during the televised event were Udo Jürgens, Andreas Bourani, Cassandra Steen, Culture Beat, DJ Bobo, Frida Gold, Glasperlenspiel, Hermes House Band, Jimi Jamison, Johnny Logan, Marianne Rosenberg, the Boss Hoss, and the Scorpions. Kim performed 'Cambodia' and 'Kids in America'.

The Snapshots & Greatest Hits tour started on 6 March 2012 at the Volkshaus in Zurich, Switzerland. With 10 dates in Germany until 15 March this was a short tour, although followed by three more dates in October: one at Amsterdam's Paradiso and two in France. Like the Come Out and Play tour, all the concerts lasted for around two hours. Each concert started with the sound of the intro 'Dream Sequence', with filmed footage from Kim and Ricky's childhood. The concerts delivered exactly what was promised: Kim and her band played various tracks from the *Snapshots* album and Kim's greatest hits. The band members, playing together for a few years by now, all got a chance to shine. Guitarist Neil Jones displayed his skills with amazing guitar solos on 'Water on Glass' and 'Can't Get Enough (Of Your Love)'; Steve Power did a great keyboard solo as an introduction to 'Sleeping Satellite'; Nick Beggs gave an impressive bass solo in the middle of 'The Second Time', followed by Johnny Atkinson's drum solo; and Scarlett, Ricky and Kim delivered a beautiful acoustic set. With just their harmonies and Ricky's guitar-playing they captivated audiences.

IT'S ALRIGHT
Written by Anthony Mortimer
Produced by Alex G
Released: 19 August 2011
Chart position: 98 (Germany)

East 17 released 'It's Alright' in November 1993 as the sixth single from debut album *Walthamstow*. The band had already accumulated an avid fan following, but this was their biggest hit in the UK so far, peaking at No.3. The single then certified platinum in Australia and Germany.

To some it seemed strange that Kim would want to cover this song, but as she explained herself, she really liked a lot of the music that was coming out in the early 1990s.

Kim at home, 2010 © Katrien Vercaigne

© Sean J. Vincent

Kim: "East 17's song 'It's Alright' I think is a magnificent pop song. I remember the beginning of the Nineties, it was either you're into Brit Pop, like Suede and Blur or Oasis, or you were really into the boy bands, like New Kids on the Block, Take That and East 17. I loved both schools, I loved what Blur and Suede and everyone were doing, but I really was a bit of a sucker for a boy band. My favourite I think was East 17. I loved all their tattoos, shaved heads and streetwise attitude. They were kind of the bad boys of boy bands, and I liked that. It was really fun to sing their song." [6]

'It's Alright' was remixed by Groove Coverage, a German dance band consisting of Axel Konrad, DJ Novus, Melanie Munch and Verena Rehm. Ole Wierk and Axel Konrad produce the band. They delivered two versions: a remix of four minutes 23 seconds, and a remix edit clocking in at three minutes. These two versions were only released on digital platforms as extra tracks with the next single, 'To France'.

The music video was filmed at the stunning Grand Hotel Kameha in Bonn, with Nikolaj Georgiew directing.

IN BETWEEN DAYS
Written by Robert James Smith
Produced by Alex Rethwisch

The Cure released 'In Between Days' as the lead single from their sixth album *The Head on the Door* in July 1985. The single certified silver, having sold over 200,000 copies in the UK. Lyrical themes of ageing, loss and fear were not reflected in the music, which even in The Cure's version were poppy and upbeat.

Kim recorded her version with Heiko Fischer (guitar), Paul Kaiser (drums) and Lisa Rethwisch (backing vocals). It was produced by Alex Rethwisch. All four are members of Stanfour, a German rock band formed in 2004 on the island of Föhr, where they live. Kim's version emphasised the driving beat of the drums and the song's melody, played on keyboards.

Kim: "In 1980, it was a year before my career began, and I'd just left art college, I was living at home but I was spending quite a lot of time going to clubs and hanging out at parties my mates were having. It was the post-punk, new wave era and you'd turn up at parties and all you would hear were Siouxsie and the Banshees or Joy Division or the Cure. I loved the dark, gothic stream that ran through that sound but amongst all of that were these great melodies, and The Cure were great at making pop records and went on to have hit after hit as they discovered they were actually a great pop band. They emerged from their gothic roots and made these fantastic records. I loved Robert's styling, I loved the way he'd look like he was rifling through his Dad's old clothes and borrowing his Mum's lipstick …he made a great pop star!" [7]

CHAPTER 19: SNAPSHOTS

ABOUT YOU NOW
Written by Cathy Dennis and Lukasz Gottwald
Produced by Alex Rethwisch

Snapshots presents songs from all five decades between 1960 and 2010, and 'About You Now' was the youngest song of them all, released in 2007 by British girl group Sugababes. The song was nominated for a Brit Award for Best British Single. It was also the first track by a British pop act to top the singles chart in the UK based solely on digital downloads. The single also reached No.1 in Germany, Hungary, Poland, and the Czech Republic.

Another track recorded with the members of Stanfour, backing vocals were provided by Lisa Rethwisch, Scarlett and Ricky, as well as Kim.

Kim: "'About you now' by the Sugababes is the most recent song I've covered, co-written by Cathy Dennis, whom I greatly admire. It's simply a great pop record, and I've always loved girl bands anyway. My mother was in one of the first girl bands in the UK, the Vernons Girls, who were singing and dancing on the very first pop music shows in the UK - *Oh Boy* **and** *The 6-5 Special***. I remember growing up thinking girl bands are very cool. I loved the Supremes, the Shangri-las and especially the Ronettes. Later, in the Eighties, the Modettes, Bananarama and Sister Sledge, and the All Saints in the 1990s. The Sugababes are really cool. I just love the way they present themselves, great at singing harmonies and having fun! When it's done well it's really exciting, and the Sugababes do it with style." [8]**

During the Snapshots & Greatest Hits tour in 2012, Kim and Scarlett performed 'About You Now' as a duet, trading harmonies.

SLEEPING SATELLITE
Written by Tasmin Archer, John Beck & John Hughes
Produced by Alex Rethwisch
Released: 19 August 2011
Chart position: 98 (Germany)

The original version of 'Sleeping Satellite' was recorded in 1992 by Tasmin Archer. It was her debut , propelling her to stardom almost overnight. The single went to No.1 in the UK and Ireland and became a top-10 hit in many European countries. The lyrics of the song question the fact that we travel to space while ignoring the environmental needs of the planet – a theme close to Kim's heart.

Kim: "'Sleeping Satellite' was a huge hit for Tasmin Archer in 1992 and I absolutely loved the song. It was a huge hit in America as well. Everyone

loved the song. There was a serious theme, talking very much about the environment and the damage we are doing, and of how mankind is in search of adventure beyond our own planet, when its focus should be back here on planet Earth." [9]

'Sleeping Satellite' was edited for the single release and 39 seconds shorter than the album version. The music video was filmed at the Grand Hotel Kameha in Bonn, with Nikolaj Georgiew directing. In the video, Kim is seen lip-synching the song in a room, with images from throughout her career projected behind her.

Kim also performed the song on a handful of TV programmes, including German show *Fernsehgarten* and *The Voice Of Poland*. Together with Ricky, she also did a tour of various German radio stations to perform the song acoustically.

TO FRANCE
Written by Mike Oldfield
Produced by Ricky Wilde & Andrew Murray
Released: 2 December 2011

Mike Oldfield released 'To France' in 1984. The song features vocals by Maggie Reilly, who also appeared on his song 'Moonlight Shadow' a year earlier.

At the beginning of the century, when Napster was a popular music filesharing service, his track was often miscredited to Kim Wilde, so it was interesting that she decided to record the song for real a decade later.

Kim: "In 1984, Mike Oldfield released 'To France' with Maggie Reilly. She's such a great vocalist, but I was already a huge fan of Mike Oldfield - we used to play his records at home, particularly 'Tubular Bells' of course. Everyone loves that album, as they should, and 'Ommadawn' and I remember my Dad bringing this album home, putting it on the record player and just all of us absolutely loving it, except my Mum who hated bagpipes. But I was always a huge fan of Mike Oldfield and this song has the most incredible melody. I think when people ask, 'How did you choose the songs for the album?', one of the answers would have to be that I focus very much on how strong the melody was." [10]

'To France' was released as a digital download single in December 2011, Ricky creating a 'Christmas edit' with added bells.

CHAPTER 19: SNAPSHOTS

A LITTLE RESPECT
Written by Vince Clarke & Andy Bell
Produced by Alex G

British duo Erasure - Andy Bell and Vince Clarke - released 'A Little Respect' in September 1988, the third single from their third album, *The Innocents*. It was their biggest UK hit since 'Sometimes' two years earlier.

Kim Wilde started performing the song during live concerts in 2009. Since then, it's regularly appeared on her live setlists. Kim also played it as one of her 'Secret Songs' during her radio show on Magic 105.4 FM.

Kim: "This song actually reminds me of dancing to it in various clubs during the late Eighties. Performing this song live has been one of the greatest experiences on stage - hearing the audience take over the chorus is pure magic."

The song was an obvious candidate for *Snapshots*. On the album it sounds a little poppier than the band-supported live version, starting with a guitar arpeggio performed by Bernd Klimpel that wouldn't be out of place on a U2 album.

Kim: "'A Little Respect' is a great song by Vince Clarke and Andy Bell. It came out in 1988, which was a really important year for me. I had my album *Close* out, which did really well, and I was on tour with Michael Jackson on the Bad Tour. Every time I hear this song it just takes me back to that fantastic time in my career, and it was wonderful to hear from Andy himself how much he loved my cover version." [11]

REMEMBER ME
Written by Nickolas Ashford & Valerie Simpson
Produced by Ricky Wilde & Andrew Murray

Diana Ross released the single 'Remember Me' in 1970. Written by Motown collaborators Ashford & Simpson, the song presents the view of a spurned woman who requests that her ex-boyfriend remembers her for all the positive things she had brought to his life. Although not a hit in Europe, it did reach No.16 in the US Billboard Hot 100 and No.7 in the UK.

Kim recorded her version in Ricky's studio in Hertfordshire, with Neil Jones on guitar and Andrew Murray on keyboards. Kim, Ricky and Scarlett provided backing vocals.

Kim: "In 1970 I was 10 years old, really mad about music even at that age. I was very lucky because there was a lot of very cool music being played in the house. My Dad had an amazing record collection, so I remember a lot of Motown being played and remember loving Diana Ross's voice particularly.

In 1970 she released 'Remember Me'. I already knew her songs from earlier, but really particularly loved this one. And of course, years later I went on to record 'You Keep Me Hangin' On' by Diana Ross & The Supremes, so I feel an affinity with her because of that in a way. Diana is my all-time favourite female vocalist."[12]

Kim's version of 'Remember Me' was remixed by Vinny Vero and Steve Migliore. They delivered five different mixes: a single mix, club mix, dub mix, instrumental, and synthapella. Surprisingly, these remixes were never released.

ANYONE WHO HAD A HEART
Written by Burt Bacharach & Hal David
Produced by Ricky Wilde & Andrew Murray

'Anyone Who Had a Heart' was presented to American singer Dionne Warwick in unfinished form while she, Burt Bacharach and Hal David were rehearsing in Bacharach's apartment in Manhattan for an upcoming recording session. The song was eventually recorded and released in November 1963. It peaked at No.8 in the US Billboard Hot 100 singles chart in January 1964.

A scout for British producer George Martin discovered the song and suggested Shirley Bassey record it. Martin gave the song to Cilla Black, who recorded her version at Abbey Road Studios in London, with George Martin producing. In February 1964, Dionne Warwick's version charted in the UK almost simultaneously with Cilla Black's version, but it was the latter who scored the biggest hit, reaching the top of the chart at the end of the month, while Warwick's version stalled at No.42. A third version, recorded by Mary May, only made the chart one week, at No.49.

The fact that Cilla Black's version remained the best-known version in the UK was not surprising. Through the years, Kim mentioned Cilla Black's 'Anyone Who Had A Heart' as a song that meant a lot to her. She remembered hearing the song on the radio when she was just eight years old.

Kim: "The radio was on all the time [at home] and I used to listen to all these amazing songs that were the soundtrack to our lives: I vividly recall hearing Cilla Black singing 'Anyone Who Had A Heart', thinking it was the most wonderful song I'd ever heard, especially Cilla's emotional voice." [13]

Kim's version was produced by Andrew Murray and Ricky, the latter providing all the music. The ambient soundtrack with lots of echo and reverb gave it a modern twist, while all the attention was on Kim's clear and emotional vocal performance.

Kim: "When I started researching some of the songs on the *Snapshots* album I was really staggered to realise I was so young and yet this song had such a big

impact on such a small little person. I grew up with this song being one of the most precious songs I can think of, so I wasn't in any rush to record it - I was in awe of it so much. But when *Snapshots* came around, I just thought, 'This is the time to do this song, if you're ever gonna have a crack at this song, it's gotta be now or never.' So I went into the studio with Rick, and it was quite an emotional thing to do, but we did it (laughs) and I'm so chuffed, so delighted with the way we've interpreted that song. It's just wonderful. It's real dream come true stuff. So many songs on the album had long journeys to get to the album. They weren't just picked out randomly, like, 'Oh, I fancy that or maybe I'll do that one.' There's real stories to them and I think that's what makes the album so special." [14]

WONDERFUL LIFE
Written by Colin Vearncombe
Produced by Ricky Wilde & Andrew Murray

Colin Vearncombe, using the band name Black, wrote 'Wonderful Life' after a particularly disastrous year (1985): he had been in a car crash, was dropped by a record company, his mother had a serious illness, his first marriage ended, and he became homeless. The phrase 'It's a wonderful, wonderful life' was sarcastically meant. When the single was released on an independent label in 1986, he was noticed by A&M Records, who offered him a contract. Upon the re-release of 'Wonderful Life' in 1987, it became a worldwide hit. Ironically, the lyrics were often taken literally: most people thought the song was meant to praise the good things in life. - which is why it appeared in adverts for insurance companies, hotels and airlines.

'Wonderful Life' had been covered many times by artists around the world, with varying degrees of success. Dutch singer Mathilde Santing created a ballad version which became a hit in the Netherlands in 1999 and Tina Cousins scored a hit with her dance-oriented version in 2005. But there were also many anonymous rock and techno versions that sunk like a stone. Kim managed to create a version that was notably different: a beautiful pop song, made more special by her own melancholy vocals.

Kim: "1987 was a really important year for me. I did a cover version of 'You Keep Me Hangin' On' with my brother Ricky and it went to No.1 in America. This was just an astonishing moment in my life, but I remember amongst all the pop music around at the time - Madonna with hit after hit, and Michael Jackson, Rick Astley, they were all putting out this fantastic power pop music - but somehow this really subtle song managed to do really, really well in the charts, and it was called 'Wonderful Life' by Black, and I absolutely loved the song and remember travelling to the airport to go and do some promotion in Europe and hearing about the news of 'You Keep Me Hangin' On' going to No.1, and hearing this song on the radio, thinking, 'Yeah, everything really is very wonderful right now', so it was sort of like a soundtrack to that period of time for me." [15]

Kim: "It was only when I started singing it myself that I tuned in to the more melancholy feeling of the song and appreciated the irony of those beautiful lyrics."

'Wonderful Life' was performed live during the Snapshots & Greatest Hits tour in 2012. During an acoustic performance, Kim, Scarlett and Ricky also incorporated lines from another song called 'Wonderful Life', released in 2010 by Hurts.

THEY DON'T KNOW
Written by Kirsty MacColl
Produced by Alex Rethwisch

Kim included 'They Don't Know' as a tribute to Kirsty MacColl, whom she was friends with at the start of her career. Kirsty MacColl recorded the track in 1979. It was a popular song on the radio at the time of release, but because of a dispute between Kirsty and her record label at the time, the single wasn't shipped and promoted properly in shops, causing it to miss the UK chart entirely. When Tracey Ullman recorded the song in 1983, MacColl reprised her original 'Bay-ay-be-ee' at the start of the third verse. This version peaked at No.2 in the UK singles chart.

Recorded with the Stanfour quartet, Kim's version is a short and breezy track, lasting just two and a half minutes.

Kim: "[Kirsty MacColl] played a great role in launching my career in 1981. Taking up 'They Don't Know' is a way of thanking her." [16]

Kim: "It was released just before my career kicked off and Kirsty is the same age as me - I remember thinking, 'Wow! She's so young, she's 20 years old, she's writing these great songs, she's on the radio, she's so positive, so gutsy', so I wanted really to be like Kirsty MacColl. I subsequently got to know her, and for a while we were both dating guys in the same band, Tenpole Tudor, which was great fun! No, not Eddie, you don't date someone like Eddie. She came to the very first rehearsals I did in North London for my very first tour. I've got lovely photographs that I took of her at that time." [17]

Kim: "'They Don't Know' was written by Kirsty MacColl and we were contemporaries back in the early Eighties, but before that I was a fan of hers. I heard the song on the radio when I was still living at home. I remember being in my bedroom, listening to it, wondering who recorded it, and finding out it was someone of my own age, but not only she'd recorded it, but she'd written it. I was very impressed by Kirsty and I met her later and we became good friends. My version is a tribute to her, and a thank you for some beautiful memories." [18]

BEAUTIFUL ONES
Written by Brett Lewis Anderson & Richard John Oakes
Produced by Ricky Wilde & Andrew Murray

'Beautiful Ones' was recorded by British band Suede for their third album, *Coming Up*, released as the second single from the album in October 1996. It reached No.8 in the UK and also reached the singles charts in Scandinavia.

Although Kim's version sounded a little richer than the pointed version by Suede, it is probably the cover version that remains closest to the original version. For her fans this was probably the most surprising cover version on the album, never expecting a Brit Pop track.

Kim: "At the beginning of the Nineties I was still recording and making albums, but my career had started to be a bit quieter - more time for me to sit back a little bit, see what everybody else was doing. It was a really interesting time for British pop music, the Brit Pop thing was exploding with bands like Suede and Blur and Oasis. They made some really great pop songs amongst all the posturing and the attitude, which was very entertaining. I love the way that they embraced their Brit Pop heritage. So I thought I'd nick it back off them and as a pop person myself, underline its pop credentials. I think 'Beautiful Ones' is a great pop record!" [19]

Kim: "The biggest headache was given to me by 'Beautiful Ones' by Suede. I really love Suede and this song too. Nevertheless, I had to fight an inner battle with myself whether I was really going to do it. But in the end, I think we got something new out of the song. However, it will not be for everyone…like Marmite!" [20]

JUST WHAT I NEEDED
Written by Ric Ocasek
Produced by Alex Rethwisch

American rock band The Cars released 'Just What I Needed' in 1978 on their self-titled debut album. It was the band's debut single and a hit in various territories, most notably France, where it peaked at No.4.

Kim's version changed a bit between the 'rough demo mix' included on a promotional CD for *Snapshots*, and the eventual album version. Several

Kim live at Musical Dome, Cologne (Germany), 21 February 2011 © Marcel Rijs

[bottom] Neil Jones, Kim and Nick Beggs live at Paradiso, Amsterdam (Netherlands), 3 October 2012 © Marcel Rijs

Scarlett, Kim and Ricky during an acoustic set live at Paradiso, Amsterdam (Netherlands), 3 October 2012 © Marcel Rijs

sections of the song were moved around, a surprise to those who listened to the promotional version in the weeks before the album's release.

Kim: "'Just What I Needed' was released in 1978. I was 18, increasingly getting into pop music. I loved the punk rock scene, but (also) loved the sort of post-punk, new wave scene. The Cars were in that sort of genre, post-punk, new wave, definitely rock'n'roll, and very pop. They seemed to combine all the elements of music I loved the most. I just loved Ben Orr's vocals and his beautiful face. It was just a few years before I started recording myself, so they were a huge influence, not just on myself but also on my brother, Ricky." [21]

EVER FALLEN IN LOVE (WITH SOMEONE)
Written by Pete Shelley
Produced by Ricky Wilde & Andrew Murray
Released: 24 February 2012

Pete Shelley from Buzzcocks wrote 'Ever Fallen in Love (With Someone You Shouldn't've)' after watching the movie *Guys and Dolls*, in which the character Adelaide says to Sky Masterson, 'Wait till you fall in love with someone you shouldn't have'. This inspired the lyric, written the next day. The single was released in September 1978 and became the Manchester punk band's biggest hit, peaking at No.12 in the UK.

In 1986, Fine Young Cannibals recorded a cover version, simply titled 'Ever Fallen in Love', for the soundtrack of the movie *Something Wild*. This version reached No.9 in the UK but was also an international hit. It was subsequently included on their second album, 1988's *The Raw and the Cooked*.

Kim's version was recorded with her band and represents the 'live sound' of Kim Wilde best: rocking drums, stabbing guitar chords and a keyboard-driven melody line to drive the song along.

Kim: "In 1978 it was a really interesting time, to say the least, in the UK for pop music. Punk rock was exploding, the Sex Pistols were causing all kinds of mayhem and upsetting all the grown-ups. I wasn't much of a rebel myself, but I loved that they were, and causing so much upset and being so rude and hilarious. Buzzcocks were a band that seemed a little bit friendlier than the others; Pete Shelley always had a very nice smile on his face and never seemed quite so angry. He wrote this song, and I remember I really loved it at the time. The punk scene was transformational and influenced so many things, especially pop music. 'Kids in America' was very influenced by that punk attitude, but also by new wave, pop and rock." [22]

The song was released simply as 'Ever Fallen in Love', coupled with non-album cover version 'Spirit In The Sky' (see below) as a double-A-side download single in February 2012.

KOOKS (with Hal Fowler)
Written by David Bowie
Produced by Ricky Wilde

David Bowie wrote the song 'Kooks' for new-born son Duncan Jones. It was first recorded for the BBC's *In Concert* radio show on 3 June 1971 and broadcast on 20 June, then recorded for the BBC's *Sounds Of The Seventies* radio show on 21 September 1971 and broadcast two weeks later. The studio recording on the album *Hunky Dory* was finally released on 17 December 1971.

British band Danny Wilson recorded a version of the song in 1991.

Kim sings this song together with her husband Hal, his first appearance on a Kim Wilde track. With Ricky performing all the instruments and producing, it is one of the most charming, least complicated tracks on the album.

Kim: "In 1971 I was 11 years old, and one of the best things about my life at that time was my parents' record collection. There were amazing albums in there, my Mum had all the really iconic women like Joni Mitchell, Carole King, Aretha Franklin, Dusty Springfield, and my father had all the rock'n'roll stuff. He also had quite a lot of classical music. I particularly remember The Who's *Tommy*, which would go on to become a very important album for me, and one of the albums I loved most of all was *Hunky Dory* by David Bowie. I used to really love every song on that, especially 'Life on Mars', which was so incredible. But there was one song on the album, 'Kooks', which I was really touched by because it was a song Bowie had written for his son. Bowie didn't look like the kind of guy that would be writing lullabies to children at the time, but I really connected with the song very strongly, so for the *Snapshots* album I thought, 'Wouldn't it be great to sing that with my husband'. He's got a beautiful voice and has sung professionally for many years in the West End. We sang this together for our children, Harry and Rose." [23]

FOREVER YOUNG
Written by Bernhard Lloyd, Marian Gold & Frank Mertens
Produced by Alex Rethwisch

Having released two up-tempo singles in 1984 – the worldwide hit 'Big in Japan' and the engaging 'Sounds Like A Melody' – German band Alphaville released the title track of debut album *Forever Young*. The song, written by the band, was certified silver in the UK and gold in Denmark, Germany and Italy. It also gave them a second hit in the USA.

Recording a cover version of 'Forever Young' wasn't Kim's own idea: it was suggested to her by Scarlett, who proposed the song to be performed during the Come Out and Play tour. Seeing the audience response to this song, it was decided to record a studio version to be included on an exclusive edition of *Snapshots* for German chain of entertainment stores Saturn.

Kim: "I played this song in February and March 2011 during the Come out and Play tour in Germany. The song was released in 1984 by German rock/synthpop band Alphaville - in the same year I released my album *Teases & Dares*. I can't claim it made a big impression on me then. In fact, I only understood what a great song it was when my niece and backing singer Scarlett proposed it for the tour. It has a wistful and at the same time powerful quality, and the audience seems to have a special connection to it. It doesn't matter that we all get old, when we stay 'Forever Young' in our hearts." [24]

I'LL STAND BY YOU
Written by Chrissie Hynde, Tom Kelly & Billy Steinberg

The Pretenders recorded 'I'll Stand By You' for their sixth album 'Last of the Independents' in 1994. Chrissie Hynde wrote the song with the American songwriting team of Tom Kelly and Billy Steinberg. The single became a worldwide hit, reaching No.10 in the UK and No.16 in the US. On BBC programme *Songwriters Circle*, Hynde mentioned her embarrassment at having set out to write a 'hit'. She added that she felt better about the song after Noel Gallagher said he wished he'd written it.

Kim started performing the song live in 2008, recording a studio version during sessions for *Snapshots*. It was released as an extra track of the album on digital downloads from iTunes and other platforms.

SPIRIT IN THE SKY
Written by Norman Greenbaum
Released: 24 February 2012

Norman Greenbaum recorded and released 'Spirit in the Sky' in 1969, writing the song after seeing a gospel song on television, thinking he would be able to write one himself. Despite his Jewish background, the song makes several references to Jesus. The recording was a combination of gospel and rock music. It became a worldwide hit, reaching No.1 in several countries, including the UK. A version by Doctor and the Medics also reached No.1 in the UK in 1986.

Kim recorded her version for a 'double A-side' single (combined with 'Ever Fallen In Love'), released digitally in February 2012, 10 days before the start of her Snapshots & Greatest Hits tour, during which she also performed the song live. Her version leans towards 'glam rock', with added electronic sound effects.

A BEAUTIFUL HOUSE (with Reflekt)
Written by Jean Fontaine, Jacko Peake and Kim Wilde
Released: August 2012

Reflekt were an English dance act consisting of DJ's Seb Fontaine and Jay Peake. They had a club hit in 2004 with 'Need to Feel Loved' featuring Delline Bass. The single was also a minor chart hit in the UK, Belgium and the Netherlands. In 2012 they wrote and recorded 'A Beautiful House' with Kim. The single was released on digital platforms in August, featuring remixes by Antillas & Dankann. Another remix was made by a young Dutch remixer called Erik Arbores, who was just 14 at the time. This remix wasn't released because Arbores signed with a different record company just after creating the remix.

Erik Arbores: "I said to my parents I'm making a remix for Kim Wilde. They were very enthusiastic: she's very famous, you know! But that music is from before I was born, ha ha. Although I did know 'Kids in America' from a computer game." [25]

'A Beautiful House' made an impact in the UK club charts when it was released, but didn't cross over to the official singles chart.

EVERY TIME I SEE YOU I GO WILD (with B.E.F.)
Written by Stevie Wonder, Sylvia Moy & Henry Moy
Released: 19 August 2013

Stevie Wonder recorded this song for his eighth studio album, *I Was Made to Love Her*, released in August 1967. It also appeared on the B-side of 'I'm Wondering' in September 1967.

Kim performed the song live in concert with B.E.F. in October 2012. The concert was followed by the release of B.E.F.'s album 'Music of Quality and Distinction Vol. 3: Dark' on 27 May 2013. The album opened with Kim's version of this song.
Martyn Ware: "Kim's vocals on this are staggeringly brilliant. I honestly believe it could well be her best-ever performance. And several people have mentioned to me they believe this is the case as well." [26]
Kim: "Now at last I get to work on a B.E.F. project, how fantastic! The Stevie Wonder track Martyn sent was unknown to me, but I've always been a huge

Stevie fan. Both Martyn and I are really excited with the result of 'I Go Wild'. (...) I am so proud to be part of the continuing B.E.F. story." [27]

This song was eventually chosen to be a single, released on 19 August 2013. There are nine different versions of the track: the album version, an edit of the album version, and an instrumental version of the album version, a radio edit, an Echoes full length remix (8'35), an Echoes remix (3'23) and an edit of the Echoes remix (2'53), a Black Asteroid remix, and a Black Asteroid instrumental remix.

Kim recorded a video for the release, directed by Paul D, a multi-award winning filmmaker. The video showed Kim fighting zombies, vampires, werewolves and demons to get to the man she loves. The video was shot on location at a Victorian cemetery and in a trendy nightclub in London. The cast of the video also included 'Dark Morte' ('Best Goth Model' on World Goth Day 2012) and Paul Ewan ('Cockneys vs Zombies'). [28]

Kim: "I was dressed in black PVC, killing ghouls and zombies. They really twisted my arm to do it. There's nothing easy about spending a whole day in 11-inch heels and black PVC when you're 53 - I can tell you that. But being able to work with people who wrote 'We Don't Need That Fascist Groove Thing', which got banned from Radio 1... I loved that at the time, it was so ridiculous. The irony that Radio 1 took it upon themselves to dictate what we could listen to in the name of their opposition to dictators! Hilarious!" [29]

I BELIEVE (with DJ Bobo)
Written by René Baumann & Axel Breitung
Released: 20 September 2013

'I Believe' was originally released on Swiss singer, songwriter and producer DJ Bobo's 2003 album *Visions*. It was released as a single and reached No.13 in Switzerland and No. 18 in Germany. His 2013 album *Reloaded* featured new versions of a selection of his songs, including several duets with artists like Swedish singer Jessica Folcker and Romanian singer Inna, while Kim made an appearance on a remade version of 'I Believe'.

CHAPTER 20:
WILDE WINTER SONGBOOK

Released: 11 November 2013
Chart position: 169 (UK)

On 13 December 2012, Magic Radio organised a Christmas party for all its employees at the O2 in London. Kim and Ricky were among the guests, singing 'Kids in America' and 'Rockin' Around the Christmas Tree' on stage. During the evening, Kim joined in the party and drank a few vodka cocktails with cranberry and lychee cordial. She left the party, by her own account 'slightly over-refreshed', to catch the train back from Kings Cross to Welwyn North. What happened next became an overnight internet sensation.

At some point during the journey, Kim and Ricky decided it would be a good idea to serenade the passengers. After all, Ricky was carrying his guitar, and it was Christmas! So they got up and started to play 'Kids in America' right there and then.

Case Eames, who was also on the train, was surprised when she recognised Kim, and started filming the impromptu performance. As Kim proceeded to walk towards her, she probably realised she was being filmed, but obviously didn't care. After a brief silence she proceeded to sing 'Rockin' Around the Christmas Tree', the second of two songs she performed during the train ride.

Kim: "We got on the train, and I said to Rick, 'Come on, it's Christmas, I've got antlers, you have got a guitar, what can possibly go wrong?'. I saw a girl filming halfway through, but I was extremely drunk, and at that point I really didn't care that she was filming. I thought, she will only show her Mum anyway. Then we got home and the phone started. And my husband went online and started watching the clicks go up on the viewings. Before we knew it, within a few weeks, two million people had watched me absolutely smashed." [1]

Kim: "Bless Case Eames, she got in touch with us and said, 'I've got this on film and I'm not gonna put it out unless you're okay with it, which I thought was so sweet of her to do. Rick and I had a chat about it, and we said, 'Oh sod it, we've really come this far'. It felt like a race, you couldn't hold this horse back. If I'd had seen it first, I probably would have said no. The talking stuff was just so humiliating. But anyway, out it went, huge views, and worries about how it would be perceived, worries that were unfounded as it turned out, bless all the great people that made us feel like it was just a fun Christmas thing to do. And this is why I have a great fondness for antlers, because I believe the only reason I got away with it was (because I was) wearing them." [2]

While Kim and Ricky made their way home, Case decided to post the video she'd recorded on YouTube, and with that, a new 'viral video' was born. A few things made it a hilarious watch: the typically stern and uninterested looks of fellow passengers, the antlers worn by Kim, and Rick falling over at one point – but still carrying on.

The day after the train ride, Kim was astonished to find that the video was attracting lots of views and the response was actually quite favourable. Within days, over a million people had watched the video.

Kim: "Truly, I am overwhelmed and confused at such a huge reaction to my night out on the tiles. Making me giggle a lot." [3]

The seed was sown for a new project. Kim had been toying with the idea of recording a Christmas album for some time, but this incident plus the release of Tracey Thorn's album *Tinsel and Lights* around this time ignited the spark that started the project for real. In January, when the UK experienced some snowfall, she quickly made video recordings around her house to be used for the music videos that would be made for the new album. No music had been recorded yet, so these were just images of Kim walking around in the snow.

Ricky: "We recorded the album during the summer. We had a plan to have a Christmas album come out, because we'd never done that before, and it seemed like a good time because of the train incident, especially because we had such a surprisingly wonderful response about that. We thought 'well, let's just embrace it, let's run with it'. Then we just spent the whole of the summer recording *Wilde Winter Songbook*." [4]

Kim: "I was very inspired by Tracey Thorn from Everything But the Girl. She made a beautiful album that was Christmas-inspired and made it her own. She didn't go down any obvious roads. I felt inspired to do the same." [5]

Kim: "I'm a huge fan of Christmas. I'm releasing a Christmas album, which came from hearing Tracey Thorn's *Tinsel and Lights*. I told her on Twitter how inspirational it was and, as soon as last Christmas was out of the way, I started writing on the piano. The album's got six original songs and six old favourites. I've kept away from religion, as I don't have strong religious views, and that took out a lot of choices for covers. 'Winter Wonderland' is on there, and there's a song based on a poem my husband Hal wrote." [6]

After the train incident, Kim joined Tony Hadley to set a world record in a plane for the Comic Relief charity event, singing their way into the record books after performing the highest-ever concert on 10 March 2013. The Spandau Ballet frontman and Kim put on an acoustic show for 128 passengers on a Boeing 767 at 43,000 feet (13km), beating the previous world record of 42,080 feet (12.8km) held by singer James Blunt.

CHAPTER 20: WILDE WINTER SONGBOOK

Kim: "I'm becoming an old hand at performing on public transport, in fact I'm getting a bit of a taste for it, so when British Airways asked me to play at 43,000ft, I simply couldn't resist. It was great fun and I'm proud to have been a part of it." [7]

In May, an Australian tour with Nik Kershaw was announced. Australian news outlets reacted with enthusiasm. It was Nik's first Australian tour since The Riddle back in 1985. Several telephone interviews followed, Kim looking forward to touring Australia again, and touring with Nik Kershaw making it an extra enjoyable prospect.

Kim: "We've been on the same record label before, back in the days of MCA. He's always been a bit of a reluctant pop star; it never sat easily on his shoulders. It's only in recent years that he's been able to come out and sing his songs again, in a kind of retro set-up, but I think he's surprised himself with how much he's enjoyed it. He recorded a brilliant new album in recent years [*Eight*] as well as playing his old classics. He's sung on a couple of albums I've recorded in recent years, so he's become a good friend and feels like part of our extended family." [8]

The duo played five shows in five days between 16 and 20 October, in Brisbane, Mornington, Melbourne, Sydney and Perth, each time performing a full set.

Earlier in the year, Chrissy Amphlett, singer of the band Divinyls passed away, leading to Kim performing their hit single 'I Touch Myself' by way of a tribute.

Kim: "I love that song, I heard what happened to Chrissy, she's the same age as me, I wanted to do it as a special tribute to her for Australia." [9]

At the end of each concert, Kim and Nik appeared on stage together to perform Pink's recent hit single 'Try'. In between concerts, they managed to squeeze in a few radio and TV interviews. It was a busy week, but a week well spent.

In October 2013, Kim Wilde started her own syndicated radio show, the Kim Wilde 80s show. The first radio station to broadcast the show was RPR1 in Germany. It was soon picked up by other stations in Australia, Canada, Cyprus, Denmark, Estonia, Norway and, in 2021, Qatar. The shows could be customised to fit local jingles and formats, the content filled to the brim with hits from the 1980's. Kim's introductions made sure listeners kept hanging on to the stations offering the show.

In November 2013, *Wilde Winter Songbook* was released, her collection of six original songs and six versions of existing Christmas songs.

Kim: "It's been a real labour of love. (...) Christmas can be a wonderful time but also a very lonely time for some, and this isn't just your cliché constantly upbeat album - it reflects all the different emotions Christmas can bring, good and bad." [10]

Kim live at the O2 Academy, Birmingham (UK), 19 December 2013 © Katrien Vercaigne

Kim live at Cultuurpodium Boerderij, Zoetermeer (Netherlands), 4 October 2015 © Katrien Vercaigne

Kim live at Tivoli Vredenburg, Utrecht (Netherlands), 16 October 2016 © Katrien Vercaigne

While *Never Say Never*, *Come Out and Play* and *Snapshots* had all been released on the European mainland only, *Wilde Winter Songbook* was Kim's first UK album release since 1995's *Now & Forever*. As a result, she promoted the album on UK shows like *BBC Breakfast* and *This Morning*. The most appealing piece of promotion was for the *Chris Evans Breakfast Show* on BBC Radio 2, where Kim, Ricky, Scarlett and Neil Jones performed 'White Winter Hymnal' and 'You Came', and were joined by Cliff Richard for renditions of his first hit, 1958'S 'Move It', and Marty Wilde's 1959 hit 'A Teenager In Love'.

It was also the first album released on Kim's own label, Wildeflower Records. The album's release was supported by 12 videos – one for each song.

Kim: "We made the choice to make 12 clips, whatever comes, whether the album is successful or not, we just did it! My manager Sean Vincent filmed the vast majority; a few songs are animated too. We even made a clip in which our dog Jessica has a comedy role! ['Hey Mr Snowman']."[11]

Reviews of the album were favourable: *The Guardian* wrote: "Wilde's purpose with this album is to spread joy, and she goes about it with relish." [12] Australian website *The Music* offered: "Christmas albums are rightfully dreaded, like the arrival of Drunk Auntie Beryl at lunchtime. But 'Wilde Winter Songbook' shocks and delights by being slightly tipsy and in great spirits." [13]

In December, Kim followed up the release of *Wilde Winter Songbook* with live dates in the UK, entitled Kim Wilde's Christmas Party. The first of these, on 18 December 2013, took place in Bristol at the Colston Hall, where she kicked off her first live tour in 1982.

Kim: "I played my first gig in Bristol and it was filmed for a TV documentary called *First Time Out*, which centred on me playing at the Colston Hall, so it will be quite emotional for me to be coming back to the city where, in many ways, it all began." [14]

The other shows took place in Birmingham and London on 19 and 21 December respectively. The festive shows were performed with her band and were similar to the Snapshots & Greatest Hits set, but with added Christmas songs. 'Hey Mister Snowman', 'New Life', 'Hope' and 'White Winter Hymnal' were performed during the main show. The encore, complete with snow falling, consisted of 'Merry Xmas Everybody', 'I Wish It Could Be Christmas Every Day', 'Rockin' Around the Christmas Tree', and 'Kids in America'.

An unexpected live show happened just before the UK live dates, when Kim reached the Dutch village of Saasveld, where locals organised a big concert, with Kim as the headliner. Having organised concerts with Dutch band Normaal for a few years, Rolf Woolderink and his friends wanted to do something special. For Kim, it was a surprise to appear in the middle of the Dutch countryside, but being so close to Germany, Saasveld was the perfect place to draw in visitors from various countries. The concert was a great success.

In the new year, Kim Wilde joined the Rock Meets Classic tour, an extravaganza also featuring Midge Ure, Joe Lynn Turner, Uriah Heep, and Alice Cooper. They played 20 dates between 9 March and 5 April 2014. Even before the tour, Kim said she had a lot in common with Alice Cooper.

Kim: "When I'm putting on my makeup, morphing out of Mrs Fowler into Kim Wilde... I mean, that's what Alice Cooper does, doesn't he – he morphs from being, you know, on hole 17 of the golf course to being this fantastic rock god. Our lives are very grounded, but on stage we fly!" [15]

Kim joined Alice Cooper on stage to sing 'Poison' and 'School's Out' with him. She blended in very well with the 'heavy' rock stars during this tour, which might have been a surprise to the audiences.

Kim reprised her train singing adventure when the Gatwick Express celebrated its 30th birthday on 8 May 2014. Together with acoustic guitarist Steve Streater, she performed three songs on the train ('You Keep Me Hangin' On', 'You Came' and 'Kids in America') and one at Gatwick Airport (a reprise of 'Kids in America') to a delighted audience. They certainly responded more than her fellow passengers in December 2012.

Kim reprised her Christmas concerts in a very special way in December 2014, when she performed live at Knebworth House three times for an audience of 100 people: two performances on 14 December and an added performance two days earlier. During these performances she presented 'Deck the Halls' with the Knebworth Community Chorus.

In February 2015, Steve Strange passed away. Since his appearance on the Here & Now tour in 2002, he had reformed Visage with Steve Barnacle, Robin Simon and Lauren Duvall, and released an album in 2013, *Hearts and Knives*. Another album with remakes of old Visage tracks, *Orchestra* appeared in 2014. He died while holidaying in Sharm-el-Sheikh, Egypt, and Kim wrote a tribute on her website.

Kim: "Steve Strange will be remembered as the most elegant and beautiful of the New Romantics at the beginning of the Eighties, and 'Fade to Grey' one of the very best, most influential records of the decade. I shall remember him for his humour and generous spirit; he really was a very lovely man." [16]

In November 2015, Kim was one of the artists appearing with the Welsh Pops Orchestra to sing the songs of Visage, the band that made Steve Strange famous. Together with Ricky she performed 'You Keep Me Hangin' On', 'Cambodia', 'Kids in America' and Visage hit 'Mind Of A Toy' – the only time she performed this song. Other artists involved included Howard Jones, Jimmy Somerville and Boy George.

Also in November, a deluxe version of *Wilde Winter Songbook* was released in the UK, featuring six bonus tracks and a DVD featuring videos for all 16 songs. To support the release, Kim did two more intimate concerts at Knebworth House on 12 and 13 December, before performing 'Kim Wilde's Christmas Party' at Holmfirth's Picturedrome on 16 December, and London's Coronet on 18 December. The London concert featured guest stars Steve Norman from Spandau Ballet, Clare Grogan from Altered Images, and Glenn Gregory from Heaven 17.

Earlier in 2015, Kim was honoured with the BASCA 'Gold Badge Award' to recognize her contribution to the UK music industry.

The year ended with Kim's niece Scarlett going away to Australia to study art for a year. It meant that Kim had to find a different backing vocalist, and she was found in the shape of Izzy Chase. As a session vocalist she had already worked with Ellie Goulding, Rod Stewart, and Boy George. During the year 2016 she would perform live with Kim and her band in Europe and the UK.

The year 2016 started relatively quiet. While her radio shows were still rolling on, Kim did not play any gigs until the festival season started in May. She did find time to record a track for the soundtrack of the movie *Eddie the Eagle*, a sports comedy drama film about Eddie Edwards, who in 1988 became the first competitor to represent Great Britain in Olympic ski jumping, only to finish last at the event. The soundtrack album was released in March 2016.

On 2 October 2016, Steve Byrd passed away suddenly, suffering a heart attack in Munich, Germany. Having contributed to Kim's live and recorded work between 1982 and 1995, tributes flooded in via Twitter and on official fansite wilde-life.com
Kim: "RIP Guitar man, we shared a lot of extraordinary days." [17]
Ricky: "He was an incredible guitarist and such a great talent. RIP Steve." [18]
Richard Blanshard: "He had a wicked sense of humour, and when Steve began to write with Kim, they produced magical material. (...) We will all miss his spirit, his talent, his humour, enthusiasm and his friendship." [19]

In October 2016, Kim started a new tradition of touring the Netherlands. Having established contact with new promoter, Peter Boone Music Productions, she was booked for six venues across the country for seven sold-out gigs. Hertfordshire-based singer/songwriter Lawrence Hill was the support act, his first gigs outside the UK, having first caught Kim's attention when he was playing live locally. It was her co-manager Nick Boyles who offered him the support slot during the Dutch tour. With his songs he made an impression on the audiences, so much so that he would join Kim again during her next Dutch tour a year later.

Kim's set started with an intro featuring samples from 'Cambodia', 'Never Trust a Stranger', 'You Came' and 'You Keep Me Hangin' On', before a rocking live version of 'King of the World'. An acoustic set by Kim and Ricky featured 'If I Can't Have You' and 'Hey Mister Heartache', after which they were joined by Lawrence Hill for

CHAPTER 20: WILDE WINTER SONGBOOK

'Chequered Love' and 'It's Here'. Other remarkable songs during this tour included cover versions of Talk Talk's 'It's My Life' and Dead Or Alive's 'You Spin Me Round (Like a Record)'.

A month later, Kim undertook a live tour in Australia, with Howard Jones. Like the tour with Nik Kershaw in 2013, having two big names from the 1980s on the bill was a way to fill the big Australian clubs. Since Scarlett was already in Australia, it was easy for her to rejoin the band while on a break from her studies. Howard and Kim each had their own sets, and they ended each concert with an acapella rendition of the Beach Boys' 'God Only Knows', performed by Kim, Ricky, Scarlett and Howard.

Howard Jones: "We just wanted to do something together. It was a celebration of 50 years of the *Pet Sounds* album and the amazing writing of Brian Wilson, so we're doing the amazing song 'God Only Knows', acapella. And there's people crying in the audience and phoning people up, holding their phones up to relatives, it's an amazing reaction." [20]

Australian reviewers were positive: the *Spotlight Report* website wrote: "The real highlight of the night was the final song. A duet between the co-headliners singing Jones' favourite song; 'God Only Knows' by The Beach Boys. The affinity these two pop stars have for each other, and for music shone through like the sun." [21] And the *Internal Jukebox* website added: "Kim Wilde and Howard Jones didn't just rely on the retro trend to have a good show, they brought the house down with passion and amazing talent." [22]

And then 2016 ended with the announcement that Marty Wilde was to receive an MBE from the Queen, for his services to popular music.

Marty: "I thought it was a tax form, because it was a brown envelope, but it was a letter from the Prime Minister!" [23]

He received the honour at Buckingham Palace, together with Joyce, Roxanne and Kim, on 5 May 2017.

Marty: "I'm 100 per cent a royalist and I think the Queen is fantastic. When she pinned on the medal, she asked me if I was still going strong. It was a surreal moment - one I could never have imagined when I started out singing for a quid and a bowl of spaghetti." [24]

Kim: "Growing up, the Queen and Elvis were like Jesus and Mary in our house. We arrived not knowing if the Queen would be doing the honours, but when a young usher gave us the nod that she was there, we became quite emotional. It made all the difference that our Queen pinned the MBE on Dad's lapel that day." [25]

Kim: "I'm so proud. My Dad's a pioneer. He was one of the first ever-pop stars. And to think that my Dad was right there at the very beginning… this is a great, great day, not least of all because we got to spend the afternoon with our beloved Queen." [26]

Near the end of 2016, Nick Boyles announced that he would step back as Kim's manager. Having been with her since 1981, it had been a long and interesting run, but he didn't feel he was ready to commit to another project. And there was a project on the horizon: a new album was already being worked on. Some changes had to be made. Sean Vincent, who had already worked with Kim for several years as her soundman during live concerts and creating music videos for the entire *Wilde Winter Songbook* project, stepped up, managing her from 2017.

After a quiet first half of the year, Kim played festivals in Denmark, the UK, Germany and Switzerland during the summer. In November 2017, Kim did another tour of the Netherlands, again with Lawrence Hill as her support act. An absolute highlight was her concert in Tilburg, which took place on her birthday, 18 November. All through the concert, audience members gave her flowers and gifts, the outpouring of love and appreciation from the crowd tangible.

By the end of 2017, Kim was ready to end the Christmas part of her career with a bang: together with Lawnmower Deth she recorded 'F U Kristmas!', a loud and tongue-firmly-in-cheek anti-Christmas song. For fans who felt *Wilde Winter Songbook* was a tad too schmaltzy, this single explored the other end of the spectrum. It cleared the way for 2018, when Kim was ready to release a whole new album and give her career another boost.

Before that, however, there was the small matter of the Wilde Wild Xmas Show, at the O2 Ritz in Manchester on 22 December 2017, featuring support acts Toyah, Carol Decker from T'Pau and Dr & the Medics, after which Kim performed live with special guests Lawnmower Deth, the only time they performed 'F U Kristmas' together on stage.

Pete Lee: "You can expect a very nervous punk metal band. We've done some pretty big shows in the past 10 years since we got back together. We've also done quite a few small ones. But this is different to any other show we've ever done and is an entirely different audience. We will be us, we don't change for anyone, nor are we capable of doing so, nor does Kim want us to, but I think we may make a few people cry." [27]

Kim and the band not only performed 'F U Kristmas', but also a version of 'Kids in America', and then, together with all the supporting artists, 'Merry Xmas Everybody' and 'I Wish It Could Be Christmas Everyday'.

WINTER WONDERLAND (with Rick Astley)
Written by Felix Bernard & Richard B. Smith
Produced by Ricky Wilde

'Wilde Winter Songbook' opens with a traditional winter song. It was written in 1934 by Richard Smith, who was reportedly inspired when he saw his local

Honesdale Central Park covered in snow. The original recording by Richard Himber and his Hotel Ritz-Carlton Orchestra was quickly followed by Guy Lombardo having the biggest hit of 1934 with his version. Since then, more than 150 artists have recorded the song.

Kim's version was recorded with her band, with added vocals by Rick Astley, her fellow pop star and a colleague at Magic Radio at the time.

Kim: "It was great to work with him. He's not only a charming man, his voice mixes perfectly with mine." [28]

Kim: "Felix Bernard and Richard B. Smith wrote 'Winter Wonderland' in 1934, since when over 150 artistes have covered this song; so I was determined to try to bring something new to the table for this much-loved Christmas classic. I asked Rick Astley to join me singing the main melody, while I take the third harmony above throughout the song until right at the end. Having sung with Rick live on a few occasions before and loving every moment, I was over the moon when he accepted my invitation to come down to RAK recording studio to duet with me. 'Winter Wonderland' is a hopelessly romantic and quintessential Christmas song, and one I've especially loved since singing it live with Status Quo on QuoFestive 2011. I think Rick Astley's and my voice go perfectly together; like a hot cup of tea and a digestive biscuit! [29]

The video was filmed at London's Winter Wonderland, the annual Christmas amusement park at Hyde Park in London, with Kim and Rick on a merry-go-round, on the dodgems, and near the ice skating rink.

HOPE
Written by Kim & Ricky Wilde & Mark Cummins
Produced by Ricky Wilde

The first original composition on the album did exactly what the title promised: even the most cynical person would melt hearing this song. In fact, the lyrics encourage the listener: '*Don't listen to the cynical / Who say things never change / And believe there are miracles / That can happen every day*'.

The song was originally written during Kim's hiatus from music by Ricky and Mark Cummins. It had different lyrics and was called 'Christmas Song'. Having not actually released it previously, Ricky proposed the song for the Christmas album, but Kim wanted to work a little on the lyrics, so she changed them.

Kim: "Ricky sent this backing track to me early on in the project – it was originally a Christmas song he'd had hidden away on his computer for some years. The message of hope sometimes seems like a naïve concept in our increasingly cynical and violent world, but in my world – and many others – hope is a source of great strength. My daughter, Rose, and her best friend,

Emily Ilott, came to sing backing vocals; young voices symbolising the hope for tomorrow's generation. Sentimental? Well, at Christmas time I think I might be forgiven. [30]

The track was remixed by Electric Penguins, a band consisting of Mark Cummins, Sean Quinn and Paul Murphy. Originally offered as an exclusive download on December 2013 for subscribers on Kim's e-mail list, it was included on the deluxe edition of *Wilde Winter Songbook* in 2015.

The video was filmed in Kim's living room with her band, performing the song. Some of the video footage from January 2013 was also used, with Kim's back garden covered in snow.

ONE
Written by Kim Wilde
Produced by Ricky Wilde

The first song written for *Wilde Winter Songbook*, appropriately titled, this accomplished, intimate track, featuring piano by Kim and a string arrangement from drummer Jonathan Atkinson, describes the feeling of celebrating Christmas together perfectly, and also refers to Christmas decorations. '*One by one / Out from the box they'll come / Shiny as new / Memories of Christmases past we've been through / Me and you / We are one*'.

Kim: "Last Christmas, via Twitter, I became aware of a new Christmas album by Tracey Thorn called *Tinsel and Lights*. Having always been a fan of hers since the early Eighties in her post-punk band The Marine Girls, then after with Ben Watt in Everything But the Girl, I immediately got myself a copy. Tracey had written a beautiful new song called 'Joy', which I fell in love with. Completely inspired, I decided then and there that I too wanted to create my very own Christmas album. I sat down at my piano and wrote this song – the first song for the album – and recreating the piano part at RAK Studios in front of my hugely talented band was a nerve-racking experience. The beautiful and tender string arrangement by my drummer, Jonathan Atkinson, touches my heart every time I listen to it." [31]

Kim: "I love my tree Christmas decorations and take special care with them, putting them all away very carefully every year. I have ones that remind me of Christmas markets in Germany, ones I bought for Harry and Rose, and fans have given me beautiful ones, just lovely pieces. Very personal. I think Christmas decorations have a lot of potency and a lot of power with memories of Christmas's past. When I slip off this mortal coil it will be my box of Christmas decorations that will be the most coveted thing I would be handing down. 'One' was also a song written about going through life with my husband

Hal, a love song to him. Sometimes it's tough at Christmas, it's not always a box of perfect Christmas decorations, and there is a melancholy in the song that reflects that." [32]

'One' was performed live only once, during a concert In Saasveld in the Netherlands on 14 December 2013. Kim appears in the music video alone, singing the song and playing the piano in her living room.

HAVE YOURSELF A MERRY LITTLE CHRISTMAS
Written by Hugh Martin & Ralph Blane
Produced by Ricky Wilde

Written in 1943 for the movie *Meet Me In St Louis*, 'Have Yourself A Merry Little Christmas' first appeared in a scene in which a family is distraught by a father's plans to move to New York City for a job promotion, leaving behind their beloved home in St Louis, Missouri. In a scene set on Christmas Eve, Judy Garland's character, Esther, sings the song to cheer up her despondent five-year-old sister, Tootie, played by Margaret O'Brien. Some of the lines in the original draft of lyrics had to be changed because Garland, co-star Tom Drake and director Vincente Minelli thought they were too depressing. For example, '*It may be your last / Next year we may all be living in the past*' became '*Let your heart be light / Next year all our troubles will be out of sight*'. Since the original version, many artists have recorded the song, including Frank Sinatra, Bing Crosby, Ella Fitzgerald, The Pretenders, Amy Grant and Luther Vandross. **Kim: "I grew up hearing this song by the great Judy Garland. The lyrics, although on the face of it quite upbeat, have an underlying melancholy which really appeals to me. Christmas can be a happy time for friends and family, but often life has different plans. I love the optimism of this song; in spite of anything life throws at you, 'Have Yourself a Merry Little Christmas!'"** [33]

In the world of Kim Wilde, 'Have Yourself A Merry Little Christmas' has an interesting history. She actually recorded a version of this song in the 1990s. A cassette of this recording was auctioned during a Fan Meeting in March 1996. It is a quiet version featuring keyboards, quiet drums and Kim's beautiful vocals. And Kim performed the song live during a Christmas concert in Germany on 10 December 2006, with acoustic backing by Nick Beggs, Perry ap Gwynnedd and Ricky.

The version recorded for *Wilde Winter Songbook* is playful and upbeat, and this was underscored by the music video, which showed Kim and her band – plus Kim's dog Jessica – as cartoon characters. It was created by Ian Holmes, the lighting and video designer for Kim's live shows since 2009.

Kim subsequently recorded another version of 'Have Yourself A Merry Little Christmas' as a duet with Tony Hadley on a deluxe version of his *Christmas Album* in 2016.

Kim and Neil Jones live at Cultuurpodium Boerderij, Zoetermeer (Netherlands), 4 October 2015 © Katrien Vercaigne

Kim live at the O2 Academy, Birmingham (UK), 19 December 2013 © Katrien Vercaigne

Kim live at Cultuurpodium Boerderij, Zoetermeer (Netherlands), 4 October 2015 © Katrien Vercaigne

WINTER SONG
Written by Sara Bareilles & Ingrid Michaelson
Produced by Ricky Wilde

In 2008, this song was released on a holiday compilation album, *The Hotel Café Presents Winter Songs*, featuring various female artists. Bareilles and Michaelson, who wrote the song, performed it as well. Although it was just a minor hit in Canada, where the album was released (it peaked at No.97 in the Canadian Hot 100), the track reached No.2 in Ireland in 2011. That year, the song was given a new lease of life when a group of Twitter users recorded the song as a charity single. All proceeds of the charity recording went to the Neonatal Unit of Holles Street Hospital in Dublin. While the single by 'Twitterers and the Twitterettes of the Parish of Twitter' reached its peak position at No.8 in Ireland on 8 December 2011, the original version went to No.2 the same week.

Kim heard the song online and wanted to record her own version. She sings most of the vocals, with subtle musical backing on bass, keyboards, guitar by Ricky, while Scarlett contributes backing vocals.

Kim: "This beautiful song by Sara Bereilles captivated me when I first heard it. Ricky came up with an idea to use 'vocoder' harmonies, as well as adding his own to create a 'hymn-like' quality, which I love. The pauses in the song allow for quiet reflection, like a prayer. There are no religious references at all on this album, I leave that to each individual. I have my own opinions about spirituality which might become clear as you listen to this album...or then again, might not."[34]

Originally, only a so-called 'lyric video' was made for this song, the lyrics of the song projected over wintry images. On the DVD of the deluxe edition of *Wilde Winter Songbook*, a compilation of video footage from other music videos appeared.

NEW LIFE
Written by Kim Wilde & Ricky Wilde
Produced by Ricky Wilde

Starting with the sonogram of the heartbeat of Ricky's daughter-in-law's unborn child, this song was dedicated to new life in the Wilde family. Both Kim's sister Roxanne and Ricky's daughter-in-law Lissy were pregnant over Christmas 2012, and this inspired the track. *'But you don't know / Sweet little thing / Safely inside / You don't know of the joy you'll bring into our lives / Or of the love that surrounds you on this winter's night / You are new, new life.'* The vocal harmonies near the end are intricate and moving, and the guitar solo, courtesy of Neil Jones, ends the track all too soon.

Kim: "Ricky sent this beautiful melody to me late one night as I lay in bed. As my husband Hal was sleeping, I put my earphones on and felt inspired to write the lyrics immediately. 'New Life' as a title came immediately, as over the previous Christmas we had a huge family get-together on Boxing Day, and both my sister Roxanne and her husband Richie, and Ricky's son Marty and his fiancé Lissy were both pregnant and expecting a baby the following summer. This song is a lullaby to the unborn babies who have yet to make their mark on the world, bringing so much love and joy, and is a wonderful memory of a family Christmas spent together." [35]

Kim: "Scarlett came up with this beautiful sort of playground backing vocals at the end. She captures the energy and joy of children running about in a playground. Her voice is amazing, the way it soars upwards towards the end always catches my breath!"

The music video starts with a picture of a pregnant Roxanne and Lissy, taken during a family gathering at Kim's home, and ends with pictures of them with their newborn babies. In between, Kim and her band perform the song in Kim's living room.

WHITE WINTER HYMNAL (with Marty Wilde)
Written by Robin Pecknold
Produced by Ricky Wilde

Fleet Foxes released this song as their first single in July 2008. The mysterious lyrics don't reveal much, but the harmonies on the song are exquisite.

Kim quickly picked up on this, and since the Wildes were always into singing harmonies, it was a great idea to get together and sing this song, Kim, Ricky, Scarlett and Dad Marty recording together.

On 8 November 2013, Kim, Ricky and Scarlett premiered their version of the song during a live performance on Chris Evans' show on BBC Radio 2. Three days later, the music video, recorded in Kim's home and directed by Sean Vincent, was published via YouTube.

Kim: "I first heard this song when I saw the Fleet Foxes perform it at Glastonbury in 2011 and loved it straight away. I remember as children my Dad and Mum would encourage Ricky and me to take harmonies on Everly Brothers songs. Finding a harmony in any song became second nature to me from an early age, and I went on to do the majority of all backing vocals on my records. Like the Fleet Foxes, we were all big fans of harmony-based bands and artistes, loving Bryan Wilson and the Beach Boys, Simon and

Garfunkel, and Crosby, Stills and Nash, among others. I knew my Dad would love the quirky eccentricity of this song, along with the sublime melody and harmonies. My brother, Ricky, takes third harmony, and so the three of us are taken back to where it all started, together with Ricky's daughter Scarlett, who's harmony work carries on the family tradition." [36]

Kim: "I love its darker aspects. I thought it would be really interesting for my father to sing some lyrics he doesn't normally sing. I wasn't that surprised when he said yes. He's always had an extremely open mind." [37]

Scarlett, Marty, Kim and Ricky appear in the video, sat close to each other near the hearth in Kim's living room.

BURN GOLD/SILENT NIGHT (with Hal Fowler)
Written by Kim Wilde & Hal Fowler
Produced by Ricky Wilde

The Christmas carol 'Silent Night' was composed by Franz Xaver Gruber and written by Joseph Mohr as 'Stille Nacht, Heilige Nacht' in Austria in 1818. Whenever artists recorded Christmas albums, 'Silent Night' usually made an appearance. The song was recorded by Bing Crosby, Julie Andrews, Simon & Garfunkel, the Carpenters, Sinead O'Connor, Mariah Carey, and Justin Bieber, to name a few.

Kim performed 'Silent Night' live during her Christmas concert in Kirchbrombach in December 2006 and Christmas concerts at Knebworth House in December 2014, together with the Knebworth Community Chorus. But on *Wilde Winter Songbook*, 'Silent Night' was combined with 'Burn Gold', based on a poem written by Hal Fowler.

Hal's poem involves a beautiful description of nature and trees waiting throughout the winter. *'Let's learn from them / Both you and I / Lay low and silent for a while / Wait for the promise of our spring to come / Then shine our colours on everyone'*, the poem concludes, before a verse of 'Silent Night'. Anyone who has heard 'Silent Night' a million times before will listen to it quite differently after this interpretation.

Kim: "I have a box of poems from my husband, and one of them I adapted as the song 'Burn Gold' on my last album." [38]

Kim: "This is the first song I've written with my husband, Hal, who has written many beautiful poems over the years we've been married - I keep them all in a special box .The song began with a simple piano part I came up with to evoke the snow falling silently on a still, cold, winter's night...'Silent Night'. Hal heard me working with the idea and suggested adding another theme; based on some poems he had written several years back, they combined beautifully. Hal also sings with me, making this song especially personal to both of us." [39]

Kim: "The song was inspired by a poem my husband wrote and our life together: the spring we met, the summer of our children, the autumn of life challenges, and the winter of regeneration. The song is inspired by the many trees we have planted together and ends with my all-time favourite Christmas song." [40]

The track was remixed by Electric Penguins. Originally offered as an exclusive download in December 2013 for subscribers on Kim's e-mail list, it was included on the deluxe edition of *Wilde Winter Songbook* in 2015.

SONG FOR BERYL
Written by Kim & Ricky Wilde & Mark Cummins
Produced by Ricky Wilde

Just like 'Hope', this song was originally written by Ricky and Mark Cummins with different lyrics. Kim rewrote the lyrics as a dedication to her late friend Beryl Askew. It is the most personal track on the album and a beautiful tribute.
Kim: "There's a song about an old lady I knew, who I used to garden for in some sheltered accommodation near where we live... a game gal who liked a glass of wine, who became housebound as she got older, and we were with her until the end of her life. I've simply called it 'Song For Beryl'." [41]
Kim: "Beryl was already in her late 70's when we first came to know her, and became a great friend of our family. We met whilst making a community garden in our village, and she would take care of Harry and Rose while I got on with the planting! Beryl lived alone in sheltered accommodation and was increasingly less mobile before becoming house-bound. We formed a close bond and shared good times and bad. I know she'll be at the great 'pub in the sky' enjoying a glass of white wine as she hears this song, written especially for her." [42]

The music video tells a little story, starting in Kim's kitchen, where she looks outside. She goes to the garden centre to buy a tree and then plants it in her back garden. As she walks away with dog Jessica by her side, the tag on the tree reads 'Beryl'. The video ends with a photograph of Kim's old friend.

LET IT SNOW
Written by Sammy Cahn & Jule Steyne
Produced by Ricky Wilde

First recorded for RCA Victor in 1945 by Vaughn Monroe, 'Let It Snow' became a popular hit, reaching No.1 on the US Billboard Bestsellers music chart in late January and through February 1946. Since then, many artists have recorded the song, including Frank Sinatra, Dean Martin, Carly Simon, Rod Stewart, and Kylie Minogue.

Kim's version, recorded with her band, has a certain warmth to it. Neil Jones' guitar solo incorporates a portion of the melody of 'Rudolph the Red-Nosed Reindeer', a Christmas hit for Gene Autry in 1949.

Kim: "I have always loved the snow, yep; I'm one of those people who secretly pray for it every Christmas, while everyone around me curses the white stuff. I have always wondered what this song might be like approached from the perspective of sweethearts getting really hot by the fire, so I tapped into my Marilyn 'Some Like it Hot' mode before singing ... I almost blushed when I got to the part, 'And I've got some corn for poppin'! Neil Jones, our lead guitarist, has created a most beautiful and subtle solo and, in my opinion, raised the bar impossibly high for all those who'll come to record this song in the future. Our keyboard player, Stevie Power, has done a great job of arranging the song as well as strings, breathing original life into a classic recorded so many times over the years." [43]

The music video starts with Kim entering the RAK Studios building in London and features 'behind the scenes' footage from Kim and the band in the studio. They perform the song in Kim's living room, comparable to other music videos for this album.

HEY MISTER SNOWMAN
Written by Kim Wilde
Produced by Ricky Wilde

An upbeat little song with harmonies that evoke the Andrews Sisters, in a sublime way. 'Hey Mister Snowman' is one of many songs on the album with a winter theme, its protagonist wanting to talk to a snowman in order to feel better.

Kim: "This was the last song written for the album. I woke up very early one morning with the whole song in my head, and sneaked downstairs to write it all down on my computer before I forgot anything. I have always been a big fan of the Andrews Sisters, loving their tight and clever harmony work, often injected with a large helping of humour. I sang the song over breakfast to my

children Harry and Rose that same morning...they both exchanged worried glances. Neil Jones has again created a sublime guitar solo, and Scarlett cleverly takes on some very challenging harmony work. Sounds easy... it isn't!" [44]

A promotional CD-single featured a 'radio edit' of the song, which while the same length deletes the spoken word dialogue between Scarlett and Kim from the intro.

The music video is filmed in black and white and depicts Kim and guests inside a car. With Kim behind the wheel, other passengers are Scarlett, Neil Jones, Kim's daughter Rose and dog Jessica.

In December 2013, Kim, Scarlett and Rick performed an acoustic version of 'Hey Mister Snowman' on German TV show *Guten Morgen Deutschland*. In December 2015, they appeared on UK programme *Loose Women* to perform an acoustic medley of 'Hey Mister Snowman' and 'Rockin' Around the Christmas Tree'.

A German version of the song entitled 'Hey Lieber Schneemann' was posted on YouTube by Jonas 'The Music Man' in October 2020. It was sung by his daughter Selma, with lyrics by Dirk Holterman.

ROCKIN' AROUND THE CHRISTMAS TREE (with Nik Kershaw)
Written by Johnny Marks
Produced by Ricky Wilde

When you say Kim Wilde and Christmas, 'Rockin' Around the Christmas Tree' usually comes up, thanks to the single with Mel Smith from 1987. Including the song on *Wilde Winter Songbook* was almost a given, but it needed a fresh angle, so Nik Kershaw was invited to be Kim's singing partner on this version. He also contributes a guitar solo.

Kim: "Me and this song go back a long way, starting when 'Comic Relief' asked comedian Mel Smith and I to record it to support the first Red Nose Day in 1987. It reached No.3 in the UK charts and has been played on the radio every Christmas since. More recently my brother Ricky and I were caught belting this tune out on a train from London's Kings Cross to Potters Bar. We had both been to a rather wonderful party hosted by Magic FM 105.4 and were in a somewhat over-refreshed state...the rest, as they, is history. This time I'm joined by my dear friend Nik Kershaw, who not only turns in a rather fab vocal, but also plays an equally fab guitar solo to boot! A huge hats off to the KW band - Rick, Neil Jones, Stevie P and Jonny A - for putting the 'Rock' into 'Rockin'!" [45]

The music video was recorded as a revisit of Kim & Rick's 'over-refreshed' train ride. Only this time the train is decorated and there are a few more people around:

Kim's band, Nik Kershaw, Case Eames, Mandy and Nick Boyles. The video is dedicated to the memory of Mel Smith, who passed away in July 2013.

Kim: "We rented a disused railway carriage fairly locally, and all turned up and recreated the Christmas where Rick and I had a drunken sing-song on a train from London to Potters Bar, except we did the whole thing absolutely sober! We managed to get Nik Kershaw to wear antlers, which I wasn't sure he'd be up for, and together with my band, family and friends we filmed one of the happiest and sweetest videos of my career! We invited Case Eames, who videod us originally in our drunken state and had put it on the internet, where it eventually notched up almost three million views, a wonderful turning of the tables."

KEEPING THE DREAM ALIVE
Written by Stefan Zauner & Aron Strobel
Produced by Ricky Wilde

Originally recorded as 'So Lang' Man Träume Noch Leben Kann' in 1987, German band Münchener Freiheit recorded the song in English as 'Keeping The Dream Alive' in 1988. Although the band had already tried to get international success, ditching the 'Münchener' from their name and releasing several German singles in English, 'Keeping The Dream Alive' remained their only international hit, peaking at No.14 in the UK singles chart and No.20 in Ireland. Although the lyrics do not mention snow or Christmas, it still receives a lot of airplay at Christmas time in Britain, and can be found on many festive compilation albums.

Kim recorded her version as a bonus track for the deluxe edition of *Wilde Winter Songbook*, with a string arrangement by Jonathan and Tom Atkinson.

The video starts with photos and videos of Kim and Ricky during their childhood, who sing the song before a dark background, while images from throughout Kim's career are projected.

Kim: The video has footage of Ricky and me as small babies, toddlers, slightly older children, and moments in our professional life. Sean Vincent created a beautiful narrative of our lives together in the video, much of it unseen cine film filmed by my Dad many years ago, and also some early live footage. We dedicated that video to Mickie Most, who first realised Ricky's huge potential as a writer and producer and of course my own potential as a pop star! It feels like Ricky and I have shared an amazing dream all these years, and we intend to keep the dream alive!"

ISOBEL'S DREAM
Written by Kim & Ricky Wilde
Produced by Ricky Wilde

Inspired by the children's book *Isobel and the Land of the Pink Bears*, which Kim read as a child, she finally found a copy of the book online, having searched for it since the summer of 2012. The lyric of the song roughly refers to the story of the book.

A spoken word section starts with Rose reading a portion of the book, Kim taking over after a few lines. '*There was once upon a time a little girl called Isobel / One night a snowy white cloud came sailing towards her window / Like a crystal ship that sparkled in the air / 'I've come to take you on a journey,' said a quiet voice / 'Where?' she asked. / 'To the land of dreams, except these ones come true if you want them to.*"

Kim: "I recently acquired a book I'd had as a child, a book that got me through quite a tricky time in our lives. We found ourselves at seven or eight years old in a boarding school for a period of time, which was really tough for both of us. And that book was really important. It was one of my lifelines at that time. (…) I'd lost it for many years and went on the internet and rediscovered it. Lo and behold, it turned up in the post and it was like someone had come back from the dead. It was just an astonishing thing to open those pages again, and then of course the lyrics flooded out as soon as I heard the beautiful music Rick had composed. The song also features the speaking voice of my daughter Rose merging with mine, making this a very personal song." [46]

DECK THE HALLS (ANGELS SING)
Trad., with additions by Kim & Ricky Wilde
Produced by Ricky Wilde

Christmas carol 'Deck the Halls' is based on a Welsh melody, dating back to the 16th century. The English lyrics were written by Scottish musician Thomas Oliphant. They first appeared in 1862, in Volume 2 of *Welsh Melodies* a set of four volumes authored by John Thomas, including Welsh words by John Jones (Talhaiarn) and English words by Oliphant. The repeated 'fa la la' goes back to the earlier Welsh and may originate from medieval ballads.

In Kim's version, one verse of the Christmas carol is used and then launches into the 'Angels Sing' segment. Kim performed the song live at Knebworth House on December 12 and 14, 2014 for the first time, with added vocals by the Knebworth Community Chorus. During further Christmas concerts in December 2015, she again performed the song.

A studio recording, recorded with London Contemporary Voices, appears on the deluxe edition of *Wilde Winter Songbook* released in 2015. They also recorded a music video together at the Asylum in South London, an artist-run community arts centre and former chapel, on 28 September 2015, with Sean Vincent directing.

Kim performed the song for BBC TV programme *Songs Of Praise* in December 2015, as part of a short documentary about the origins of the song.

LAST CHRISTMAS
Written by George Michael
Produced by Ricky Wilde

'Last Christmas' could be seen as the ultimate Christmas song. Since its release in 1984 it has become so essential that radio stations can't avoid the song in December. Although the original version recorded by Wham! is hard to beat, it has been covered many times.

Kim's version is beautiful because of its simplicity. It is performed by Kim, Ricky and Scarlett, with just keyboards and guitar to accompany their voices.
Kim: "We kept this classic Christmas song very simple, just three-part harmony with Ricky, Scarlett and myself, guitar and piano. This was an homage to George Michael from us."

LAS CARTAS (with Chico & the Gypsies)
Written by Dominic James Miller & Gordon Sumner
Produced by Thorsten Schotten, Tony O'Melley & Christian Geller

Jahloul 'Chico' Bouchikhi formed Chico & the Gypsies in 1992 after leaving the band Gipsy Kings, who enjoyed an international breakthrough when they recorded the song 'Bamboleo'. With his new band he continued to have success.

In June 2014, they released the album *Chico & the Gypsies & International Friends*, featuring duets with various artists, including Kim. She sings on the track 'Las Cartas', an adaptation of Sting's 1993 song 'Shape of my Heart'. The album reached No.60 in France.

LOVE WILL KEEP US TOGETHER
Written by Howard Greenfield & Neil Sedaka
Produced by Ricky Wilde

Neil Sedaka recorded 'Love Will Keep Us Together' after writing it with Howard Greenfield in 1973. Originally the song was written with Diana Ross in mind, but it was the duo Captain & Tennille who made the song famous in 1975. Their version became the best-selling single of the year in the USA and topped the charts in Canada and Australia as well.

The version by Kim Wilde was recorded for the album *80's Re:Covered*, released in September 2015, on which 12 artists best known for their success in the 1980s recorded exclusive cover versions of songs from the 1970s and 1980s. Remarkably, the album was only released in South America.

WITHOUT YOUR LOVE
Written by Glenn Gregory, Berenice Scott & Gary Barlow
Produced by Berenice Scott & Glenn Gregory

'Without Your Love' was written for the soundtrack of the movie of *Eddie the Eagle*. With many male artists contributing to the soundtrack – Holly Johnson, Howard Jones, Marc Almond, Midge Ure, Andy Bell, Paul Young and Go West, to name but a few – Kim's contribution comes as a breath of fresh air.

The music is largely electronic, and created by Berenice Scott (daughter of Robin Scott, aka M) and Heaven 17's Glenn Gregory, who also wrote and produced the track.

F U KRISTMAS! (with Lawnmower Deth)
Written by Pete Lee, Paddy O'Maley, Steve Nesfield, Kim & Ricky Wilde
Produced by Ricky Wilde

Kim had been a fan of Lawnmower Deth's cover version of 'Kids in America' since she first heard it. The band asked Kim to join them on stage during Download Festival in 2016. They didn't just play 'Kids in America' together, Kim also joined in on Lawnmower Deth classics 'Egg Sandwich' and 'Watch Out Grandma'. This surreal moment was followed by a possibly even more surreal collaboration: the track 'F U Kristmas', released in December 2017.

This is a different kind of Christmas song. Kim offers: "*I love winter round the tree / Spending time with family / Joy and children spreading laughter / Peace at Christmas forever after*", after which Lawnmower Deth's lead singer Pete Lee cuts in with "*Wreck the halls with rows of folly / Hate the season for the jolly*". According to him, 'F U Kristmas' was 'the greatest project [the band has] been involved in'. The song was described as an 'anti-Christmas song' and 'punk and thrash-metal crossover number with thrashing riffs and hardcore vocals'.

Kim: "I've heard several covers [of 'Kids in America'], but my favourite is always Lawnmower Deth's version. I heard they'd done it, then I saw it on YouTube and loved that. It's completely bonkers and the energy of it, but they did it in the early 90s, before social media took over, so I never got to meet

them. When anyone asked me, it was a no-brainer, I'd always say them. I ended up meeting them and doing Download Festival with them a few years ago, which was really good fun. I got to know their music more and ended up singing some of their songs with them. Then this last Christmas, we made our inappropriate Christmas homage, which was called 'F U Kristmas!'. To my great shame, but also great pride, it was me that came up with the idea of calling it that. I thought while I was singing it, 'No one's ever going to play this, but I don't give a fuck!'" [47]

Pete Lee: "Once Kim and I had drunk beer and decided we were going to do this, Steve wrote the track, but naturally back then it was sounding very, very different. Once we had a backbone in place, I wrote the lyrics. It's the first time for us we have worked in a collaborative way, so it was a whole new thing. Steve recorded the track at home in his home studio, and now of course this can be circulated without anyone leaving the house. Things basically spent six months travelling between Steve, myself, Kim and Ricky, the chorus became the verse, the verse the chorus, a hook was added, and so on. The final step was actually getting together to record the vocals at Ricky's studio, and before you know it, we had a finished track. And very pleased we are with it too." [48]

Pete Lee: "It wasn't a polar leap to ask Kim to join us at Download Festival in 2016. Now, working on a Christmas single together, some would say it's the most bizarre juxtaposition since KLF and Extreme Noise Terror at the Brits. I prefer a bunch of loveable chancers married with pure pop royalty." [49]

A promotional CD-single featured a 'clean mix' and a 'sweary mix'. A video to accompany the song, directed by Sean Vincent, was released on Kim's official YouTube channel on 1 December 2017.

INTERVIEW: CASE EAMES

Please tell us a little bit about yourself...
I was born in 1984 and had grown up with Kim Wilde, from being a famous singer with her tunes being played so often on the radio and on TV - on things like *Top of the Pops* to her gardening shows later on in her career. I'm a big music lover and my usual station of choice is Magic FM. I often found myself listening to Kim's Sunday slot on the radio over the years from my early 20s, when I lived in South London on the way to do my food shopping to when I moved to Hertfordshire to commute into London, working at the weekend.

How did you get to film Kim and Ricky on the train after their Christmas party?

CHAPTER 20: WILDE WINTER SONGBOOK

At the time I was doing two jobs - one as a performing tour guide impersonating Nell Gwynne at the Theatre Royal, Drury Lane, another as a follow spot operator backstage at the London Palladium. The day it happened I was down to work from 10am-10pm, a bit of a slog, and to make matters worse my now-wife Shelley was very unwell in hospital with suspected meningitis! I hopped in and out of town from Potters Bar twice that day to see her on my breaks. My boss let me have the matinee off to see her, but couldn't find the cover for the evening show, so I had to go back to work. It was hugely worrying and exhausting! Thankfully it wasn't meningitis and she ended up being okay. Finally, after two guided tours, a hospital visit and an anxious evening show, I was going back home to her. And when I stepped on the train sometime after 10pm, I couldn't get a bloomin' seat, having to stand in the aisle.

I was aware that the Magic FM party was that week, because the DJs had been talking about it on the radio. Soon as I got on, I almost instantly spotted Ricky's massive guitar on the parcel shelf above him, and he was chatting away to a blonde woman in sparkly antlers. I knew that voice so well from all those times listening to her chatting on the show I was so fond of, and thought, 'She really sounds like Kim Wilde!'. Then I saw Ricky get his guitar and was like, 'Oh God, I'm really not in the mood for a busker today'. But when he got it down and, because I thought it might be her, it was a no-brainer - I had to press record to see what was about to happen. Then my bad mood disappeared...

As grumpy as those people looked in the foreground, behind the camera people were enjoying it more, including myself, needing some old-fashioned Christmas cheer. I sang along, laughed and cheered. It was absolutely wonderful.

When I got home, I couldn't believe what I'd witnessed. I put the video on Facebook for my friends, it started to go a bit nuts, and I had second thoughts and took it off - worried it could do Kim damage. So the next morning I sent her a tweet: '@kimwilde made my night! Had the longest shittest day and you made me so happy on the train last night. You are brilliant!' She replied, '@case_84. Not often I'm on a train with @wildericky and a handy guitar! Wasn't that little bot a star?'

I couldn't believe she replied, so decided to send her a private message. I told her I'd filmed the whole thing, and would she mind if I posted it on YouTube. She said to go for it, so with her permission, I did.

When you posted the video, did you expect the amount of views it eventually got? What were those first few days like?

After loading it, the numbers multiplied throughout the day. I think it hit about 250,000 in the first 24 hours. My phone went crazy with all the comments and sharing. Then I started getting enquiries from newspapers and TV, so quickly found an agent to help out. It went on for days. I couldn't believe it made the national news, and everywhere Kim is known it was talked about on TV shows like *This Morning* as well. I was often referred to as 'someone with a camera' or 'a girl filmed it', but it was pretty exciting when one actually mentioned me by name.

One massive thing Kim and I have in common is our ridiculous love for Christmas and positivity. As the video went crazy, we began to message each other a bit, mostly in disbelief as it hit so many views, and then just joyously about our mutual excitement for Christmas. Even the hashtag #antlers got trending at one point.

It's hard to believe this was eight years ago now, and every year it gets attention again. I think it really cheers people up, and that makes me so happy!

A year later you appeared on the video for 'Rockin' Around the Christmas Tree' with Kim and Nik Kershaw. How did that come about and what are your memories of filming this?

Kim decided to make her own spoof version of the event, and I believe it was her brother Ricky who got in touch to see if we wanted to be part of the fun. Shelley and I of course leapt at the chance. We had a total ball. Most of the people playing the passengers in the video were Kim and Ricky's mates, and we all piled into a cold, disused railway station to shoot it. It was great to finally meet Kim and Ricky properly and just laugh about it all. They were so good humoured about it, and it was nice that what happened turned into such a positive thing for their careers. We both got matching antlers from Kim, and she and Ricky signed a giant bauble, which we get out every year when we decorate the house at Christmas.

Every Christmas the clip comes 'round again and it gets played on TV or talked about in some way. Who wouldn't want to get a bit merry at Christmas and have a sing-song? I was even interviewed on a clip show for Channel 5 last year, *When Christmas Goes Horribly Wrong*. A nerve-racking first for me!

What is your favourite Kim Wilde song?

Well, I love 'Rockin Around the Christmas Tree' and 'Kids in America' of course, but I'm also a fan of 'You Keep Me Hangin' On'.

What do you like most about Kim as an artist and a person?

Kim is one of the warmest, kindest people you'll meet. She's totally down to earth (when she's not looking for aliens) and brilliant fun. I'd happily sit in a carriage with her and Ricky any day of the week. She's the kind of person that if you went on a night out with her, it would never be boring.

CHAPTER 21:
HERE COME THE ALIENS

Released: 16 March 2018
Chart positions: 21 (UK), 34 (Austria), 48 (Belgium), 68 (France), 11 (Germany), 74 (Netherlands) 10 (Switzerland)

On 25 June 2009, the world was shocked when American pop star Michael Jackson died. Jackson had been rehearsing for his planned concert residency of 50 concerts at the O2 in London in 2009 and 2010. He was found in his room, not breathing and with a weak pulse, later attributed to acute propofol and benzodiazepine intoxication. It caused an outpouring of grief from fans and celebrities, many of them being asked to comment on Jackson's sudden passing. Kim wrote a piece for her website, published on 1 July.

Kim: "When I was told of the death of Michael Jackson, I couldn't really take it in; I heard heard it late in the evening on Thursday 25 June 2009. By the time Friday morning came around I could feel a deep and gnawing sadness growing inside me, and I spent the next day playing his records as loudly as possible. Whenever his name is mentioned, or his music played I am transported back to a magical time in my life, forever grateful of the opportunity to tour with him on the Bad Tour in 1988, and for the amazing music he left us all with." [1]

The next night, a UFO was reported in the sky above Hertfordshire, with the event reported by a local newspaper [2]. Kim witnessed the UFO above her back garden. She only spoke about the event publicly over a year later in the German *Bild* newspaper.

Kim: "A year ago I saw a UFO. I know it sounds crazy, but it was in my backyard. These lights came from the south east, then they stopped and then they danced. If you do not believe me, it was also mentioned in our local paper. I was not the only one who has seen it. It was a day after Michael Jackson died." [3]

After that first occasion, the subject came up a few times in other interviews.

Kim: "It was 26 June, the day after Michael Jackson died, and me and my mate were in the garden and we saw bright lights in the sky. I have to say there's not a day gone by that I don't think about what the hell it was. It was so huge, two of them, going zig-zag for 10 minutes, and I could feel the momentum and knew it was really massive. It could be some advanced technology that someone developed somewhere, but I've a feeling it wasn't." [4]

Kim: "We were sat outside in the garden, me and my husband and one of my close friends. We'd spent the evening in A&E with our little boy, who had

suspected swine flu. So it wasn't a typical Friday night and suddenly noticing lights after the second bottle of Pinot! We put Harry on the sofa, to keep an eye on him, and went outside. It was still dusk but there was some low cloud. I noticed a very bright light coming up from the south east at the bottom of our garden, which faces on to fields, and some helicopters. I thought: 'Here we go, they're chasing someone'. Then the helicopters went over our roof, disappeared, and it all fell quiet. I'm sat there and saw this incredibly bright light still shining and static, behind low cloud in the way the moon shines behind clouds. I noticed it was unusual that it would be there. I got my friend to come down to the field and we looked up to see what it was. We thought it was perhaps a light from nearby Knebworth House, or someone was pointing lights into the sky, or letting off Chinese lanterns. But it didn't tick any of those boxes. It was silent and huge, and stayed there for a minute or two before zooming over from an 11 o'clock position, to a one or two o'clock position. It stayed there for a little while, zoomed straight back to 11, then did this two o'clock, 11 o'clock dance, with a smaller one following it. We couldn't actually see them, but the light they made was so bright and it was such a bizarre thing to see in the sky. I thought I was going mad. I'm so glad, in retrospect, there were two other people who saw it. It was inexplicable and extraordinary. That was on the Friday, and the following Monday the story made the local paper - someone else had seen it and managed to take a photograph of a sphere in the sky. Then I met other people locally who also saw something up there that night. It was observed by quite a lot of people. It was an astonishing thing to see, and still amazes me. I had a very strong sense that it wasn't a threatening thing - it was a benevolent feeling I had. I had a sense it was watching us." [5]

The encounter inspired what was to become *Here Come the Aliens*. Writing for the album started as early as 2012, but because Kim also worked on her Christmas album, that project was prioritised. Work on the new album progressed over the next few years, until it was finally announced in December 2017. 'Here Come the Aliens' was given a worldwide release in March 2018. That included the UK, where Kim hadn't released an original studio album since *Now & Forever* in 1995.

Kim: "On the back of [*Anyplace, Anywhere, Anytime* with Nena] we ended up recording a couple of original albums which were released in Germany which I'm really proud of, but I didn't feel it was appropriate to release them here because we didn't have the same momentum. Certainly there wasn't any great enthusiasm on anyone's part to get them released here. But this time it's different. It's a real commitment to be back in the UK, which is where it all started for me." [6]

Some of the album was recorded at RAK Studios in London.

Kim: "Recording the album there was a pilgrimage. It was there that the

CHAPTER 21: HERE COME THE ALIENS

legendary Mickie Most launched my career. The studio has not changed. Mickie changed our lives and it was a magical time. It was 1980, I'd just left art college and was dreaming of being a pop star. I turned 57 this year. It's very hard now to think I'm pushing 60 and I was only 20 when I first walked into the building." [7]

Kim: "I found the emotions of being there (at RAK) a little overwhelming from time to time. We recorded most of the tracks with my band there, but ended up doing a lot of the vocals in the Doghouse Studio, which is Ricky's studio, in a more intimate setting." [8]

The sleeve of the album featured, for the very first time, not a photograph of Kim, but a piece of artwork featuring her. The painting was created by Scarlett. The image was inspired by the Italian movie poster for *Earth vs. The Flying Saucers*, a 1956 movie starring Hugh Marlowe and Joan Taylor. The poster for *La Terra Contro I Dischi Volanti*, as it was called in Italian, bears some resemblance to the LP artwork, although Big Ben in the background is replaced by Amsterdam's Paradiso venue.

Kim: "My niece is studying art and is also my backing singer. She's very talented so I knew the artwork would be in safe hands. I saw some of her work and it was amazing, so I'd told her about my UFO experience, and she decided to go retro and create a fantasy sci-fi world for me." [9]

The album was released on CD and a yellow vinyl LP. In Germany, a limited-edition boxset of the album was released, containing the CD and yellow vinyl LP plus two art prints and a square canvas image of the album sleeve. Later in the year, a limited-edition red vinyl LP was released, and for Record Store Day in Germany a picture disc LP was available in selected record shops.

While promoting the album, Kim repeatedly spoke about what happened to her during that evening on 26 June 2009. It had a profound effect on her.

Kim: "I've thought about it pretty much every day since. I'm always looking up at the sky to see if anything else unusual is going on up there. (...) I wouldn't blame the aliens if they came down and flung us all off the earth, but I have a strong, positive faith in the human race, in spite of the terrible things that I observe. I'm still holding a flag of hope out for us, that we can learn from our mistakes and clear our mess up." [10]

Dutch magazine *Lust for Life* described the album as 'a solid rock record with great harmonies, nice guitar riffs, beautiful synth melodies and a singer who's just as enthusiastic as she was almost 40 years ago.'' [11] The UK's *Classic Pop* magazine added: "Wilde is still down with the kids, and often in unexpected ways. There's still reason to keep hangin' on." [12] *Record Collector*, also in the UK, remarked: "It's been some time since anyone made a frothy but smart pop record like Kim Wilde used to, so it's especially pleasing to find the woman herself answering the call." [13]

*Kim live at Tivoli Vredenburg, Utrecht (Netherlands),
17 November 2018 © Katrien Vercaigne*

Kim live at Tivoli Vredenburg, Utrecht (Netherlands), 17 November 2018 © Katrien Vercaigne

© Sean J. Vincent

And the *Express & Star* newspaper in the UK accurately remarked: "Disco, new wave, electro and glam rock all get an outing here, and spread throughout the record are also a sweet collection of popular culture Easter eggs." [14]

First single, 'Pop Don't Stop', was released on 30 January 2018. BBC Radio 2 made it their record of the week, and for the first time in a long while, a new Kim Wilde single was regularly played on the station.

Kim: "I haven't heard my record on the radio so much since the Eighties. It's a thrill to turn on the radio and hear my song coming out, especially as it is a duet with my brother Ricky. He's always sung on my albums and he's always had a beautiful voice – one of pop's best kept secrets, and now everyone knows!" [15]

Promotion for the album and the ensuing tour took place primarily in March, with countless radio interviews in the UK and a couple of appearances on German TV. Most notably, Kim, Scarlett, Rick and Neil Jones performed an acoustic version of 'Pop Don't Stop' on German channel ARD's *Morgenmagazin*.

The album's release coincided with a tour in the UK consisting of 19 dates between 30 March and 30 April. Although Kim was never big on costume changes, the tour was all about the right look. She worked with costume designer Christopher Wilmer, who previously worked with her on the video for 'Every Time I See You I Go Wild', to get the perfect sci-fi themed look.

For the first time, Kim toured with two drummers: Johnny Atkinson and Emily Dolan Davies. The other members of the band were the same: Ricky, Scarlett, Paul Cooper, Steve Power and Neil Jones.

In October 2018, a deluxe edition of *Here Come the Aliens* was released. This version added a second disc, with two new tracks, three remixes created by Ricky Wilde and three live tracks from the Here Come the Aliens UK tour.

The release coincided with the European leg of the tour, taking Kim and her band through Germany, Austria, Slovakia, Belgium and the Netherlands on 25 dates between 2 October and 24 November 2018. A notable change was the inclusion of album tracks 'Solstice' and 'Cyber.Nation.War', which were left out during the UK leg.

Descriptions of the tour in the press were elated: "You notice the positive chemistry and the ease between the family members throughout the show."[16] "After a middle section with quieter and new songs like 'Solstice', 'Rosetta' and 'Cyber.Nation.War.' almost no one sat during 'Chequered Love'." [17] "Fireworks such as the Supremes cover 'You Keep Me Hanging On', 'You Came' dedicated to true fans and the indispensable 'Kids in America' make for a brilliant conclusion to a memorable concert." [18]

A more unexpected collaboration happened in 2018, when Ricky and Kim collaborated with Denise Harrison on short film *This is Depression*. Harrison had started a blog of the same name to write about a particularly difficult period in her life. When the idea came around to create a short film, there was only the problem that she had never made a film before. Via social media she got in contact with illustrator Juli Dosad and Miguel Letang. The soundtrack would be provided by Ricky.

Denise Harrison: "The soundtrack for the film was written by singer/songwriter legend Ricky Wilde, and we had crossed paths when he messaged me to tell me how moved he had been by my blog. We kept in touch after that, so when he heard I was trying to put together a soundtrack for the film, not only did he offer to write it, he asked his sister – Eighties pop sensation Kim Wilde – to sing the lead vocals." [19]

This is Depression premiered in Manchester in 2018 and featured at film festivals in 2019. It won Best Animation in America and in October 2019 won Best Adaptation at the Discover Film Awards at the Prince Charles Cinema in London.

On 16 August 2019, live album *Aliens Live* was released, a collection of songs recorded during both legs of the tour in 2018. Each track was taken from a different city.

Kim: "People say to me, 'You've sung 'Kids in America' hundreds of times, thousands of times, don't you get bored of it?'. You know what, the audience make it fresh for us every single time. It's their energy that keeps that song alive, not just mine and the band. They give it straight back to us, and we've tried to capture that magic on this album. There's a special unity that happens at a live gig, which is rare in life." [20]

In November 2019, Kim and her band toured the Netherlands and Belgium, as had become tradition. The Return of the Aliens Tour, as it was called, started on 14 November and ended 10 days later.

Fans in Germany and the UK were treated to Christmas concerts in December, in a tour called Wilde Winter Acoustic. Neil Jones, Ricky, Scarlett and Kim performed a selection of songs from *Wilde Winter Songbook* as well as seven big hits.

1969
Written by Ricky & Kim Wilde
Produced by Ricky Wilde

The album *Here Come the Aliens* starts with a song that immediately picks up on the theme. Listening to short samples of music – two years later identified as the track 'Numinous' – electronic sounds and an electric guitar suddenly break the relative calm and Kim sings about seeing the Moon Landing in 1969 on black and white television, before treading the familiar theme, touched upon in previous songs written by Kim, of humans destroying their own planet from the second verse.

'Here Come the Aliens' teases the chorus, citing the album title and intimating that aliens have tried to warn us and are now ready to invade and chuck us off the planet. It's a serious message but brought in a playful way, not uncommon for Kim Wilde songs.

Kim: "1969 is a song that has a few influences. First of all, I was nine years old when man landed on the Moon and I was there watching it with my Mum and Dad, as a little girl, on the TV and I could not believe my eyes. It had a massive impact on me. I've been fascinated by the Moon and all things to do with space ever since. It was further compounded by a UFO sighting in 2009. 'Here Come the Aliens' was also inspired by that. '1969' is a song about the aliens coming down and kicking us off the planet, because we've made such a mess of things." [21]

A remix of 'Stereo Shot', '1969' and 'Different Story' appeared on the deluxe edition of *Here Come the Aliens*. Entitled the 'Numinous Mix', it was created by Ricky Wilde.

POP DON'T STOP
Written by Kim, Ricky & Scarlett Wilde
Produced by Ricky Wilde
Released: 30 January 2018

The lead single of *Here Come the Aliens* was released six weeks ahead of the album. The song is a tribute to pop music, without getting sentimental. It certainly packs a punch right from the start, and comes with a catchy chorus that is instantly memorable.

Kim: "'Pop Don't Stop' is an homage to pop music from Ricky and I, thanking it so much for all the inspiration and meaning it's given our lives, and still does!" [22]

Different versions of the song exist. The 12" remix created by Ricky, features musical quotes from The Buggles' 'Video Killed the Radio Star', 'View From a Bridge', 'Kids in America', Tears for Fears' 'Shout', 'Cambodia', and Bronski Beat's 'Smalltown Boy'. Some of these were cut from the album and single version, but it's obvious that the track pays homage to legendary pop music from the 1980s.

The artwork for the single featured a portrait of Kim and Ricky, created by Scarlett. While the artwork for the LP was based on the film poster of *La Terra Contro I Dischi Volanti*, the artwork for this single was based on an alternative poster for the same movie. Scarlett cleverly replaced the faces of Hugh Marlowe and Joan Taylor with Ricky and Kim's.

The song also came with a music video, directed by Sean Vincent, a combination of a 'performance' video by Kim and her band, and shots of Kim in various pop-related guises: as a hip-hop artist, a guitar goddess, and a Siouxsie Sioux lookalike.
Sean Vincent: "The idea for the video came from a couple of conversations myself and Kim had. The first of which was talking about referencing Elvis Costello song 'Pump it Up'. We felt there was a similarity between that and 'Pop Don't Stop', and when we remembered the video – just him and the band and a really cool white background, and Elvis doing his unique performance to camera - we used that as a visual reference. And then there are the different looks Kim sings (about) in the chorus – hip-hop, rock, punk, funk - and that came about quite early in the discussion about the video. It was obvious this was the main focus for the clip. Kim was really up for it; it was a really good fun thing to do with costume and make-up, especially when Kim was made up to look like Siouxsie Sioux - incredible!" [23]

KANDY KRUSH
Written by Kim Wilde, Frederick Thomander, Anders Wikström & Ricky Wilde
Produced by Ricky Wilde
Released: 16 March 2018

Those who are familiar with Billy Idol's music output of the 1980s will recognise the pastiche of his hit 'White Wedding' in the intro. Indeed, Kim confessed that the song was inspired by him.[24] Written in Sweden with Frederick Thomander and Anders Wikström of the Epicentre songwriting team, it was released as the second single from the album.
Kim: "It's a rock/pop track, inspired by playing live with my band. When I wrote the song with Frederick and Anders in Stockholm, we listened to Billy Idol's 'White Wedding' as inspiration." [25]

'Kandy Krush' was remixed by Ricky Wilde, who created a radio mix and 12" mix, nicknamed the 'Push the Button Mix'. There were also three remixes by Wideboys (a radio mix, a club mix and a dub mix) and one by Dan Peters (the DMFP Remix).

The video was again directed by Sean Vincent, this time focusing very much on Kim and her band.
Sean: "The idea behind the 'Kandy Krush' video was two-fold: one, we wanted to show the band doing their thing live and looking as cool as possible - Kim with straight hair, PVC outfit, the band completely rocking out, all looking amazing - and then the other thing was to do this thing called the Spike Lee dolly shot, which is a favourite shot Spike Lee does in all his films, where

basically the camera is mounted on a dolly and so is the talent. And then they move together. You have to go past something so you can get that sense of movement. In this case we built a corridor of lights, and Kim and the band were on the dolly with the camera, and it went back and forth." [26]

STEREO SHOT
Written by Ricky & Scarlett Wilde
Produced by Ricky Wilde

Scarlett Wilde recorded a handful of songs together with her band Scarlett Feeva around 2012. The band didn't take off as hoped, but some of the songs transformed into Kim Wilde tracks. This was one of them. The lyrics of 'Stereo Shot' are very much about music and the production of music.
Kim: "'Stereo Shot' was written by my brother Ricky and his daughter Scarlett, who also did the artwork for the album. Scarlett's had a massive input on this project and totally understands and gets where I'm coming from. She wrote this song inspired by the power and magic of production, which of course has played a massive part in my recording career through Ricky's inspired work. The song talks about the way that sounds make you feel: '*With pure addiction feed your kicks for sound*'."

A remix of 'Stereo Shot', '1969' and 'Different Story' appeared on the deluxe edition of *Here Come the Aliens*. Entitled the 'Numinous Mix', it was created by Ricky Wilde.

During the Here Come the Aliens tour, 'Stereo Shot' was the first song on the setlist, with a rousing extended intro that excited the audience wherever Kim and her band played.

YOURS 'TIL THE END
Written by Ricky Wilde & Neil Jones
Produced by Ricky Wilde

Two elements in this song hark back to the 1980s: the chorus, featuring a chant that is similar to the one in Duran Duran's 1984 hit 'The Reflex', and a bass-line inspired by late bass player Mick Karn of the band Japan.
Kim: "A sort of a Duran Duran inspired pop tune, with lots of backing vocals I put in which were inspired from the song 'The Reflex'. You'll know what I mean when you have a listen to it." [27]

Ricky created the 'Infinity Mix', which was included on the deluxe edition of *Here Come the Aliens*.

CHAPTER 21: HERE COME THE ALIENS

SOLSTICE
Written by Ricky, Scarlett & Kim Wilde
Produced by Ricky Wilde

In June 2014, teenagers Charleigh Disbrey (15) and Mert Karaoglan (18) jumped in front of a train near Elstree and Borehamwood station in Hertfordshire, where Kim lives. This tragic event inspired the song 'Solstice'. This ballad is the emotional highpoint of the album, describing the feelings of those left behind. '*Why couldn't you share your pain? / I thought you could tell me everything / Now it's too late, too late, it's too late / Your lives had just begun, why do they end as one?*'.

Kim: "Ricky, Scarlett and myself wrote 'Solstice' after some really tragic stories we were hearing about a few years back, dealing with teenage suicide. Feeling utterly helpless we wrote this really hard-hitting ballad as a response. Elton John's 'Don't Let the Sun Go Down On Me" inspired the backing vocals, which run throughout the song, sung by Ricky. A very personal song, and it often chokes me up just listening to it." [28]

ADDICTED TO YOU
Written by Sean Vincent, Roxanne & Ricky Wilde
Produced by Ricky Wilde

Originally included as a bonus track on the deluxe version of *Come Out and Play* in 2011, 'Addicted to You' was re-recorded for *Here Come the Aliens*, this time produced by Ricky and played by Kim's own band.

Kim: "This song was inspired by New Order's 'Blue Monday' or Kylie's 'Can't Get You Out of my Head', with a bit of Gary Numan's frosty synth lines thrown in for good measure. It was a song I recorded on the *Come Out and Play* bundle but we all felt it was such a great track, it needed to be reworked and put on *Here Come the Aliens*." [29]

BIRTHDAY
Written by Ricky & Scarlett Wilde & Shane Lee
Produced by Ricky Wilde
Released: 22 June 2018

Another track reworked from an original recording by Scarlett Feeva, 'Birthday' is a lively track that reminds the listener to live life to the fullest. '*You gotta jump like it's your birthday / You gotta shout like there's no tomorrow / This is now / Gotta show 'em how to party, the night is yours*'.

Kim: "'Birthday was inspired by, amongst others, a band called the Sounds, and of course a bit of Blondie, and 'Birthday' really talks about living like it's your birthday every day of your life, every day can be a reason to celebrate something!"[30]

The single version is edited, cutting almost a minute from the original album version. The 'Wilde Party Mix', created by Ricky, clocks in at six minutes and changes the song into a space-like track.

The music video for 'Birthday' shows video footage from Kim's live tour in 2018. An extended music video for the 'Wilde Party Mix' is very different and shows Kim singing the song with headphones on and images of the sun and earth spinning around.

CYBER.NATION.WAR
Written by Ricky & Kim Wilde
Produced by Ricky Wilde

Written as a criticism of keyboard warriors, those always active on social media in a bid to spread negativity. Scientists have repeatedly pointed out that besides the 'bright side' of social media (connecting like-minded individuals, creating opportunities for people to be heard) there is also a 'dark side'. Cyber-bullying, addictive use, trolling, fake news and privacy abuse are only a few examples of this 'dark side'.

With 'Cyber.Nation.War' Kim addresses this fact, aiming specifically at those who use their online time to spread hate. '*Your cowardly malicious lies / Cause only devastation to everybody's lives / You'd never say it to their face / And never know the consequences 'til it's all too late / So tell me how do you sleep at night?*' **Kim:** "'Cyber, Nation, War, three separate words, which help to describe my feelings about social media sometimes. You know, the haters, the one that have nothing good to say. Why do that? I just don't understand, and they can cause so much pain for so many people. Why go to war with each other every day on social media? There's too much war and hate already in this world."

The original album version was followed a few months later by the 'Keyboard Warrior Mix', created by Ricky, and included on the deluxe edition of *Here Come the Aliens*. This version became the basis for the live performance of the track in the second leg of the Here Come the Aliens tour.

DIFFERENT STORY
Written by Kim Wilde, Frederick Thomander & Anders Wikström
Produced by Ricky Wilde

Kim: "We came up with this defiant pop song which really just says 'Let me get on with it, please don't chip in with what you think I should be doing. How many people in your life do you know who keep telling you how to live it? It's really annoying, isn't it?" [31]

A remix of 'Stereo Shot', '1969' and 'Different Story' appeared on the deluxe edition of *Here Come the Aliens*. Entitled the 'Numinous Mix', it was created by Ricky Wilde.

ROCK THE PARADISO
Written by Ricky, Scarlett & Kim Wilde
Produced by Ricky Wilde

'Rock the Paradiso' was originally called 'Amsterdam' and recorded by Scarlett's band Scarlett Feeva in 2010. The lyrics were slightly changed to become an ode to the converted church in Amsterdam where Kim had performed live a few times.

Anyone who has heard 'She Sells Sanctuary' by the Cult a few times will be delighted by the intro of this track, a pastiche of that song's intro.

Kim: "Because the Paradiso in Amsterdam is one of our favourite venues. The atmosphere there is special, and they know - just like in all of the Netherlands - how to rock out!"

Kim: "The Paradiso building facade features on the album sleeve, with Scarlett's amazing artwork. You can see it just tucked behind my face." [32]

ROSETTA (with Frida Sundemo)
Written by Kim & Ricky Wilde
Produced by Ricky Wilde

The album closes with a ballad to Rosetta, the space probe which brought us new understanding of comets. It seems both Wilde siblings are deeply fascinated by the whole idea of space.

Kim: "There's a song on my album called 'Rosetta', about the satellite that launched in 2004 and was on its way to the comet Tschurjumow-Gerassimenko for 10 years. Its mission was to find out more about the origin of mankind. The song is about not having to go so far to find that information, as I believe the answers about mankind's origins are to be found here on earth, deep within us." [33]

Kim live at Tivoli Vredenburg, Utrecht (Netherlands), 17 November 2018 © Katrien Vercaigne

Kim live at Parkpop Saturday Night, Den Haag (Netherlands), 23 June 2018
© Marcel Rijs

© Sean J. Vincent

© Sean J. Vincent

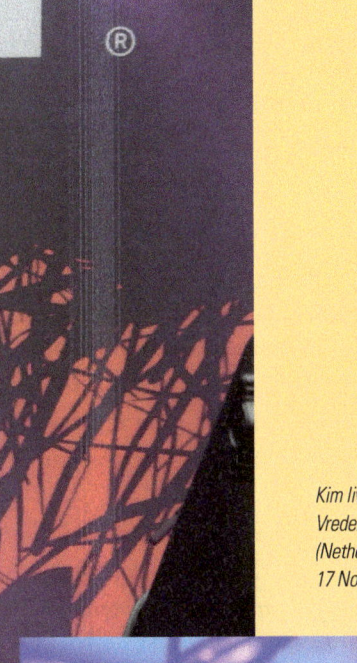

Kim live at Tivoli Vredenburg, Utrecht (Netherlands), 17 November 2018

Frida Sundemo, who appears as a guest on this track, is a Swedish singer, songwriter and producer. She released debut album *Dear, Let It Out* in 2010, followed by *For You, Love* in 2013 and *Flashbacks & Futures* in 2017. Kim and Ricky got to know her music and were delighted when she agreed to appear on this track.

Kim: "I asked Frida Sundemo, who we're huge fans of, and she said yes and did the duet with me for this song, which questions the meaning of life. Why are we here? It doesn't really come up with any answers, but I think asks some really good questions." [34]

During live performances of 'Rosetta' in 2018 and 2019, Ricky sang Frida's parts, which were greeted with applause by the audience.

AMOUREUX DES RÊVES (with Laurent Voulzy)
Written by Ricky Wilde, Steve Lee & Kim Wilde
Produced by Ricky Wilde

Kim's duet with Laurent Voulzy in 1985 – 'Les Nuits Sans Kim Wilde' – was a big milestone in France. For years afterwards, interviewers in France were curious if this collaboration would be followed up by the pair. Kim mentioned a few times that she wanted to record more songs with Laurent, but nothing ever came of it. Until 2018, when suddenly, seemingly out of nowhere, this song appeared on the deluxe edition of *Here Come the Aliens*.

In 'Amoureux Des Rêves' (translated as 'Dream Lover'), the tables are turned. While Kim had a few spoken words on Laurent's track, here Laurent spoke a few words on Kim's track. It is actually quite a speech: '*Oh, j'ai tant rêvé d'être ton rêve / Enfin je suis dans ton coeur / Enfin je viens dans ta vie / Réel, irréel*', which translates as: '*Oh, I have dreamed for so long of being your dream / Finally, I am in your heart / Finally, I come in your life / Real, unreal*'.

For the knowing fan, this song is a direct response to the 'Nights without Kim Wilde' that Laurent experienced three decades earlier. '*You're a dream lover / Whatever you got, you gotta gimme some*', she sings, and it's everything Laurent dreamed of - a fantasy love affair has come full circle.

Although Kim and Laurent never performed the song together, Kim did perform 'Amoureux des Rêves' on French TV programme *Les Enfants de la Télé* on 11 November 2018 with Ricky and a band of French musicians. Kim and Ricky also performed an acoustic version of the song on two occasions: on 7 November 2018 in the office of *Elle* magazine, streamed live on Facebook, and on 16 November 2018 on RFM Radio in France.

CHAPTER 21: HERE COME THE ALIENS

FIGHT TEMPTATION
Written by Ricky & Scarlett Wilde & Peredur ap Gwynedd
Produced by Ricky Wilde

Scarlett released 'Fight Temptation' on a promotional CD in 2009, and the song was accompanied by a music video that was posted on YouTube. She appears in the video with her band Scarlett Feeva.

The song was recorded by Kim for the deluxe edition of *Here Come the Aliens*, featuring Perry ap Gwynedd on guitar.

INTERVIEW: STEVE NORMAN

When did you first meet Kim?

I'm not exactly sure when or where we first met, possibly with Steve Strange at Club for Heroes or most probably at the Camden Palace back in the early Eighties. However, I do remember having a relaxed chat with Kim at a private party when she told me off for wearing a string vest. She made it clear to me that it was time to drop the string vest. She was honest and ever so slightly brutal, but it was made clear that vest had to go. And so it was gone. Just like that. Relegated to New Romantic sartorial folklore history. At the dodgy end. Like a mullet that has passed its sell-by date. Bless you for that, sweetie! P.S. For anyone that misses that string vest… blame Kim. She made me do it!

The New Romantic scene was pretty vibrant in the early 1980s, with Spandau Ballet, Adam Ant, Steve Strange and others around. I know that Adam and Steve had a 'romantic' date with Kim at some point. Did others have this inclination, as far as you know?

Er… no. And I couldn't possibly comment if I did. I somehow doubt, however, that Kim's relationship with our dearly missed pal, Steve Strange was anything more than them being just good friends. As he and I were. The thought makes me chuckle. It wouldn't surprise me if there was also a little PR trickery going on in some cases. I mean, it can't harm anyone's reputation being 'papped' about town with the dazzling and delightful Kimmi on your arm, can it?

You've played with Kim's band on a few occasions. What were they like to work with?

The band are an absolute joy to work with, and such talented musicians. There's always a relaxed, family atmosphere backstage, which makes it easier for guest artists/musicians like me to get creative and have fun. Rubbing shoulders onstage and throwing shapes with Ricky is a must. And I don't mind finding myself sandwiched between a couple of Wildes, be they Ricky, Kim, Scarlett or indeed the great man himself, Marty.

What do you admire most about Kim as an artist and person?

Kim has managed to keep her feet on the ground throughout her career. Of course, she has her family with her, she is not alone. But even so, you could forgive her for having a little bit of an ego given the fine body of work she has produced over the decades. But she simply doesn't have one that you would notice. She is the same person on and off stage. Ricky's the same. I love that.

What is your favourite Kim Wilde track?

I'm torn between the Billy Idol-esque 'Kandy Krush' and the gently disarming charm of 'One'. I think 'Here Come the Aliens' is exceptional. The whole album is supercharged, with or without tongue-in-cheekiness. Love those cheeky nods'n'winks to other artists - T.Rex, Duran Duran, Thin Lizzy, and so on... even if they ran out of room for Spandau. Besides 'Aliens', our go-to Christmas album in our house is no longer Michael Buble's. It's Kimmi and co's *Wilde Winter Songbook*. I keep getting drawn to 'One', but the whole album is truly beautiful.

© Sean J. Vincent

© Sean J. Vincent

CHAPTER 22:
SHINE ON

At the end of 2017, Cherry Red bought the entire discographies of 13 artists as part of Warner Music Group's divestment programme. Acts such as Marc Almond, Howard Jones, Mel & Kim and Renaissance had already received a reissue treatment as a result, but because Kim had released a new album in 2018, they were asked to hold off on re-releasing Kim's first three albums, which were acquired by Cherry Red as part of the deal.

In 2019, it was time for Cherry Red to act on their new possession. Having received all the master-tapes from Kim's time with RAK Records between 1981 and 1983, there was ample material to choose from. During the summer of 2019, those masters were digitised and sifted through, resulting in a lavish deluxe release of all three LPs in January 2020.

Besides the original albums with associated single edits and B-sides, a lot of previously unreleased material saw the light of day. All three albums came with a DVD disc, featuring tie-in music videos and a handsome selection of TV performances, licensed from the BBC archives. The original LPs were also reproduced: Cherry Pop released *Kim Wilde* on yellow vinyl, *Select* on white vinyl, and *Catch as Catch Can* on blue vinyl.

Cherry Red also released quadruple-CD boxset *Marty: A Lifetime in Music 1968-2019* in 2019, offering a generous selection of rare Marty Wilde tracks. Not only did it contain all his singles - A- and B-sides - but also a live performance from Radio Luxembourg in 1959 and a disc of 32 previously unreleased demos. The 133-track set was a dream for Marty Wilde collectors and a good and thorough introduction to his work for the uninitiated.

Next up would be a new Kim Wilde *Greatest Hits* compilation album in the autumn, a project she was looking forward to.

Kim: "The *Greatest Hits* is taking me, personally, on a journey I haven't gone down for a while. I very rarely sit around and examine my legacy and my past or listen to my old songs. And that's been a really emotional journey, going back and knowing how my life panned out, side by side with those songs. It brings back lots of memories for me. I am proud that somehow I have survived with my sense of humour intact. I take what I do very seriously, but don't take myself too seriously at all."[1]

However, in March 2020 the world ground to a halt as the Covid-19 virus caused a worldwide pandemic. People had to adjust to a different way of life. All the things accepted as 'normal' were suddenly replaced by working from home, getting out of the house as little as possible, and closure of schools, shopping centres, theatres and sports facilities. Several countries, including the UK, went into a state of lockdown, and Kim's Greatest Hits tour, set to start in Sweden in April and other European countries in the autumn, had to be postponed until 2021. As the year progressed, there was further uncertainty. The virus wasn't going to be a quick, passing phenomenon.

However, the demand for music was on the rise. Scarlett Wilde decided to release the songs she recorded a decade earlier via website Bandcamp. Her versions of songs like 'Stereo Shot', 'Fight Temptation' and 'Birthday', together with seven more tracks, became available to fans. And in May, Kim released a video of 'Numinous', a song recorded during the sessions for *Here Come the Aliens*.

More good news followed when Marty announced his new album, *Running Together*. The title track was released in May, with a video recorded during lockdown. Two years in the making, the album featured original compositions by Marty, including two familiar songs: a version of 'Love Me, Love My Dog', written with Peter Shelley (who had a UK top-three hit with it in 1975), and a version of 'Cambodia', written for Kim with Ricky. All the other songs, including the title track, were written, recorded and released for the first time. And the song '60s World', a duet with Kim, was released as the second single from the album.

Marty: "It's the album I always wanted to write. I've hand-picked each track to depict my journey. It's a musical slice of history. I recorded with youngest daughter Roxanne as I wanted her to perform the songs that needed that woman's touch, and they were written especially for her."[2]

Kim and Marty promoted the album together, something made easier by the coronavirus pandemic, as they were able to do several interviews for television from their own homes. Kim and her family filmed lockdown videos for title track 'Running Together' and the duet '60s World', father and eldest daughter appearing on several TV programmes in the UK for short interviews – sometimes joined by Roxanne, who sang five tracks on the album and added backing vocals on seven more tracks.

Meanwhile, a 'socially-distanced' concert, experienced by less audience members than usual, was held by Marty at Cricket St Thomas Hotel in Chard, Somerset on 3 October 2020. Kim and Roxanne joined him on stage for what would be their only live concert during that strange year.

For the third annual National Album Day on 10 October 2020, Kim and Marty were chosen as ambassadors, along with artists such as Billy Ocean, La Roux, Toyah Willcox, ABC's Martin Fry, T'Pau's Carol Decker, Jazzie B, and Ward Thomas.

Originally Kim was going to spend her 60th birthday in the Netherlands, during another annual tour in that country. Instead, she spent the day at home,

CHAPTER 22: SHINE ON

surrounded by family. And shortly before turning 60, she got another tattoo, this time with daughter Rose.

Kim: "A hot-air balloon tattoo is now emblazoned on our left arms. It's a symbol that means a lot to Rose and me. It represents a magical moment that happened to us a few years ago. But it's too personal to reveal."[3]

A pre-recorded acoustic concert by Kim, Scarlett and Ricky Wilde plus guitarist Neil Jones premiered on YouTube on 18 December 2020. The concert was made available in support of the Stagehand and Crew Nation charities, raising money for those in the entertainment industry affected by a total absence of concerts and festivals during the year.

In January 2021, Boy George announced his new album *Cool Karaoke Vol. 1*, which featured a duet with Kim, entitled 'Name and Number'. They also recorded 'Shine On' as a duet for Kim's forthcoming compilation album. Kim and Boy George were never strangers, having met regularly through the years. But recording music together was something they'd never managed.

Boy George: "It's really nice. I've thought about doing something with Kim a lot and just never got around to it. I've been trying to widen my creative chain over the last couple of years."[4]

The compilation album *Pop Don't Stop: Greatest Hits* was finally released in the summer of 2021. The album – a double-CD pack - was a collection of single versions of all her hits between 1981 and 2021. The collection also added two new tracks. One was 'Shine On', another duet with Boy George, the other was 'You're My Karma', a duet with Tom Aspaul. A collector's edition added three more CDs, featuring all the remaining singles, a generous selection of B-sides and 12 remixes, most of which had never been released on CD before. Two DVD discs completed the collectors' edition, featuring for the first time all of Kim's music videos from 1981 to 2021.

It is hard to overestimate the impact Kim Wilde has had on pop music. She's had more hits than most female solo singers, she succeeded in conquering the top spot in the American singles chart, and together with her family she has composed songs that are still played regularly on the radio, decades after they were released. She developed her songwriting while she was in the public eye and became a successful live act, having toured with all the big names of the pop world. Kim also proved successful in other areas, such as horticulture, writing and presenting. To some it may sound like a success story that came easily, but the reality is that it involved a lot of hard work.

Kim: "My career was like a rollercoaster, adapting to the lows after the highs was my biggest challenge over the years... that and growing up in public, which became very much easier after I got married".

© Sean J. Vincent

Marty in 2020. © Wilde Productions

Kim, Marty and Roxanne in 2020. © Wilde Productions

The Wildes have never taken their success for granted. They grafted for it and treated their careers as a regular job. Behind all the glamour in the world of showbusiness, there are numerous stories of excess, drug abuse, and even criminal behaviour. But in the case of the Wilde family, you will hear most of all how down to earth they are.

Kim: "My father always said fame is a tool of the trade. You have to accept and use it graciously. He always handled it well and didn't get big-headed and think of himself as superior to anybody else'" [5]

When you see Marty Wilde live, still performing beyond his 80th birthday, you see a man who feels right at home on stage, laughing and telling jokes with his audiences, all over the UK. If Kim follows in her father's footsteps, her story looks likely to continue for a few more decades – and if the past decades are any indication, there are a few more surprises in store.

NUMINOUS
Written by Kim & Ricky Wilde
Produced by Ricky Wilde

Recorded during the sessions for the album *Here Come the Aliens*, 'Numinous' was released as a music video on 14 May 2020. The song opens with a quote from Christopher Hitchens (spoken by Hal Fowler) and at the end samples the melody of Kim's 1983 song 'Stay Awhile'. Parts of the song can be heard in the intro of the song '1969', but the full song was unreleased until 2021's *Pop Don't Stop: Greatest Hits* compilation.

RUNNING TOGETHER (Marty Wilde)
Written by Marty Wilde
Produced by Marty Wilde

Released as a video on YouTube on 15 May 2020 and a download single two weeks later, the title track of Marty's new album, *Running Together*, was released in October 2020.

Marty supported the release of the single with various radio interviews and a music video, created during the UK lockdown following the Covid-19 virus pandemic. All the members of The Wildcats, backing vocalists Roxanne and Kim, and Marty himself were filmed separately in their back gardens, the footage merged into one beautiful music video.

Marty: "When I wrote it, it was quite a serious song for me in some ways. It was dedicated to... it was written about my family, all my family, my wife and

my children, and doing things together. I was at a charity event I was invited to and watched all these runners, and as I watched them, I remember seeing these two people holding hands, and thought, 'Wow'. Running together is something you can say about life - it can be your marriage, it can be you and your family, it could be you and your football team. Two people are stronger than one person, nearly every time. 'Running Together' is about people." [6]

60'S WORLD
Written by Marty Wilde
Produced by Marty Wilde

Described in the press as Kim and Marty's first-ever duet, the song appeared on Marty's album *Running Together* and was released digitally two months ahead of its release.
Marty: "'60's World' is my way of celebrating Joyce, the woman that I've loved and who's been the rock of our family for 60 years. It's 60 years since the start of the decade, 60 years we've been married, and 60 years since our gorgeous Kim was born. Every day of my life has been special with Joyce and the family, and I wanted to go back to 1960, where it all began. And what better way to celebrate than by bringing back the sound of the Sixties with a modern twist."[7]

The original version was released on a promotional CD for the album. In this version, Kim sings, '*Oh, won't you be my baby*'. That line was then replaced by '*Back in the '60s, baby*' on the version eventually released.

A 7" vinyl single (the first vinyl single for both Kim and Marty since the 1990s) was released in December 2020 in a very limited edition, in combination with a double-vinyl LP of *Running Together*. A limited edition of 300 copies sold out within a week.

The music video was recorded in Kim's and Marty's back garden, during the pandemic lockdown. For the first time, Kim was in the director's seat, filming Marty at his home, not far from hers, in Tewin, Hertfordshire.
Kim: "We made the '60s World' clip earlier in the summer. I went over to Dad's garden, socially distanced, and became a director for the first time in my life. Having been directed many times for so many videos, I suddenly found myself on the other side of the camera, which was huge fun... and I discovered I was pretty good at it too! Then I went back to my garden, and my daughter Rose filmed me sitting amongst the daisies. I channelled Julie Felix, with flowers in my hair, strumming a guitar for an authentic '60s vibe." [8]

THE WIRE (RICKY WILDE REMIX)
Written by Nina Boldt, Laura Fares & Jon Wide
Produced by Oscillian
Remixed by Ricky Wilde

Nina Boldt is a German synthpop singer based in London. On 5 June 2020 she released her second album, *Synthian*, featuring two tracks written with Ricky Wilde: 'Runaway' and 'Gave Up on Us'. Two months later, an album of remixes was released across digital platforms, featuring Ricky's remix of one of the other tracks on the album, 'The Wire'.

Although Kim didn't appear on the original track, she contributed vocals to this remixed version.

Nina: "I had no idea Kim was going to sing on 'The Wire' remix. It was such a happy surprise when Ricky sent the remix back to me. He said he played it to Kim, and she loved the song so much that she had to sing on it. What a powerful duo, those two! I absolutely love what they've done with it."[9]

SHINE ON
Written by Fredrik Thomander, Ricky & Kim Wilde
Produced by Ricky Wilde & Fredrik Thomander

Recorded at Palma Music Studios in Majorca, 'Shine On' was a new track for the *Pop Don't Stop: Greatest Hits* album. A rather serious song, it opens with the sound of a heart-rate monitor and the lyrics, '*Every day a battle for two / Fight against the chemical demons / Who control the fire in you*'.

Fredrik Thomander: "This is not the first time I've worked with Kim. I produced a few of her songs over the past 10 years. But it is really special this time as she's about to celebrate her 60th birthday and is bringing out her Greatest Hits to mark this milestone in her life and career. She came down for the best part of a week, and we wrote a new single for the album, recording a number of tracks. She's amazing. Her voice is just like it was when she was 19 - she's still got that great range and enthusiasm."[10]

Although originally recorded as a solo song, Kim eventually recorded it as a duet with Boy George for inclusion on 2021 greatest hits compilation *Pop Don't Stop: Greatest Hits*. A music video for the song was recorded on 18 March 2021.

CHAPTER 22: SHINE ON

YOU'RE MY KARMA
Written by Ricky Wilde & Scarlett Wilde

Ricky and Scarlett wrote this summery George Michael-inspired song whilst in lockdown. Kim fell in love with it, and together with help from music man Lee Bennett was introduced to acclaimed UK artist Tom Aspaul. After a Zoom video meet-up, they decided to swap songs (as happened with Boy George) to create the second new and original track included on *Pop Don't Stop: Greatest Hits*.

W.M. (INITIAL TALK REMIX)
Written by Tom Aspaul, Gil Lewis, Clare Maguire & Finlay Robson
Produced by Gil Lewis

This duet with Kim features on Tom Aspaul's remix album, *Black Country Disothèque*, released on 16 April 2021.

NAME AND NUMBER

Premiered on YouTube on 14 January 2021 as part of Boy George's album, *Cool Karaoke Vol. 1*, Boy George and Kim Wilde recorded their duet in the autumn of 2020, with a video to follow to celebrate George's 60th Birthday.
Boy George: "It's unashamedly Eighties, and nothing like the music I made in the Eighties, which makes it fun!"[11]

CHAPTER 1

1. Simon Button, *Where are they now...? Donna singer Marty Wilde.* Daily Express(UK), 10 September 2016 https://www.express.co.uk/life-style/life/708040/Where-are-they-now-Donna-singer-Marty-Wilde
2. Katherine Hassell, *Marty Wilde: 'Passing on my love of music was my greatest gift.'* The Guardian (UK), 6 October 2017. https://www.theguardian.com/lifeandstyle/2017/oct/06/marty-wilde-passing-on-my-love-of-music-was-my-greatest-gift
3. *The Marty Wilde Story Interview by Iain McNay.* Cherry Red Records (UK), 31 January 2019 https://www.youtube.com/watch?v=iVLQVCpGpDI
4. *The Retros Legends Interviews - Marty Wilde.* YouTube, 13 August 2020. https://www.youtube.com/watch?v=DN_YZJq2Zpk
5. David Toop, *The past master in idol speculation.* The Times (UK), 7 August 1989
6. *Mr. Parnes, Shillings & Pence.* Channel 4 (UK), broadcast in 1986. https://www.youtube.com/watch?v=dJu3F3pVf08
7. *Mr. Parnes, Shillings & Pence.* Channel 4 (UK), broadcast in 1986. https://www.youtube.com/watch?v=dJu3F3pVf08
8. *Mr. Parnes, Shillings & Pence.* Channel 4 (UK), broadcast in 1986. https://www.youtube.com/watch?v=dJu3F3pVf08
9. *Mr. Parnes, Shillings & Pence.* Rock History: unique interviews from inside the British Music business, 11 October 2012. http://www.rockhistory.co.uk/cd-parnes-shillings-pence/
10. *Jukebox Heroes.* BBC (UK), broadcast on 17 July 2001 https://www.youtube.com/watch?v=ebl5tWv796g https://www.youtube.com/watch?v=OOmMSC_Qfes https://www.youtube.com/watch?v=twTrz_TnMkY
11. Jenny Itzcovitz & Simon Fine, *Sixtyplusurfers Interview: Marty Wilde.* Sixtyplusurfers.co.uk website (UK), September 2020. http://www.sixtyplusurfers.co.uk/entertainment-and-books/
12. http://ohboy.org.uk/tv-series/diary/december/item/50-friday-12th
13. *The Marty Wilde Story Interview by Iain McNay.* Cherry Red Records (UK), 31 January 2019 https://www.youtube.com/watch?v=iVLQVCpGpDI
14. *Wilde plays it straight.* Picturegoer (UK), 28 March 1959.
15. Donald Seaman, *What went on behind this kiss!* Daily Express (UK), 3 December 1959
16. *News in brief: Marty Wilde married.* The Times (UK), 3 December 1959.
17. *Marty's £60 Ring Disappears.* Liverpool Echo (UK), 17 September 1960.
18. *He's Gone Wilde.* Daily News (New York, USA), 22 January 1960.
19. Joe Warwick, *Kim's early Wilde dining.* The Times (UK), 18 July 1998. https://www.wilde-life.com/articles/1998/kims-early-wilde-dining
20. Rachael Bletchly, *Marty Wilde tells of life in the spotlight as he heads on tour at 80.* Mirror (UK), 12 April 2019. https://www.mirror.co.uk/3am/marty-wilde-tells-life-spotlight-14304370
21. Sheila Jenner, *When the fans stopped screaming.* Daily Herald (UK), 1 March 1963. https://www.wilde-life.com/articles/1960-1980/when-the-fans-stopped-screaming
22. Andrew Easton, BBC Radio Hereford & Worcester (UK), broadcast 13 July 2020.
23. *£104,000 contract for Marty Wilde.* Daily Express (UK), 26 January 1960.

END NOTES

24. Katherine Hassell, *Marty Wilde: 'Passing on my love of music was my greatest gift'*. The Guardian (UK), 6 October 2017. https://www.theguardian.com/lifeandstyle/2017/oct/06/marty-wilde-passing-on-my-love-of-music-was-my-greatest-gift
25. James Thomas, *Is Marty Wilde finished?* Daily Express (UK), 7 November 1960.

CHAPTER 2

1. *Jukebox Heroes*. BBC (UK), broadcast on 17 July 2001 https://www.youtube.com/watch?v=ebl5tWv796g https://www.youtube.com/watch?v=OOmMSC_Qfes https://www.youtube.com/watch?v=twTrz_TnMkY
2. Judith Simons, *Father and daughter*. Woman's weekly (UK), 16 July 1996 https://www.wilde-life.com/articles/1996/father-and-daughter
3. *Eye trouble hits pop singer Marty*. Daily Express (UK), 11 April 1961.
4. Mette Rou Lund, *Kim Wilde: 6 snapshots from my life*. Femina (Denmark), 21 November 2011. https://www.wilde-life.com/articles/2011/kim-wilde-6-snapshots-from-my-life
5. *Jukebox Heroes*. BBC (UK), broadcast on 17 July 2001 https://www.youtube.com/watch?v=ebl5tWv796g https://www.youtube.com/watch?v=OOmMSC_Qfes https://www.youtube.com/watch?v=twTrz_TnMkY
6. *The Marty Wilde Story Interview by Iain McNay*. Cherry Red Records (UK), 31 January 2019 https://www.youtube.com/watch?v=iVLQVCpGpDI
7. *This is your life: Marty Wilde*. BBC (UK), broadcast 15 December 1982. https://www.youtube.com/watch?v=X2KVMiqqBHo
8. Judith Simons, *Father and daughter*. Woman's weekly (UK), 16 July 1996 https://www.wilde-life.com/articles/1996/father-and-daughter
9. *Kim Wilde Fan Club News*, vol. 2, no. 3, 1983. https://www.wilde-life.com/discography/fanclub/volume-2-no-3
10. Jenny Itzcovitz & Simon Fine, *Sixtyplusurfers Interview: Marty Wilde*. Sixtyplusurfers.co.uk website (UK), September 2020. http://www.sixtyplusurfers.co.uk/entertainment-and-books/
11. *This is your life: Marty Wilde*. BBC (UK), broadcast 15 December 1982. https://www.youtube.com/watch?v=X2KVMiqqBHo
12. Sandra Deeble, *Marty Wilde still rocking at 80*. Hertfordshire Life (UK), 18 December 2019. https://www.hertfordshirelife.co.uk/people/marty-wilde-still-rocking-at-80-1-6431200
13. Richard Webber, *My first home: Kim Wilde*. Daily Mail (UK), 17 January 2004. https://www.wilde-life.com/articles/2004/my-first-home-kim-wilde
14. *My childhood home: Kim Wilde*. Waitrose weekend magazine (UK) 5 April 2012. https://www.wilde-life.com/articles/2012/my-childhood-home-kim-wilde
15. *Contender: Ricky Wilde*. Disc (UK), 28 April 1973. https://www.wilde-life.com/articles/1960-1980/contender-ricky-wilde
16. Sweden Chart Archive, https://drive.google.com/file/d/1TFKburGy5c0JoBkFE4UiG5le_fRRJasG/view
17. *Kim Wilde bares her childhood soul to Pop Shop*, Pop Shop (UK), 1990. https://www.wilde-life.com/articles/1990/kim-wilde-bares-her-childhood-soul-to-pop-shop
18. Jillian Hughes, *Milde thing!* Juke (Australia), 6 November 1982. https://www.wilde-life.com/articles/1982/milde-thing-0

19. *The Marty Wilde Story Interview by Iain McNay*. Cherry Red Records (UK), 31 January 2019 https://www.youtube.com/watch?v=iVLQVCpGpDI
20. Kim Wilde & Nik Kershaw Tour of Australia 2013 tour programme.
21. *Me & Mrs Jones*. Vintage TV (UK), broadcast 11 September 2010. https://www.wilde-life.com/radio-tv/2010/me-mrs-jones
22. Uwe Schmalenbach, *Die Fans und der Garten geben Kraft*. Grünschreiber (Germany), January 2014. https://www.wilde-life.com/articles/2014/the-fans-and-the-garden-give-strength
23. Valerie Mabbs, *Stay as sweet as you are…* Record Mirror (UK), 31 March 1973. http://pop45.blogspot.com/2008/06/ricky-wilde-record-mirror-interview.html

CHAPTER 3

1. *Hitlåtens historia*. SVT (Sweden), broadcast 24 January 2012. https://www.wilde-life.com/radio-tv/2012/hitlatens-historia
2. Unsung Heroes podcast, 16 January 2020. https://podcasts.apple.com/gb/podcast/ricky-wildes-unsung-heroes-with-jake-wood-lee-bennett/id1494271662
3. *The Marty Wilde Story Interview by Iain McNay*, Cherry Red Records (UK), 31 January 2019 https://www.youtube.com/watch?v=iVLQVCpGpDI
4. *Kim Wilde: how we made Kids in America*. The Guardian (UK), 30 January 2017 https://www.theguardian.com/music/2017/jan/30/kim-wilde-how-we-made-kids-in-america
5. Unsung Heroes podcast, 16 January 2020. https://podcasts.apple.com/gb/podcast/ricky-wildes-unsung-heroes-with-jake-wood-lee-bennett/id1494271662
6. *Kim Wilde: how we made Kids in America*. The Guardian (UK), 30 January 2017 https://www.theguardian.com/music/2017/jan/30/kim-wilde-how-we-made-kids-in-america
7. *Kim Wilde chats to RAK Blog about her new winter album Wilde Winter Songbook*. The Rak Blog (UK), 28 November 2013. https://www.wilde-life.com/articles/2013/kim-wilde-chats-to-rak-blog-about-her-new-winter-album-wilde-winter-songbook
8. *The Official Fan Club For Kim Wilde: Introductory Magazine*. https://www.wilde-life.com/discography/fanclub/the-official-fan-club-for-kim-wilde-introductory-magazine
9. Judith Simons, *Wilde about Marty's girl*. Daily Express (UK), 12 January 1981. https://www.wilde-life.com/articles/1981/wilde-about-martys-girl
10. Nick Kent, *I'm a wild one says Kim*. Daily Mirror (UK), 14 January 1981. https://www.wilde-life.com/articles/1981/im-a-wild-one-says-kim
11. Mickie Most Interview rush for 'I love the 80s', BBC (UK), January 2001.

CHAPTER 4

1. *KIM WILDE: Kim Wilde (Rak)* Smash Hits (UK), 23 July 1981. https://www.wilde-life.com/articles/1981/review-kim-wilde-5
2. *Kim Wilde*. Top (Belgium), June 1981. https://www.wilde-life.com/articles/1981/review-kim-wilde-0
3. *Heroes, Kim have future*. The Age (Australia), 10 September 1981. https://www.wilde-life.com/articles/1981/review-kim-wilde-23
4. *Frequenstar*, M6 (France), broadcast 5 October 1992. https://www.wilde-life.com/radio-tv/1992/frequenstar

END NOTES

5. *Tracks of my years*. BBC Radio 2 (UK), broadcast 6 April 2005. https://www.wilde-life.com/radio-tv/2005/tracks-of-my-years-1
6. *Clare Grogan interview*. This Is Not Retro website (UK), 2002. https://www.thisisnotretro.com/interviews/altered-images-clare-grogan-interview-2002/
7. *Vasa Carapi?, Sto te tata pusta samu?* Džuboks (Yugoslavia), 11 September 1981 https://www.wilde-life.com/articles/1981/why-does-your-daddy-let-you-go-alone
8. Mickie Most Interview rush for 'I love the 80s', BBC (UK), January 2001.
9. Paul Morley, *WILDE: Sex kitten or reluctant starlet?* New Musical Express (UK), 19 September 1981. https://www.wilde-life.com/articles/1981/wilde-sex-kitten-or-reluctant-starlet
10. *The Official Fan Club For Kim Wilde: Introductory Magazine*. https://www.wilde-life.com/discography/fanclub/the-official-fan-club-for-kim-wilde-introductory-magazine
11. Marty Wilde, *Solid Gold* (CD). Select Records SRCD 01

CHAPTER 5

1. *Frequenstar*, M6 (France), broadcast 5 October 1992. https://www.wilde-life.com/radio-tv/1992/frequenstar
2. Rick Sky, *Kim Mild! Sex kitten of rock is a family girl at heart*. Daily Star (UK), 14 December 1981 https://www.wilde-life.com/articles/1981/kim-mild-sex-kitten-of-rock-is-a-family-girl-at-heart
3. *Threw huge surprise party to thank mum and dad*. The Weekly News (UK), 18 December 1982 https://www.wilde-life.com/articles/1982/threw-huge-surprise-party-to-thank-mum-and-dad
4. Mickie Most Interview rush for 'I love the 80s', BBC (UK), January 2001.
5. Kim Wilde, *Steve Strange (1959-2015)*. KimWilde.com, 13 February 2015 https://web.archive.org/web/20150422042646/http://www.kimwilde.com/latest-news/steve-strange-1959-2015 (archived)
6. Steve Strange, *Blitzed!*. London: Orion Books, cop. 2002. ISBN 0752847201
7. *Kim Wilde Fan Club News*, vol. 2, no. 2, 1983. https://www.wilde-life.com/discography/fanclub/volume-2-no-2
8. Julia Meyer-Hermann & Annette Schmiede, *"Ich weiss, wie sich verzweiflung anfühlt".* FreundinDonna (Germany), January 2012. https://www.wilde-life.com/articles/2011/i-know-how-despair-feels
9. Teddy Jamieson, *Kim Wilde on Adam Ant, Christmas and the enduring power of 1980s pop*. Herald Scotland (UK), 5 December 2015. https://www.wilde-life.com/articles/2015/kim-wilde-on-adam-ant-christmas-and-the-enduring-power-of-1980s-pop
10. Tim Lewis, *Kim Wilde: 'I don't see ghosts, but I did see a UFO once'*. The Observer (UK), 8 December 2013. https://www.wilde-life.com/articles/2013/kim-wilde-i-dont-see-ghosts-but-i-did-see-a-ufo-once
11. Judith Simons, *After 18 years - a new rocker round the house!* Daily Express (UK), 11 April 1980. https://www.wilde-life.com/articles/1960-1980/after-18-years-a-new-rocker-round-the-house
12. *Het mysterie van Kim Wilde*. Muziek Expres (Netherlands), June 1982 https://www.wilde-life.com/articles/1982/the-mystery-of-kim-wilde
13. *Kim Wilde, Select*. Popfoto (Netherlands), July 1982. https://www.wilde-life.com/articles/1982/review-select-3
14. *Kim Wilde, Select*. Top (Belgium), June 1982. https://www.wilde-life.com/articles/1982/review-select-0

15. *Kim Wilde: Select.* Sounds (Germany), June 1982. https://www.wilde-life.com/articles/1982/review-select-13
16. Teddy Jamieson, *Kim Wilde on Adam Ant, Christmas and the enduring power of 1980s pop.* Herald Scotland (UK) 5 December 2015. https://www.wilde-life.com/articles/2015/kim-wilde-on-adam-ant-christmas-and-the-enduring-power-of-1980s-pop
17. Steve Byrd, *Steve's story*, part 4. Kimwildetv.com website. https://web.archive.org/web/20080705165908/http://www.kimwildetv.com/kim-wilde-tv-steve-byrd.php#WTVByrdStory04 (archived)
18. Ross Benson, *A walk on the Wilde side as Kim takes the family show on the road.* Daily Express (UK), 13 September 1982 https://www.wilde-life.com/articles/1982/a-walk-on-the-wilde-side-as-kim-takes-the-family-show-on-the-road
19. Chris Dymond, *Kim's ready now to go on tour.* The Citizen (UK), 5 October 1982. https://www.wilde-life.com/articles/1982/kims-ready-now-to-go-on-tour
20. *These boots are made for luck!* Blue Jeans (UK), 22 January 1983 https://www.wilde-life.com/articles/1983/these-boots-are-made-for-luck
21. *First Time Out*, Thames Television, broadcast 31 December 1982. https://www.wilde-life.com/radio-tv/1982/first-time-out
22. *Kim Wilde at the Dominion.* Daily Express (UK), 29 October 1982. https://www.wilde-life.com/articles/1982/kim-wilde-at-the-dominion
23. *Kim Live.* Popcorn (Germany), November 1982. https://www.wilde-life.com/articles/1982/kim-live
24. Ron Blansjaar, *Succes Kim Wilde live waargemaakt.* Utrechts Nieuwsblad (Netherlands), 15 November 1982. https://www.wilde-life.com/articles/1982/success-kim-wilde-realized-live
25. *Kim's alone in the wild world of pop.* Evening post (UK), 31 December 1982. https://www.wilde-life.com/articles/1982/kims-alone-in-the-wild-world-of-pop
26. *Kim Wilde Fan Club News*, vol. 2, no. 3, 1983. https://www.wilde-life.com/discography/fanclub/volume-2-no-3
27. *Kim Wilde Fan Club News*, vol. 2, no. 3, 1983. https://www.wilde-life.com/discography/fanclub/volume-2-no-3
28. *Kim wird wieder wild.* Bravo (Germany), 5 August 1982. https://www.wilde-life.com/articles/1982/kim-becomes-wild-again
29. *Kim Wilde, View from a bridge.* Smash Hits (UK), 15 April 1982. https://www.wilde-life.com/articles/1982/review-view-from-a-bridge-0
30. *A Wilde family affair.* Daily Mail (UK), 3 April 1982. https://www.wilde-life.com/articles/1982/review-view-from-a-bridge
31. *Kim Wilde 80er Show*, RPR1 (Germany), broadcast 17 June 2015
32. *Kim Wilde Fan Club News*, vol. 2, no. 3, 1983. https://www.wilde-life.com/discography/fanclub/volume-2-no-3
33. *Kim Wilde Fan Club News*, vol. 2, no. 3, 1983. https://www.wilde-life.com/discography/fanclub/volume-2-no-3
34. *Kim Wilde Fan Club News*, vol. 2, no. 3, 1983. https://www.wilde-life.com/discography/fanclub/volume-2-no-3

END NOTES

35. Simone Schlegel, *Kim Wilde: Die Lady mit Mikrofon und Gießkanne*. Centaur (Germany), March 2009. https://www.wilde-life.com/articles/2009/kim-wilde-the-lady-with-microphone-and-watering-can
36. Margit Ritti, *Am 17. Dezember stellt sie im "Musikladen" ihren neuen Song "Cambodia" vor: Kim Wilde*. Bravo (Germany), 16 December 1981. https://www.wilde-life.com/articles/1981/on-december-17-she-presents-her-new-song-cambodia-in-musikladen-kim-wilde
37. *Kim Wilde Fan Club News*, vol. 2, no. 1, 1982. https://www.wilde-life.com/discography/fanclub/volume-2-no-1
38. Marcel Rijs, *Select* liner notes. Cherry Pop, 2020. PCRPOPT213

CHAPTER 6

1. Ray Coleman, *Midem '83 performance: The Galas*. Music & Video Week (UK), 12 February 1983. https://www.wilde-life.com/articles/1983/midem-83-performance-the-galas
2. Douglas McPherson, *Flashback: Kim Wilde recalls being star-struck at the BPI Awards in 1983*. The Telegraph Magazine (UK), 31 March 2018. https://www.wilde-life.com/articles/2018/flashback-kim-wilde-recalls-being-star-struck-at-the-bpi-awards-in-1983
3. *Kim Wilde Fan Club News*, vol. 2, no. 2, 1983. https://www.wilde-life.com/discography/fanclub/volume-2-no-2
4. Douglas McPherson, *Flashback: Kim Wilde recalls being star-struck at the BPI Awards in 1983*. The Telegraph Magazine (UK), 31 March 2018. https://www.wilde-life.com/articles/2018/flashback-kim-wilde-recalls-being-star-struck-at-the-bpi-awards-in-1983
5. Paul Simper, *Return of the love blonde*. No. 1 (UK), 16 July 1983. https://www.wilde-life.com/articles/1983/return-of-the-love-blonde
6. *Kim Wilde, Catch As Catch Can*. Record Mirror (UK), 19 November 1983. https://www.wilde-life.com/articles/1983/review-catch-as-catch-can-5
7. *Kim Wilde / 'Catch As Catch Can'* Hitkrant (Netherlands), 17 November 1983. https://www.wilde-life.com/articles/1983/review-catch-as-catch-can-4
8. *Catch As Catch Can, Kim Wilde*. Hamburger Morgenpost (Germany), 5 November 1983. https://www.wilde-life.com/articles/1983/review-catch-as-catch-can-16
9. *Mit Kim auf Tournee*. Bravo (Germany), 29 December 1983. https://www.wilde-life.com/articles/1983/on-tour-with-kim
10. *Confident Kim - after a struggle*. The Advertiser (UK), January 1987. https://www.wilde-life.com/articles/1987/confident-kim-after-a-struggle
11. Maxime Chavanne, *Kim Wilde prise aux pieges*. Salut! (France), 21 December 1983. https://www.wilde-life.com/articles/1983/kim-wilde-taken-in-traps
12. Jorgen Christiansen, *Mig sexet? Du må vaere gal!* Vi Unge (Denmark), October 1983. https://www.wilde-life.com/articles/1983/me-sexy-you-must-be-crazy
13. Mark Paytress, *Kim Wilde*. Record Collector (UK), September 1993. https://www.wilde-life.com/articles/1993/kim-wilde-0
14. Karen Swayne, *Singles*. No. 1 (UK), 30 July 1983. https://www.wilde-life.com/articles/1983/review-love-blonde-3
15. Simon Scott, *Blondes have more fun*. Melody Maker (UK), 20 August 1983. https://www.wilde-life.com/articles/1983/blondes-have-more-fun

16. *Kim swingt sexy*. Popcorn (Germany), September 1983. https://www.wilde-life.com/articles/1983/kim-swings-sexy
17. Tim Jones, *Rare!* Record Collector (UK), March 2002. https://www.wilde-life.com/articles/2002/rare
18. Martin Townsend, *The Wilde style*. No. 1 (UK), 6 October 1984. https://www.wilde-life.com/articles/1984/the-wilde-style

CHAPTER 7

1. *Kim Wilde Fan Club News*, vol. 2, no. 2, 1983. https://www.wilde-life.com/discography/fanclub/volume-2-no-2
2. Jim Reid, *Is this woman ruder than Frankie?* Record Mirror (UK), 5 January 1985 https://www.wilde-life.com/articles/1985/is-this-woman-ruder-than-frankie
3. 'There's nothing wrong with sex.'... Juke (Australia), 24 January 1987 https://www.wilde-life.com/articles/1987/theres-nothing-wrong-with-sex
4. Tom Watkins, *Let's make lots of money: secrets of a rich, fat, gay, lucky bastard*. London: Virgin Books, 2016. ISBN 9780753541968.
5. Kim Wilde Interview rush for 'I love the 80s', BBC (UK), January 2001.
6. Tom Watkins, *Let's make lots of money: secrets of a rich, fat, gay, lucky bastard*. London: Virgin Books, 2016. ISBN 9780753541968.
7. *Kim Wilde Fan Club magazine*, vol. 9, no. 2, 1990. https://www.wilde-life.com/discography/fanclub/volume-9-no-2
8. Jane Dudley, *Call of the Wilde*. Yorkshire Post Magazine (UK), 28 April 2001. https://www.wilde-life.com/articles/2001/call-of-the-wilde
9. Christophe Genet, *Kim Wilde*. Jukebox (France), 1987 https://www.wilde-life.com/articles/1987/kim-wilde-7
10. *Snapshot*. Popcorn (Germany), November 1984. https://www.wilde-life.com/articles/1984/snapshot
11. Unsung Heroes podcast, 9 January 2020. https://podcasts.apple.com/gb/podcast/ricky-wildes-unsung-heroes-with-jake-wood-lee-bennett/id1494271662
12. Steve Byrd, *Steve's story - part 4*. Kimwildetv.com website. https://web.archive.org/web/20081115121000/http://www.kimwildetv.com/kim-wilde-tv-steve-byrd.php#WTVByrdStory04
13. *Raging Wilde*. Patches (UK), 1985. https://www.wilde-life.com/articles/1985/raging-wilde
14. Steve Byrd, *Steve's story, part 4*. Kimwildetv.com website. https://web.archive.org/web/20080705165908/http://www.kimwildetv.com/kim-wilde-tv-steve-byrd.php#WTVByrdStory04 (archived)
15. Benjamin Locoge, *Laurent Voulzy & Kim Wilde: Une histoire sans fin*. Paris Match (France), 17 February 2011 https://www.wilde-life.com/articles/2011/laurent-voulzy-kim-wilde-a-history-without-end
16. *Laurent Voulzy face à nos lecteurs*. La Voix du Nord (France), 30 January 2013. https://www.lavoixdunord.fr/art/region/laurent-voulzy-face-a-nos-lecteurs-video-ia0b0n994814
17. Foreword by Kim Wilde. Alain Wodrascka, Alain Souchon, Laurent Voulzy: Destins et mots croisés. Éditions Carpentier, 2005. ISBN 9782841673469.

END NOTES

CHAPTER 8

1. *Kim Wilde Fan Club Magazine*, vol. 5, no. 2, December 1985. https://www.wilde-life.com/sites/default/files/fanclubvol5_no2.pdf
2. Steve Byrd, *Steve's story, part 4*. Kimwildetv.com website. https://web.archive.org/web/20080705165908/http://www.kimwildetv.com/kim-wilde-tv-steve-byrd.php#WTVByrdStory04 (archived)
3. *Kim Wilde: Another Step (MCA)*. Smash Hits (UK), 5 November 1986. https://www.wilde-life.com/articles/1986/review-another-step-5
4. *Kim Wilde: Another Step*. Melody Maker (UK), 1 November 1986. https://www.wilde-life.com/articles/1986/review-another-step-2
5. *Elpee van de week*. Hitkrant (Netherlands), 1 November 1986. https://www.wilde-life.com/articles/1986/review-another-step-3
6. Gordon Smart, *'Leona's magic will give her an amazing career in the States,' says Kim Wilde*. The Sun (UK), 29 March 2008 https://www.wilde-life.com/articles/2008/leonas-magic-will-give-her-an-amazing-career-in-the-states-says-kim-wilde
7. Sinéad McIntyre and Richard Simpson, *Leona Lewis becomes the first British woman to top US charts for more than 20 years*. Daily Mail (UK), 27 March 2008 https://www.wilde-life.com/articles/2008/leona-lewis-becomes-the-first-british-woman-to-top-us-charts-for-more-than-20-years
8. *Kim Wilde thrilled for Leona*. Welwyn & Hatfield Times (UK), 28 March 2008. https://www.wilde-life.com/articles/2008/kim-wilde-thrilled-for-leona
9. Joe Bangay, *The Roxy Book*. London: Sidgwick & Jackson, cop. 1987. ISBN 0283996021.
10. Kim Wilde, *My country memories*. Country Living (UK), May 2005. https://www.wilde-life.com/articles/2005/my-country-memories
11. *Frequenstar*. M6 (France), broadcast 5 October 1992. https://www.wilde-life.com/radio-tv/1992/frequenstar
12. *Kim Wilde Fan Club magazine*, vol. 6, no. 3, 1987 https://www.wilde-life.com/discography/fanclub/volume-6-no-3
13. *Godfather of Pop interview: Junior Giscombe*. Classic Pop (UK), May 2019. https://www.classicpopmag.com/2019/05/godfather-of-pop-interview-junior-giscombe/
14. *Kim Wilde Fan Club magazine*, vol. 6, no. 3, 1987 https://www.wilde-life.com/discography/fanclub/volume-6-no-3
15. Music Box, broadcast in 1987.
16. Helen Ballard, *Just Wilde about Kim*. The Sun (UK), 8 January 1987. https://www.wilde-life.com/articles/1987/just-wilde-about-kim
17. *Kim Wilde Fan Club magazine*, vol. 7, no. 1, 1987. https://www.wilde-life.com/discography/fanclub/volume-7-no-1
18. Ann Scanlon, *Some like it hot*. Sounds (UK), 19 September 1987. https://www.wilde-life.com/articles/1987/some-like-it-hot
19. Track by track analysis by Calvin Hayes and Mike Nocito, 'Turn Back The Clock' CD, EMI, 2008.
20. *Wogan*. BBC (UK), broadcast 23 November 1987. https://www.wilde-life.com/radio-tv/1987/wogan-0

21. *Kim Wilde Fan Club magazine*, vol. 7, no. 1, 1987. https://www.wilde-life.com/discography/fanclub/volume-7-no-1
22. Sophie Delassien, *Françoise Hardy: "La première fois que j'ai vu Michel Berger…"*. L'obs (France), 10 November 2013. https://www.nouvelobs.com/culture/20131110.OBS4864/francoise-hardy-la-premiere-fois-que-j-ai-vu-michel-berger.html
23. Patrice Le Nen, *Kim Wilde: "Le jardinage était ma thérapie"*. BonWeek (France), 26 October 2006. https://www.wilde-life.com/articles/2006/kim-wilde-gardening-was-my-therapy

CHAPTER 9

1. Unsung Heroes podcast, 12 March 2020. https://podcasts.apple.com/gb/podcast/ricky-wildes-unsung-heroes-with-jake-wood-lee-bennett/id1494271662
2. Unsung Heroes podcast, 16 January 2020. https://podcasts.apple.com/gb/podcast/ricky-wildes-unsung-heroes-with-jake-wood-lee-bennett/id1494271662
3. *Kim Wilde Fan Club magazine*, vol. 8, no. 1, 1988. https://www.wilde-life.com/discography/fanclub/volume-8-no-1
4. *Kim Wilde: Close (MCA)*. Smash Hits (UK), 1988. https://www.wilde-life.com/articles/1988/review-close-7
5. *Kim Wilde: Close, MCA*. Boston Globe (USA), 20 October 1988. https://www.wilde-life.com/articles/1988/review-close-13
6. *Steve Byrd, Steve's story - part 4*. Kimwildetv.com website. https://web.archive.org/web/20081115121000/http://www.kimwildetv.com/kim-wilde-tv-steve-byrd.php#WTVByrdStory04
7. Lesley-Ann Jones, *I'm the star here but Michael only asked to meet my little sister*. Today (UK), 30 June 1988 https://www.wilde-life.com/articles/1988/im-the-star-here-but-michael-only-asked-to-meet-my-little-sister
8. Kirsa Kurz, *Kim Wilde: "Never Say Never"*. NDR2 website (Germany), 14 September 2006. https://www.wilde-life.com/articles/2006/kim-wilde-never-say-never-1
9. *On the air*. Super Channel (UK), broadcast 20 June 1990. https://www.wilde-life.com/radio-tv/1990/on-the-air
10. Lesley-Ann Jones, *I'm the star here but Michael only asked to meet my little sister*. Today (UK), 30 June 1988 https://www.wilde-life.com/articles/1988/im-the-star-here-but-michael-only-asked-to-meet-my-little-sister
11. *"People usually think I'm a girl who just looks like Kim Wilde!"* Look-In (UK), 13 August 1988 https://www.wilde-life.com/articles/1988/people-usually-think-im-a-girl-who-just-looks-like-kim-wilde
12. Kim Wilde, *Dear Diary*. Just Seventeen (UK), 10 August 1988 https://www.wilde-life.com/articles/1988/dear-diary
13. Ian Watson, *Now that's what I call an Eighties pop comeback*. Evening Standard Magazine (UK), 2 November 2001. https://www.wilde-life.com/articles/2001/now-thats-what-i-call-an-eighties-pop-comeback
14. Marcel Rijs, *Kim answers fan questions - A Wilde Life exclusive!* Wilde-Life.com, 21 July 2007. https://www.wilde-life.com/articles/2007/kim-answers-fan-questions-a-wilde-life-exclusive

END NOTES

15. Sofia Zagzoule, *'Michael Jackson was very gentle and sweet.'* Closer (UK), 29 May 2018. https://www.wilde-life.com/articles/2018/michael-jackson-was-very-gentle-and-sweet
16. *RTL Nachtshow*. RTL (Germany), broadcast 10 June 1994. https://www.wilde-life.com/radio-tv/1994/rtl-nachtshow
17. *Vader Kim Wilde rockt op z'n 50ste*. Hitkrant (Netherlands), 20 May 1989. https://www.wilde-life.com/articles/1989/father-kim-wilde-rocks-at-his-50th
18. Facebook Track by Track commentary, published 3 September 2013 https://www.thinglink.com/scene/431161908834336768?buttonSource=viewLimits
19. *Toppop*. AVRO (Netherlands), broadcast 25 April 1988. https://www.wilde-life.com/radio-tv/1988/toppop-0
20. *You Came, Kim Wilde*. In: Werner Köhler, Thomas Steinberg, The story behind the song: Die 80er Jahre, cop. 2010. ISBN 978-3-7973-1225-9
21. Unsung Heroes podcast, 9 January 2020. https://podcasts.apple.com/gb/podcast/ricky-wildes-unsung-heroes-with-jake-wood-lee-bennett/id1494271662
22. Facebook Track by Track commentary, published 3 September 2013 https://www.thinglink.com/scene/431161908834336768?buttonSource=viewLimits
23. *You Came, Kim Wilde*. In: Werner Köhler, Thomas Steinberg, The story behind the song: Die 80er Jahre, cop. 2010. ISBN 978-3-7973-1225-9
24. Lodewijk Rijff, *Kim Wilde: de kater na het feestje*. Veronica (Netherlands), 25 March 1989. https://www.wilde-life.com/articles/1989/kim-wilde-the-hangover-after-the-party
25. Facebook Track by Track commentary, published 3 September 2013 https://www.thinglink.com/scene/431161908834336768?buttonSource=viewLimits
26. Facebook Track by Track commentary, published 3 September 2013 https://www.thinglink.com/scene/431161908834336768?buttonSource=viewLimits
27. Unsung Heroes podcast, 16 January 2020. https://podcasts.apple.com/gb/podcast/ricky-wildes-unsung-heroes-with-jake-wood-lee-bennett/id1494271662
28. Facebook Track by Track commentary, published 3 September 2013 https://www.thinglink.com/scene/431161908834336768?buttonSource=viewLimits
29. Bernadette Clohesy, *What I know about men*. Sunday Life, Sun-Herald Magazine (Australia), 13 October 2013. https://www.wilde-life.com/articles/2013/what-i-know-about-men
30. Facebook Track by Track commentary, published 3 September 2013 https://www.thinglink.com/scene/431161908834336768?buttonSource=viewLimits
31. Griselda Visser, *Kim: de wilde haren kwijt*. Veronica (Netherlands), 21 May 1988. https://www.wilde-life.com/articles/1988/kim-lost-her-wild-streak
32. *Het grote Kim Wilde interview*. Hitkrant (Netherlands), 18 June 1988 https://www.wilde-life.com/articles/1988/the-big-kim-wilde-interview-too-much-has-gone-wrong-that-wont-happen-to-me-again
33. Facebook Track by Track commentary, published 3 September 2013 https://www.thinglink.com/scene/431161908834336768?buttonSource=viewLimits
34. *Kim Wilde Fan Club magazine*, vol. 8, no. 1, 1988. https://www.wilde-life.com/discography/fanclub/volume-8-no-1
35. Kim Wilde, Facebook Track by Track commentary, published 3 September 2013

36. Unsung Heroes podcast, 16 January 2020 https://podcasts.apple.com/gb/podcast/ricky-wildes-unsung-heroes-with-jake-wood-lee-bennett/id1494271662

CHAPTER 10

1. *Kim Wilde 10 years on*. ITV (UK), 8 November 1990. https://www.wilde-life.com/radio-tv/1990/kim-wilde-10-years-on
2. *Kim Wilde: Love Moves (MCA/WEA)*. Hitkrant (Netherlands), 16 June 1990. https://www.wilde-life.com/articles/1990/review-love-moves-3
3. *Driven Wilde by 80's Nostalgia*. The Music website (Australia), 18 October 2016. https://www.wilde-life.com/articles/2016/driven-wilde-by-80s-nostalgia
4. Kirsa Kurz, *Kim Wilde: "Never Say Never"*. NDR2 website (Germany), 14 September 2006. https://www.wilde-life.com/articles/2006/kim-wilde-never-say-never-1
5. *Kim Wilde Fan Club magazine*, Xmas 1990. https://www.wilde-life.com/discography/fanclub/christmas-1990
6. *Kim Wilde talks about her new album "Love Is"*, MCA Records KIM 6 CD, 1992
7. DeeJay. RAI 1 (Italy), broadcast in 1990. https://www.wilde-life.com/radio-tv/1990/dee-jay
8. 'It's here' limited edition 7" box set, MCA Records KIMB12, released 1990.
9. *Kim Wilde Special*. Nordic Channel (Sweden), broadcast 26 September 1990. https://www.wilde-life.com/radio-tv/1990/kim-wilde-special
10. *Kim m'a dit...* [unknown] (France), 1990 https://www.wilde-life.com/articles/1990/kim-told-me
11. Cors v.d. Berg, *'Al mijn songs zijn bladzijden uit m'n dagboek'*. Hitkrant (Netherlands), 12 May 1990. https://www.wilde-life.com/articles/1990/kim-wilde-plays-kylie-during-her-vacuuming-all-my-songs-are-pages-from-my-diary
12. *Kim Wilde Special*. Nordic Channel (Sweden), broadcast 26 September 1990. https://www.wilde-life.com/radio-tv/1990/kim-wilde-special

CHAPTER 11

1. Judy McGuire, *Kim confesses: How I cured my blues*. Sunday - News of the World magazine (UK), 16 August 1992 https://www.wilde-life.com/articles/1992/kim-confesses-how-i-cured-my-blues
2. Rebecca Hardy, *'Fame gave me a breakdown' Pop-star-turned-gardener Kim Wilde on her darkest days - and how a drunken singsong led to her first Christmas album*. Daily Mail website (UK), 29 November 2013. https://www.wilde-life.com/articles/2013/fame-gave-me-a-breakdown-pop-star-turned-gardener-kim-wilde-on-her-darkest-days-and
3. Corinna Honan, *Princess Anne's my ideal*. Daily Mail (UK), 28 May 1992 https://www.wilde-life.com/articles/1992/princess-annes-my-ideal
4. Corinna Honan, *How Kim Wilde fell for the 'lout' who sent her up*. Daily Mail (UK), 2 July 1993. https://www.wilde-life.com/articles/1993/how-kim-wilde-fell-for-the-lout-who-sent-her-up
5. Judy McGuire, *Kim confesses: How I cured my blues*. Sunday - News of the World magazine (UK), 16 August 1992. https://www.wilde-life.com/articles/1992/kim-confesses-how-i-cured-my-blues
6. *Questionnaire: Kim Wilde*. Radio Times (UK), 26 May 2001. https://www.wilde-life.com/articles/2001/questionnaire-kim-wilde
7. *Kim Wilde Fan Club magazine*, Christmas 1991. https://www.wilde-life.com/discography/fanclub/christmas-1991

END NOTES

8. *Kim Wilde talks about her new album "Love Is"*. MCA Records, 1992. KIM 6 https://www.wilde-life.com/articles/1992/kim-wilde-talks-about-her-new-album-love-is
9. Chrissy Iley, *Making me Wilde*. Vox (UK), September 1992. https://www.wilde-life.com/articles/1992/making-me-wilde
10. Chrissy Iley, *Making me Wilde*. Vox (UK), September 1992. https://www.wilde-life.com/articles/1992/making-me-wilde
11. *Kim Wilde Fan Club magazine*, Christmas 1992. https://www.wilde-life.com/discography/fanclub/christmas-1992
12. Marcel Rijs, *Kim answers fan questions - A Wilde Life Exclusive!* Wilde-Life.com, 21 July 2007. https://www.wilde-life.com/articles/2007/kim-answers-fan-questions-a-wilde-life-exclusive
13. *Kim Wilde talks about her new album "Love Is"*. MCA Records, 1992. KIM 6 https://www.wilde-life.com/articles/1992/kim-wilde-talks-about-her-new-album-love-is
14. Irene Linders, *Kim Wilde: 'Ik was gefrustreerd en erg ongelukkig'*. Hitkrant (Netherlands), 23 May 1992
15. *Kim Wilde talks about her new album "Love Is"*. MCA Records, 1992. KIM 6 https://www.wilde-life.com/articles/1992/kim-wilde-talks-about-her-new-album-love-is
16. *Kim Wilde talks about her new album "Love Is"*. MCA Records, 1992. KIM 6 https://www.wilde-life.com/articles/1992/kim-wilde-talks-about-her-new-album-love-is
17. *Payshagg talks to Kim Wilde*. https://www.youtube.com/watch?v=7FpX8rCNlIg
18. *Laurent Voulzy face à nos lecteurs*. La Voix du Nord (France), 30 January 2013. https://www.lavoixdunord.fr/art/region/laurent-voulzy-face-a-nos-lecteurs-video-ia0b0n994814

CHAPTER 12

1. Nick McGrath, *Kim Wilde: My life in travel*. Daily Telegraph (UK), 3 January 2020. https://www.wilde-life.com/articles/2020/kim-wilde-my-life-in-travel
2. Mark Paytress, *Kim Wilde*. Record Collector (UK), September 1993 https://www.wilde-life.com/articles/1993/kim-wilde-0
3. Nik Garifalakis, *Born to survive*. Sunday Herald Sun (Australia), 17 October 1993 https://www.wilde-life.com/articles/1993/born-to-survive
4. Jane Rocca, *Alex Dimitriades: Mum taught me that to be a trailblazer, you can't always play by the rules*. The Sydney Morning Herald (Australia), 22 September 2017. https://www.smh.com.au/lifestyle/life-and-relationships/alex-dimitriades-mum-taught-me-that-to-be-a-trailblazer-you-cant-always-play-by-the-rules-20170921-gym5r4.html
5. Andy Coulson, *Thank Evans for my new life: Breakfast date was a turning point, says Kim*. Daily Mail (UK), 10 January 1994. https://www.wilde-life.com/articles/1994/thank-evans-for-my-new-life-breakfast-date-was-a-turning-point-says-kim
6. Chris Evans, *It's not what you think*. Harper Collins 2009. ISBN 978-0-00-732723-2
7. Andy Coulson, *Chris Evans: Truth about the women in my life*. The Sun (UK), 14 April 1994 https://www.wilde-life.com/articles/1994/chris-evans-truth-about-the-women-in-my-life
8. Andy Coulson, *Karaoke Kim n the sunny side of the slopes*. Daily Mail (UK), 8 January 1994 https://www.wilde-life.com/articles/1994/karaoke-kim-on-the-sunny-side-of-the-slopes
9. Prue Rushton, *Wilde Card*. Cleo (Australia), May 1994 https://www.wilde-life.com/articles/1994/wilde-card

10. Lisa Verrico, *My hols: Kim Wilde*. The Times (UK), 11 March 2018. https://www.wilde-life.com/articles/2018/my-hols-kim-wilde
11. Leipziger Volkszeitung (Germany), 6 June 1994. https://www.wilde-life.com/articles/1994/beguiling-leather-lady-kim-bathes-in-rhythm-and-cheering
12. *Kim Wilde*. Oor (Netherlands), 12 February 1994. https://www.wilde-life.com/articles/1994/review-kim-wilde-live-at-vredenburg-utrecht-4-february-1994
13. Cors van den Berg, *'Tot mijn 20ste had ik weinig geluk in de liefde'*. Hitkrant (Netherlands), 4 September 1993. https://www.wilde-life.com/articles/1993/until-i-was-20-i-had-little-luck-in-love
14. Mark Paytress, *Kim Wilde*. Record Collector (UK), September 1993. https://www.wilde-life.com/articles/1993/kim-wilde
15. Graeme Kay, *Celebrity date: Kim Wilde*. More! (UK), September 1993 https://www.wilde-life.com/articles/1993/celebrity-date-kim-wilde
16. Interview on Finnish radio, broadcast 29 October 1993.
17. Nik Garifalakis, *Born to survive*. Sunday Herald Sun (Australia), 17 October 1993. https://www.wilde-life.com/articles/1993/born-to-survive
18. Cors van den Berg, *'Tot mijn 20ste had ik weinig geluk in de liefde'*. Hitkrant (Netherlands), 4 September 1993. https://www.wilde-life.com/articles/1993/until-i-was-20-i-had-little-luck-in-love
19. Cors van den Berg, *'Tot mijn 20ste had ik weinig geluk in de liefde'*. Hitkrant (Netherlands), 4 September 1993. https://www.wilde-life.com/articles/1993/until-i-was-20-i-had-little-luck-in-love
20. *Kim Wilde Fan Club Magazine*, February 1995. https://www.wilde-life.com/discography/fanclub/february-1995

CHAPTER 13

1. Patrick Toxværd-Larsen, *Wilde thing*. Ekstra Bladet (Denmark), 19 May 1994 https://www.wilde-life.com/articles/1994/wilde-thing
2. *Kim Wilde Fan Club magazine*, February 1995. https://www.wilde-life.com/discography/fanclub/february-1995
3. *Don't forget your Ferrari*. Daily Mirror (UK), 27 February 1995 https://www.wilde-life.com/articles/1995/dont-forget-your-ferrari
4. *Kim Wilde Fan Club magazine*, Christmas 1995. https://www.wilde-life.com/discography/fanclub/christmas-1995
5. *Kim Wilde Fan Club magazine*, Christmas 1995. https://www.wilde-life.com/discography/fanclub/christmas-1995
6. Bart Giepmans, *Kim Wilde kiest voor soul*. Primeur (Netherlands), 8 December 1995. https://www.wilde-life.com/articles/1995/kim-wilde-chooses-soul
7. Ramona de Roij, *The Complete Kim Wilde Interview - 26 October 1995*. Ramona de Roij, cop. 1995.
8. Bart Giepmans, *Kim Wilde kiest voor soul*. Primeur (Netherlands), 8 December 1995. https://www.wilde-life.com/articles/1995/kim-wilde-chooses-soul
9. *Kim Wilde: Now & Forever (MCA)*. Beat (Norway), October 1995. https://www.wilde-life.com/articles/1995/review-now-forever-2

END NOTES

10. David Quantick, *Kim Wilde: Now & Forever*. Q (UK), October 1995. https://www.wilde-life.com/articles/1995/review-now-forever-0
11. Quentin Harrison, *Interview: Kim Wilde's Enthralling & Enduring Brand of Pop Don't Stop*. Albumism website (USA), 7 April 2018. https://www.wilde-life.com/articles/2018/interview-kim-wildes-enthralling-enduring-brand-of-pop-dont-stop
12. Carmen Bruegmann, *Wilde times!* Women (UK), 23 January 1996 https://www.wilde-life.com/articles/1996/wilde-times
13. Bart Giepmans, *Kim Wilde kiest voor soul*. Primeur (Netherlands), 8 December 1995. https://www.wilde-life.com/articles/1995/kim-wilde-chooses-soul
14. Jakobien Huisman, *Rijk, mooi, single en dol op rollerbladen!* Flair (Belgium), 1995 https://www.wilde-life.com/articles/1995/rich-beautiful-single-and-loves-rollerblading
15. *Kim Wilde Fan Club magazine*, Christmas 1995. https://www.wilde-life.com/discography/fanclub/christmas-1995
16. *Kim Wilde Fan Club magazine*, Christmas 1995. https://www.wilde-life.com/discography/fanclub/christmas-1995
17. *Kim Wilde Fan Club magazine*, Christmas 1995. https://www.wilde-life.com/discography/fanclub/christmas-1995
18. *Kim Wilde Fan Club magazine*, Christmas 1995. https://www.wilde-life.com/discography/fanclub/christmas-1995
19. *Kim Wilde Fan Club magazine*, Christmas 1995. https://www.wilde-life.com/discography/fanclub/christmas-1995
20. *Kim Wilde Fan Club magazine*, Christmas 1995. https://www.wilde-life.com/discography/fanclub/christmas-1995
21. *Kim Wilde Fan Club magazine*, Christmas 1995. https://www.wilde-life.com/discography/fanclub/christmas-1995
22. *Kim Wilde Fan Club magazine*, Christmas 1995. https://www.wilde-life.com/discography/fanclub/christmas-1995
23. Ramona de Roij, *The Complete Kim Wilde Interview - 26 October 1995*. Ramona de Roij, cop. 1995.
24. Bart Giepmans, *Kim Wilde kiest voor soul*. Primeur (Netherlands), 8 December 1995. https://www.wilde-life.com/articles/1995/kim-wilde-chooses-soul
25. *Kim Wilde Fan Club magazine*, Christmas 1995. https://www.wilde-life.com/discography/fanclub/christmas-1995

CHAPTER 14

1. Jill Parsons, *Marriage, men and Kim... the single-minded success story*. Daily Express (UK), 2 December 1995 https://www.wilde-life.com/articles/1995/marriage-men-and-kim-the-single-minded-success-story
2. *Electric Circus*. BBC (UK), broadcast 2 February 1996. https://www.wilde-life.com/radio-tv/1996/electric-circus
3. *Kim Wilde Fan Club magazine*, Summer 1996. https://www.wilde-life.com/discography/fanclub/summer-1996
4. John Finn, *Wilde no more*. Applause (UK), August 1996 https://www.wilde-life.com/articles/1996/wilde-no-more

5. *Tommy*. ThisIsTheatre.com. http://www.thisistheatre.com/londonshows/tommy.html
6. Henk van der Meijden, *Tommy is thuis: Musical nu met Nederlandse steun in première op West-End*. De Telegraaf (Netherlands), 9 March 1996. https://www.wilde-life.com/articles/1996/tommy-is-home-musical-premiere-on-west-end-with-dutch-support
7. Lester Middlehurst, *Now I'm the wrong side of 30, I can't expect to be called a sex kitten. But it is nice when I am*. Daily Mail (UK), 17 August 1996. https://www.wilde-life.com/articles/1996/now-im-the-wrong-side-of-30-i-cant-expect-to-be-called-a-sex-kitten-but-it-is-nice
8. *Tommy: a new musical* theatre program, 1996.
9. Andrew G. Marshall, *Revelations: 'It was just a tiny kiss to the lips'* The Independent (UK), 15 July 1997 https://www.wilde-life.com/articles/1997/revelations-it-was-just-a-tiny-kiss-to-the-lips
10. *Sex Trugs And A Rockery Role*. Hertfordshire Life (UK), August 2002. https://www.wilde-life.com/articles/2002/sex-trugs-and-a-rockery-role
11. Anne de Courey, *Hal, just Wilde about his Kim*. Daily Mail (UK), 22 November 1996. https://www.wilde-life.com/articles/1996/hal-just-wilde-about-his-kim
12. Sarah Waterfall, *The personality test: Kim Wilde*. Hello! (UK), 30 October 2001. https://www.wilde-life.com/articles/2001/the-personality-test-kim-wilde
13. John Earls, *The second time*. Classic Pop (UK), November 2013. https://www.wilde-life.com/articles/2013/the-second-time
14. Zeena Moolla, *Kim Wilde, the former pop star and her actor husband Hal introduce new baby Rose at their home in Hertfordshire*. OK! (UK), 18 February 2000. https://www.wilde-life.com/articles/2000/kim-wilde-the-former-pop-star-and-her-actor-husband-hal-introduce-new-baby-rose-at
15. Betty Brisk, *'Mullets are bad, nasty things'*. The Sun (UK), 16 November 2011. https://www.wilde-life.com/articles/2011/mullets-are-bad-nasty-things
16. Anne de Courey, *Hal, just Wilde about his Kim*. Daily Mail (UK), 22 November 1996. https://www.wilde-life.com/articles/1996/hal-just-wilde-about-his-kim
17. *Kim Wilde Fan Club magazine*, Christmas 1996. https://www.wilde-life.com/discography/fanclub/christmas-1996
18. Sarah Smith, *In the closet with Kim Wilde*. Sunday Express Magazine (UK), 19 October 2003. https://www.wilde-life.com/articles/2003/in-the-closet-with-kim-wilde
19. *Kim Wilde Fan Club magazine*, Christmas 1996. https://www.wilde-life.com/discography/fanclub/christmas-1996
20. *Traditional style for the bride who used to rock and roll*. Daily Telegraph (UK), 2 September 1996. https://www.wilde-life.com/articles/1996/traditional-style-for-the-bride-who-used-to-rock-and-roll
21. *Kim Wilde Fan Club magazine*, Christmas 1996. https://www.wilde-life.com/discography/fanclub/christmas-1996
22. *Traditional style for the bride who used to rock and roll*. Daily Telegraph (UK), 2 September 1996. https://www.wilde-life.com/articles/1996/traditional-style-for-the-bride-who-used-to-rock-and-roll
23. *A fairytale ending for the girl who thought she'd never find true love : Kim Wilde marries co-star Hal Fowler*. Hello! (UK), 14 September 1996. https://www.wllde-life.com/articles/1996/a-fairytale-ending-for-the-girl-who-thought-shed-never-find-true-love-kim-wilde

END NOTES

24. *Kim Wilde... likes to pack light, turn the phone off and keep a close eye on the kids.* The Sun Herald (Australia), 16 October 2011. https://www.wilde-life.com/articles/2011/kim-wilde-likes-to-pack-light-turn-the-phone-off-and-keep-a-close-eye-on-the-kids
25. Nicola Pittam, *I can't wait to have a Wilde child! Bride Kim's vow*. The Sun (UK), 2 September 1996. https://www.wilde-life.com/articles/1996/i-cant-wait-to-have-a-wilde-child-bride-kims-vow
26. Jane Dudley, *Call of the Wilde*. Yorkshire Post Magazine (UK), 28 April 2001. https://www.wilde-life.com/articles/2001/call-of-the-wilde
27. Tricia Welch, *Former pop star and 'Better Gardens' presenter Kim Wilde is photographed in the grounds of Capel Manor*. OK! (UK), 26 May 2000. https://www.wilde-life.com/articles/2000/former-pop-star-and-better-gardens-presenter-kim-wilde-is-photographed-in-the-grounds
28. Polly Graham, *Tommy's time comes too late to save the show*. Daily Mail (UK), February 17, 1997. https://www.wilde-life.com/articles/1997/tommys-time-comes-too-late-to-save-the-show
29. Michael Carr, *'Kids in America' singer Kim Wilde: "I'd Rather Be 55 Than 25"*. Music Feeds website (Australia), 9 November 2016. https://www.wilde-life.com/articles/2016/kids-in-america-singer-kim-wilde-id-rather-be-55-than-25
30. *Kim Wilde Fan Club magazine*, Christmas 1996. https://www.wilde-life.com/discography/fanclub/christmas-1996

CHAPTER 15

1. Sally Staples, *In conversation: Planting companions*. [unknown magazine] (UK), 1997 https://www.wilde-life.com/articles/1997/in-conversation-planting-companions
2. *From pop charts to pot plants*. Star Awards (UK), 25 February 2005 https://www.wilde-life.com/articles/2005/from-pop-charts-to-pot-plants
3. Zeena Moolla, *Kim Wilde, the former pop star and her actor husband Hal introduce new baby Rose at their home in Hertfordshire*. OK! (UK), 18 February 2000. https://www.wilde-life.com/articles/2000/kim-wilde-the-former-pop-star-and-her-actor-husband-hal-introduce-new-baby-rose-at
4. Kim Wilde, *Gardening has given me just as much pleasure as being a pop star - now I can't wait to see the Show*. Daily Mail (UK), 9 March 2004. https://www.wilde-life.com/articles/2004/gardening-has-give-me-just-as-much-pleasure-as-being-a-pop-star-now-i-cant-wait-to
5. *Wilde child has a boy!* Sunday Mirror (UK), 4 January 1998 https://www.wilde-life.com/articles/1998/wilde-child-has-a-boy
6. Julia Lawrence, *Oh brother*. Daily Mail Weekend Magazine (UK), 11 April 1998 https://www.wilde-life.com/articles/1998/oh-brother
7. Lisa O'Carroll, *Kim Wilde flowers as she lands a TV garden show*. Daily Mail (UK) 30 June 1999. https://www.wilde-life.com/articles/1999/kim-wilde-flowers-as-she-lands-a-tv-garden-show
8. Nick Pryer, *TV gardeners 'don't know their onions'*. Daily Telegraph (UK), 2 July 1999. https://www.wilde-life.com/articles/1999/tv-gardeners-dont-know-their-onions
9. Tiffany Daneff, *Gardening is not something to get on your high horse about*. Daily Telegraph (UK), 31 December 1999. https://www.wilde-life.com/articles/1999/gardening-is-not-something-to-get-on-your-high-horse-about
10. *Better Gardens*, Channel 4 (UK), broadcast 13 February 2000. https://www.wilde-life.com/radio-tv/2000/better-gardens-3

11. Caroline Tilston, *Where the wilde things are.* Junior Magazine (UK) June 2004. https://www.wilde-life.com/articles/2004/where-the-wilde-things-are
12. Zeena Moolla, *Kim Wilde, the former pop star and her actor husband Hal introduce new baby Rose at their home in Hertfordshire.* OK! (UK), 18 February 2000. https://www.wilde-life.com/articles/2000/kim-wilde-the-former-pop-star-and-her-actor-husband-hal-introduce-new-baby-rose-at
13. Simon Price, *Kim Wilde: We're the kids in the potting shed...* The Independent (UK), 4 November 2001. https://www.wilde-life.com/articles/2001/kim-wilde-were-the-kids-in-the-potting-shed
14. *Wilde about new arrival.* The Herald (UK), 15 January 2000. https://www.wilde-life.com/articles/2000/wilde-about-new-arrival
15. Dimestars, *Living For The Weekend* CD booklet. Polydor Records, 2001. DSUK 7.
16. *Wilde about gardens.* Seven days (UK), 16 April 2000. https://www.wilde-life.com/articles/2000/wilde-about-gardens
17. *Wilde about the Eighties.* South Wales Echo (UK), 21 September 2001. https://www.wilde-life.com/articles/2001/wilde-about-the-eighties
18. [Marcel Rijs], *Review: Fabba and Kim Wilde throw a party.* KimWilde.com, 15 January 2001. https://web.archive.org/web/20010212081255fw_/http://kimwilde.com/news28.htm (archived)
19. Freeserve online chat, 1 March 2001. https://www.wilde-life.com/articles/2001/transcript-of-the-freeserve-online-chat
20. *Open house with Gloria Hunniford.* Channel 5 (UK), broadcast 16 July 2001. https://www.wilde-life.com/radio-tv/2001/open-house-with-gloria-hunniford
21. Fiona Webster, *Pop star to earth mother.* Sunday Magazine (UK), 15 April 2001. https://www.wilde-life.com/articles/2001/pop-star-to-earth-mother
22. *Spotlight: Garden Invaders.* Gardeners World (UK), April 2001. https://www.wilde-life.com/articles/2001/spotlight-garden-invaders
23. Ros Drinkwater, *Just Wilde about Alice.* Sunday Business Post (Ireland), 29 July 2001. https://www.wilde-life.com/articles/2001/just-wilde-about-alice
24. Alan Jewell, *A place to play for peace.* Daily Post (UK) 25 October 2001. https://www.wilde-life.com/articles/2001/a-place-to-play-for-peace
25. David Dunn, *Wilde flowers.* The Star (UK), 8 November 2001. https://www.wilde-life.com/articles/2001/wilde-flowers
26. *Kim's making a pop comeback.* Wales on Sunday (UK), 22 July 2001. https://www.wilde-life.com/articles/2001/kims-making-a-pop-comeback
27. *Sex Trugs and a Rockery Role.* Hertfordshire Life (UK), August 2002. https://www.wilde-life.com/articles/2002/sex-trugs-and-a-rockery-role
28. David Dunn, *Wilde flowers.* The Star (UK), 8 November 2001. https://www.wilde-life.com/articles/2001/wilde-flowers
29. *Kim Wilde fährt im Astra-Renntaxi.* DTM website (Germany), 30 June 2002. https://www.wilde-life.com/articles/2002/kim-wilde-drives-in-the-astra-racing-taxi
30. *Thundersley: Hobbit garden created.* Essex Chronicle (UK), 28 April 2003. https://www.wilde-life.com/articles/2003/thundersley-hobbit-garden-created
31. *A magical garden for Little Haven hospice.* Green Fingers Appeal website (UK), 7 April 2003. https://www.wilde-life.com/articles/2003/a-magical-garden-for-little-haven-hospice

END NOTES

32. Alan Air, *Wilde about Cumbria*. Cumbria & Lake District Life (UK), August 2002. https://www.wilde-life.com/articles/2002/wilde-about-cumbria
33. Lisa Verico, *Here and Now*. The Times (UK), 20 December 2002. https://www.wilde-life.com/articles/2002/review-here-and-now
34. Simon Briggs, *The best and worst of 1980s relics*. Daily Telegraph (UK), 16 December 2002. https://www.wilde-life.com/articles/2002/the-best-and-worst-of-1980s-relics
35. *Truth behind my pap pix: Kim Wilde*. Sunday Mirror (UK), 5 October 2003. https://www.wilde-life.com/articles/2003/truth-behind-my-pap-pix-kim-wilde
36. *My therapy*. Daily Express (UK), 23 December 2002. https://www.wilde-life.com/articles/2002/my-therapy
37. Caesilia Ryborz, *Kim Wilde - Never Say Never*. Vrouw.nl website (Netherlands), 5 September 2006. https://www.wilde-life.com/articles/2006/kim-wilde-never-say-never
38. *Kim Wilde: 'Vous ne pouvez pas vous prendre au sérieux quand vous chantez "Kids in America" à 41 ans!'* Télé Ciné Revue (Belgium), 28 March 2002. https://www.wilde-life.com/articles/2002/kim-wilde-you-cant-take-yourself-too-seriously-when-you-sing-kids-in-america-at-41
39. *Still Wilde*. Annabelle (Switzerland), 11 December 2002. https://www.wilde-life.com/articles/2002/still-wilde
40. *"The Feeling Modified" - info*. Readymade website, 2002. http://www.readymade.de/feeling_info_en.html
41. Frank Ipach, *Readymade: The Feeling Modified. CD-Review*. Hooked on Music (Germany), 27 July 2002. https://www.hooked-on-music.de/review/readymade-the-feeling-modified/1744
42. *Das Comeback von Kim Wilde: Wilde Times*. Braunschweiger Zeitung (Germany), 9 March 2007. https://www.wilde-life.com/articles/2007/the-comeback-of-kim-wilde-wilde-times
43. *Nathan Moore feat. Kim Wilde: "If There Was Love"*. Nathan Moore website, July 2002. https://web.archive.org/web/20020811073245/http://www.nathanmoore.co.uk/0001/html/music08_07_02.html (archived)

CHAPTER 16

1. *Back from the Wilde-rness*. Evening Chronicle (UK), 15 August 2003. https://www.wilde-life.com/articles/2003/back-from-the-wilde-rness
2. *Paul Young, Here & Now Australia*. Paul Young website, 15 November 2003. https://web.archive.org/web/20031206012025fw_/http://www.paul-young.com/news/h&naustralia.htm (archived)
3. Kim Wilde, *Australian Tour Diary*. KimWilde.com, 13 November 2003. https://web.archive.org/web/20031204024205/http://www.kimwilde.com/news/australiandiary.html (archived)
4. Kim Wilde, *Australian Tour Diary*. KimWilde.com, 13 November 2003. https://web.archive.org/web/20031204024205/http://www.kimwilde.com/news/australiandiary.html (archived)
5. Blaise Tapp, *Here And Now at M.E.N. Arena*. Manchester Online Website (UK), 18 December 2003. https://www.wilde-life.com/articles/2003/here-and-now-at-men-arena
6. Kate Lowery, *Show of hits and misses*. Evening Chronicle (UK), 18 December 2003. https://www.wilde-life.com/articles/2003/show-of-hits-and-misses
7. *Fame was a bore, now I love my life*. Sunday Express (UK), 14 March 2004. https://www.wilde-life.com/articles/2004/fame-was-a-bore-now-i-love-my-life

8. Gary Ryan, *Here and Now Tour @ Manchester*. Manchester Evening News (UK), 4 December 2004. https://www.wilde-life.com/articles/2004/here-and-now-tour-manchester
9. David Dunn and Graham Walker, *Mighty Midge still wows fans as he extracts charity cash*. The Star (UK), 11 December 2004. https://www.wilde-life.com/articles/2004/mighty-midge-still-wows-fans-as-he-extracts-charity-cash
10. *Wilde in the country*. Red Magazine (UK), September 2004. https://www.wilde-life.com/articles/2004/wilde-in-the-country-0
11. *Hoping to strike it lucky at Chelsea*. Welwyn & Hatfield Times (UK), 20 April 2005. https://www.wilde-life.com/articles/2005/hoping-to-strike-it-lucky-at-chelsea
12. *Wilde flowers*. Sunday Mirror (UK), 2 July 2005. https://www.wilde-life.com/articles/2005/wilde-flowers-0
13. *Interview: Kim Wilde*. Bol.com website (Netherlands), 1 October 2006. https://www.wilde-life.com/articles/2006/bolcom-interview
14. *Keith Middleton*. BBC Radio Shropshire (UK), broadcast 26 November 2011. https://www.wilde-life.com/radio-tv/2011/keith-middleton
15. *RHS Chelsea Flower Show*. BBC (UK), broadcast 23 May 2005. https://www.wilde-life.com/radio-tv/2005/rhs-chelsea-flower-show-0
16. *Slate expectations*. Daily Telegraph (UK), 7 May 2005. https://www.wilde-life.com/articles/2005/slate-expectations
17. *Tour message from Kim Wilde*. KimWilde.com, 17 December 2004. https://web.archive.org/web/20050205070515/http://kimwilde.com/blog2/pivot/entry.php?id=135#body (archived)
18. *RHS Chelsea Flower Show*. BBC (UK), broadcast 23 May 2005. https://www.wilde-life.com/radio-tv/2005/rhs-chelsea-flower-show-0
19. *The Cumbrian Fellside Garden*. Leaflet, 2005. https://www.wilde-life.com/expos/chelsea2005/intro/majestic.html
20. *Wilde flowers*. News & Star (UK), 25 May 2005. https://www.wilde-life.com/articles/2005/wilde-flowers
21. *People with Andrew Pierce*. The Times (UK), 25 May 2005. https://www.wilde-life.com/articles/2005/people-with-andrew-pierce
22. *LK Today*. ITV (UK), broadcast 25 May 2005. https://www.wilde-life.com/radio-tv/2005/lk-today

CHAPTER 17

1. *Kim Wilde, 2005*. In: Gilbert Blecken, Destination Pop: 36 Interviews aus 18 Jahren, 2007.
2. *Wilde about her garden*. Daily Ireland (Ireland), 7 April 2006. https://www.wilde-life.com/articles/2006/wilde-about-her-garden
3. *A date with Kim Wilde: the 'Never Say Never' interview*. 'Never Say Never' Bonus DVD, EMI, 2006. https://www.wilde-life.com/articles/2006/a-date-with-kim-wilde-the-never-say-never-interview-transcript
4. *A date with Kim Wilde: the 'Never Say Never' interview*. 'Never Say Never' Bonus DVD, EMI, 2006. https://www.wilde-life.com/articles/2006/a-date-with-kim-wilde-the-never-say-never-interview-transcript
5. Marcel Rijs, *Kim answers fan questions - A Wilde Life Exclusive!* Wilde Life website, 21 July 2007. https://www.wilde-life.com/articles/2007/kim-answers-fan-questions-a-wilde-life-exclusive

END NOTES

6. *Domino Day*. SBS6 (Netherlands), broadcast 17 November 2006.
7. *Kim Wilde* [Interview], 2007 https://www.wilde-life.com/expos/perfectgirltour/index.html
8. *Stars of Europe*. VRT (Belgium), broadcast 24 March 2007.
9. Dicky and Dolly, *Interview: Kim Wilde*. Gaydarradio.com website (UK), 23 March 2008. https://www.wilde-life.com/articles/2008/interview-kim-wilde
10. *Kim Wilde* [Interview], 2007 https://www.wilde-life.com/expos/perfectgirltour/index.html
11. *Could it be a Wilde wedding?* Daily Express (UK), 23 January 2008. https://www.wilde-life.com/articles/2008/could-it-be-a-wilde-wedding
12. *Sopot Festival 2008*. Wikipedia (Polish). https://pl.wikipedia.org/wiki/Sopot_Festival_2008
13. *Wilde memories*. The Northern Echo (UK), 7 May 2009. https://www.wilde-life.com/articles/2009/wilde-memories
14. *Kim Wilde Night of the Proms tour diary*. KimWilde.com, December 2008.
15. *Kim Wilde Night of the Proms tour diary*. KimWilde.com, December 2008.
16. Jürgen Moises, *Family thing: a worldwise Kim Wilde in the Muffathalle*. Süddeutsche Zeitung (Germany), 26 March 2009. https://www.wilde-life.com/articles/2009/family-thing-a-worldwise-kim-wilde-in-the-muffathalle
17. *"It's all about the old hits"*. Mannheimer Morgen (Germany), 27 March 2009. https://www.wilde-life.com/articles/2009/its-all-about-the-old-hits
18. Daniel Honsack, *Kim Wilde in rock uniform*. Allgemeine Zeitung (Germany), 30 March 2009. https://www.wilde-life.com/articles/2009/kim-wilde-in-rock-uniform
19. *Kim Wilde interviewed*. Welove.de website (Germany), October 2006. https://www.wilde-life.com/articles/2006/kim-wilde-interviewed
20. Marcel Rijs, *Wilde Life Exclusive: Ian Finch*. Wilde Life website, 24 November 2006. https://www.wilde-life.com/articles/2006/wilde-life-exclusive-ian-finch
21. *A date with Kim Wilde: the 'Never Say Never' interview*. 'Never Say Never' Bonus DVD, EMI, 2006. https://www.wilde-life.com/articles/2006/a-date-with-kim-wilde-the-never-say-never-interview-transcript
22. *Neue Helden* (Germany), broadcast 15 February 2007. https://www.wilde-life.com/radio-tv/2007/neue-helden
23. *A date with Kim Wilde: the 'Never Say Never' interview*. 'Never Say Never' Bonus DVD, EMI, 2006. https://www.wilde-life.com/articles/2006/a-date-with-kim-wilde-the-never-say-never-interview-transcript
24. Michael Eichhammer, *Kim Wilde never says never*. Teleschau (Switzerland), 9 September 2006. https://www.wilde-life.com/articles/2006/kim-wilde-never-says-never
25. *Kim Wilde: "Entre le public gay et moi c'est avant tout une histoire d'honnêteté"* CitéGay website (France), 12 October 2006. https://www.wilde-life.com/articles/2006/kim-wilde-between-the-gay-audience-and-me-theres-above-all-a-whole-history-of-honesty
26. Michael Eichhammer, *Kim Wilde never says never*. Teleschau (Switzerland), 9 September 2006. https://www.wilde-life.com/articles/2006/kim-wilde-never-says-never
27. *A date with Kim Wilde: the 'Never Say Never' interview*. 'Never Say Never' Bonus DVD, EMI, 2006. https://www.wilde-life.com/articles/2006/a-date-with-kim-wilde-the-never-say-never-interview-transcript

28. *Kim Wilde: "Entre le public gay et moi c'est avant tout une histoire d'honnêté".* CitéGay.com (France), 12 October 2006. https://www.wilde-life.com/articles/2006/kim-wilde-between-the-gay-audience-and-me-theres-above-all-a-whole-history-of-honesty
29. Martin Schlögl, *Kim Wilde - Never Say Never.* Frankfurther Neue Presse (Germany), 14 September 2006. https://www.wilde-life.com/articles/2006/kim-wilde-never-say-never-0
30. *Song of the month October 2010: Snow Patrol - Chasing Cars.* LazyRocker.com, 3 October 2010.

CHAPTER 18

1. *Wilde Life.* Hotline: Virgin Trains magazine (UK), April 2010. https://www.wilde-life.com/articles/2010/wilde-life
2. *Music Special.* Sat1 (Germany), broadcast 2 September 2010. https://www.wilde-life.com/radio-tv/2010/music-special
3. *Interview with Kim Wilde.* Absolute (UK), 13 October 2010. https://www.wilde-life.com/radio-tv/2010/absolute
4. Doreen Hübler, *Happy Birthday to you: Kim Wilde feierte in Dresden ihren 50.* Sächsische Zeitung (Germany), 19 November 2010. https://www.wilde-life.com/articles/2010/happy-birthday-to-you-kim-wilde-celebrated-her-50th-in-dresden
5. Doreen Hübler, *Happy Birthday to you: Kim Wilde feierte in Dresden ihren 50.* Sächsische Zeitung (Germany), 19 November 2010. https://www.wilde-life.com/articles/2010/happy-birthday-to-you-kim-wilde-celebrated-her-50th-in-dresden
6. Christine Staab, *Endlich habe ich wieder Zeit für mich.* Meins (Germany), 7 March 2018. https://www.wilde-life.com/articles/2018/finally-i-have-time-for-myself
7. Catherine Butler, *Like mother like daughter.* Woman & Home (UK), April 2011. https://www.wilde-life.com/articles/2011/like-mother-like-daughter
8. Peter Müller, *Das Richtige tun im richtigen Moment - Kim Wilde auf "Come out and play"-Tour in der Alten Oper gefeiert - "Kids in America" als Zugabe.* Gelnhäuser Tageblatt (Germany), 25 February 2011. https://www.wilde-life.com/articles/2011/doing-the-right-thing-at-the-right-moment-kim-wilde-on-come-out-and-play-tour-in-the
9. B.Z., 24 February 2011. https://www.wilde-life.com/articles/2011/kim-wildes-blonde-hair-is-blowing-again
10. *Gesehen: Kim Wilde in Mannheim.* Regiomusik.de, 28 February 2011. https://www.wilde-life.com/articles/2011/seen-kim-wilde-in-mannheim
11. Joss Danjean, *Mes nuits avec Kim Wilde.* Modzik (France), March 2011. https://www.wilde-life.com/articles/2011/my-nights-with-kim-wilde
12. *Kim Wilde: Comeback of a power woman - Come out and play interview.* Vip-chicks website (Germany), 17 August 2010. https://www.wilde-life.com/articles/2010/kim-wilde-comeback-of-a-power-woman-come-out-and-play-interview
13. Franck Cizaire, *My nights with Kim Wilde.* Jukebox (France), May 2011. https://www.wilde-life.com/articles/2011/my-nights-with-kim-wilde-0
14. *Kim Wilde: Comeback of a power woman - Come out and play interview.* Vip-chicks website (Germany), 17 August 2010. https://www.wilde-life.com/articles/2010/kim-wilde-comeback-of-a-power-woman-come-out-and-play-interview

END NOTES

15. *Music Special*. Sat1 (Germany), broadcast 2 September 2010. https://www.wilde-life.com/radio-tv/2010/music-special
16. *Kim Wilde: Comeback of a power woman - Come out and play interview*. Vip-chicks website (Germany), 17 August 2010. https://www.wilde-life.com/articles/2010/kim-wilde-comeback-of-a-power-woman-come-out-and-play-interview
17. *Kim Wilde: Comeback of a power woman - Come out and play interview*. Vip-chicks website (Germany), 17 August 2010. https://www.wilde-life.com/articles/2010/kim-wilde-comeback-of-a-power-woman-come-out-and-play-interview
18. Samir H. Köck, *Kim Wilde: Die Ikone spielt*. Die Presse (Germany), 2 September 2010. https://www.wilde-life.com/articles/2010/kim-wilde-kim-plays
19. *Interview: Kim Wilde*. Inqueery website (Germany), 27 October 2010. https://www.wilde-life.com/articles/2010/interview-kim-wilde-0
20. *Kim Wilde: Comeback of a power woman - Come out and play interview*. Vip-chicks website (Germany), 17 August 2010. https://www.wilde-life.com/articles/2010/kim-wilde-comeback-of-a-power-woman-come-out-and-play-interview
21. *Kim Wilde: Comeback of a power woman - Come out and play interview*. Vip-chicks website (Germany), 17 August 2010. https://www.wilde-life.com/articles/2010/kim-wilde-comeback-of-a-power-woman-come-out-and-play-interview
22. *Kim Wilde: Comeback of a power woman - Come out and play interview*. Vip-chicks website (Germany), 17 August 2010. https://www.wilde-life.com/articles/2010/kim-wilde-comeback-of-a-power-woman-come-out-and-play-interview
23. *Kim Wilde: Comeback of a power woman - Come out and play interview*. Vip-chicks website (Germany), 17 August 2010. https://www.wilde-life.com/articles/2010/kim-wilde-comeback-of-a-power-woman-come-out-and-play-interview
24. *Kim Wilde: Comeback of a power woman - Come out and play interview*. Vip-chicks website (Germany), 17 August 2010. https://www.wilde-life.com/articles/2010/kim-wilde-comeback-of-a-power-woman-come-out-and-play-interview
25. *Kim Wilde: Comeback of a power woman - Come out and play interview*. Vip-chicks website (Germany), 17 August 2010. https://www.wilde-life.com/articles/2010/kim-wilde-comeback-of-a-power-woman-come-out-and-play-interview
26. *Kim Wilde: Comeback of a power woman - Come out and play interview*. Vip-chicks website (Germany), 17 August 2010. https://www.wilde-life.com/articles/2010/kim-wilde-comeback-of-a-power-woman-come-out-and-play-interview

CHAPTER 19

1. Nadin Hüdaverdi, *Kim Wilde: "Blondie-Hits sind mir heilig"*. Kölner Stadt Anzeiger website (Germany), 10 October 2011. https://www.wilde-life.com/articles/2011/blondie-hits-are-sacred-to-me
2. *Kim Wilde dreht Musikvideos in Bonn*. General Anzeiger (Germany), 1 July 2011. https://www.wilde-life.com/articles/2011/kim-wilde-records-music-videos-in-bonn
3. DRS3 Radio (Switzerland), 21 August 2011. https://www.wilde-life.com/radio-tv/2011/drs3-radio

4. Jude Rogers, *"I'm Not Ready To Hang Up My Pop Hat" - Kim Wilde interviewed*. The Quietus (UK), 6 December 2013. https://www.wilde-life.com/articles/2013/im-not-ready-to-hang-up-my-pop-hat-kim-wilde-interviewed
5. *BBC Breakfast*. BBC (UK), broadcast 24 November 2011. https://www.wilde-life.com/radio-tv/2011/bbc-breakfast
6. Track by Track: It's Alright. YouTube, 2 September 2011. https://www.youtube.com/watch?v=Ec-2AVC-jYc
7. Track by track commentary, Sony Music, 2011.
8. Track by track commentary, Sony Music, 2011.
9. Track By Track: Sleeping Satellite. YouTube, 31 August 2011. https://www.youtube.com/watch?v=Ls54HEJDBOA
10. Track By Track: To France. YouTube, 8 September 2011. https://www.youtube.com/watch?v=LpPl-zXLOeE
11. Track by track commentary, Sony Music, 2011.
12. Track by track commentary, Sony Music, 2011.
13. Growing up in the hit factory. Sunday Times (UK), 21 July 2002. https://www.wilde-life.com/articles/2002/growing-up-in-the-hit-factory
14. Track by track commentary, Sony Music, 2011.
15. Track by track commentary, Sony Music, 2011.
16. Pascal Vuille, "Une chanson est une carte postale sonore". Le Nouvelliste (Switzerland), 5 September 2011. https://www.wilde-life.com/articles/2011/a-song-is-a-sound-postcard
17. Tracks of my years. BBC Radio 2 (UK), broadcast on 6 April 2005. https://www.wilde-life.com/radio/2005/tracks-of-my-years-1
18. Track by track commentary, Sony Music, 2011.
19. Track By Track: Beautiful Ones. YouTube, 6 September 2011. https://www.youtube.com/watch?v=2PusdCzpTT4
20. Volker Probst, *Im Bett mit Kim Wilde*. NTV website (Germany), 26 August 2011. https://www.n-tv.de/leute/musik/Im-Bett-mit-Kim-Wilde-article4140976.html
21. Track by track commentary, Sony Music, 2011.
22. Track by track commentary, Sony Music, 2011.
23. Track by track commentary, Sony Music, 2011.
24. Kim Wilde, *Snapshots* CD booklet. Sony Music Columbia SevenOne, 2011. 8 86979 41172
25. *Wonderkind Erik (14) maakt remix voor Kim Wilde*. Algemeen Dagblad (Netherlands), 22 May 2012. https://www.wilde-life.com/articles/2012/prodigy-erik-14-makes-remix-for-kim-wilde
26. B.E.F., *Music of Quality & Distinction Volume 3*, track by track commentary.
27. B.E.F., *Music Of Quality And Distinction Volume 3: Dark*. CD Booklet. Wall of Sound, 2013. WOS120CDX
28. *Paul D directs Kim Wilde in horror music video*. Horror-fix.com website (UK), 6 August 2013. https://www.wilde-life.com/articles/2013/paul-d-directs-kim-wilde-in-horror-music-video
29. ude Rogers, *"I'm Not Ready To Hang Up My Pop Hat" - Kim Wilde interviewed*. The Quietus (UK), 6 December 2013. https://www.wilde-life.com/articles/2013/im-not-ready-to-hang-up-my-pop-hat-kim-wilde-interviewed

END NOTES

CHAPTER 20

1. *Kim Wilde was mortified by drunk busking film.* Express (UK), 2 September 2013. https://www.wilde-life.com/articles/2013/kim-wilde-was-mortified-by-drunk-busking-film
2. Unsung Heroes podcast, 13 December 2020. https://podcasts.apple.com/gb/podcast/ricky-wildes-unsung-heroes-with-jake-wood-lee-bennett/id1494271662
3. Kim Wilde on Twitter, 14 December 2012, 6:04 PM. https://twitter.com/kimwilde/status/279632918173872129
4. Unsung Heroes podcast, 13 December 2020. https://podcasts.apple.com/gb/podcast/ricky-wildes-unsung-heroes-with-jake-wood-lee-bennett/id1494271662
5. *Driven Wilde By '80s Nostalgia.* The Music website (Australia), 18 October 2016. https://www.wilde-life.com/articles/2016/driven-wilde-by-80s-nostalgia
6. John Earls, *The second time.* Classic Pop (UK), November/December 2013. https://www.wilde-life.com/articles/2013/the-second-time
7. *Kim Wilde and Tony Hadley set highest gig record.* BBC website (UK), 11 March 2013. https://www.bbc.com/news/entertainment-arts-21739619
8. *Interview: Kim Wilde.* Scene magazine (Australia), 6 May 2013. https://www.wilde-life.com/articles/2013/interview-kim-wilde
9. Cameron Adams, *Kim Wilde to play Chrissy Amphlett's I Touch Myself on tour.* Adelaide Now website (Australia), 17 October 2013. https://www.wilde-life.com/articles/2013/kim-wilde-to-play-chrissy-amphletts-i-touch-myself-on-tour
10. Elisabeth Joyce, *Whatever happened to the 80s Wilde child?* Express & Star Weekend (UK), 28 September 2013. https://www.wilde-life.com/articles/2013/whatever-happened-to-the-80s-wilde-child
11. Uwe Schmalenbach, *Die Fans und der Garten geben Kraft.* Grunschreiber (Germany), January 2014. https://www.wilde-life.com/articles/2014/the-fans-and-the-garden-give-strength
12. Caroline Sullivan, *Kim Wilde: Wilde Winter Songbook - review.* The Guardian (UK), 12 December 2013. https://www.theguardian.com/music/2013/dec/12/kim-wilde-wilde-winter-songbook-review
13. Mac McNaughton, *Kim Wilde / Wilde Winter Songbook.* The Music (Australia), 9 December 2013. https://themusic.com.au/reviews/kim-wilde-wilde-winter-songbook-mac-mcnaughton/COQbGh0cHx4/09-12-13/
14. David Marks, *Eighties Wilde child makes a festive return to Bristol.* Bristol Post Weekend magazine (UK), 14 December 2013. https://www.wilde-life.com/articles/2013/eighties-wilde-child-makes-a-festive-return-to-bristol
15. Jude Rogers, *"I'm Not Ready To Hang Up My Pop Hat" - Kim Wilde Interviewed.* The Quietus (UK), 6 December 2013. https://www.wilde-life.com/articles/2013/im-not-ready-to-hang-up-my-pop-hat-kim-wilde-interviewed
16. Kim Wilde, *Steve Strange (1959-2015).* KimWilde.com, 13 February 2015 https://web.archive.org/web/20150422042646/http://www.kimwilde.com/latest-news/steve-strange-1959-2015 (archived)
17. Kim Wilde on Twitter, 4 October 2016, 10:05 PM. https://twitter.com/kimwilde/status/783397613894787073
18. Ricky Wilde on Twitter, 4 October 2016. 12:06 AM. https://twitter.com/Wildericky/status/783065603011665920

19. *Steve Byrd*, by Richard Blanshard. Wilde Life website, 4 October 2016. https://www.wilde-life.com/news/2016/steve-byrd-by-richard-blanshard
20. *Today Extra*. Channel 9 (Australia), broadcast 12 November 2016. https://www.wilde-life.com/radio-tv/2016/today-extra
21. *Howard Jones & Kim Wilde live @ Enmore theatre, 04/11/16*. Spotlight Report website (Australia), 6 November 2016. https://spotlightreport.net/on-the-spot-2/concert_reviews/howard-jones-kim-wilde-enmore-theatre-041116
22. *Live Review: Kim Wilde & Howard Jones - Rooty Hill RSL 5.11.16* Internal Jukebox (Australia), 6 November 2016. http://theinternaljukebox.blogspot.com/2016/11/live-review-kim-wilde-howard-jones.html
23. Giles Sheldrick, *Rocker Marty collects gong on Wilde day at the Palace*. https://www.wilde-life.com/articles/2017/rocker-marty-collects-gong-on-wilde-day-at-the-palace
24. Rachael Bletchly, *He's back on the road at 80, but Marty's no Wilde boy*. Daily Express (UK), 13 April 2019. https://www.wilde-life.com/articles/2019/hes-back-on-the-road-at-80-but-martys-no-wilde-boy
25. *My life through a lens*. Daily Mail Weekend (UK), 10 October 2020. https://www.wilde-life.com/articles/2020/my-life-through-a-lens-singer-marty-wilde-81-and-his-pop-star-daughter-kim-59-share
26. *ITV News*. ITV (UK), broadcast 5 May 2017. https://www.wilde-life.com/radio-tv/2017/itv-news
27. *Interview: Pete Lee - Lawnmower Deth*. The Rockpit (Australia), 18 December 2017. https://www.therockpit.net/2017/interview-pete-lee-lawnmower-deth/
28. *Optreden in Twents dorpje wennen voor Kim Wilde*. Nieuws.nl website (Netherlands), 15 December 2013. https://www.wilde-life.com/articles/2013/kim-wilde-needs-to-adjust-before-performance-at-village-in-twente
29. Kim Wilde, Track by track. Kimwilde.com (UK), 11 November 2013. https://www.wilde-life.com/articles/2013/track-by-track
30. Kim Wilde, Track by track. Kimwilde.com (UK), 11 November 2013. https://www.wilde-life.com/articles/2013/track-by-track
31. Kim Wilde, Track by track. Kimwilde.com (UK), 11 November 2013. https://www.wilde-life.com/articles/2013/track-by-track
32. Unsung Heroes podcast, 13 December 2020. https://podcasts.apple.com/gb/podcast/ricky-wildes-unsung-heroes-with-jake-wood-lee-bennett/id1494271662
33. Kim Wilde, Track by track. Kimwilde.com (UK), 11 November 2013. https://www.wilde-life.com/articles/2013/track-by-track
34. Kim Wilde, Track by track. Kimwilde.com (UK), 11 November 2013. https://www.wilde-life.com/articles/2013/track-by-track
35. Kim Wilde, Track by track. Kimwilde.com (UK), 11 November 2013. https://www.wilde-life.com/articles/2013/track-by-track
36. Kim Wilde, Track by track. Kimwilde.com (UK), 11 November 2013. https://www.wilde-life.com/articles/2013/track-by-track
37. Teddy Jamieson, *Kim Wilde on Adam Ant, Christmas and the enduring power of 1980s pop*. Herald Scotland (UK) 5 December 2015. https://www.wilde-life.com/articles/2015/kim-wilde-on-adam-ant-christmas-and-the-enduring-power-of-1980s-pop

END NOTES

38. Olivia Buxton, *Inside the head of… Kim Wilde*. Daily Mail (UK), 5 March 2016. https://www.wilde-life.com/articles/2016/inside-the-head-of-kim-wilde
39. Kim Wilde, Track by track. Kimwilde.com (UK), 11 November 2013. https://www.wilde-life.com/articles/2013/track-by-track
40. *Ihren runden Geburtstag verbringt sie mit der Familie*. Stuttgarter Nachrichten (Germany), 18 November 2020. https://www.wilde-life.com/articles/2020/she-spends-her-milestone-birthday-with-the-family
41. Jude Rogers, *"I'm Not Ready To Hang Up My Pop Hat" - Kim Wilde Interviewed*. The Quietus (UK), 6 December 2013. https://www.wilde-life.com/articles/2013/im-not-ready-to-hang-up-my-pop-hat-kim-wilde-interviewed
42. Kim Wilde, Track by track. Kimwilde.com (UK), 11 November 2013. https://www.wilde-life.com/articles/2013/track-by-track
43. Kim Wilde, Track by track. Kimwilde.com (UK), 11 November 2013. https://www.wilde-life.com/articles/2013/track-by-track
44. Kim Wilde, Track by track. Kimwilde.com (UK), 11 November 2013. https://www.wilde-life.com/articles/2013/track-by-track
45. Kim Wilde, Track by track. Kimwilde.com (UK), 11 November 2013. https://www.wilde-life.com/articles/2013/track-by-track
46. Unsung Heroes podcast, 13 December 2020. https://podcasts.apple.com/gb/podcast/ricky-wildes-unsung-heroes-with-jake-wood-lee-bennett/id1494271662
47. *The story behind the song: Kids in America by Kim Wilde*. Team Rock website (UK), 20 February 2018. https://www.wilde-life.com/articles/2018/the-story-behind-the-song-kids-in-america-by-kim-wilde
48. *Interview: Pete Lee - Lawnmower Deth*. The Rockpit (Australia), 18 December 2017. https://www.therockpit.net/2017/interview-pete-lee-lawnmower-deth/
49. *Kim Wilde to team up with thrash metal band for anti-Christmas single*. Belfast Telegraph, 30 November 2017. https://www.belfasttelegraph.co.uk/entertainment/music/news/kim-wilde-to-team-up-with-thrash-metal-band-for-anti-christmas-single-36367912.html

CHAPTER 21

1. Kim Wilde, *Michael Jackson (1958-2009)*. KimWilde.com, 1 July 2009. https://web.archive.org/web/20090707003620/http://www.kimwilde.com/blog/michaeljackson.html (archived)
2. *UFO spotted hovering in Hertfordshire*. The Telegraph, 1 July 2009. https://www.telegraph.co.uk/news/newstopics/howaboutthat/5707336/UFO-spotted-hovering-in-Hertfordshire.html
3. *Kim Wildes irre UFO-Beichte*. Bild (Germany), 26 November 2010. https://www.wilde-life.com/articles/2010/kim-wildes-crazy-ufo-confession
4. Tim Lewis, *Kim Wilde: 'I don't see ghosts, but I did see a UFO once'*. The Observer (UK), 8 December 2013. https://www.wilde-life.com/articles/2013/kim-wilde-i-dont-see-ghosts-but-i-did-see-a-ufo-once
5. David Burke, *Close encounters of the Wilde kind*. Classic Pop (UK), March 2018. https://www.wilde-life.com/articles/2018/close-encounters-of-the-wilde-kind

6. John Anson, *Kim Wilde on new album Here Come The Aliens and UK tour calling at Preston Guild Hall and the Lowry, Salford Quays*. Lancashire Telegraph (UK), 9 February 2018. https://www.wilde-life.com/articles/2018/kim-wilde-on-new-album-here-come-the-aliens-and-uk-tour-calling-at-preston-guild-hall
7. Marion McMullen, *I was in the garden and I saw these lights and I felt absolutely they were not of this world*. The Chronicle (UK), 2 March 2018. https://www.wilde-life.com/articles/2018/i-was-in-the-garden-and-i-saw-these-lights-and-i-felt-absolutely-they-were-not-of
8. Duncan Seaman, *Out of this world*. Yorkshire Post (UK), 23 March 2018. https://www.wilde-life.com/articles/2018/out-of-this-world
9. Marion McMullen, *I was in the garden and I saw these lights and I felt absolutely they were not of this world*. The Chronicle (UK), 2 March 2018. https://www.wilde-life.com/articles/2018/i-was-in-the-garden-and-i-saw-these-lights-and-i-felt-absolutely-they-were-not-of
10. David Burke, *Close encounters of the Wilde kind*. Classic Pop (UK), March 2018. https://www.wilde-life.com/articles/2018/close-encounters-of-the-wilde-kind
11. Esmee de Gooyer, *Kim Wilde - Here Come The Aliens*. Lust For Life (Netherlands), March 2018. https://www.wilde-life.com/articles/2018/review-here-come-the-aliens-8
12. Wyndham Wallace, *Kim Wilde - Here Come The Aliens*. Classic Pop (UK), March 2018. https://www.wilde-life.com/articles/2018/review-here-come-the-aliens-9
13. Terry Staunton, *Kim Wilde / Here Come The Aliens*. Record Collector (UK), April 2018. https://www.wilde-life.com/articles/2018/review-here-come-the-aliens-11
14. Leigh Sanders, *Kim Wilde, Here Come The Aliens - album review*. Express & Star (UK), 15 March 2018. https://www.wilde-life.com/articles/2018/review-here-come-the-aliens-4
15. Gordon Barr, *My greatest success is that I've managed to keep a sense of humour*. The Chronicle (UK), 13 April 2018. https://www.wilde-life.com/articles/2018/my-greatest-success-is-that-ive-managed-to-keep-a-sense-of-humour
16. Oliver Plischek, *"Family Business" - Kim Wilde mit "Aliens"-Tour in der Ottakringer Brauerei!* Mein Bezirk website (Austria), 28 October 2018. https://www.wilde-life.com/articles/2018/family-business-kim-wilde-with-aliens-tour-in-the-ottakringer-brewery
17. Yannick Höppner, *Pop-Ikone Kim Wilde rockt die Columbiahalle*. Berliner Morgenpost (Germany), 14 October 2018. https://www.wilde-life.com/articles/2018/pop-icon-kim-wilde-rocks-the-columbiahalle
18. *Da rocken selbst die Aliens mit*. Lübecker Nachrichten (Germany), 11 October 2018. https://www.wilde-life.com/articles/2018/even-the-aliens-are-rocking
19. *Our film story: This Is Depression - the blog that led to a movie*. Film Stories website (UK), 8 April 2020. https://www.filmstories.co.uk/features/our-film-story-the-blog-that-led-to-a-movie/
20. Unsung Heroes podcast, 16 January 2020. https://podcasts.apple.com/gb/podcast/ricky-wildes-unsung-heroes-with-jake-wood-lee-bennett/id1494271662
21. Track by track interview: "1969". YouTube, 10 March 2018. https://www.youtube.com/watch?v=NRel-HpMreE
22. Track by track interview: "Pop Don't Stop". YouTube, 1 March 2018. https://www.youtube.com/watch?v=HIBVX5Dk-vU
23. Kim Wilde - The Making of "Pop Don't Stop". YouTube, 9 February 2018. https://www.youtube.com/watch?v=R_ZhalPDdaI

END NOTES

24. Kim Wilde on Twitter, 24 March 2018, 2:41 PM https://twitter.com/kimwilde/status/977540995675049985
25. *BBC Breakfast*. BBC (UK), broadcast 14 March 2018. https://www.wilde-life.com/radio-tv/2018/bbc-breakfast
26. Kandy Krush - Behind the scenes. YouTube, 14 May 2018. https://www.youtube.com/watch?v=J2cIgo1IFmE
27. Track by track interview: "Yours 'Til The End". YouTube, 24 March 2018. https://www.youtube.com/watch?v=9kccbexQZT0
28. Track by track interview: "Solstice". YouTube, 23 March 2018. https://www.youtube.com/watch?v=YxX27C_xQvg
29. Track by Track interview: "Addicted To You". YouTube, 23 March 2018. https://www.youtube.com/watch?v=pHiaGEKJudw
30. Track by track interview: "Birthday". YouTube, 12 March 2018. https://www.youtube.com/watch?v=oL2KI0laUIk
31. Track by track interview: "Different story". YouTube, 23 March 2018. https://www.youtube.com/watch?v=hn884tXW1SE
32. Track by track interview: "Paradiso", YouTube, 23 March 2018. https://www.youtube.com/watch?v=dvV8z6hgE_M
33. Stefan Adrian, *"Ich war in den 80ern dabei, erinnere mich aber trotzdem"*. Galore (Germany), May 2018. https://www.wilde-life.com/articles/2018/i-was-there-in-the-eighties-but-i-still-remember
34. Track by track interview: "Rosetta". YouTube, 23 March 2018. https://www.youtube.com/watch?v=RBYH9gXnGR8

CHAPTER 22

1. Alex Green, *Kim Wilde: I'm proud I have survived with my sense of humour intact*. The Irish News (UK), 17 January 2020. https://www.wilde-life.com/articles/2020/kim-wilde-im-proud-i-have-survived-with-my-sense-of-humour-intact
2. Mark Jefferies, *The Wilde Bunch: Marty's first duet with daughter Kim*. Daily Mirror (UK), 8 August 2020. https://www.wilde-life.com/articles/2020/the-wilde-bunch-martys-first-duet-with-daughter-kim
3. *Kim Wilde: Ein Tattoo zum 60. Geburtstag - Unser Interview*. Klatsch-Tratsch.de website (Germany), 16 November 2020. https://www.wilde-life.com/articles/2020/kim-wilde-a-60th-birthday-tattoo-our-interview
4. *Weekend: With an upcoming Culture Club gig and solo album in the mix, Boy George is busy*. Metro (UK), 20 November 2020. https://www.metro.news/weekend-with-an-upcoming-culture-club-gig-and-solo-album-in-the-mix-boy-george-is-busy/2227214/
5. *Kim hopes the psychic is right*. Herald Sun (Australia), 2 July 1992. https://www.wilde-life.com/articles/1992/kim-hopes-the-psychic-is-right
6. *Memory Lane 80s*. Sky TV (UK), broadcast July 18, 2020. https://www.wilde-life.com/radio-tv/2020/memory-lane-80s
7. Mark Jefferies, *The Wilde Bunch: Marty's first duet with daughter Kim*. Daily Mirror (UK), 8 August 2020. https://www.wilde-life.com/articles/2020/the-wilde-bunch-martys-first-duet-with-daughter-kim

8. *Kim Wilde 'inspired' by father Marty after his 'dramatic health scare'*. Evening Express (UK), 11 August 2020. https://www.wilde-life.com/articles/2020/kim-wilde-inspired-by-father-marty-after-his-dramatic-health-scare
9. *Synthwave star NINA: 'I couldn't believe Kim Wilde wanted to duet with me!'*. Retropop website (UK), 1 February 2021. https://retropopmagazine.com/exclusive-synthwave-star-nina-i-couldnt-believe-kim-wilde-wanted-to-duet-with-me/
10. *Kim goes wild for Majorca after recording session*. Majorca Daily Bulletin (Spain), 11 March 2020. https://www.wilde-life.com/articles/2020/kim-goes-wild-for-majorca-after-recording-session
11. Stephen Daw, *20 Questions with Boy George: How His 'Compulsion to Create' Led to a Global Live Show*. Billboard (, 7 December 2020. https://www.billboard.com/index.php/articles/news/pride/9495299/boy-george-20-questions-rainbows-in-the-dark-stream

ACKNOWLEDGEMENTS

Most of the quotes in this book are from the sources you find in the end notes. Quotes without an end note were newly contributed by Kim, exclusively for this book.

I would like to thank first of all Neil Cossar and all at This Day In Music Books without whom this book would never have come about.

Special thanks to Katrien Vercaigne for her inspiration and guidance during this project, as well as her exceptional photography through the years.

Many thanks to Nick Beggs, Richard Blanshard, Anton Corbijn, Case Eames, Greg Masuak, Steve Norman, Sabrina Winter and Martin Zandstra for taking their time to answer my questions.

I also want to thank Melanie Almond, Nick Boyles, Robert Hoetink, Graham Hunter, Juan Larraz, Walter Luijckx, Pierre Mathis, Bart Moons, Tom Parker, Mateusz Piechaczek, Edwina Smith, Sean Vincent and Joyce, Kim, Marty, Ricky, Roxanne and Scarlett Wilde.

And of course, thank you to Annet Rijs, Camilla and Odilia for love and support.

"Don't let your dreams escape, the future's ours to shape"

Milton Keynes UK
Ingram Content Group UK Ltd.
UKHW021229180224
437983UK00002B/35